THE FRENCH REVOLUTION

The French Revolution was one of the greatest events in world history, filled with remarkable characters and dramatic events. From its beginning in 1789 to the Reign of Terror in 1793–94, and through the ups and downs of the Directory era that followed, the Revolution showed humanity at its optimistic best and its violent worst; it transformed the lives of all who experienced it.

The French Revolution: Faith, Desire, and Politics offers a fresh treatment of this perennially popular and hugely significant topic, introducing a bold interpretation of the Revolution that highlights the key role that religion and sexuality played in determining the shape of the Revolution. These were issues that occupied the minds and helped shape the actions of women and men; from the pornographic pamphlets about Queen Marie-Antoinette to the puritanical morality of revolutionary leader Maximilien Robespierre, from the revolutionary catechisms that children learned and to the anathemas hurled on the Revolution from clandestine priests in the countryside. The people who lived through the French Revolution were surrounded by messages about gender, sex, religion and faith, concerns which did not exist outside of the events of the Revolution.

This book is an essential resource for students of the French Revolution, History of Catholicism and Women and Gender.

Noah Shusterman teaches at Temple University, USA and the Chinese University of Hong Kong. His previous works include *Religion and the Politics of Time: Holidays from Louis XVI to Napoleon* (2010).

WITHDRAWN

THE FRENCH REVOLUTION

Faith, Desire, and Politics

Noah Shusterman

Routledge
Taylor & Francis Group

LONDON AND NEW YORK

First published 2014
by Routledge
2 Park Square, Milton Park, Abingdon, Oxon OX14 4RN

and by Routledge
711 Third Avenue, New York, NY 10017

Routledge is an imprint of the Taylor & Francis Group, an informa business

British Library Cataloguing in Publication Data
A catalogue record for this book is available from the British Library

Library of Congress Cataloging in Publication Data
Shusterman, Noah.
The French Revolution: faith, desire, and politics / Noah C Shusterman.
    pages cm
1. France – History – Revolution, 1789–99. 2. France – History – Revolution,
1789–99–Religious aspects. 3. France – History – Revolution, 1789–99–Social
aspects. 4. France – Church history – 18th century. 5. Sex role – France –
History – 18th century. I. Title.
DC148.S495 2013
944.04 – dc23   2013007134

ISBN: 978-0-415-66020-4 (hbk)
ISBN: 978-0-415-66021-1 (pbk)
ISBN: 978-0-203-79580-4 (ebk)

Typeset in Garamond
by Cenveo Publisher Services

MIX
Paper from
responsible sources
FSC
www.fsc.org   FSC® C013056

Printed and bound in Great Britain by
TJ International Ltd, Padstow, Cornwall

CONTENTS

List of figures and maps   vi
Acknowledgments   vii
Brief chronology of the French Revolution   viii

Introduction   1

1   Religious culture, popular culture: life in Old Regime France   6

2   The liberal Revolution of 1789 (spring 1789–spring 1790)   23

3   The Civil Constitution of the Clergy
    (summer 1790–spring 1791)   55

4   The king's flight and the decline of the French monarchy
    (summer 1791–summer 1792)   88

5   The end of the monarchy and the September Massacres
    (summer 1792–fall 1792)   119

6   The new French republic and its rivalries (fall 1792–summer 1793)   143

7   The federalist revolt, the Vendée, and the start of the
    Terror (summer 1793–fall 1793)   175

8   The Reign of Terror (fall 1793–summer 1794)   204

9   After the Terror (fall 1794–1799)   235

Guide to further reading   255

Index   258

FIGURES AND MAPS

Figures

2.1	The storming of the Bastille	37
2.2	The aftermath of the storming of the Bastille	38
2.3	The women of Paris bring the royal family to Paris	52
3.1	Patriotic discipline	81
4.1	The royal family leaving the Tuileries	90
5.1	The September Massacres	136
6.1	The execution of Louis XVI	154
7.1	The assassination of Marat	180
7.2	The sentencing of the Girondins	199

Maps

1.1	The provinces of Old Regime France	7
1.2	The dioceses of Old Regime France	8
3.1	The departments of France	58
3.2	The geography of oath taking	78
4.1	The king's flight to Varennes	91
7.1	The fighting in the Vendée	183
8.1	The Vendéans' trek	212

ACKNOWLEDGMENTS

As is often the case with history books, the time it takes to write them can seem longer than the events they describe. Though I only devoted myself to this book full time in 2010, the intellectual development that led me to it began far earlier. I especially look to Dale Van Kley and William Sewell, both of whom I worked with at the University of Chicago, and Peter Sahlins, my dissertation advisor at Berkeley. At Temple, I would like to thank Richard Immerman, Kathy Biddick, Peter Logan, and Richard Libowitz for their feedback; Laura Levitt and David Watt for their friendship and support; and the students in my French Revolution classes for indulging me in what must have seemed like some rather specific obsessions. I would also like to thank the audiences for my talks at the 2007 and 2011 meetings of the Western Society for French History and the 2011 talk at the Center for the Study of Force and Diplomacy for all of their suggestions and advice. Temple University provided some early research funding as this project was starting to take shape. In Philadelphia, my friends have been a consistent source of support, and I would specifically like to thank Bill Hangley and Audra Wolfe. At Routledge, I owe my gratitude to Michael Strang, Vicky Peters, and Laura Mothersole, all of whom patiently helped me through the writing process. The anonymous readers of the proposal and the manuscript all offered valuable advice.

The illustrations in this book are courtesy of the University of Pennsylvania Library's Special Collections. I would like to thank them for the permission to reproduce these images, and to thank their staff for being so helpful and accommodating.

My family has been more patient with me than I had any right in asking them to be; I thank all of them, especially my wife Helen Cheung. While writing the book, we had one "Z" come into our life and another leave it. Two years after our son Zachary was born my stepfather Al Zielenski, "Grandpa Z," passed away. Grandpa Z would have been an excellent historian, had he not been wise enough to choose a far more practical career path. Here's hoping that his youngest grandson will grow up with both his curiosity and his wisdom.

BRIEF CHRONOLOGY OF THE FRENCH REVOLUTION

1789

May 5: Estates-General opens in Versailles

June 17: Third Estate constitutes itself as the National Assembly

June 20: Tennis Court Oath

June 27: Louis XVI calls on the first and second Estates to meet with the National Assembly

July 9: National Assembly rechristens itself the National Constituent Assembly

July 11: Louis XVI dismisses Necker

July 14: Storming of the Bastille

July–August: Great Fear

August 4: Nobility in National Assembly agrees to wide-ranging measures abolishing privileges

August 11: Decree enacting most of the agreements from the night of August 4

August 27: National Constituent Assembly passes the Declaration of the Rights of Man

October 5–6: Women's March to Versailles

October 19: National Assembly's first session in Paris

November 2: Nationalization of church property

November 9: National Assembly's first session in the salle du Manège

1790

January 28: National Assembly grants French citizenship to Jews of southern France (but not Alsace)

February 26: Division of France into 83 departments

May 10: Riots in Montauban pitting Catholics against Protestants

June 13: Violence between Protestants and Catholics in Nîmes

July 12: National Constituent Assembly approves the Civil Constitution of the Clergy

July 14: Festival of the Federation

July 22: Louis XVI officially sanctions the Civil Constitution of the Clergy

October 30: Bishops in the National Constituent Assembly issue the *Exposition of Principles*

November 27: National Constituent Assembly decree calls for all ecclesiastics to swear an oath implying acceptance of the Civil Constitution of the Clergy

December 26: King Louis XVI sanctions the decree of November 27

December 27: Ecclesiastical deputies who support the Civil Constitution of the Clergy take their oath in the National Assembly

1791

January 3–4: All ecclesiastical deputies called on to take the oath to the Civil Constitution of the Clergy; most refuse

February 24: Talleyrand ordains first constitutional bishops

March 10: Pius VI officially condemns Civil Constitution of the Clergy

April 2: Death of Mirabeau

June 20: Louis XVI and his family attempt to flee Paris

July 17: Champ de Mars Massacre

September 27: National Assembly grants citizenship to Jews of Alsace

September 30: Last session of the National Constituent Assembly

October 1: First session of the National Legislative Assembly

October 9: National Legislative Assembly hears report on the Vendée

October 16: Massacres in Avignon

November 29: National Legislative Assembly issues decree calling for all refractory priests to swear oath or be considered suspects

December 19: Louis XVI vetoes decree of November 29

1792

January 19: Brissot speaks in favor of war against the Austrian Empire; start of movement toward war

April 20: France declares war on the Austrian Empire

April 28: War begins

May 27: National Legislative Assembly issues decree calling for deportation of refractory priests

June 11: Louis XVI vetoes decree of May 27

June 20: Crowd invades Tuileries

July 11: National Legislative Assembly declares the fatherland in danger

July 25: Brunswick Manifesto threatens France, should anything happen to the royal family

August 10: The "Second Revolution" – the crowd storms the Tuileries; the royal family takes shelter in the National Assembly, which suspends the monarchy, and calls for a Convention

August 26: National Legislative Assembly issues decree calling for deportation of refractory priests

September 2: Fall of Verdun

September 2–5: September Massacres

September 20: French victory at the Battle of Valmy

September 21–22: First sessions of the Convention, which declares France a republic

November 20: Discovery of the *armoire de fer*

1793

January 3: Execution of Louis XVI

February 24: Conscription of 300,000 men for the army

March 11: Start of the uprising in the Vendée

April 1: Betrayal of Dumouriez

April 6: Creation of the Committee of Public Safety

May 31–June 2: Expulsion of the Girondins from the Convention

June 7: Start of the federalist revolt

June 18: Vendéans take Angers

June 29: Vendéan defeat at Nantes

July 13: Assassination of Marat; retreat of federalist troops marching from Normandy toward Paris

July 27: Robespierre enters the Committee of Public Safety

August 1: Convention announces scorched earth policy in the Vendée

August 23: Convention decrees the *Levée en masse*

August 28: Execution of General Custine

September 5: Convention declares Terror the "Order of the Day"

September 17: Law of Suspects

September 22: First day of the Year II

October–November: De-Christianization movement

October 9/18 Vendémiaire: Recapture of Lyon

October 10/19 Vendémiaire: Government declared "Revolutionary until peace"

October 12/21 Vendémiaire: Convention calls for the destruction of Lyon

October 16/25 Vendémiaire: Execution of Marie-Antoinette; French troops defeat Austrians at Battle of Wattignies

October 17/26 Vendémiaire: Vendéans defeated at Cholet, cross Loire

October 21/30 Vendémiaire: Decree calling for deportation of refractory priests

October 30/9 Brumaire: Decree closing all women's political clubs

October 31/10 Brumaire: Execution of Girondins

November 7/17 Brumaire: Execution of Philippe-Egalité; clerical deputies to the Convention renounce their vows

November 8/18 Brumaire: Execution of Madame Roland

November 13/23 Brumaire: Vendéans defeated at Granville

November 16/26 Brumaire: First *noyade* in Nantes

December 7/17 Frimaire: Death of Bara in the fighting in the Vendée

December 12/22 Frimaire: Defeat and quasi-destruction of Vendéans at Le Mans

December 23/3 Nivôse: Destruction of remains of the Vendéan army at Savenay

1794

January 11/22 Nivôse: Second *noyade* in Nantes

February 5/17 Pluviôse: Robespierre's speech on Political Morality

March 24/4 Germinal: Execution of the Hébertists

April 5/16: Execution of the Dantonists

April 13/24: Execution of Chaumette, Gobel

May 18/29: Floréal Battle of Tourcoing

June 8/20: Prairial Festival of the Supreme Being

June 10/22 Prairial: Law of 22 Prairial

June 26/8: Messidor: Battle of Fleurus

July 27/9 Thermidor: Fall of Robespierre

July 28/10 Thermidor: Execution of Robespierre and his allies

September 18/2nd *jour complémentaire*: Convention decrees that no religious ministers will receive a state salary

Year III

November 11/21 Brumaire: *Muscadins* attack the Jacobin club

November 12/22 Brumaire: Convention closes the Jacobin club

December 16/26 Frimaire: Execution of Carrier

1795

February 17/29 Pluviôse: Amnesty for Vendéans

April 1/12 Germinal: A largely female crowd invades the Convention; deportation of Billaud-Varenne, Barère, Collot d'Herbois

May 20/1 Prairial: Insurrection in Paris calling for "Bread and the Constitution of 1793"; people invade the Convention and kill one deputy

June 26/8 Messidor: Start of émigré uprising in Quiberon

Year IV

October 25/3 Brumaire: Convention's final decrees against refractory priests and émigrés
October 26/4 Brumaire: Start of the Directory

1796

March 2/12 Ventôse: Napoleon Bonaparte becomes head of the Army of Italy
March 30/10 Germinal: Babeuf begins his conspiracy
May 15/26 Floréal: Bonaparte enters Milan

Year V

December 4/14 Frimaire: Relaxation of laws of 3 Brumaire IV against refractory priests

1797

January 15/26 Nivôse: First theophilanthropist gathering in Paris
May 27/8 Prairial: Execution of Babeuf
June 27/9 Messidor: Further relaxation of laws of 3 Brumaire IV against refractory priests
August 24/7 Fructidor: Revocation of laws on deportation of refractory priests
September 4/18 Fructidor: Coup d'état moves Directory to the left
September 5/19 Fructidor: Reinstatement of laws against refractory priests and émigrés

Year VI

October 17/26 Vendémiaire: Treaty of Campo Formio between Bonaparte and Austria.

1798

April 3/14 Germinal: Directors' decree on the republican calendar
May 11: Coup d'état of 22 Floréal
July 2/14 Messidor: Bonaparte's troops take Alexandria
July 21/3 Thermidor: Battle of the Pyramids
July 24/6 Thermidor: Bonaparte enters Cairo
August 1/14 Thermidor: English destroy Bonaparte's fleet in Egypt
August–September/Thermidor–Fructidor: Laws on the republican calendar

1799/Year VIII

October 16/24 Vendémiaire: Bonaparte arrives in Paris
November 9/18 Brumaire: Napoleon Bonaparte's coup d'état

The republican months (each lasts 30 days, divided into three ten-day *décades*)

Vendémiaire: September–October
Brumaire: October–November
Frimaire: November–December
Nivôse: December–January
Pluviôse: January–February
Ventôse: February–March
Germinal: March–April
Floréal: April–May
Prairial: May–June
Messidor: June–July
Thermidor: July–August
Fructidor: August–September

Complementary days: mid-September. There were five complementary days most years, six in leap years. During the radical Revolution, they were known as the *sans-culottides*.

INTRODUCTION

Toward the end of the semester, I like to give the students in my course on the French Revolution an exercise: if they had to teach the French Revolution but could only include five events, which five would they choose?

The exercise is not easy, given the many worthy possibilities. Among the more famous events of the Revolution, the storming of the Bastille in July 1789 is a strong choice; the king's execution in January 1793 is another. But many events that are less well known today had a major impact at the time. The passage of the Declaration of the Rights of Man changed the legal framework of the kingdom; the revolt of August 10, 1792 abolished the monarchy. Then there was the start of the war against Austria, or of the civil war in western France, and the key French victories in those wars that saved the Revolution: at Valmy or Fleurus, at Nantes or Cholet. Students more focused on biographical explanations look to the different leaders of the Revolution: the rise and fall of the Girondins or of Robespierre; the assassination of Marat, stabbed as he sat in his bathtub; even the rise of Napoleon Bonaparte – these events, too, deserve consideration, given the impact that those men had on their world. All of which is to say that "not easy" is an understatement. Even limiting the timeframe from the start of the Revolution in 1789 until the end of the Reign of Terror in 1794, "impossible" is more like it.

Even if there is no perfect five, as an intellectual endeavor, the exercise does much good. It lets students shape their own stories of the Revolution, while giving attention to some old-fashioned chronology. It makes students weigh the relative importance of chance in historical events (they often ask, "What if such-and-such had *not* happened?"). And, as they approach the end of the course, it lets students take stock of the huge amount they have learned. The French Revolution was a complicated, even bewildering event for the people who lived through it. Teaching it today is a balancing act – you never want to confuse your students, nor your readers. But you do not want to make things seem simple if they were not. During the years that make up the subject matter of this book, things were not simple at all.

Besides, even in less tumultuous times, and with less complex events, people disagree about causes. And so the students make their own decisions about what events led the French Revolution to take the shape it took; then they get to argue with each other over their lists, asking each other how it is that they left, say, the Women's March to Versailles, or perhaps the king's attempt to flee France, out of the top five.

One item that rarely fails to make the students' top five, though, is the Civil Constitution of the Clergy. Passed in the summer of 1790, this law was not, to be sure, one of the Revolution's sexier events. There are no famous paintings depicting its signing, no oft-quoted statements about it. The text of the law reads like an administrative restructuring of a bureaucracy. Its goals were to reshape the Catholic Church in France and to limit the influence that the church had in society. France was a Catholic country, and not only did many French citizens look to the church for guidance, but many of the most powerful men in the church were powerful in the political world as well – not surprising when one considers that in the years before the Revolution, France's most powerful leaders came from a small number of aristocratic families. In the court of public opinion, though, France's Catholic Church – also known as the "Gallican Church" – had been taking quite a beating in the decades leading up to the Revolution. Popular eighteenth-century French writers had been openly hostile to the Gallican Church, portraying it as hypocritical, greedy, and lazy. Licentious priests were stock characters in the pornographic novels of the day. The intellectual movement known as the Enlightenment had made anti-clericalism one of its main principles. The leading writers of the Enlightenment disagreed among themselves on the importance of faith, but they all agreed that the religious institutions that they saw – *especially* the Catholic Church – were holding society back.

The revolutionary legislature included a large number of Catholic clerics – mostly priests, but some bishops as well – but it included a far larger number of men who considered themselves to be followers of the Enlightenment. So it was clear to all involved that with the coming of the Revolution, there would be some changes for the Gallican Church. But while no one expected the leaders of the church to go along with every proposed change, neither did anyone expect the tenacity with which half of the church – and a large part of the population – resisted the changes and, specifically, resisted the Civil Constitution of the Clergy.

The first year of the French Revolution had gone surprisingly smoothly. From mid-1789 through mid-1790, the legislature and the king, together, had transformed France from an absolutist monarchy to a constitutional monarchy; they had reshaped the legal and political framework of French society. They had done this with relatively little opposition, given the scope of the changes. There was a "counter-revolution," at that early point in the Revolution, but it amounted to little more than a small number of disgruntled aristocrats. By early 1791, however, things had changed. Roughly half of France's priests had rejected the Civil Constitution of the Clergy; the government was trying to replace the priests who refused their allegiance, and those replacements had to face down hostile crowds, often relying on military help just to celebrate mass. Villages, towns, communities were expressing their hostility to the government. The counter-revolution was now a popular movement, based in opposition to the Revolution's religious policies, and the Revolution would never regain the enthusiasm and the relative unity that it had before the Civil Constitution of the Clergy.

Instead, France would become more and more polarized. As the government in Paris became more radical the opposition became more extreme, until, by 1793, the Vendée region of western France erupted into all-out civil war. Troops sent from Paris to quash the rebellion found themselves fighting against peasants who seemed to rise up in armies one day only to disappear into the countryside the next. The rebel armies fought in the name of "God and the king," calling for the return of their priests and the restoration of their old religion – the religion that the Civil Constitution of the Clergy, in their minds, had attacked. The revolutionary forces, though, had their own sort of religion: the new religion of the Revolution, much less organized, much less systematic, but one that had its own martyrs, its own beliefs, even its own catechisms and rituals.

In much of France, women played prominent roles in the opposition to the Civil Constitution of the Clergy. Priests who opposed it boasted of the support they received from pious women willing to put their lives at risk in defense of their faith. Supporters of the Civil Constitution complained of the crowds of women whom the priests had "misled," or even "seduced," by playing on women's fears and emotions. The revolutionaries were facing opposition that, in their minds, was threatening the progress of the Revolution and keeping people enslaved to superstition. But could people be forced to "free themselves from superstition"? And if so, how?

On this point, the arguments between my students would also rage, and they tended to be more heated than the debates over the top fives. The religious clashes of the French Revolution bring up some fundamental questions about what freedom of religion means. Some students argued for the women's right to choose whatever religious beliefs they wanted and to act accordingly; other students, more cynical about the role of religion in society, thought that too many women were letting themselves be tricked by the church, and particularly by the men leading the church. All agreed that these were not only questions that remain relevant – what exactly is freedom of religion? And when do claims about religious freedom cloak other demands for political power? – but that these issues went to the heart of the French Revolution. People made decisions based on their religious beliefs, or at least, on what they considered to be their religious beliefs; people behaved in ways they felt corresponded with the appropriate relations

3

between women and men. And not only "ordinary" people – politicians, generals, even the king, would all make decisions that they thought would save their souls, or would preserve (or create) what they saw as the appropriate relationship between women and men.

Questions of gender and sexuality, like questions of religion, intertwined with questions of politics at the highest level. Even before the Revolution, there were newspapers and books devoted to portraying famous people – especially the queen, Marie-Antoinette – in unflattering ways. Many of these papers were downright pornographic. Some even had images. These portrayals of the queen helped shape popular opinions of the royal family, perhaps as much as their financial policies did. As the Revolution advanced, the gossip about the queen only got stronger. But the revolutionaries themselves were not immune, as gossip about each revolutionary leader could make or break their careers – dependent as they were on their popularity among an at times fickle public.

The importance of religion in the French Revolution – and particularly in the reactions to the Civil Constitution of the Clergy – were there to see from the start. Many historians, though, have chosen not to see it, just as until the last few decades scholars were quick to ignore the gossip about the queen. Instead, they tried to uncover what was "really" going on – be it questions of social class, of political philosophy, of the centralizing state. Historians, though, have to determine what motivated people, not what *should* have motivated people. Some of what motivated people during the French Revolution deals with the noblest of human endeavors: liberty for oppressed peoples, freedom of speech, the rule of law, and, to some, the salvation of the soul. But some of what motivated people during the French Revolution belongs to a far lower class of motivations: petty jealousies, sexual gossip, protection of privileges and wealth. There are episodes from the Revolution which bring up implications worthy of the most abstract philosophical debates, and episodes that seem more worthy of an article in *People* magazine.

The first chapter of this book gives a glimpse into what life was like in France before the Revolution came along. Given the importance of religion and sexuality in the French Revolution, it is worth exploring what role they had traditionally played in French society. The rest of the book deals with the Revolution itself, from its start in 1789 through the end of the Reign of Terror in 1794 and the Directory era that followed. Like any history of the Revolution, it can only tell part of the story. My goal has been to tell the most important parts, but some readers will disagree with my assessments of what was more or less important. Some will be surprised at how little attention Danton receives; others will be shocked – if not scandalized – at how few details there are on the external war. Unlike most recent histories of the Revolution, this book does not cover the Haitian Revolution or other developments in France's colonies. Some historians will be surprised at the extent to which I engage with some of the classic nineteenth-century histories of the Revolution, including accounts by Jean Jaurès, Edgar Quinet, Adolphe Thiers, and especially Jules Michelet, rather than relying on more modern scholarship. My goal is not to denigrate twentieth- and twenty-first-century historians of the Revolution, who have added immensely to our knowledge of the Revolution and corrected many of the errors in earlier accounts. Without the work of recent historians like Nigel Aston, Suzanne Desan, Timothy Tackett, Lynn Hunt, and Dale Van Kley, this book would have been impossible. But the classic accounts still have much to teach us, and receive far less attention than they merit. This book attempts to show that the old histories of the Revolution are still relevant.

Given my interpretation of the Revolution, I have focused more than most other historians on events where religion and gender played a major role. This book is not, however, a history of religion and gender during the French Revolution; it is a history of the French Revolution, based on the view that religion and gender were key to how the Revolution unfolded. The distinction might seem minute, but it has important implications for what is, and is not, in this book. There were religious developments which had little impact on the Revolution, which are therefore not included; nor is there any attempt to trace, say, the history of prostitution during the Revolution, nor to quantify the rate of out of wedlock births. There were events which were crucial to the Revolution, but where other motivations held sway – questions of wealth, of nationalism, of privilege – which are in the book. There were other events and developments, though, which seem to have little to do with religion or with sexuality at first glance, but turn out to be far more complicated than they appear. Above all, I have tried to retain the drama of the events themselves. For the people who lived through the French Revolution, these were tumultuous times: dangerous and promising, liberating and deadly. Exciting developments deserve exciting books.

1

RELIGIOUS CULTURE, POPULAR CULTURE

Life in Old Regime France

The France that stood on the verge of revolution in the 1780s did not know that it was standing on the verge of revolution. Nor did it know, in the way that we do now, what a revolution entails. Many of France's inhabitants knew that some things were changing, about which they were concerned or not, happy or not; and there were things that were not changing, about which they were concerned or not, happy or not. By the standards of eighteenth-century Europe France was a large kingdom, and it was not expected that reforms that pleased one group would please others, nor was it expected that traditions that favored one group would enjoy the approval of the rest of society. And make no mistake – countless traditions existed designed to benefit certain parts of the kingdom, traditions that the holders had to defend jealously. Among the most notable at the time was the relative tax exemption for members of the nobility. But while that tax exemption was a prime example of the nature of privilege that the wealthiest members of French society enjoyed, it grew as much out of the fractured nature of French laws and regulations as it did out of the long tradition of social inequality. Different towns had different rights, depending largely on how long they had been part of the kingdom. Different neighborhoods – particularly in Paris – had different regulations concerning who could work at what job and how much they could expect to be paid. Peasants in some regions paid much lower taxes than peasants in other regions. But do not expect the origins or causes of the Revolution to come from the most downtrodden of the peasants, or the most poorly paid of the workers. The most privileged could feel threatened when those privileges were attacked – and, moreover, they tended to have more resources with which to defend them.

What is today known as *la France métropolitaine*, or mainland France, has for most of the last two centuries enjoyed relatively stable boundaries. Aside from the provinces of Alsace and Lorraine, which were part of Germany from 1870 until the end of the First World War, and the occupation of France during the Second World War, the roughly hexagonal shape of modern

France has become established enough to forget that it was a lengthy process establishing it. Many parts of mainland France had some legacy of independence from the French crown, whether that went back to the seventeenth century, as was the case for some parts of eastern France, or back to the medieval era, as was the case for Provence, Brittany, and other regions. Some parts of France still had governing institutions that predated that region's incorporation into the kingdom, institutions which coexisted with more recent government bodies. The various boundaries that covered France, from the dioceses of the Catholic Church to the administrative units known as *généralités* to the traditional provincial borders, rarely coincided. Local political institutions varied both in name and in influence.

Eighteenth-century France was far more than just the hexagon, however. The French crown ruled over a large number of colonies, from North and

Map 1.1 The provinces of Old Regime France. Many of France's provinces traced their history to a time before they were part of the kingdom of France.

Map 1.2 The dioceses of Old Regime France. Note the many small dioceses in southern France, and the lack of correspondence between these boundaries and the provincial boundaries in Map 1.1.

South America to parts of India to Africa. Its most lucrative colonies were in the Caribbean, where the economy was based on sugar cultivation, and where slaves made up the majority of the population. Not everyone in the hexagon was happy about the existence of slavery in the colonies, but under the monarchy the debates over ending slavery were little more than discussions between intellectuals; the crown had no desire to end slavery, and the local elites in the colonies had little interest in any such reforms.

Paris was France's largest city, and had been for quite some time. Sitting astride the Seine River, roughly equidistant from the Atlantic Ocean and France's northwest borders, Paris had a population of roughly 600,000 people in 1789. Paris had been France's capital and the home of its kings throughout most of French history. During the seventeenth century

King Louis XIV moved the royal court to the nearby town of Versailles, to be away from Paris's crowds and the dangers he felt they posed. Versailles did not replace Paris as France's center of gravity, however; Paris remained not only France's largest city, but its most commercially and intellectually dynamic city.

For all of its diversity, France was still a Catholic kingdom, and it is hard to overemphasize the importance of Catholicism not only in shaping the kingdom that entered the Revolution, but also in influencing the shape that Revolution would take. Because of this importance, it is worth explaining something about what "Catholic kingdom" means in this context. It does not mean that there were no non-Catholics in France. There were significant populations of Protestants, particularly Huguenots, who made up as much as two percent of the population. The city of Nîmes had a large Huguenot population, although French Protestantism had become largely rural by the eighteenth century. Relations between Protestant communities and their Catholic neighbors were not the deadly rivalries they had been in the sixteenth century, but tensions remained in many areas where the two religions lived in proximity with each other. Legally, Protestantism was forbidden in France (with the exception of Alsace, which had a noteworthy Lutheran population). There had been a fair amount of government repression of Protestantism during the first half of the eighteenth century, but by the second half of the century such policies had lost most of their public support. A 1787 edict gave Huguenots more rights – including a legal right to marry – although it did not grant Huguenots the right to practice their religion publicly.

Paris and Bordeaux also had significant Jewish communities, as did Alsace. None of these communities were particularly large – there were perhaps 40,000 Jews in France in 1789 – though, as one historian has recently noted, Jews did exercise a fascination among thinkers beyond their numbers.[1] The Jewish communities in Paris and Bordeaux were relatively wealthy and integrated into the local societies. The Alsatian Jews were mostly rural, spoke Yiddish, and were less integrated with the surrounding population. Though Judaism was tolerated, Jews themselves were prohibited from many trades and from owning land.

The term "Catholic nation" also does not mean that everyone who was not Protestant or Jewish was a believing and practicing Catholic. Many people, while not necessarily declared atheists or unbelievers, were increasingly removed from the beliefs of Catholicism. That does not, however, mean that they had given up all of the customs and practices that had evolved along with Catholicism. Some religious holidays were the occasions for festivities in which all people took part, no matter their beliefs.

For millions of French people, the Catholic Church shaped not only their faith but also their social lives – their "patterns of social interaction," to use an academic term. Peasants who spent most of their time on their farms were most likely to see neighbors on Sundays and on religious holidays, whether at church in the morning or, for men, later that day at the tavern. While bishops and priests often complained about the proximity of taverns to churches, most parishioners saw no contradiction between morning mass and afternoon libations. It is not a given that the prevalence of Catholicism represented a deep piety. The historian John McManners notes that

> there is difficulty in disentangling religion and custom, for this was a social order in which human relationships evolved and secular business was transacted within a religious cadre; often, one can only guess at the relevance of the religious reference in the minds of ordinary people.[2]

Here, we are up against the limits of the historical craft; practices, such as church attendance, are easier to document than the thoughts going through the heads of those who attended.

The Catholic Church had official control over the religious life of French Catholics, but that control was not always as easy to enforce as the church would have liked. For one thing, there were a number of divisions within French Catholicism. The French church did have a long tradition of autonomy from the pope, a tradition known as Gallicanism. Almost all French Catholics were part of the Gallican Church, although here belonging or not belonging depended on where one lived, not on the nature of one's beliefs. But it was not always clear what Gallicanism meant in practice. While the pope had only limited authority over French Catholics, there was no one man who played the role of "French pope."

By the eighteenth century, the leaders of the Gallican Church spent much of their time dealing with internal divisions. Sometimes this was because of the frequent quarrels between the high clergy – the archbishops and bishops of France – and the lower clergy, which included the 60,000 or so parish priests who brought the church into all but the smallest villages. At other times, the divisions revolved around the battles between the Jesuits, a well-established religious order with strong ties to Rome, and the Jansenists, a loosely structured movement that favored a more rigorous, ascetic form of Catholicism. The Jansenist movement had begun in the seventeenth century. Around the turn of the eighteenth century French Jansenism had run afoul of both the king and the pope, both of whom set out to destroy the movement. Neither succeeded: Jansenism survived through the eighteenth century, at least until most of its energy was diverted to more political issues by the 1780s. Jansenism even outlasted the Jesuits in France, who were expelled from the kingdom in the 1760s. The pressure on Jansenists from both Rome and Versailles would shape the movement, though. As hostility to Jansenism became a requirement for anyone the king might appoint as bishop, Jansenism became more hostile to the episcopacy and more supportive of the lower clergy.

In some places, these intra-church quarrels played a major role in the daily life of French Catholics. In Paris, in particular, the repeated battles between a heavily Jansenist population and an archbishop hostile to Jansenism played out for many decades; during the 1740s the archbishop went so far as to refuse last rites to Catholics who could not prove their hostility to Jansenism. These battles would do much to politicize the population of Paris and strengthen its hostility to the church hierarchy. In most of France, however, these debates had little to no effect on religious life. Catholics went to church, as they always had, and as they imagined they always would. Catholic parents baptized their children at the local church, young couples got married there, and that was where people's funerals took place, before the burial in the adjacent graveyard. The church bells that rang out on these occasions gave sound to the cycle of life, just as those same bells, ringing out on holidays, gave sound to the cycle of the seasons. Springtime holidays celebrating the resurrection of Jesus occurred just as the earth was coming back to life, while fall holidays like All Saints' Day and the Day of the Dead came when the earth's fertility was coming to its annual end. These mixtures of meanings – the "agro-liturgical calendar," as the historian François Lebrun calls it – show just how difficult it is to separate religious life from other aspects of life in early modern France, be they agricultural, economic, or social.[3]

It is important, therefore, to make a distinction between official Catholicism and the religion that people practiced. Many of the folk traditions that had arisen around various saints did not enjoy the approval of church leaders. Many of the men in the French clergy, whether parish priests in small villages or wealthy bishops, were as concerned about excessive or inappropriate celebrations as they were about those who did not attend mass at all. One priest who had just arrived at his village in southeast France found that the villagers welcomed Lent by having a newlywed bride light fires in front of people's doors at night, so that the following day all of the horned animals in the village could walk through the ashes.[4] In this case as in countless others, villagers saw nothing wrong with the practice – this was how they had always practiced their religion, and how they imagined they always would. Priests were often shocked and scandalized, seeing in these traditions not expressions of Christian faith but the remnants of paganism and superstition. There were limits, however, to the extent to which the men in the church could do anything about those traditions. A priest in a village was caught between two allegiances – to the villagers he saw regularly, and to the church hierarchy whom he represented to those villagers. Priests had to choose their battles, and many came to accept the "superstitions" they saw around them.

Then there were those in eighteenth-century French society who saw the whole thing as superstitious – not just the more obscure practices, but Catholicism itself, Christianity itself, even religion itself. The period is commonly referred to as the "age of Enlightenment," and the chorus of those praising the virtues of rationality and science over faith and tradition grew throughout the eighteenth century. The leaders of this movement, referred to as the *philosophes*, differed on the specifics of their views. Some saw in religion a source of order, others saw merely a means of blinding the population. But all saw in the Catholic Church itself a despotic institution that kept society from progressing. The battle cry to *"écraser l'infame"* – "crush that hideous thing" – became the motto of a movement that tried to free eighteenth-century society from the reins of traditional beliefs. The man who coined that battle cry was Voltaire, a philosopher, novelist, playwright and one of the Enlightenment's biggest stars. Unlike some more radical philosophers of the Enlightenment, Voltaire was no atheist – and he feared a society where atheism was common. Religion exists, he wrote, "to keep mankind in order, and to make men merit the goodness of God by their virtue."[5] For *philosophes* like Voltaire, the value of a religion – as with any other custom or tradition – lay in its utility for society. By that measure, the Catholic Church fell short. Voltaire saw in the Catholic Church a collection of lazy men who abused their power and lived off the work of others.

For all of the Enlightenment's criticisms of the Catholic Church, it is best seen as an optimistic movement. The *philosophes* believed that men, by using their reason, could improve the society in which they lived. They also believed that the spread of knowledge would help society advance. Much of that knowledge would be spread through the written word, but there were also institutions that rose up throughout France, as well as elsewhere in Europe, designed to help spread Enlightenment. There were official academies in most French cities, where leading men (and sometimes women) could gather to discuss the ideas of the day. There were also the more informal salons in Paris, where select members of high society would gather. Those salons were often hosted by women, although not everyone appreciated the prominent role that women played there. By the end of the Old Regime a backlash had begun against these women and the influence they wielded, led in part by Jean-Jacques Rousseau, a Swiss writer and philosopher. For Rousseau, men should be "active and strong." Women, on the other hand, should be "passive and weak," and concentrate on their domestic duties, leaving the world of politics to men.[6]

Rousseau was an extremely popular writer during the second half of the eighteenth century, though he fits oddly with the other leaders of the Enlightenment, most of whom focused on the importance of rationality. Rousseau was more sentimental. Surprisingly, he was as popular with women as he was with men – if not more so. Though he advocated that women be restricted to domestic roles, he also emphasized how important those domestic roles were in shaping citizens. "A home whose mistress is absent," he wrote, "is a body without a soul which soon falls into corruption."[7] Rousseau's arguments against sending infants out to wet nurses led many educated women to start breastfeeding their children. Some recent scholars have seen a certain logic to the way that women at the time embraced Rousseau and his philosophy, despite its apparent misogyny. Still, for those writers at the time who advocated increasing women's rights, Rousseau's popularity with women posed a problem. Thus the *philosophe* Condorcet, who in 1787 advocated giving women full rights of citizenship:

> I am afraid of antagonizing women if they ever read this piece. For I speak of their rights to equality, and not of their sway over men; they may suspect me of a secret desire to diminish their power. Ever since Rousseau won their approval by declaring that women are destined only to take care of us and to torment us, I cannot hope to gain their support.[8]

Whether the philosophers of the Enlightenment were a cause or just a symptom, many people were moving away from the Catholic Church in the second half of the eighteenth century. Quantitative historians have done what they can to measure this shift, and have come up with some impressive findings: the language in which people wrote their wills began to have less reference to Christianity; fewer parents named their children after saints; even the naming of boats showed a movement away from names based in religion to names evoking the sea itself. Numbers can rarely explain everything, however, and some historians have argued that this was not a "decline" of Catholicism, but rather a shift from a more ostentatious spirituality toward a more internalized piety. It is hard not to see *some* sort of decline, however, in religious practices – or, at least, an increased boldness with which growing numbers of people expressed their independence from the church. That independence does not, however, mean that people were abandoning all the practices that the church had instituted – and this is where things get complicated. Just because someone gave up church attendance on Sunday does not mean that they gave up Sunday rest; just because they no longer believed in Christ does not mean that they stopped celebrating Christmas. If rent was due on All Saints' Day, it was due on All Saints' Day, whether one worshipped the saints or not.

Those arguing that the Enlightenment was less a cause of all of these declines than a symptom find much support in what we now know about the extent to which the ideas, and more importantly the texts, of the Enlightenment spread. The Enlightenment was a movement of the wealthy. The overwhelming mass of the population had never heard of Voltaire or Rousseau, and the radical works of the Enlightenment rarely, if ever, managed to reach the peasants living in the countryside. And eighteenth-century France was still, overwhelmingly, a rural and agricultural society. Less than 20 percent of France's population lived in cities in 1789.[9] Aside from Paris's 600,000 or so inhabitants, the other major cities – Marseilles, Bordeaux, Lyon – ranged from 80,000 to 140,000, in a kingdom whose total population hovered somewhere around 27 million.

The social structure that existed among those 27 million people is not easy to describe, due less to lack of information than to debates over the proper way to classify. For quite some time, historians thought that the cause of the Revolution was the advance of a rising industrial capitalist class, or *bourgeoisie*, that had grown in economic power during the course of the seventeenth and eighteenth centuries. According to this inter-pretation, the Revolution represented the now economically dominant bourgeoisie's takeover of political power. But things were not that simple. To start with, trying to figure out just what that "rising social class" was, or who was in it, is hardly a straightforward endeavor. It is not just that the term "bourgeois" meant something fundamentally different in the eighteenth century than it does today. Historians are not sure that there was anything like what people today would call a bourgeoisie – that is, a wealthy urban class, more interested in commerce and industry than in the landed wealth so dear to the nobility.

What we can say is that there was a nobility, which contained less than two percent of the population. The nobility existed not only as a social class, however, but also as an *order*. According to the traditional scheme that existed, France had three orders (also known as estates): clergy, nobility, and commoners. According to tradition, this corresponded to those who pray, those who fight, and those who work. But this simple scheme hides some major divisions. The nobility had long since ceased to be a "warrior nobility" where knights led battles on horseback. Many in the nobility now lived at the king's court in Versailles, made wealthy by the taxes that peasants paid to them. Others, however, were nobility by blood and by name, but had little wealth to speak of. In the western province of Brittany, some of these poorer members of the nobility wore wooden swords, symbolizing at once their exalted rank and their lowly finances. In other words, the links that we expect to see between rank and wealth are not always there. Being a member of the nobility was a legal status, determined primarily by birth. And while most members of the nobility would have preferred to see noble status be determined exclusively by birth, those born out of the nobility but who made enough money were able to buy their way in – much to the chagrin of older, poorer members of the nobility who preferred the traditional values of birth and military service over the rising influence of commercial society.

It was not only the nobility that was growing; the population as a whole was growing over the course of the eighteenth century. The century even saw an increase in births out of wedlock. At the beginning of the century, the percentage of children born out of wedlock was lower than one percent in most of the kingdom (with the notable exception of regions where a large number of troops were stationed). By the end of the century those numbers were quite a bit higher – particularly in the larger cities. Nantes saw its rate of illegitimate births rise to ten percent by the end of the Old Regime, and Paris's rate was twice that.[10] Much of this rise was due to the increasing mobility in society. Many people in Paris, at the end of the century, were not from Paris. Farther from their roots, they were farther removed from the institutions that would have prevented illegitimate births: the church, which would have pressured young people not to have sex until marriage, and extended families that would exert enough social pressure to make sure that the couple married if the woman did become pregnant. The century also saw an increased use of contraception. There were some early condoms, although they did not catch on in the general population. The most common form of contraception was simply *coitus interruptus*, a practice that seems to have spread from the upper classes down through the ranks of the lower classes over the course of the century. Married couples had for generations tried to limit their number of offspring. In rural areas, these attempts at "family planning" were the result of the lack of available land; typically, offspring would live at home until well into their twenties, when a couple could have a farm of their own.

Sexuality had long been more than just a private matter. It was a social concern, one that not only interested people quite a bit, but that was dealt with in ways that would strike many people today as surprisingly public. In some areas, this was as simple as a lack of private bedrooms for married couples; for people who did grow up in one-room houses, "sex ed" was a constant presence from infancy on. Theologians criticized the practice of having the whole family sleep in the same bed, but they were powerless to prevent children in rural areas from learning the facts of life while taking care of the animals. Catholic guides of behavior outlined – albeit in Latin, where only the most educated could read it – just what sexual behaviors were and were not permitted.

It was not only family members and priests who pried into people's sexual behavior. A marriage should be quickly followed by a pregnant wife; if that did not happen, the newlyweds' neighbors would often subject them to rituals known as *charivaris*, intended at once to humiliate the couple and to spur them into action. The actual ritual varied from place to place, from event to event, but some traditions were fairly widespread – especially the practice of making the husband ride backwards on a donkey while neighbors banged on drums and sang. Widowers who remarried were sometimes subject to these rituals as well, as their remarriage was thought to jeopardize other men's ability to find wives.

Such concerns were not limited to the lower classes. Among the wealthier literate classes, the eighteenth century saw a major rise in pornographic books, although they were known at the time as "philosophical books" – a classification that ranged from meditations on epistemology to tales of the adventures of young prostitutes (the latter, frequently enough, with illustrations). Other novels, while less graphic, still revolved around the sort of sexual adventures that would have scandalized earlier centuries.

Women who could tried to remain celibate until marriage, or at least until marriage was impending. It was common for couples to begin sleeping together as their wedding approached; and it was common for couples who had begun sleeping together to suddenly become engaged. In tight-knit communities it might not be easy for a man to avoid marrying a woman who was pregnant with his child. Young women were expected to protect their maidenhood, however, and could expect to be blamed for becoming pregnant, even when they had been raped.

Legally, women who became pregnant outside of wedlock were entitled to financial support from their lover. In practice, this rarely happened. If the man was married, for instance, the woman could not seek financial support from him. There was a certain twisted logic behind this: it was only in cases of fraud or deceit, and specifically the promise of marriage, that a woman had the right to bring her complaint to the courts. If the man was already married, there could be no promise of marriage – at least, no believable one, "and the woman can only complain about her own lack of virtue."[11]

The Catholic Church took sexual behavior seriously and recognized the power of sexual desire. Catholic theologians were especially scandalized by the contraceptive practices spreading among married couples. While some theologians had begun to accept, even praise, sexual pleasure within marriage, intercourse was still only meant to be done for the purpose of pro-creating, and one Catholic writer went so far as to claim that "cheating nature" was as sinful as incest, or the rape of a nun.[12] But the church could do little to stem the tide of changing behaviors, and the periodic well-publicized shortcomings of various clerics did little to shore up the church's public reputation. Many of the most pornographic novels even featured members of the clergy in various states of undress. The popular novel *Therese Philosophe* managed to use relatively few pages to show not only the way that priests would seduce nuns and female parishioners alike, but also to poke fun at the Jesuits' supposed penchant for sodomy over vaginal intercourse. Portraying priests as sex-crazed sodomites was a good way to sell books; it may have changed some people's views of the clerical profession, but it seems more likely that those who read such novels already held pretty low opinions of the Catholic Church.

The increasing numbers of illegitimate births and the spread of pornographic literature led various people at the time to complain about a decline in society's morality. Some historians have gone so far as to talk of a "sexual revolution" during the eighteenth century. Things are not so simple, however. Many of the women who found themselves pregnant out of wedlock were desperate and destitute with few options, taken advantage of by older and wealthier men.[13] By eighteenth-century standards, however, such behavior did reflect a declining morality, making it seem to contemporaries that something was changing, even if it wasn't a revolution. There was still a huge portion of the population that clung to old models of behavior, insisting on proper conduct between the sexes, and restricted contact between men and women (and between boys and girls growing up). To these people, the world was changing for the worse. And there was no shortage of people who were shocked by developments. Most people continued to behave as they always had, and had trouble accepting the changes going on around them. Other people tried to have it both ways, claiming for themselves an upright morality but showing what seemed like a more than passing interest in the actions of the more sexually liberated of their contemporaries.

Unlike the Catholic Church, the government authorities paid only passing attention to enforcing codes of morality. On occasion, and usually after repeated pleadings from the church, the king or one of the local prominent institutions would issue some sort of decree or ordinance that denounced, in impressive terms, whatever particular behavior the church was concerned about. Depending on time and place, this issue could be anything from excessive drinking to opening stores during mass. But true government enforcement would have required not only decrees but also a significant contribution of manpower, and the royal authorities never took that step. They could not compete with the church's 60,000 or so parish priests, nor did they wish to do so. From the government's perspective, it was far easier to have the Catholic Church handle issues of morality. The government did, at times, act to enforce "confessional uniformity" and restrict the activities of Protestants or Jews. Such activity fell under the king's traditional role; at coronation ceremonies the French king's vow included a promise to "exterminate ... the heretics" in the kingdom, a catch-all term that had long been taken to mean the Huguenots. Sometimes the restrictions took the form of outright repression or religious persecution. In two infamous cases in the 1760s, the government executed two Protestants, Jean Calas and the Chevalier de La Barre, under conditions that scandalized much of French society. But the government was not unaware of these scandals and the discontent that they caused. At his 1774 coronation Louis XVI chose to mumble through that part of the oath.[14]

In any case, the royal authorities had other things to deal with (or, to use the French idiom, they had "other cats to whip"). In a kingdom as large as France, it was not easy to keep everything together. The king's first task was to protect the population from foreign invasions. France had been quite successful at this for some time, although that did not keep people from worrying about it. The complementary task was invading other nations, an activity at which France had had mixed results in the preceding centuries. Louis XIV, king of France from the mid-seventeenth century until 1715, had expanded France's boundaries somewhat, although the excesses of several wars had brought a series of crises at the end of his reign. Over the eighteenth century, France got involved in several wars, including the Seven Years War (1754–63) and the American Revolution. Traditionally it allied itself against Austria, which was ruled by the Habsburg dynasty (and whose territories far exceeded the boundaries of today's Austria); its other main rival was England. Since 1635 French diplomacy had been conducted in terms of national interests even when that meant siding with Protestants against other Catholic kingdoms.

By the eighteenth century, the biggest impact of the wars was the way that they strained the kingdom's finances. The government ran on taxes, and the only consistent means the government had found of raising more money was increasing those taxes. The very system of collecting taxes was horribly inefficient, benefiting the private collectors (known as "tax farmers") more than the royal state. But the government never had the power to attack those tax farmers head on.

Historically, the most powerful political institution in France other than the monarchy was the Estates-General. This body would meet to discuss taxation, present the kingdom's grievances to the king, and establish a dialogue between the king and his subjects. The nature of any decision made by the three estates was never clear, however, nor was it clear whether the king was obliged to listen to the Estates-General. Despite the vagueness of its mandate, it was the closest thing that France had to any sort of representative government. But since 1614, it had not met. This led to the "parlements" serving as a de facto voice for popular concerns. Technically, the parlements were law courts, and the men who sat on these courts owned their positions, or "offices." There were thirteen of these courts in France, the largest of which was in Paris. During the seventeenth century, as Louis XIV increased his own power, the parlements' role decreased. During the eighteenth century the parlements played a key role in expressing grievances and resisting royal authority (including defending the cause of the Jansenists). By the end of the century the parlement of Paris had significant political strength – if not enough to enact the changes that they wanted, at least enough to prevent the king's projects from being successful.

There are two ways to look at the impact of the parlements' role in eighteenth-century France. Some saw in the parlements a defense of liberties and a bulwark against an overly intrusive government; others saw a selfish group bent only on protecting their own privileges and preventing any effective modernization of the political system, including the tax system. Its influence over the population, especially in the capital, gave the parlement a level of authority that far surpassed any traditional court.

The role of a king in a large kingdom like France is not always easy to define. The king was responsible for the well-being of his people, and after protecting them from foreign invasion, keeping them from starvation was at the top of the list of his responsibilities. The king often referred to himself as the father of his subjects; it was a term that most kings took seriously, as did their subjects, though different kings handled their obligations differently. Some, like Louis XIV, immersed themselves in the details of the job; others, like Louis XV, preferred immersing themselves in the accompanying perks. By the end of Louis XV's reign, he spent most of his days hunting. The people of France were mostly not concerned with the hunting, but they were concerned with his sexual behavior. Kings traditionally had mistresses, and this had not usually been a problem; but the prominent role that his mistresses the Madame de Pompadour and the Madame du Barry played was a frequent source of discontent among the king's subjects. Frequently, critics attributed misdeeds by the crown to those closest to him, such as powerful ministers, confessors, or mistresses. Mmes de Pompadour and du Barry were by no means Louis XV's only mistresses, but they were the ones around whom the most discontent centered.

Louis XV's mistresses were among the most visible of a small number of women who were able to wield a great deal of influence, by occupying influential (if unofficial) positions. They were particularly resented because of the perceived illegitimacy of their position, especially when people thought that they were abusing their influence over the king by advocating particular political causes or particular politicians. But any woman in a public position, and particularly one able to wield influence, was subject to criticism from her peers – including the women who ran the Enlightenment salons in Paris. Under previous kings, the French not only tolerated but even seemed to endorse a certain amount of sexual profligacy on the part of their kings. With Louis XV, however, people believed he was letting his libido get in the way of his rule.

The opposite was true of Louis XVI, Louis XV's grandson. Born in 1756, the future Louis XVI was his parents' second oldest son and, as such, not originally slated for kingship. His older brother's death in 1761 followed by his father's death in 1765 made him next in line, and also made the choice of his wife the subject of considerable speculation. That choice was not a popular one among many French people, as Marie-Antoinette was a Habsburg princess from Austria – France's traditional rival. The 1770 marriage of Louis XVI and Marie-Antoinette, therefore, represented a change in political alliances, one that displeased many people in France. French people at the time typically referred to Marie-Antoinette as *l'autrichienne*, a word that does translate as "Austrian woman" but whose last two syllables, *chienne*, literally mean "female dog" and figuratively mean pretty much what an English speaker would expect. It was not a term of endearment.

The two were both in their teens when they married. This young age did not change French expectations; and when the young princess did not conceive right away, this led to open speculation on the sexuality of both the young prince and his wife. The cause was most likely a case of phimosis, or an abnormally developed foreskin, which made intercourse painful for the king and prevented the couple from consummating their relationship for seven years. A small surgery would eventually fix the problem, and the couple had their first child in 1778. By that point people's ideas were set. Louis XVI would forever be associated with an inability to satisfy his wife; the hostility toward her quickly became associated with the wildest rumors about her sexuality. These rumours took especially harsh forms during the Revolution, but they were present from the beginning. Often, critics spread rumors of her sexual activities with her female companions, including the Princesse de Lamballe, a young widow devoted to the queen. One 1783 book purported to provide descriptions of the queen's nighttime wanderings around Versailles along with her servants and her ladies-in-waiting. Those walks, the book claimed, would turn into large orgies.[15] Such speculation found an eager audience among the people of Paris, but was by no means limited to the lower classes. It did not help that one of the most powerful men in the French church, the Cardinal de Rohan, apparently believed not only that the queen's support – and perhaps more – was there in return for the gift of an extravagant diamond necklace, but also that she was willing to meet him in the middle of the night, in an obscure part of the woods near the palace at Versailles, in order to make the exchange. As it turned out, she was not; the cardinal had been duped by a group of con artists, and his humiliation would soon become known throughout the kingdom. Marie-Antoinette had never had any wish to see the cardinal, let alone to take things any further. Yet when news spread, as the "diamond necklace affair" dominated discussion, people were quick to blame the queen, although there was no evidence that she had done anything wrong.[16]

Louis XVI was unable to quell the rumors that existed during his era, nor did his course of action save him from the second-guessing of historians. His hesitancy in consummating his relationship with his wife would be followed by a hesitancy in making any major decision. His policies swung wildly over the course of his reign, depending on which minister was most influential that year. He initiated some major reforms, including the loosening of guild regulations and the liberalization of the grain trade. When those reforms met with resistance, however, he did not have the fortitude to see them through, and would place severe limitations on the proposed reform, along with making a change in the ministerial ranks, especially a new favorite installed in the position of controller general, the most prominent ministerial position in the kingdom.

French kings did not have to acknowledge the existence of other political institutions whose power did not come from the king himself. It was not a "constitutional monarchy," as existed in England at the time. In 1766, Louis XV told the parlements that "sovereign power resides in my person only," and that "public order in its entirety emanates from me ... the rights and interests of the nation, which some dare to regard as a separate body from the monarch, are necessarily united with my rights and interests, and repose only in my hands."[17] But even the most basic aspects of governance required cooperation between royal officials and local notables. In all of these relationships there were possibilities for resistance, particularly given the lax nature of the last two kings of Old Regime France. But it was not only resistance to the crown that led to the Revolution. Instead, it was that most basic of all governmental needs: money. By the 1780s, the crown was running out. Financing the French assistance in the American Revolution had been expensive, and the debt had never quite gone away. The king had borrowed what money he could. A rationalizing of the tax code would have helped, but the king did not have the political strength to pull that off. The only option he had was to raise taxes in an ad hoc and temporary manner, yet even that idea turned out to be unworkable. The parlement of Paris eventually refused to register any more tax increases unless the king agreed to call the Estates-General.

In August of 1788, the king gave in. He called for the Estates-General to meet in 1789. He also called for the people of France to tell him, and to tell the Estates-General, what they wanted. In a renewal of an old tradition, the people began gathering their complaints, writing out their *cahiers de doléances* (literally, "notebooks of grievances"), from the cities and from the villages, from the rich, from the less rich, and to some extent, even from the poor. In the months that followed Louis XVI's calling of the Estates-General, the people of France produced thousands of *cahiers*, listing everything that they wanted changed in the kingdom. From today's perspective, the complaints tended to be relatively minor. No one called for a republic, or the end of the monarchy. Most of the peasants had more tangible goals – fewer taxes, an end to some of the obligations that they had to the local aristocrats, perhaps a better system of weights and measures. But in a kingdom as large as France, it was not expected that reforms that pleased one group would please others. Each group was now fighting for what they thought was right, and from every corner the expectations were different – but from every corner the expectations were high.

Notes

1 Ronald Schechter, "The Jewish Question in Eighteenth-Century France," *Eighteenth-Century Studies* 32:1 (1998), p. 86.

2 John McManners, *Church and Society in Eighteenth-Century France*, 2 vols. (Oxford, 1998), II:104.

3 François Lebrun, *Croyances et cultures dans la France d'ancien régime* (Paris, 2001), pp. 97–102.

4 Jean-Pierre Gutton, *La Sociabilité villageoise dans la France d'ancien régime* (Paris, 1979), p. 285.

5 Voltaire, "The Ecclesiastical Ministry," *The Philosophical Dictionary*, available at http://history.hanover.edu/texts/voltaire/voleccle.html.

6 Jean-Jacques Rousseau, *Emile, or On Education*, trans. and ed. Christopher Kelly and Allan Bloom, *The Collected Writings of Rousseau*, vol. 13 (Lebanon, NH, 2010), p. 532.

7 Jean-Jacques Rousseau, *Politics and the Arts: Letter to M. d'Alembert on the Theatre*, trans. Allan Bloom (Ithaca, 1960), p. 87.

8 Jean-Antoine-Nicolas de Caritat, marquis de Condorcet, *Oeuvres de Condorcet*, ed. Condorcet O'Connor and M. F. Arago, (Paris, 1847), IX: 20.

9 Jeremy Popkin, *A History of Modern France* (New Jersey, 2001), p. 9.

10 McManners, *Church and Society*, I:294.

11 Fournel, *Traité de la séduction considéré dans son ordre judiciaire* (Paris, 1781), p. 7.

12 McManners, *Church and Society*, II:302.

13 Cissie Fairchilds, "Female Sexual Attitudes and the Rise of Illegitimacy: A Case Study," *Journal of Interdisciplinary History* 8:4 (Spring 1978), pp. 627–67.

14 See McManners, *Church and Society*, I:15.

15 Sarah Maza, *Private Lives and Public Affairs: The Causes Célèbres of Prerevolutionary France* (California, 1993), p. 208. The book was suppressed in 1783, but became very popular after 1789.

16 Maza, *Private Lives*, p. 185.

17 Keith Michael Baker, ed., *The Old Regime and the French Revolution* (Chicago, 1987), p. 49.

2

THE LIBERAL REVOLUTION OF 1789
(SPRING 1789–SPRING 1790)

January 1789. France was somewhere between a state of political excitement and a more general apprehension: apprehension, due in large part to the poor harvest of 1788 and the scarcity and expense of bread across the kingdom; excitement, from King Louis XVI's announcement that the Estates-General would meet for the first time since 1614. By the end of January the king had even announced the elections to the Estates-General and called for his subjects to compile their grievances for his attention.[1] Change was coming.

But in other ways, France in 1789 was a lot like France in 1779. It was a lot like France had been for decades, perhaps for a century. It was still a monarchy, still an absolute monarchy, and any limits on the king's authority were vague at best. It was still a society of orders, where birth determined wealth and legal status. It was still a kingdom of provinces, with its conflicting jurisdictions, where different regions had not only different traditions and languages but also different laws and institutions. It was still a Catholic kingdom, where the lines between crime and sin were not always clear and where the power of the Catholic Church entered all realms of society.

By the end of 1789, things had changed. The parlements were gone. The provinces' legal existence was gone. One set of laws now governed the entire kingdom. And while those laws were not yet all written, that process was underway enough to make it clear that France was no longer an absolute monarchy, but a constitutional monarchy. It would still have a king, but his power would be limited by laws guaranteeing certain rights to the population. The Catholic Church would lose both its monopoly on official worship and most of its property. And Louis XVI had even approved these measures. He had done so with a heavy heart, and with the eighteenth-century equivalent of his fingers crossed behind his back, but the king did not present himself as the opponent of the Revolution. He had even acceded to the request of the women of Paris that he leave Versailles and move into the Tuileries Palace in the center of Paris.

In other words, France at the end of 1789 was no longer the same country. A revolution had taken place.

It is tempting to see in the light of all of 1789's accomplishments the causes of those events. But it was not the lack of civil rights, the excessive power of the Catholic Church, or the confusion of provincial institutions that caused the Revolution. Or at least they are not what caused the fall of the Old Regime. One of the keys to understanding the French Revolution is that the reasons for the fall of the Old Regime have only indirect relationships with the events and developments of the Revolution. The Old Regime fell for that most banal of reasons: it was out of money.

The monarchy had been in economic difficulties ever since the American Revolution. While the French armies under the marquis de Lafayette played a key role in helping the Americans (and, more importantly for France, in striking a blow at England), it had come at a steep price for the crown. Wars were expensive. And in the late eighteenth century, the money that the French government spent on the war was money that it could not afford to spend.

In true Old Regime fashion, the tax system was unwieldy and complicated, with different rules for different regions, with vastly unequal burdens. The biggest inequality: the nobility, the richest group in the kingdom, were exempt from most taxes. The Catholic Church, with its vast wealth, was also theoretically exempt, although it "chose" to give the king its "free gift" after negotiating with the king's agents about just how much that free gift should include. But that gift never reflected the real wealth of the church's holdings.

There were, then, major structural reasons preventing the kingdom from being economically healthy. But the economy and the politics of the economy sometimes parted ways. It was, of course, quite expensive to run a kingdom like France – with its sprawling administration and its legions of regulators and its armies – but that did not stop many French people from seeing the cause of the kingdom's economic woes in the king's own extravagant displays of wealth at Versailles. People found events like the diamond necklace affair believable because they reflected the views of the royal family, and particularly the queen, as greedy and unsympathetic to the difficulties of the population. It was impossible for the king to call for a rationalization of the tax structure, or to ask for any more sacrifices from his subjects, when neither he nor the queen seemed to be making any sacrifices of their own.

The economy and the politics of the economy also parted ways when it came to how – or rather, who – should fix it. People would see particular politicians as potential saviors or as dangerous villains.

In the category of villain, few could match the queen. It was she, and not her husband, whom the French tended to blame for the court's excesses, or for any unpopular changes in policy. As the diamond necklace affair had shown, she wound up playing the villain in any story that involved her – even when she had done nothing wrong.

In the category of hero, in early 1789, few could match Jacques Necker. A Swiss Protestant, Necker had been the director-general of finances from 1777 until 1781. He was not, perhaps, the typical hero of the day. At a time when people blamed royal ministers for the king's decisions, Necker was a popular minister. He had won the people's hearts when he managed to pay for France's participation in the American Revolution without increasing taxation. That he had accomplished this by deferring the debt payments would matter in the long run, but not the short: he was wily enough to see, before others did, that crucial distinction between the economy and the politics of the economy.

Whether he really had any success in fixing France's financial system is questionable; he was more successful at winning the war of public opinion than he was at getting the kingdom's finances in order. Such a task would have required a more thorough overhaul of the financial system. If any such overhaul was possible, it would have only been with the full support of the king. Necker, however, never had that full support. The king removed Necker from his duties in 1781, a move that many people at the time blamed less on the king than the queen. It is far from clear, though, that Necker would have done things that much differently than the men who replaced him.

Again, the issues that the French economy faced were structural ones. For years, for decades, the government had been meeting its financial needs by borrowing money or adding on ad hoc taxes. But borrowing money would only defer the problem, which would then return with interest – literally. By the 1780s, one of the crown's largest expenses was the interest that it had to pay on loans that it had already taken out. During the middle of the century the crown had introduced several new temporary taxes on landed property, and had done so again in the 1780s. But those taxes met with the inevitable opposition, and that opposition would limit the revenue that the crown could raise.

In a kingdom which needed money, and where the wealthiest paid the fewest taxes, it can be hard to sympathize with the nobility's opposition to new taxes. But the nobility's opposition to the new taxes did have a certain logic to it. Nobles would attack any new tax on issues of principle. That principle? That the taxes were unfair not because of the demands that they made, but because of how the crown imposed them.[2] Aristocrats who argued against tax reform rarely argued that the nobility should not be paying more taxes; they argued that it was beyond the king's authority to reform the tax structure without their help. Or, as the nobles who made up one of the most important courts in France told the king in 1775, "the right to tax your subjects or modify their taxes arbitrarily and at will [would] give rise to a despotism odious to France and shameful for a free nation."[3]

There is one basic point worth highlighting in this debate between the crown and the parlements, between the "despots" and the "aristocrats." Behind the specifics of their mutual acrimony lay a divided ruling class. The most radical phases of the Revolution have the feel of a true uprising of the poor and downtrodden. But it was not the actions of the poor and downtrodden that led to the Revolution breaking out in the first place, or that led to the fall of the Old Regime. It was the fights among the elites of the society that prevented the resolution of the economic crisis of the 1780s.

The opposition to the crown had an ace up its sleeve when it came to tax policies. The king could not legally raise the taxes on his own. He could do many things on his own, according to the rules of the kingdom. He could exile the parlements, he could send people to prison, but he could not raise taxes on his own. So the parlement of Paris eventually made any increase of taxes – even ad hoc increases – dependent on the king calling the Estates-General. This Louis XVI tried hard to avoid, changing ministers, unsuccessfully seeking backdoor approval from groups with only tenuous claims to the relevant authority. None of these tactics succeeded.

There were two main reasons for the king's failure, his inability to avoid calling the Estates-General. On the one hand, here as elsewhere Louis XVI proved unwilling to stick with any of the policies that his ministers enacted. Louis XVI was never a king who had the will to stick with controversial decisions. On the other hand, it is not clear, even in retrospect, that any political solution existed that would have been palatable to enough people to succeed. A more resolute king might have been able to push through the needed reforms; a more resolute king might also have sparked an even more violent response. In the end, the king needed the money, and he had no chance of raising it without working with the parlements. So, reluctantly, in 1788 Louis XVI called for the meeting of the Estates-General to take place the following year. There was no way to know it at the time, but in calling for the Estates-General Louis XVI was putting in place dynamics that neither he nor the parlements could control.

The Estates-General

It is hard to recapture the excitement that greeted the meeting of the Estates-General in May of 1789, the first meeting of the Estates-General in anyone's lifetime. It was an excitement that spread across the kingdom, that reached every village – but none of those villages, none of the provincial cities, could match the excitement in Versailles, where the Estates-General would actually meet.

Versailles, suddenly, was filled with new men from all corners of the kingdom, ready to step onto the world stage, ready to step into the pages of history. For those who watched the events – however closely – it was a seemingly endless flow of personalities, of agendas, far too many, it must have seemed, to keep them straight. The historian writing today can pick and choose among these men, knowing which ones would go on to become famous, and which ones did not, which ones can be safely ignored – yet still the number bewilders.

Some faces were already famous. The stars were there: Louis XVI, but also his ministers, fading stars of a past day. Only one minister seemed to offer any hope for the future, only one minister earned the love of the people: Necker. Among the nobles, there were the rich established families who were already famous. There was the duc d'Orléans, the king's fourth cousin but first rival, at Versailles with the rest of the deputies, but very much with his own agenda. If any of his fellow deputies from the nobility outshone him, it would only be Lafayette, that hero of the New World, hoping to bring his glory back to his homeland, hoping to recreate in France that which he had helped create in America.

Lafayette and Orléans were the stars of the nobility, they were also the extreme avant-garde, the most willing to move in a new direction – what would soon become the extreme *left* of the nobility, when all of the deputies in the Estates-General started sitting left to right by ideology. These soon-to-be left-wing nobles were men of old money, but new ideas. They had each, to some extent, embraced the notion that the times were changing. Those changes might make them a bit less rich, but they could afford it. At the other end? The most conservative nobles were often the poorest nobles. Brittany's nobility, one of the kingdom's most conservative, had chosen to boycott the events altogether.

The clergy, too, sent its share of men, its range of opinions, to the party. It had sent bishops, men born into the nobility – distinguishable from their cousins in the nobility's delegation only by their clothing. Men like La Fare, the bishop of Nancy in eastern France. Still young, he had barely managed to get himself elected from his diocese. Once there, however, he was given the privilege of giving the Estates-General's opening sermon. There, too, was the Cardinal Rohan, the same Cardinal Rohan who had been played for a dupe in the diamond necklace affair, yet had somehow kept his credibility among the men who were given the privilege to vote for him. Then there were men like Boisgelin, the talented and ambitious 57-year-old archbishop of Aix. Boisgelin had paid close attention to the rising new ideas of his day, even if he did not agree with them. Unlike the blanket dismissals of some of his colleagues in the church, though, Boisgelin had taken the time to try to understand those ideas. For some time he had been trying to win himself a place in the royal government, without ever having succeeded. The Estates-General offered Boisgelin a different path to prominence, less dependent on patronage and court politics, and he jumped at it. He campaigned as a patriot, as a supporter of new ideas, rather than simply a defender of the status quo. Boisgelin was willing to accept that developments to come might limit the Catholic Church's power and influence – provided, that is, that they did not limit his own.

Most of the first estate deputies, though, did not have the rank of a La Fare, of a Boisgelin – nor did they have their wealth or prestige. The bishops had all been born into the nobility and shared the second estate's ideas and lifestyles. Many of the deputies, however, were from the lower clergy – particularly the parish priests who brought the Catholic Church to nearly every village and neighborhood in the kingdom. While the bishops shared the same backgrounds as the deputies from the second estate, parish priests were far closer in background and beliefs to the third estate.

Half of the deputies were from the third estate: men who were not from the nobility nor from the clergy (though there were exceptions). According to the traditional scheme of orders, the third estate represented the rest of society, but these deputies were hardly a true cross-section of that society. They were an educated lot, the third estate deputies, with lawyers especially well represented. Most were unknown on the national scene, arriving from their towns, their provincial cities, as the local big fish in their little pond, hoping to stand out in the sea of men that had descended on Versailles.

There was Jean Sylvain Bailly, an astronomer, an intellectual. His goal in the waning days of the Old Regime was to become Paris's answer to Benjamin Franklin, linking politics, science, and intellectual life with the social life of the salons and the court. He entered the Estates-General with enough of a reputation to make people take notice of his actions. It was Paris itself that sent Bailly to the Estates-General, but even the king knew who Bailly was in 1789, knew him as an "honest man." Paris also sent the 49-year-old Armand-Gaston Camus. Like Bailly, Camus had taken part in the world of letters, but Camus's primary focus was politics. A prominent Jansenist, by 1789 Camus had already taken part in many of the quarrels between the parlements and the king's ministers, as well as the quarrels between his fellow Jansenists and their opponents.

Then there was Antoine Barnave, a young man from a Protestant family in the Dauphiné, where France approaches the Alps. As a 10-year-old boy, he and his mother had been thrown out of a theater box reserved for an aristocrat; as a grown man, he would claim that since that incident he was committed to "raise the caste to which he belonged from the state of humiliation to which it seemed condemned."[4] An intelligent man with a powerful voice, he would become one of the most powerful orators of the first years of the Revolution.

Jérôme Pétion arrived from nearby Chartres. Handsome and well spoken, he brought with him a commitment to the people who faced daily humiliations, in the hope of "inspiring in them the sentiment of dignity."[5] His ideas, in 1789, would quickly put him at the far left, where he would find himself allied with a curious, soft-spoken man named Maximilien Robespierre, also a man of the left, a man of ideas and a certain intransigence, but who seemed in 1789 altogether lacking the sort of panache or vigor that would make him stand out above the crowd.

Then there was the Abbé Sieyes. Completely unknown two years earlier, he arrived at the Estates-General as one of the most famous men in the kingdom, thanks to a pamphlet he had written. Most of the men who managed to make themselves stand out did so by speaking well, by inspiring people with their voices, their vitality, with their pride and their utter lack of self-doubt. But Sieyes was a man of ideas, a man of books, and a man of deep-seated resentments. It was those ideas that brought the strength, the passion, to his pamphlet *What is the Third Estate?* That pamphlet, as one recent historian has put it, "managed to catch up the emotions and thoughts that were swirling around him, crystallize them into a powerful and coherent text."[6] In its immortal first lines, Sieyes wrote: "What is the third estate? Everything. What has it been until now in the political order? Nothing. What does it want to be? Something." Throughout the pamphlet, Sieyes took aim at the aristocracy, whom he considered "not part of our society at all." The third estate, wrote Sieyes, "is the nation," but in its current state "it is like a strong and robust man with one arm still in chains."

Sieyes had a religious education that had trained him well without inspiring in him any feelings of faith. He'd gone on to a career in the church despite what seemed to be a complete lack of any piety. For someone like Sieyes – intelligent and ambitious but not in the nobility – the church was one of the few ways to get ahead. And get ahead he had, to the extent that he could, due in large part to the favors done for him by various nobles. Where another man might have responded to this patronage with gratitude, for Sieyes it only nurtured his resentments – resentment toward the aristocratic patrons who had helped him, resentment toward the aristocracy in general. Thus, one of the most autobiographical passages in his pamphlet: a member of the third estate in France

> must submit to every form of contempt, insult, and humiliation. To avoid being completely crushed, what must the unlucky non-privileged person do? He has to attach himself by all kinds of contemptible actions to some magnate; he prostitutes his principles and human dignity for the possibility of claiming, in his need, the protection of a *somebody*.[7]

It was this resentment that *What is the Third Estate?* captured, and that made Sieyes one of the most recognized delegates elected to represent the third estate at the meeting of the Estates-General.

One aspect of Sieyes's argument in his pamphlet concerned a basic question: how should the Estates-General be organized? The Estates-General had last met in 1614, and it was possible to follow those guidelines, known as the "forms of 1614." The problem with the forms of 1614, however, was that they were obsolete in the world of 1789. According to the old rules, each order – the church, the nobility, and the third estate – would meet separately, and each would get one vote. These forms would not satisfy the demands of the third estate. Advocates of the third estate were not interested in having their power be equal to that of each of the other two estates, and one-half that of the other two estates together.

When the king had convoked the Estates-General, he had called for a doubling of the representation of the third estate. Given the makeup of the kingdom, even a doubling seems, from today's standards, weak. The clergy and the nobility together made up at most five percent of the kingdom, and probably less than three percent. But doubling the third estate's voting at least represented some improvement. To stick with the forms of 1614 was, in 1789, horribly anachronistic. And given the circumstances the idea probably would not have gotten much attention at all, had not the parlement of Paris officially endorsed the idea. In this one move, it alienated all but its most devoted supporters.

The parlement of Paris, along with its provincial counterparts, had led the opposition to the crown for decades. The leaders of that opposition had come to have a certain credibility with the larger population, particularly in Paris. With their endorsement of the forms of 1614, that credibility vanished, never to return.

The *timing* of the parlement's demise was therefore quite contingent. But it is hard to see the parlement's demise not coming eventually. There was a philosophical shift going on, a shift away from a belief in the wisdom of the ages and a return to tradition, a shift toward an embrace of reason and independence. The parlements had been arguing for decades that the king's authority was limited, and they defended that position by using historical arguments, by pointing to traditions, by pointing out how often earlier kings had consulted with other men, men from the nobility. For those who embraced the historical argument, the plan for the future was a return to the past – a past with a stronger Estates-General and a weaker king. As one of the king's courts wrote in 1775,

> if we are proposing measures that some call novelties, but which are really only the reestablishment of earlier rules, it is because the progress of despotism and the real innovations it is introducing every day make the reestablishment of true principles absolutely necessary.[8]

In 1789, historical arguments were on the way out. Reason was replacing tradition, abstract ideas of human rights were replacing precedents from previous centuries. For most of the men who were elected to the Estates-General, a return to the past was of no interest – or, at least, a return to the French past was of no interest. The Roman Republic, that was a past that they could use – a past when men played active roles in public life, when, as citizens, men shared in political decisions. But even more than the Roman past, the deputies looked to the ideas of the Enlightenment, and to the role that reason could play in reshaping the world. Thus Jean-Paul Marat, the journalist who would become one of the most radical voices of the Revolution, in January of 1789: "the flames of reason will chase the darkness" from people's eyes. "People of France," he wrote, "you are free, if you have the courage to be."[9]

Over the course of the Revolution, it would become clear just how radical Marat's ideas were, and what a strange character he was. Writing non-stop, always sniffing after one wild conspiracy or another, he would soon be calling for heads to roll, for the deaths of politicians with whom he had what seem like rather minor political differences. The developments of 1789, however, filled him with boundless optimism about the future. He had spent decades before the Revolution arguing against despotism, arguing on behalf of freedom, liberty, and the people. In 1789, he finally saw hope for France.

It had been a strange career, up until then, for Marat. He had tried his hand at most everything. He had been a doctor, a scientist, a philosopher, a novelist, and a political theorist. None of these endeavors had brought Marat the acknowledgment, fame, or fortune he felt he deserved. The Revolution offered a double opportunity for Marat: a chance for that fame and fortune, and a chance for society to finally take the sorts of steps that he had long been calling for.

Marat was hardly alone in seeing this double opportunity. In the last decades of the Old Regime, there was a growing crowd of men who shared Marat's double dream: the dream that society would embrace the message of reason, of the Enlightenment; and that they would be the writers and intellectuals to shape that new society. Most of that growing crowd of men would remain every bit as obscure, every bit as anonymous, during the Revolution as they had been during the Old Regime. But there were men who would find, like Marat, that the Revolution could provide the opportunity they had long been seeking. Jacques Pierre Brissot, Camille Desmoulins – both, like Marat, would make the transition from unsuccessful Old Regime writers and intellectuals to leaders of the Revolution. Brissot had spent the last decades of the Old Regime in and out of trouble, spend-ing time in prison for debts and for his writings, even working as a police spy. In 1789 he started writing newspapers and pamphlets, getting himself noticed. By 1791 he would be one of the most prominent politicians in France. Desmoulins had been an unsuccessful lawyer during the Old Regime; for want of clients, he spent his time in cafes, living off what little money his father would send him. In 1789 he found he could be a successful writer. During the Revolution these men – and there were others with similar trajectories – would quickly take to quarreling with each other. Those later quarrels, though, should not hide the similar career trajectories or the shared beliefs. All were men who had embraced the ideas of the Enlightenment, who saw Rousseau as a hero. They had their own agendas and their own ambitions, but all agreed that society should leave behind its old traditions, its old inequalities, and use the power of reason to remake the kingdom. There was now the possibility for a true reshaping of society, one that could be done along the lines of reason and without regard to traditions, but one that could also be done by a representative government.

This belief in the importance of reason would turn out to be problematic, and those problems would in turn play out in crucial ways during the course of the Revolution. The representatives of the Estates-General took it for granted that not everyone was equally possessed of the power to think rationally. Parents were required to look after their children, because they could better see what was in the children's own interest. Nor were men and women equally capable of thinking rationally, according to the views of the time. Women, many people believed, were more emotional and more easily led astray. Men had a greater capacity to think rationally, and therefore had an obligation to make certain decisions for women. Those better off and better educated also had a greater capacity to think rationally than the lower ranks of society, and therefore the obligation to make certain decisions in the name of society that others would perhaps not agree with but which were nevertheless in the interest of the good of society. In other words, there was a certain elitism built into the ideas of the Enlightenment.

Even Sieyes's *What is the Third Estate?* – with all of its anger toward the aristocracy, with all of its claims on behalf of the nation – turned out to be using the ideas of the Enlightenment not on behalf of the most downtrodden in the society, but on behalf of those most like Sieyes: educated, well-off, but excluded from the nobility. When discussing who should represent the third estate at the Estates-General, Sieyes wrote that they had to come from its "available classes," which he defined as "those classes where some sort of affluence enables men to receive a liberal education, to train their minds and to take an interest in public affairs."[10] This view of who should lead the nation was broader than the one that had existed in the Old Regime – but still a small portion of the population. It did not include the women of France; it did not include all those employed as domestic servants (a significant portion of France, especially in the cities); and it excluded those in the lowest ranks of society.

Later in the Revolution, these issues would divide the different factions of the third estate. In 1789, enthusiasm could sweep all those divisions under the rug; all in the third estate wanted a larger role in the Estates-General, a shared desire which hid the divisions between the lower ranks of the third estate and its elite in the background.

The search for leadership

What is the Third Estate? made Sieyes famous and sent him to the Estates-General as one of its most recognizable members – a surprising turn for a man who had until then been completely unknown. He would turn out to be not much of a leader, however. It was with ideas and concepts that Sieyes was most comfortable. The leadership in the Estates-General, and in all future assemblies, would require oratorical skills, the ability to speak dramatically enough to get people to listen. This was a skill that Sieyes did not have. He was also a rather solitary figure. Jacques Necker's daughter, the Madame de Stael (herself a significant political commentator in her own right in the later years of the Revolution), would later write that "the human race displeased him."[11]

Madame de Stael's father, however, would not have much more success than Sieyes in leading the Estates-General in 1789, despite the extraordinary popularity he enjoyed among the opposition. Louis XVI had recalled Necker in 1788, in an attempt both to improve the kingdom's finances and to appease the demands of the public. To the public, and to many of the deputies, Necker still represented hope. Not all of that hope would survive his disappointing speech on the first day of the Estates-General. Expecting an exciting speech on the principles of government, they received a long technical discussion of finances. Expecting resolutions in favor of the third estate, they received statements that were vague and uncertain, talks about the possibility of a limited increase in their future role.

Necker would not be the leader that the Revolution seemed to need. But who would be? In 1789, the leaders that emerged were men who came to Versailles with some renown already. Men like the marquis de Lafayette and the comte de Mirabeau. Two very different men – Lafayette, only 19 years old when he first arrived in South Carolina in 1777 to fight alongside Washington, and still in his early thirties at the start of the French Revolution, was already a celebrity. Associated with the American Revolution and the ideas which it represented, he was enough of a traditional military leader to be comfortable talking with the royal family and with members of the upper nobility. In July 1789 he would become the head of a new unit, the National Guard, responsible for maintaining order. Lafayette struggled, however, to find the support he expected from the rest of French society.

Mirabeau was a different sort of leader. Like Lafayette, he was from noble stock, yet Mirabeau arrived in Versailles as a representative of the third estate. He had come to view their cause as his own, and his own class had long since soured on him. He had spent his youth in and out of trouble, living the life of a young member of the nobility – drinking, womanizing, quarreling, and gambling. He was a rather ugly man, as a result of an early bout of smallpox that permanently damaged his face, but that disfiguration did not keep him from a series of well-publicized and scandalous romantic conquests. His actions had been enough to land him in prison and exile on a few occasions in his youth. He had mostly managed to keep himself out of trouble since his last release from prison in 1782, continuing to make a name for himself in a complicated sort of double game, sometimes criticizing the monarchy, sometimes working with it. Mirabeau would continue this double game during the early years of the Revolution, where he would emerge as one of the few leaders of the third estate to be able to talk with the royal family.

It was not only his intellect and experience, however, that led to him having such an influential role in the early phases of the Revolution. Like Barnave, Mirabeau was a first-class orator. In the Estates-General, where these newly created politicians were talking with each other for hours on end every day, trying to determine just what it meant to be a politician in France in 1789, those who could talk the most convincingly were successful. Thus it was that in 1789, Mirabeau would be the most successful in presenting himself as a leader of the Estates-General – or, as it would soon name itself, the National Assembly.

The term "National Assembly" itself represented a victory for Sieyes – for his ideas, if not for his role in the actual assembly. Always focused on the theories of government, always indifferent to the traditions of the past, Sieyes had no need to remain faithful to historical precedent in the naming of the representative body. His proposal to rename the Estates-General the National Assembly quickly gained popularity among the third estate. It took some maneuvering before the other two orders would join them. Indeed, relations between the three orders went poorly from the time they arrived at Versailles in May. The third estate felt belittled and disrespected by the other orders and by the king. But in the early weeks after being convoked, the third estate was the one order that stuck together, united by their frustration. One day – 20 June – when the third estate deputies found the doors to their assembly hall locked and guarded by soldiers, they gathered in a nearby indoor tennis court, swearing their commitment to their cause. Soon enough, members of the first two estates did join it, first a few, then a few more, until the trickle became a stream. When it became clear enough that the third estate had won the battle, the king ordered the other two estates to join it. The Estates-General was no more, replaced by the National Assembly. Soon, that name would become the "National Constituent Assembly" – or just the Constituent Assembly, for short.

The king's order that the other two orders join the National Assembly must not be read as a sign that Louis XVI was becoming a full supporter of this new political universe. Soon, indeed, there were signs that the king was going to go back on his promises. The court at Versailles was full of powerful people plotting against the National Assembly – starting with the queen herself. Some of these voices were already clamoring for Louis XVI to send the Estates-General home, to bring in troops, to quash these new developments. But the king could not make up his mind. He set plans in motion then abandoned them; there were signs all around of an impending crackdown, enough signs to make people nervous – but as yet no actual crackdown. The king brought a total of 16 army regiments into the Paris region on June 26 and July 1. The people of Paris knew that the army was arriving. They did not know why, they did not know how many – and so they feared the worst. Rumors filled the air, the people convinced that the counter-revolution was coming, that the army was going to march on the National Assembly. Some fears went farther still. Would the National Assembly be shut down? Would it be blown up, with all of the deputies inside? Would the king's brother lead an army to march on Paris, killing thousands in some sort of bloody revenge? And while events did not bear out the wildest scenarios, it was clear enough that the king was planning *some* sort of crackdown – although, given Louis XVI's patterns, it is likely that he would have abandoned the plan before it actually came into full effect.

Louis XVI eliminated any last doubts on July 11. He dismissed Necker and several other ministers, replacing them with opponents of the National Assembly. Whether the 16 army regiments were in place to occupy Paris in preparation for shutting down the National Assembly, or whether they were there in case of protests that might take place after the closing of the National Assembly – or for another reason altogether – the people of Paris knew that the soldiers were there. The members of the National Assembly also knew that the soldiers were there, and asked the king to withdraw them, and to recall Necker – requests that the king denied.

In these circumstances, the people of Paris decided that the Revolution was in peril. The people of Paris decided to fight back.

The storming of the Bastille

To hear the nineteenth-century historian Jules Michelet describe it, the population of Paris transformed itself into an army on 13 July. When the city received word of Necker's dismissal, the city sprang into action. A *de facto* leadership committee had grown out of the elections to the Estates-General; the "electors," as they were called, decided to raise a militia of 48,000 men. Rumors continued to spread. At one point Paris was convinced that an army of 15,000 soldiers was already on its way to invade the city. These were desperate times; it was hard to separate truth from exaggeration, exaggeration from falsehood. After all, people learned of the false rumors of the arriving soldiers in the same way that they learned, accurately, of Necker's dismissal. The leaders ordered people to put up barricades and to sound the alarm – via the time-tested method of ringing out the tocsin, which meant the city's bells would peal. In a city like Paris, which had bells all over – and in an era where few things were louder than those bells – it was enough to let everyone in the city know that there was cause for alarm.

To raise a militia required not just men, but also arms. Those were not easy to come by. By morning, 30,000 Parisians who had gathered to support the National Assembly had made it over to the Hôtel des Invalides in western Paris. There, they succeeded in obtaining 30,000 to 40,000 muskets, along with 20 cannons.[12] Weapons in hand, the crowd then left the Invalides and headed back to the Hôtel de Ville – the city hall, in the center of Paris – to plot their next move.

At this point, they had guns and they had cannons, but no bullets, and little gunpowder. Getting that gunpowder and ammunition would turn out to be far harder than obtaining the muskets themselves. One Parisian wrote of taking what powder he was rationed and going to a local store to purchase nails to use instead of bullets. Others marched unarmed, or with pikes, or simply with guns but no bullets, to the one place known to have a stockpile of gunpowder: the prison in eastern Paris known as the Bastille.

The fall of the Bastille, in the following days, would come to symbolize the fall of arbitrary power and the fall of despotism. As with all of the prisons of the Old Regime, being sent to the Bastille was something more complicated than just breaking a law, given the rights that parents had to have their children locked up, or the ease with which a powerful member of the nobility could have someone from the lower ranks sent there for something as minor as an insult. (Early in the century, Voltaire himself had been locked up there for a satire he had written.) The prison's imposing view, a grim fortress less than a mile from the Hôtel de Ville, added to its image as a bastion of despotism. But if despotism fell with the taking of the Bastille, it is still worth remembering that the crowd that approached the Bastille was focused not on overthrowing despotism, but much more on the task at hand: finding gunpowder and bullets.

It was not a goal that the man in charge of the Bastille, the Governor de Launey, had much sympathy for. His forces were badly outnumbered: he had around 80 army veterans and 30 Swiss guards. But his forces did have a strong tactical superiority. They, of course, had all the bullets and gunpowder they could possibly want. They were inside a fortress that was designed – like all fortresses – to resist attacks. For the last several days de Launey had been preparing for such a confrontation. It was because of these preparations that he had moved the gunpowder to the Bastille, where it could be defended. (Once there he had simply left it in the courtyard; the Swiss guards moved it underground on the 13th.) De Launey even had six carts of cobblestones delivered and brought up to the towers, to throw down at anyone attacking – a tactic more reminiscent of the thirteenth century than the eighteenth.

The actual taking of the Bastille was a long, drawn-out affair, full of smoke and gunfire and confusion. Delegates from the city's electors came several times but were unable to prevent bloodshed and, once the fighting started, they were unable to stop it. The prison had an outside gate, then an inner courtyard, and then a second round of towers surrounded by a moat. The people were able to get into the inner courtyard quite quickly, only to discover that they were sitting ducks for the Swiss guards firing

Figure 2.1 The storming of the Bastille, July 14, 1789. By the end of the day, reinforcements had come to help the protesters take over the prison. From *Révolutions de Paris*. © Penn Special Collections.

on them. To the people, it felt like a trap: they had been drawn into the courtyard only to be massacred.

The battle was a stalemate for several hours. The turning point came when reinforcements came for the attackers – not just more civilians, but troops from the French Guards loyal to the third estate, along with several cannons seized that morning from the Hôtel des Invalides. From that point on, it was clear that time was running out for the soldiers inside. They could have held out until reinforcements came for them too, but it was telling that the first soldiers to arrive as reinforcements came in on the side of the people. Indeed, the allegiance of the area's soldiers was a major question in July of 1789; the troops stationed outside of Paris might not have been the force of despotism that the people of Paris feared.

By the end of the fighting, 83 of the attackers were dead; one had been crushed by the drawbridge, most of the others shot dead after entering the courtyard. Only one of the soldiers defending the Bastille was killed during the fighting. Some would be killed that night by members of the crowd, angry at what they saw as the betrayal of luring them into the courtyard just to shoot their comrades down. De Launey, for his part, surrendered himself to be taken to the Hôtel de Ville. The surrender did not save him. Upon reaching the Hôtel de Ville the crowd succeeded in getting de Launey away from his protectors. One of de Launey's last actions was to kick one member of the crowd, an unemployed cook named Desnot, in the groin;

VUE DE LA PLACE DE GREVE LE JOUR DE LA PRISE DE LA BASTILLE.

Figure 2.2 The aftermath of the storming of the Bastille outside Paris's Hôtel de Ville. From *Révolutions de Paris.* © Penn Special Collections.

Desnot did not have to wait long for revenge. After the crowd had killed de Launey, Desnot cut off his head and placed it on a pike, which cheering crowds then paraded throughout the city.

That night and the following days were a mixture of celebration and mourning, of elation and horror. The wives of the dead men grieved for their husbands, or went out in hopes of avenging them; the people were elated at the victory, at their success, at the abolition of the prison. Members of the nobility began the first of what were to be many waves of emigration. The comte d'Artois, youngest brother of Louis XVI (and the future King Charles X), joined this first wave of departures, as did other prominent members of the nobility. Many of the aristocrats who had watched the events unfold with concern, with trepidation, now moved to outright fear.

As for the men in the National Assembly – they were torn. The day was saved but the violence involved was a bit much. The people of Paris had acted on behalf of the National Assembly, but it was the Parisians' initiative. Many deputies worried that the violence would come back to haunt the Revolution, that it would harden the forces of reaction, that it would hasten the end of any hopes of achieving a constitutional monarchy in France. When the news first reached the deputies in Versailles it was not well received.

The true impact of the storming of the Bastille would only become clear in the following days. The deputies sent a delegation to check on conditions in Paris; that delegation would report back that the city was ecstatic, that a sentiment of victory and unanimity filled Paris. For Louis XVI, who noted in his journal that "nothing" happened on July 14, over the course of the next three days he would recall Necker, he would withdraw the troops. Finally, on the 17th he visited Paris himself and appeared before the people wearing a tricolor cockade that Sylvain Bailly had presented to him. The cockade, a blue, white and red headpiece, had become a symbol of the Revolution. For the people of Paris, the king – who was not only in Paris, but wearing the cockade – was now on their side.

Again, it is clear in retrospect that the king's endorsement of revolutionary measures was not done wholeheartedly. But in July of 1789, things were less clear. People wanted to like him. They wanted to like him so much that they were willing to blame people around the king – his brothers, his advisors, and especially the queen – for any false steps the king may have taken.

The deputies in the Assembly, meanwhile – they wanted to like the people. And as the impact of the storming of the Bastille became clear, the deputies in the National Assembly had to change their views toward the people who had stormed it, even change their views on violence.

The taking of the Bastille was a Parisian event, but it was not long before its impact was felt across the kingdom. In cities across France, local supporters of the third estate had their own versions of the events in the capital. The first wave of rural reaction to the events in Versailles and Paris, however, preceded the news of the Bastille's fall.

The chronology is complicated, because in 1789 it took time for news to spread. In most cities, the first wave of political action of what would be called the "Municipal Revolution" occurred when people learned of Necker's dismissal and heard the rumors of royalist armies marching on Paris. People began to organize militias, and – as the people of Paris had done – the citizens of the provincial towns prepared to resist the arrival of royal troops. When news of the fall of the Bastille came, those concerns vanished, and the people rejoiced, in what one historian called "an explosion of enthusiasm and delight."[13]

The impact of the taking of the Bastille in the countryside went beyond this enthusiasm, it went beyond this delight; it went as far as dismantling the local governments, in some cases leading to the end of institutions that dated back centuries. Those institutions, so recently covered in the glory of tradition, were now swept aside in the name of reason and progress. In many cities and towns, the transition was peaceful. The old elites simply ceded before the crowds. In place of the old patchwork of local institutions came a new patch-work, this time of various "national committees" or "permanent committees," led by men loyal to the National Assembly. Within a few weeks, the traditional power structures that the nobility had long dominated had fallen.

The Great Fear

It was now time for the next major player to present itself: the peasantry.

France was still a rural nation, and when studying the Revolution it is easy to get lost in the details of events in Paris and Versailles. The people living in Paris at the time, however, were well aware of the enormity of the rural population and the ties between the towns and the countryside. All towns, but especially a large city like Paris, relied on the countryside for its survival; the rural areas supplied the grain that fed the urban populations. When this interrelationship functioned well, it let people in the countryside earn more than they had, and kept the cities well fed. When times were tighter, distrust reigned, people fought and even rioted over the destination of grain shipments. The peasants in the countryside believed their grain would be taken from them just to feed the cities, even if it meant that the people who had grown it would starve; the urban populations did not trust the peasantry to let the grain come to Paris and the other cities, although their strongest suspicions were aimed more at the middle-men who made money off the trade itself, rather than at the people who had grown the crops.

All of which is to say that at the start of the Revolution, the people of the cities and towns and the people of the countryside did not always have the same goal. So it is not surprising that the countryside had been relatively unimpressed with the early phases of the Revolution. Many of the aims of the deputies – ruling according to the precepts of reason, rationalizing the criminal justice system – were not issues on which the peasantry were focused. Their demands were much more tangible: peasants had asked for lower taxes and fewer obligations to the nobility.[14]

If the peasants distrusted the urban inhabitants, that distrust was nothing compared to the hatred that many of them had for the nobility. Nobles had various rights over peasants' lands, ranging from collecting rents, to monopolies on milling grains, to the right to hunt on lands that peasants were farming. This system of "seigneurial" rights had evolved in the Middle Ages, when the nobility justified its privileges based on the military protection they were supposed to provide. The eighteenth-century nobility was no longer a warrior nobility, yet they held on to their traditional rights. Even justice was in the hands of the local *seigneur*, who presided over the local courts. And if the most famous seigneurial right – the *droit de cuissage*, or the right of the local lord to sleep with peasant women before their wedding night – was a myth, that did not stop the local peasants from finding grievances to air against their local seigneurs.

These were longstanding demands, but the peasantry did realize that the political context had changed. The king's instructions that all villages compile lists of grievances had heightened people's expectations throughout the countryside. The peasantry had been expecting some sort of benefits to arrive since the calling of the Estates-General and, thus far, had been disappointed. Add to that the agricultural context, and people were quite uneasy. The 1788 harvest had been a major disappointment throughout the kingdom, the worst since the beginning of the century. Signs for the upcoming harvest were promising, but with the crops not yet ready it was still vulnerable. It was at this point that the first rumors of "brigands" began to spread throughout the kingdom.

In some ways, the rumors surrounding the brigands would start to look a bit like the rumors that spread through Paris on the eve of the taking of the Bastille. Peasants were generally aware of what was happening in Paris and Versailles, even if (as in the cities) they rarely had a reliable way of separating true information from false. They knew that key members of the nobility were fleeing France; they knew and expected those nobles to try to overturn the changes that had occurred since the start of the year. The brigands, then, could either appear as simple bands of criminals, of a kind that had been feared for years; or else they could seem more ominous still, as some sort of secret counter-revolutionary army, paid off by the aristocracy. With all the changes that had occurred in recent months, anything seemed possible. People stood waiting, armed as well as they could be, readying themselves for the brigands' arrival. As Georges Lefebvre, the foremost historian of rural France during the Revolution, points out, "what matters in seeking an explanation for the Great Fear is not so much the actual truth as what the people thought the aristocracy could and would do." And when an entire population sits waiting for the arrival of some enemy, "it would be very unusual if this enemy were not actually sighted at some time or another."[15]

Triggered by these fears of brigands, the "Great Fear," when it did break out, was an odd combination of rural riot, uprising, and generalized panic. It was violent but rarely deadly, chaotic but not without certain similarities from one region to another. There would be a "sighting" of the brigands; this could be a result of anything from a group of wandering vagabonds to clouds of dust caused by a flock of sheep, but usually it was the result of armed peasants from neighboring villages who, ironically, had come to warn of the brigands' arrival. This would lead to mass hysteria in the village. For the peasant women,

> in their imagination, it was already too late – they were raped, then murdered, their children slaughtered, their homes burnt to the ground; weeping and wailing, they fled into the woods and fields ... Sometimes, the men would follow close behind once they had buried anything of value and set the animals loose in the open country ... Preparations would be made for the defense of the village ... Everyone armed himself as best he could.[16]

When it became clear that no brigands were coming, things would calm down. But for all of its fictional basis, the Great Fear had some very real repercussions. Often, villagers chose to maintain the defense groups that they had set up. During the Great Fear, many peasants had taken the opportunity to attack the local chateau. Some they burned down; others they left intact, but burned the records listing the taxes and duties that local peasants had been required to pay.

For the men in the National Assembly, these events were troubling. The deputies had little sympathy for the traditions and customs that had long served as justifications for the particular form of unequal distribution of wealth in the French countryside. They were, however, strong believers in the importance of property, and as news of the Great Fear came to Paris and Versailles, the destruction of so many chateaux, the widespread violence, made it look like things in the countryside were spinning out of control.

This was, however, the post-Bastille National Assembly, in the aftermath of the deputies' embrace of popular violence for political ends. The Great Fear became the spark for a wide-reaching reassessment of the very shape of French law and the relationship between the classes. On the night of August 4, 1789, with news coming in to Versailles from throughout the kingdom detailing the kingdom's unrest, the deputies met and, piece by piece, proceeded to dismantle the system of land ownership that had evolved since the Middle Ages. Depending on one's perspective, it was either one of the most gallant, selfless events of the Revolution, or else a cynical, backdoor attempt to retain as much of that system as possible.

It was deputies from the nobility, and not the third estate, who took the lead on the night of August 4.

These were the men who had the most to lose from the peasants' actions, and who for generations had gained the most wealth off the peasants. The night started off with one of the kingdom's richest nobles, the duc d'Ai-guillon, along with other prominent members of the aristocracy, pledging to forgo some of their privileges. D'Aiguillon invited his fellow nobles to give up their privileges in exchange for compensation; but when his fellow aristocrat the marquis de Foucault followed, with a speech condemning the privileges that he and his fellow nobles shared, it unleashed a spread of self-sacrifice among the members of the nobility, who one by one pledged to forgo their privileges. By two o'clock that morning, when the session finally ended, the deputies had vowed to abolish virtually all of the nation's privi-leges and the entire feudal system, and those men with the most to lose had taken the lead in renouncing their privileges.

For Michelet, these were genuine acts of self-sacrifice. Many members of the nobility were already tired of the role that they played in the kingdom, tired of defending the old feudal tyranny. Their actions on the night of August 4 represented the best of the noble spirit – along with its enthu-siasm and its tenderness, the aristocracy showed "the vivacity of a noble gambler who takes pleasure in throwing away gold."[17] Jean Jaurès, in another classic history of the Revolution, had a different – and far more cynical – interpretation of that evening's events. For Jaurès, the nobles who renounced their rights had known what they were doing; they were, he noted, far better informed of events in the countryside than were their urban colleagues. They knew that many of the rights they were renouncing were ones that they had no chance of regaining. Their best chance at holding on to something resembling the lives that they had led was by making themselves popular in the countryside through their very public self-sacrifice. Their actions, therefore, were more self-interested than they appeared.[18]

Whichever interpretation is correct, the implications of the night's decisions were quite astounding. The feudal structure and the complicated patchwork of privileges that had long defined the kingdom of France were gone. Now the Assembly just had to decide what to put in their place.

The night of August 4 was a night of declarations, of proclamations, of sweeping statements and noble promises. Over the next few days, the deputies set about putting those declarations, those promises, into law. In that process, the deputies stood back from some of the extreme promises of that euphoric evening, deciding in a few cases that there would be reimbursement where previously there had been none. But the final document, the Decree of August 11, still stands as one of the turning points not only in the history of the Revolution, but in the history of France.

The decree started with a bold declaration: "The National Assembly entirely destroys the feudal regime." Privileges that the nobility enjoyed over the peasants in their regions were now gone – privileges that had existed for centuries, gone with the stroke of a pen, with the word of the National Assembly. Many – although not all – the Assembly abolished without compensation. Some of the issues that bothered peasants so much, and that peasant *cahiers* most frequently mentioned, were among the first to go – including the exclusive right to hunt that the nobility had long enjoyed, even when it meant running roughshod over peasant farmland. The decree also abolished the tithe, a tax that the peasants had long been required to give to the clergy, although it did so in a not very convincing manner, promising that there would soon be a new system in place to pay the clergy and maintaining the tithe until that time.

The most important changes in the decree, however, came later in the document. Item nine abolished all "pecuniary privileges in matters of taxation," declaring that all taxes will be "levied on all citizens and properties in the same manner and the same form." In other words, the exemptions from taxation that the nobility and the clergy had enjoyed for centuries were over. Item ten was no less dramatic an overhaul of the traditional French laws: "all the peculiar privileges, pecuniary or otherwise, of the provinces, principalities, districts [*pays*], cantons, cities and communes, are once and for all abolished and are absorbed into the law common to all Frenchmen."

In abolishing all provincial laws and privileges, the National Assembly was making a move toward both equality among people and increased power for the central government. From today's vantage point, it is easy to see the advantages of having one set of laws for the entire kingdom. To do away with the different customs was certainly a move toward simplicity. It was also a blow for the local nobilities, who invariably profited from the local laws. But, as noted above, when those local nobilities defended their privileges and traditions, it was rarely in the name of their own benefits; rather, they defended those privileges in the name of tradition, of liberty, and of providing some protection from the dangers of an overly powerful central government. These had been the traditional claims of the parlement of Paris, but those claims were increasingly foreign to the men of the National Assembly. Many deputies shared a disdain for traditional privileges, but also possessed an optimism about their own ability to use the dictates of reason to reshape their kingdom. They did not see the dangers of increasing the central government's power, so long as they felt they were doing so for the right reasons.

On August 26 the National Assembly adopted the Declaration of the Rights of Man and Citizen. This declaration shared the same spirit as the Decree of August 11, declaring the civil equality of all men and confirming the elimination of any sort of distinctions before the law. Even more than the Decree of August 11, though, the Declaration showed the influence of the Enlightenment. The sixth article's claim that "the law is the expression of the general will" was an explicit reference to Rousseau's philosophy; the first article's statement that social distinctions could only be based on public utility was a tribute to the eighteenth century's fascination with the concept of utility.

Along with civil equality, the Declaration provided guarantees for the freedom of speech and the protection of property. But the Declaration is worth a close reading. Along with its guarantees of freedoms, it also contained some strange qualifications, ways in which it restricted the rights it seemed to guarantee. The freedom of opinion was guaranteed, "even in religious matters, provided that their expression does not trouble the public order"; every citizen could speak and write what he wished, but was "accountable for abuse of this freedom in the cases determined by law." All citizens were innocent until proven guilty; but anyone summoned before the court who did not appear as required "makes himself guilty by resisting."[19] The men in the National Assembly were eager to provide the people with the freedoms that the Old Regime government had denied them; but those same deputies always kept an eye on the central government's role.

The Declaration of the Rights of Man and of the Citizen

August 26, 1789

The Representatives of the French People, constituted as a National Assembly, considering that ignorance, forgetfulness, and the disdain of the rights of Man are the sole causes of public misfortune and the corruption of Governments, have resolved to show in this solemn Declaration the natural, inalienable, and sacred rights of Man, such that this Declaration, present constantly for all Members of the social body, will constantly remind them of their rights and their obligations; such that the acts of the legislative power, and those of the executive power, can at any instant be compared with the goals of all political institutions, and be all the more respected; such that citizens' demands, henceforth founded on simple and incontestable principles, always revolve around the support of the Constitution and the happiness of all.

Consequently, the National Assembly recognizes and declares, in the presence and under the auspices of the Supreme Being, the following rights of Man and of the Citizen.

1   Men are born and remain free and equal in rights. Social distinctions can only be based on general utility.

2   The goal of every political association is the conservation of the natural and imprescriptible rights of Man. These rights are liberty, property, safety, and the resistance to oppression.

3   The source of all Sovereignty resides essentially in the Nation. No body or individual may exercise the authority that does not expressly derive from it.

4   Liberty consists in being able to do anything that does not harm others: therefore, the exercise of the natural rights of every Man has no limits other than those that assure the other Members of Society the enjoyment of those same rights. These limits can only be determined by the Law.

5   The Law only has the right to prohibit actions which harm society. Anything that is not prohibited by Law cannot be prevented, and none may be forced to do that which the Law does not command.

6   The Law is the expression of the General Will. All Citizens have the right to participate personally, or via their representatives, in its formation. It must be the same for all, in that which it protects as in that which it punishes. All Citizens being equal in its eyes are equally eligible to all dignities and to all public positions and employments, according to their capabilities, and without other distinctions than those of their virtues and their talents.

7   No Man may be accused, arrested, nor detained except for in those cases determined by the Law, and according to the forms which it has prescribed. Those who solicit, aid, execute or have executed arbitrary orders, must be punished; but any Citizen summoned or held according to the Law must obey instantly; he makes himself guilty by resisting.

8   The Law must establish only those penalties strictly and clearly necessary, and no one may be punished except by virtue of a Law established and promulgated before the crime, and applied legally.

9   All Men are presumed innocent until they are declared guilty, if it is judged indispensable to arrest him, all severity not necessary to secure his person must be severely repressed by the Law.

10   No one must be disturbed for his opinions, even in religious matters, provided that their expression does not trouble the public order established by the Law.

11   The free communication of thoughts and opinions is one of the most precious to Man: any Citizen may therefore speak, write, and print freely, but are accountable for abuse of this freedom in the cases determined by Law.

12   The assurance of the rights of Man and of the Citizen requires a public force: this force is therefore instituted for the advantage of all, and not for the particular utility of those to whom it is confided.

13   In order to sustain the public force, and for all the administrative expenses, a common contribution is indispensable: it therefore must be equally shared among all of the Citizens, in proportion to their means.

14   All Citizens have the right to determine, by themselves or via their representatives, the necessity of the public contribution, to agree to it freely, to track its use, and to determine its basis, duration, and the mode of its collection.

15   Society has the right to demand of each public Agent an account of his administration.

16   Any society in which the guarantee of these Rights is not assured, nor the separation of Powers determined, does not have a Constitution.

17   Property being a sacred and inviolable right, no one may be deprived of it, unless the public necessity, legally established, clearly demands it, and under the condition of a just and pre-established indemnity.

Perhaps the most important aspect of the Declaration, however, lies not in the content of any of the rights that it listed, but in the named holders of those rights: the *citizens* in the title. For centuries, the inhabitants of France had not been citizens, or at least their rulers had not considered them to be citizens. They had been subjects. In an absolute monarchy, subjects obeyed the king. Citizens, however, were active participants in the public and political life of the nation. The idea of being a citizen instead of a subject went back to the ancient world and the republics of Greece and Rome. There, the men of the upper classes were expected to take part in major decisions, and to be ready to fight and die for their fellow citizens. The revolutionaries' emphasis on the importance of citizenship was not only meant to expand the rights that the men of France enjoyed; it was intended to reshape the relationship between the government and the population.

The transformation of subjects into citizens would arrive in fits and starts, however. In late October, the National Assembly would introduce a distinction between "active" and "passive" citizens. To be an active citizen required that one be French (which could be established in a variety of ways); male; and that one's annual taxes were at least the equivalent of three days of unskilled labor. The distinctions did not end there. The poorest of the active citizens had only a limited say in the government; the complicated election procedures that the Assembly envisioned for future legislatures included grades of eligibility all the way up to the "silver mark" of 54 days of unskilled labor. It was in some ways a less democratic system than the one that had chosen the deputies to the Estates-General.[20]

Not everyone was pleased with this division between active and passive citizens. The distinction between rich and the poor incited the most debate, and the most ire from the left. Desmoulins, pointing out that Jesus Christ would have been a passive citizen, added that "the true active citizens are those who captured the Bastille, those who cleared the fields while the feeble clergy and the Court, despite their immense wealth, acted like plants."[21]

If the exclusion of the poor led to opposition, the exclusion of women passed with barely a notice. There were very few voices calling for women to get the right to vote.

From today's perspective, and particularly when reading in English, the word that stands out in the title of the Declaration of the Rights of Man and of the Citizen is "man," not "citizen," though neither implies the spread of rights to women. In late eighteenth-century France, few people considered making women equal to men – be it in legal status, in economic status, or in the responsibilities women had in public life. The relationship between the rights that the government was bestowing on the men it governed and the division of sexes in society, however, is more complicated than determining which rights women did and did not have. Roughly speaking, the rights that "men" enjoyed involved freedom *from* excessive government intrusion. These rights included the right to own property and the protection against arbitrary imprisonment. These rights were ones that, for many in the eighteenth century, were compatible with the societal roles that they expected women to play. Not so, the rights of citizens. The rights that citizens enjoyed involved the freedom *to* participate in the public life of the nation. For the revolutionaries, for many people in France at the time, that sort of political activity was not compatible with their view of the proper role of women in society or with their view of femininity. The revolutionaries viewed citizenship as masculine – even virile – and women had no part to play in it.[22]

The members of the National Assembly – every last one – were all men, and this surprised no one at the time. Indeed, many a deputy, many a supporter of the National Assembly, believed that one of the problems with Louis XV's reign, with Louis XVI's reign, was the excessive influence that women had. From the scandals of Louis XV's mistresses to the *salonnières* of the Enlightenment, women were leading France astray, using their excessive influence to prevent the regeneration of the kingdom. Marie-Antoinette, from this perspective, was but the most recent of a series of women who had harmed the kingdom. So beyond there not being any women in the National Assembly (a rather banal point to make about any eighteenth-century political body in Europe), there was also a particular ethos to the National Assembly that grew out of the combination of its all-male composition and the open displays of emotion that frequently ran through the Assemblies at certain times. As Rousseau had argued, politics was the work of men. Increasingly, the revolutionaries described the links that united them as the bonds of *fraternity* – the links not between fellow men, or even fellow countrymen, but between brothers.

The motto "Liberty, Equality, Fraternity" was not the Revolution's motto yet. Or at least, it was one motto among many, and in 1789 they were not yet carving it in stone. But it is not without cause that it would become the most prominent motto; it fit well with the principles of the men leading the Revolution. The full repercussions of the revolutionaries' focus on fraternity would play out later in the Revolution, but some of its early implications were there from the start. The historian Lynn Hunt has argued that the Revolution can be seen as a move from a paternal to a fraternal model of government.[23] This shift was only beginning in 1789, and the men in the Assembly hoped that they, the brothers, could also in some sense remain good sons to their "father," the king. Marat wrote in January 1789 that all of the members of the Estates-General "would only see, in the national assembly, the children of one big family, of which the monarch will show himself to be the father."[24] But family relations do not always run smooth, love can turn to hatred – and Marat himself would soon become something other than the ideal son. In 1789 the deputies were still united by their newfound bonds of fraternity. They were at times impatient sons, given Louis XVI's inconsistent support of the Revolution, but they were still willing to be won over by his more noble gestures.

If the king was the father and the deputies were brothers, how could women participate in the Revolution? If this was a Revolution for the citizens, and the citizens were men, what was left for the other half of the population to do? This was a question that both women and men faced. Some of the men's most patronizing answers were also the answers that women greeted with the most enthusiasm. Women were to be the moral guardians of the nation; they were to support their husbands; they were to provide examples of virtue which would inspire their husbands, their brothers, their neighbors. Women were to give birth to the next generation of revolutionary heroes and raise them to be true citizens. Here, too, the influence of Rousseau was strong. Not only had he argued that politics was the work of men; he had argued that women's domestic role was key to a healthy society.

Any talk of what women or men should be doing, of what they should not be doing, always runs up against the facts of what people actually did. Gender roles always have some fluidity to them. For all of the views about what women should be doing, women had long been doing things that they were not supposed to do. From the start of the Revolution, women who wanted to take part in the political process found ways to do so. They read newspapers, they attended meetings, they took part in protests in the street. Women also attended sessions of the National Assembly, whose meeting place in Versailles had space for thousands of spectators. Women found ways to make their voices heard – and if their voices were not heard as much as those of the men in the government, they were heard more than some of those men would have preferred.

There was a long tradition of political activity by women that dated back to the Old Regime. In confrontations between the population and the forces of order, there were always women rioting along with men. In these riots, a sort of division of labor between women and men had developed, where some activities were considered more appropriate for women, others for men. The storming of the Bastille was considered more appropriate for men – it involved gathering guns and ammunition in order to form an army. Women were more likely to take part when the riots were about issues that were considered "women's" issues. In eighteenth-century France those issues usually involved bread, housekeeping, and children. In the 1770s, when a governmental attempt to eliminate the restrictions on the grain trade led to a series of food riots, women were often in the front ranks of the rioters. That tradition was about to expand in the next major event of the Revolution.

The October Days

Even in the best of times, people worried about food; and when people worried about food, they mostly worried about bread. In September 1789, bread was getting harder and harder to obtain in Paris. While the events of the Great Fear had passed, people were still concerned about the vulnerability of the next harvest. During good times, the inhabitants of France – and particularly Paris – might enjoy a more varied diet. When times were tight, bread was the main source of sustenance for much of the population; it was the one thing to eat when there was only one thing to eat. The heightened political tensions did not make the bread shortages any easier to deal with, but they did make people more likely to express their discontent. By mid-September women in Paris were complaining that the men there did not understand anything about provisioning the city with bread, and that the women should play a larger role in the matter.

The women's activism in demanding more bread was a complicated issue for the men of the National Assembly. According to the traditional views, in times of dearth it was the king's responsibility to keep his subjects fed. The king was not only the kingdom's father, he was also the "first baker." In 1789 the women of Paris were, on the whole, very much supporters of the National Assembly. But there were echoes of the old paternalist model of kingship that still had a hold on people's hearts.

On October 4, women began to gather at the Hôtel de Ville, demanding bread. One of the men there was Stanislas Maillard, a man who had distinguished himself in the taking of the Bastille. He noted that the women "would not listen to reason," and that they were coming "from every direction, armed with broomsticks, lances, pitchforks, swords, pistols, and muskets" (but, again, no ammunition).[25] Eventually the women decided to march to Versailles and present their demands to the king – along with Maillard, and along with two cannons. As one woman cried out, "we're going to Versailles, to ask the king for bread for ourselves, our husbands and our children, and for the provisioning of the capital."[26]

The Women's March to Versailles – also known as the October Days – needs to be seen in the context of a convergence between the lack of bread and the political developments of 1789. The National Assembly had already presented to the king the Declaration of the Rights of Man and of the Citizen. The king had not yet signed it into law. The king had stated his concerns about the Decrees of August 11 in September; on October 4, Louis XVI would express his concerns about the Declaration of the Rights of Man to the National Assembly.

The Assembly was already debating the role that the king would play in the reshaped government. The National Assembly knew that France would have a constitutional monarchy in place of the absolutist monarchy that had existed during the Old Regime. In the fall of 1789, no one was talking about eliminating the monarchy and starting a republic. Just what role the monarch would play in that constitution, however, was one that the men of 1789 were having trouble figuring out – one that in many ways, they never would figure out. The particular bone of contention in October of 1789 concerned the king's right to veto the Assembly's legislation. The queen's insistence on her husband's absolute right to veto any legislation had led to her latest nickname, "Madame Veto," but the king too hoped to retain as much power in the legislative process as he could. It was these concerns that led to his statement to the National Assembly, and to his reservations about the Declaration of the Rights of Man. That statement did not sit well with the deputies.

The Women's March to Versailles, then, had goals beyond just the demand for bread. The marchers set out to Versailles intent on getting the king to approve the Declaration and to give up on the plan for an absolute veto. When word reached Paris that during a banquet at the royal palace soldiers in Versailles had walked all over a cockade, that news served as the spark that led the women to march. In times of such little bread, *any* banquet was seen as unpatriotic; the symbolic attack on the Revolution, via the cockade, made things that much worse.[27]

The march itself was a dreary affair, the day rainy and cold. A quick train ride today, the palace of Versailles lies 12 miles from the center of Paris, most of that distance lying beyond the city's eighteenth-century borders. There were no provisions for the marchers, many of whom had already been suffering from shortages of bread and other foods in the days and weeks leading up to the march. At one point, when the women came upon a soldier on horseback they kicked the man off his horse, which they then killed and ate on the spot.[28]

There could hardly have been more of a contrast between life in the capital and life at the king's court at Versailles. It was at this point that some people falsely claimed Marie-Antoinette spouted her famous "let them eat cake" line – a claim which belongs alongside others made about the queen, ranging from the improbable to the downright obscene. But understanding the distance between the two worlds requires nothing more than noting that at the time when the women arrived at Versailles to see their king, he was out hunting. It would take several hours before his return, and several hours after that until any of the women would be able to talk to him.

The women's arrival at Versailles was a mixture of protest and celebration, of anger and joy, of violence and reconciliation. They sang the king's praises – even, eventually, gave some words of praise to the queen. They killed two soldiers protecting Versailles and paraded their heads, once again, on pikes. They greeted with joy the king's promise to return with then to Paris.

The deputies knew enough to take advantage of the situation. They successfully pressed the king to accept the Decree of August 11 and the Declaration of the Rights of Man. They also knew not to stick around in Versailles. The National Assembly, declaring itself inseparable from the king, joined him in the move to Paris. The royal family would move to the Tuileries Palace in central Paris. The Assembly would scramble a bit for

Figure 2.3 The women of Paris bring the royal family to Paris. The "French Heroines" escorting the royal family from Versailles to Paris, which will become the king's "principal residence." From *Révolutions de Paris*. © Penn Special Collections.

space – there were few options in Paris for such a large assembly – before eventually settling in the salle du Manège, a horse-riding space adjacent to the Tuileries.

This legacy of the October Days – the government's transfer to Paris – can hardly be overestimated. Kings of France had lived at Versailles since the mid-seventeenth century. It was the fear of Parisian mobs that had led Louis XIV to seek the refuge of the countryside estate at Versailles; now the women of Paris had brought his great-great-great-grandson back to Paris. The route back was filled with the crowd's joyous cries of "long live the king" and their joy at having brought back "the baker, the baker's wife, and the baker's son." It is hard to believe, though, that the king or his family was happy about leaving Versailles. Paris had changed a great deal since Louis XIV had taken up residence in Versailles, but not in ways that would make it more tempting for a king – even if Louis XVI tried to like the Revolution, and the Revolution, at least in 1789 and 1790, tried to like Louis XVI. It just was not a good match. As for the queen, she was not pleased with the developments. She had never felt comfortable around the people, and not without reason. Long since tried and found guilty in the court of public opinion, people had not only blamed the queen for everything from the public debt to the inefficiency of the government, those same people had proved an eager audience for whatever pamphlets her rivals at the court had printed about her, no matter how scandalous, no matter how pornographic. The royal couple, along with their children, would spend the next 20 months as *de facto* prisoners in the Tuileries Palace until an ill-fated attempt to flee the city in June 1791, which would eventually be followed by their official imprisonment and finally their executions. At the end of 1789, however, the royal family and the people of Paris were able to pretend that this was all an arrangement that was for the better – the reconciliation of the well-meaning king and his devoted subjects.

The move to Paris would have a major impact on the Assembly as well. The people who had supported the Assembly on July 14 were still there to support the Assembly, but they were also able to make their desires known in a more direct manner than some of the deputies would have preferred. The galleries at the Manège were smaller than those at Versailles had been, but their occupants found ways to make themselves heard, and, in the process, made it harder for the deputies to hear each other. The National Assembly was a loud place. Women, in particular, became active audience members in the Assembly's galleries, cheering speeches they liked, and "murmuring" or even shouting the speakers down when they disapproved. The particularly male ethos of the National Assembly coexisted with an audience that was largely female – an audience which some politicians thrived on, some disliked, and others feared. Meanwhile, outside the Assembly the deputies were in the same city, the same boisterous city, as any other Parisian. By the standards of the eighteenth century, Paris was not only a large city; it was a loud city, full of church bells and markets, full of people yelling out the latest news or yelling simply to be heard. What was true inside the Assembly was true of Paris as a whole: once there, some politicians disliked the city, some feared Paris and could not wait to leave, while other politicians thrived.

The events of the following years would make the developments of 1789 appear less significant in retrospect. But for inhabitants of France, 1789 was a dramatic upheaval of so much of what they had known. The fall of the Bastille symbolized an end to a whole tradition of absolutist rule; the success of the third estate, in turn, symbolized the arrival of an era of constitutional rule. Few people, however, doubted that France would remain a monarchy. The people of France expected the king to continue to rule. Most people looked to him to rule according to a new constitution, but they expected that constitution to provide a significant role for the monarch. The France that emerged from the changes of 1789 was also still very much a Catholic kingdom. True, it was no longer officially Catholic; the Declaration of the Rights of Man had established the freedom of religious opinion for all inhabitants, within limits. The National Assembly's attempt to redefine the relationship between the Catholic Church and the nation had begun in

1789; but its most prominent reforms would come in 1790, when the central government issued the Civil Constitution of the Clergy. That legislation would end up reshaping not only the relationship between the Catholic Church and the French state, but the entire French Revolution.

Notes

1 Baker, ed., *The Old Regime*, p. 182.
2 Quoted in Baker, ed., *The Old Regime*, p. 64.
3 William Doyle, *The Origins of the French Revolution* (Oxford, 1988), p. 45.
4 Quoted in William Doyle, *The Oxford History of the French Revolution*, 2nd ed. (Oxford and New York, 2002), p. 26.
5 Jérôme Pétion, *Régles général de ma conduite* (Paris, 1792), p. 11.
6 William Sewell, *A Rhetoric of Bourgeois Revolution: The Abbé Sieyes and What is the Third Estate?* (Durham, NC, 1994), p. 7.
7 Emmanuel Joseph Sieyes, *What is the Third Estate?*, trans. M. Blondel, ed. S. E. Finer (London, 1963), pp. 51–2, 56, 57, 61.
8 Baker, ed., *The Old Regime*, p. 63.
9 Jean-Paul Marat, *Œuvres politiques, 1789–1793*, 10 vols. (Brussels, 1989–95) [henceforth *OP*], 1:3, 5.
10 Sieyes, *What is the Third Estate?*, p. 78.
11 Quoted in Sewell, *Rhetoric*, p 21.
12 Jacques Godechot, *La Prise de la Bastille* (Paris, 1965), p. 268. See also Jules Michelet, *Histoire de la Révolution française*, 2 vols. (Paris, 1979), I:144–56.
13 Georges Lefebvre, *The Coming of the French Revolution*, trans. R. R. Palmer (Princeton, 1947), p. 124.
14 John Markoff, *The Abolition of Feudalism: Peasants, Lords, and Legislators in the French Revolution* (University Park, PA, 1996), pp. 30–2.
15 Georges Lefebvre, *The Great Fear of 1789: Rural Panic in Revolutionary France*, trans. Joan White (New York, 1973), pp. 50, 60.
16 Lefebvre, *Great Fear*, p. 156.
17 Michelet, *Histoire*, I:194, 196.
18 Jean Jaurès, *Histoire socialiste de la Révolution française*, 4 vols. (Paris, 1969), I:320–7.
19 Baker, ed., *The Old Regime*, p. 239.
20 See Doyle, *Oxford History*, p. 124.
21 Quoted in http://chnm.gmu.edu/revolution/d/412/.
22 William H. Sewell, Jr., "Le Citoyen/la Citoyenne: Activity, Passivity, and the Revolutionary Concept of Citizenship," in *The French Revolution and the Creation of Modern Political Culture*, vol. 2, *The Political Culture of the French Revolution*, ed. Colin Lucas, 371–87 (Oxford, 1988), p. 119.
23 Lynn Hunt, *The Family Romance of the French Revolution* (Berkeley and Los Angeles, 1993).
24 *OP* I:47.
25 Quoted in Darline Gay Levy *et al.*, eds., *Women in Revolutionary Paris, 1789–1795* (Urbana, 1979), p. 35.
26 Baker, ed., *The Old Regime*, p. 234.
27 Doyle, *Origins*, p. 121.
28 Michelet, *Histoire*, I:222.

3

THE CIVIL CONSTITUTION OF THE CLERGY (SUMMER 1790–SPRING 1791)

On July 14, 1789, the people of Paris seized the Bastille. That event transformed the Revolution.

On July 14, 1790, the people of France set out to commemorate that event. The resulting festival would surpass the enthusiasm of 1789; it would mark the high point of the early years of the Revolution, the high point of revolutionary unity.

The commemoration was officially known as the *Fête de la fédération*, the Festival of the Federation. Despite its date, it was far more than just an anniversary or a commemoration. Throughout the kingdom, people gathered in towns and villages to honor the Revolution. In the days and weeks leading up to July 14, from every corner of the kingdom, soldiers known as *fédérés* – older soldiers, veterans of wars gone by – set out for Paris, to take part in the main celebration. That celebration by hundreds of thousands of enthusiastic citizens took place on the Champ de Mars, the fields in western Paris that, today, lie in the shadow of the Eiffel Tower but that on that day were transformed into a great hill, transformed by the sweat of Parisians who did everything they could to make the celebration as good as it could be.

To hear its supporters describe it, everyone in Paris took part in preparing the Champ de Mars. When the men the government hired were not up to the task, the citizens of the capital put their energy into the project and brought the plan to completion. With the old soldiers already on their way, with villages and towns across France greeting those soldiers, the capital was not going to let the soldiers' experience in Paris be outshone. "The whole population," according to Michelet, began working day and night: "men of all classes, of all ages, even children, all citizens, soldiers, priests, monks, actors, nuns, beautiful women, shopkeepers' wives"[1] all took part. One eyewitness, Louis Sébastien Mercier, agreed: "I saw 50,000 citizens," he wrote, "of all classes, of all ages, of all sexes, forming the most superb portrait of unity."[2] There were even women who "forgot the weakness of their sex" and pushed the wheelbarrows. Other men also noticed the women's participation. One song praised the way that their "delicate hands" had taken on so

55

much difficult work, and the zeal with which the women had set about their tasks.[3] The work began on July 7, the people completed it before the 14th.

The unity of the Parisians in constructing the scene, on the day of the festival, became the unity of the nation. In the main festival in Paris, there was a place for everyone. Soldiers marched in procession before the king who stood over them. Some deputies in the Constituent Assembly had grown weary of Louis XVI by this point, of his inconsistencies and his indecisiveness, but the soldiers were touched by the presence of the "good citizen king" – awed, even, by the sight of their monarch, their hearts filled with filial piety. The people had long seen the king as their father, even if Louis XVI was sometimes uncomfortable in that role. Lafayette, the long-time revolutionary, newly dedicated to the royal family's safety since the events of October, stood at the king's feet. Alongside him were 200 priests, showing their allegiance to the Revolution. For the sermon blessing the procession a man named Talleyrand, the bishop of Autun, rose to the altar. This would not be the last that the Revolution saw of Talleyrand, a young bishop, intelligent, ambitious, and unencumbered by religious faith. As in all of the major festivals of the Revolution, women were prominent – even if the song quoted above described their presence as the "ornament" of the festival. But as the song explained, the women should not end their parti-cipation with the preparation of the festival. "Your task is not fulfilled," the song went, calling on women to "Give us little Heroes/ worthy emulators of their fathers."[4]

In the provinces, the festivals lacked the pomp of the Parisian event, but not the enthusiasm. The provincial festivities were, as Mona Ozouf points out, syncretic events.[5] Rather than sticking to the script sent from Paris, they used that script to weave their traditions into the Revolution. People in villages celebrated their marriages and baptisms at the festival; maypoles and processions, with which people had celebrated holidays for generations, were now recast as rituals to celebrate the Revolution.

In Paris, as in the provinces, it was a festival of unity. Young and old people, new and old customs; rich and poor, men and women celebrated together. And if the heavens seemed not to cooperate – in Paris and nearby cities, it rained all day – the people danced together in the rain. The event unified monarchy, religion, and revolution. The only people excluded were the *émigrés*, the aristocrats who had begun to flee France in the aftermath of the fall of the Bastille, whose absence strengthened the unity of those who did participate. But if the émigrés did not participate, they were at least spared the fate of the enemies of the day the year before, or in Versailles the previous October. No one paraded anyone else's head on a pike.

Was this true unity? Or was the festival only a superficial way of covering over rifts that would have soon surfaced, no matter what the politicians did? Whichever was the case, the unity was not to last.

The great split in the Revolution was not between the aristocrats and the people. The Revolution would have survived that split; in 1790, the Revolution was surviving that split. But the Revolution as it existed in 1789, in the first half of 1790, would not survive the split with the Catholic Church. That split was already starting to develop in 1789. On the eve of the Festival of the Federation, the conditions for the split were in place. By the end of 1790 it would be more apparent; by early 1791, it would alienate many supporters from the Revolution. A disproportionately large number of women, even women who had been early supporters of the Revolution, would find themselves on the other side of the political divide. Soon, Catholic priests would stand along with émigrés and aristocrats as the enemies of the Revolution – blamed for the Revolution's setbacks, blamed for the "errors" of the counter-revolutionary women. By 1793, France would be in the throes of full-scale civil war.

The Festival of the Federation, for all of its pomp, for all of its importance, was not a completely isolated moment of unity. The year had started off well. In February, Louis XVI appeared at the Constituent Assembly, unannounced, unplanned, and gave one of the finest speeches of his entire reign (granted, the bar here is fairly low). The deputies, for a brief period, left behind their partisan bickering and their criticisms of the king, and let themselves get caught up in the enthusiasm of the moment.

One of the Assembly's projects that the king specifically praised was the new division of the kingdom into departments. These departments – there were 83 of them in the original plan – replaced the traditional provinces, as well as the other political jurisdictions of the Old Regime. This redrawing of the political map was, indeed, one of the Revolution's most enduring reforms; although some details have changed, they are still overall the political demarcations of France today. In its own way, the creation of the departments helped contribute as much to the unity of the nation as did the Revolution's festivals. The old provinces had existed for centuries, remnants of times when the territory was split into rival kingdoms. Some regions, like Brittany and Burgundy, had long legacies of independence, grounded in historical traditions. The departments were meant to rationalize and unify the kingdom, but they were also meant to eliminate the allegiances that people had to their provinces, and replace them with an allegiance to France; they were meant to replace the allegiances based on tradition with allegiances based on rational administration and the rights of man. For the king to approve of this new division was a promising sign.

The king's praises did not stop there. He declared himself a friend of the constitution which the Assembly was writing. It was, perhaps, self-interested praise. His magnanimous offer to the Assembly to solve the

Map 3.1 The departments of France. The departmental boundaries, 1790. Note the departments' relatively uniform size. The 1790 boundaries are very close to the boundaries that exist today.

difficult problems was also his way of advocating a strong executive and more power for the monarch in the constitution's final version. But that did not stop the deputies from rising to their feet and swearing their allegiance to the constitution, and it did not stop the series of celebrations that swept Paris, and then the provinces, over the next ten days.[6]

There is no need to exaggerate; the euphoria following the king's appearance at the Constituent Assembly, the exhilaration of the Festival of the Federation, these were not typical days. The Constituent Assembly was quickly finding itself divided into factions. Writing a constitution was not easy. The egos of the Revolution's leaders did not help matters, either, as one man after another sought to lead one faction or another. And even on the day after the Festival of the Federation, Marat was crying out warnings, telling his readers that the nation was too trusting, that their "blind confidence" would lead them straight to a new despotism.[7] But the real threats were small.

True, Marie-Antoinette was not particularly pleased with developments, or with being a de facto prisoner in Paris. But her various attempts at plotting revenge against the Revolution were not effective. She did not take up the offers of assistance from the two men who could have helped her, Mirabeau and Lafayette. She did not want to be saved by the men who had brought the Revolution.[8] She was hoping instead to be helped by her brother, the Austrian emperor, but he had his own issues to deal with. Eventually, all of Europe's monarchs would recognize the French Revolution as a threat to their power. In 1790, that was not yet the case, and most of the neighboring powers still saw the confusion of the Revolution as a chance to expand their boundaries at France's expense.

As for the émigrés, they continued to flee, and they continued to haunt the imaginations of those still in France, but they posed little real threat. The most powerful of the émigrés (including the king's brother, the comte d'Artois) did little but bicker with each other and complain about their situations. The counter-revolution, in the first half of 1790, barely existed; its lack of participants was matched only by the lack of cooperation between those participants.

There were threats to the peace in early 1790, especially in southern France. Two cities, Montauban and Nîmes, saw major violence between the Protestant and Catholic populations. In Montauban, officials inventorying church goods found themselves facing riots led by Catholic women; in Nîmes, four days of street battles between the largely Protestant national guardsmen and Catholic groups led to over 300 deaths. With the rise to prominence of several key Protestant politicians, including Barnave and Jean-Paul Rabaut de Saint-Etienne, a Protestant minister who had been elected to the Estates-General for Nîmes, and the direction that the Revolution was taking, some Catholics in Nîmes were convinced that the Revolution itself was a Protestant plot, with Catholics the main victims. They had complained in April 1790 that royal authority was non-existent, ever since the king had been taken back to Paris, and that peace and happiness were only possible if founded on the "conservation of the monarchy and the Catholic religion."[9] When violence did break out between Protestants and Catholics, the Catholics were quick to blame the Protestants, and especially quick to blame the Protestant women who encouraged soldiers to kill Catholics, even claiming that the women were paying them.[10]

For all of the violence between these two groups in Nîmes and Montauban, those fights remained local. Certain regions, certain cities could still be torn apart by fights between Protestants and Catholics, but most could not, and those tensions did not move to the rest of the kingdom. There was enough support for toleration, if not equal rights, to prevent the spread of violence between the two groups.

In early 1790, in most of the kingdom, the threats were few.

None of this stopped people from seeing threats to the Revolution rising over every horizon. In a society with a long tradition of seeing plots behind any calamity, the threat of an aristocratic plot remained active in the minds of the people of France throughout the Revolution – as it had during the Great Fear and on the eve of the taking of the Bastille. Before the counter-revolution existed in reality, it existed in the imaginations of the people from whom the aristocrats had fled.[11] It would come to have a real existence soon enough, but by then it was not the aristocrats leading it.

The major changes in the Revolution that would eventually usher in the counter-revolution were ones that the revolutionaries brought on themselves; but they were changes that the revolutionaries stumbled into, with little sense of the stakes involved. There were three main turning points in this deterioration of relations between the National Assembly and the Catholic Church. The first would come in July 1790, just days before the Festival of the Federation, when the Constituent Assembly approved the Civil Constitution of the Clergy. The next came in November, when the Assembly – impatient at the Civil Constitution's lack of progress – voted to require all of the nation's clerics to swear an oath of allegiance to the Civil Constitution. At the start of the following year, on January 3–4, events came to a head once again, as the two sides squared off in the Constituent Assembly.

The Civil Constitution of the Clergy and the oath would transform the Revolution – or, rather, it would transform the counter-revolution, providing it with a popular base that it lacked at the start of 1790, that it lacked when the crowds gathered on the Champ de Mars to celebrate the Festival of the Federation. If no other festival was ever that successful, it was because the nation was never again that unified. And if the nation was never again that unified, during the tumultuous years of the Revolution, it was because of the divisions that resulted from the Constituent Assembly's attempt to reshape the Catholic Church.

Viewed from a long-term perspective, the religious upheavals of revolutionary France can seem like something of a step backward. The direction of the eighteenth century had been toward a smaller presence of religion in everyday life: church attendance was down, births out of wedlock were up, and clerics across the kingdom were complaining. But France was still a Catholic kingdom, and it is hard to overemphasize the importance of Catholicism in shaping not only the kingdom that entered the Revolution, but the Revolution itself. The Constituent Assembly's attempt to reshape the Catholic Church turned the counter-revolution into a popular movement. It turned village against village; it turned the Revolution against the church; and it turned wives against husbands. The attempt to transform the Catholic Church was a turning point in the Revolution; it was also a turning point in the relations between the women and men who made, who opposed, who lived through that Revolution.

The Catholic Church in 1789

By the time of the Festival of the Federation, the Catholic Church had already gone through quite a few changes, starting even before the Estates-General first met. The last years of the Old Regime saw some major upheavals in the clergy, culminating in the elections to the Estates-General. Those changes are sometimes referred to as the "revolt of the curés," although the term "revolt" might be a bit too extreme. The Old Regime clergy had long been riddled with internal divisions. Some of these were divisions based on disagreements about theology or doctrine. Other divisions – equally longstanding – were between the different ranks of the clergy. The richest and most powerful men in the church were the bishops and archbishops in the richest dioceses and archdioceses. These men were all from the nobility. Some were conscientious in their duties as bishops. Others sought the position for little more than the income and prestige it brought them. A few never bothered to visit their dioceses – ever. Some were pious Catholics; others, like Talleyrand, had little if any faith.

At the other end of the hierarchy from the bishops were the parish priests, the curés, some 60,000 strong, who brought the message of the Catholic Church to almost every city neighborhood, to almost every village, throughout the kingdom. Many of these men lived on fairly modest incomes. Even the brightest among them, if they had not been born into the nobility, were blocked from ever being promoted to the rank of bishop. Many of these men would spend their whole adult lives in one parish. Some – whether because of their piety or because of their general amiability – would become valued members of that community; others – whether because of their exigency in disciplinary matters, or simply because they were drunkards – would be, at best, tolerated. Some were openly despised by their parishioners, but there was little those parishioners could do about a curé that they found wanting. Even the most ignorant parish priests, provided that their behavior was not overtly criminal, were protected from any sort of dismissal from their positions.[12]

Sexual relations between priests and female parishioners were a frequent matter of concern for theological writers, and a regular occurrence in the erotic literature of the day, but actual scandals were few. There was, however, a gender dynamic to many of the parishes in France that is worth noting – particularly for the impact that it would have after the passage of the Civil Constitution of the Clergy. France, in the eighteenth century, was moving toward gender-specific modes of religious practice. Women and men no longer practiced their faith in the same way. To point out the obvious, the Catholic priests were all men. Their most faithful and devoted parishioners, however, were women. This had not always been true; over the course of the century, however, church attendance became particularly associated with women and with female modes of piety.

Village priests had been targets of derision for decades from the writers of the Enlightenment, but they were enjoying something of a renaissance in public opinion. The *bon curé*, the good parish priest, was getting good press: people in the cities were starting to see him not just as a part of the village community (and therefore as likely to be superstitious, lazy or drunk as anyone else in the villages) but as a useful part of society, bringing education to the countryside.[13] His image was strengthened, too, by the contrast with the ostentatious wealth of the bishops. In any struggle between the parish priest and the upper echelons of the church hierarchy, public opinion was swinging toward the men in the villages.

There were many other people in the Catholic Church, including roughly 26,000 monks spread out in monasteries across France. There were also several thousand canons at the cathedrals, although their number is harder to pin down. After the bishops with their excessive riches, it was these men who were most frequently the subject of criticism. Since the start of the century, more and more people were demanding that religious institutions justify their existence based on their usefulness in society. And by that measure, the large number of canons and monks had little value, especially at a time when more and more people were writing about the value of work and the dangers of idleness. The life of a monk or a cathedral canon looked increasingly idle, made possible by the labor of the poor, for the benefit of the lazy, and providing no benefit to society.

Doctrinal and theological differences often coincided with the disputes between the upper and lower clergy. Many men in the lower clergy were advocates of a movement known as "Richerism," a movement which frequently overlapped with Jansenism. Richerism emphasized the role of the lower clergy, and criticized the excessive authority of the bishops – views that fit well with those of the third estate. And it is not surprising that the third estate's most prominent spokesman, the Abbé Sieyes, would himself come from the clergy (even if his position as abbé was a bit problematic from the perspective of the parish priests). But the biggest push for the lower clergy did not come from the popularity of Sieyes's writings, or the agitation of the lower clergy, but rather from the government, in January 1789, being able to tell the clergy how they would elect their representatives to the Estates-General.[14] Those regulations were far more democratic than anything that the Catholic Church itself would have chosen, and gave each parish priest as much say in his region's delegates as a bishop had.

The Gallican Church had little, if any, tradition of democracy. It was an institution that valued hierarchy and obedience; tradition, not equality, governed its actions, and according to those traditions, bishops would speak on behalf of their dioceses if they wished to. But it was not tradition that determined how the first estate would determine its delegates to the

Estates-General. As a result, more than 200 of the nearly 300 members of the first estate were parish priests. The elections were not a complete disaster for the bishops, 51 of whom won their elections.[15] Parish priests still tended to respect bishops who respected their pastoral duties. The bishops who had earned the respect of the priests in their dioceses (or in neighboring dioceses, for that matter – since in another break with tradition, election was not done by diocese) usually won their elections, at least when they were not too old. But alongside those bishops was a new generation of leaders from the Catholic Church. So the two representatives from the eastern region of Lorraine were one bishop and one parish priest – each representing, in his own way, the trajectories of the Old Regime clergy as it entered the Revolution. The bishop was La Fare, the man who had given the Estates-General's opening sermon. The following year he joined the ranks of the émigrés. His commitment to the traditional order, to the autonomy of the church and the power of the episcopacy, would turn out to be incompatible with the new politics. The parish priest, a man named Henri Baptiste Grégoire, would go on to be among the leaders of the Revolution, the man who did more than anyone, who tried harder than anyone, to unify religion and Revolution, Catholicism and constitutional rule (and, eventually, republicanism). Heavily influenced by Jansenism, Grégoire was convinced that the French Revolution was the work of God, even if some of his colleagues at times tried to lead it astray.

Posterity has shone brightly on Grégoire, a man whose goals in 1789 remain relevant more than two centuries later. Grégoire possessed a trait common to many of the Revolution's leaders, one that goes beyond self-confidence. He was convinced not only in the purity and the merit of his own goals, but in the absolute and complete identification of his own cause with that of the Revolution.

This self-assurance on his part would not stop his opponents from seeing him as a self-promoter, even a hypocrite. The Revolution would indeed open possibilities to him. Born outside of the nobility, he would never have been able to become a bishop in the Old Regime church. He not only represented the rise of clerical leaders from the middle class; he also represented the rising influence of those men within the church who had long called for reforms – who had called for an end to the excessive authority that bishops had over the other clerics in their dioceses, who had called for a church that was less focused on wealth and more focused on pastoral work. They called, in short, for a return to the purity of the primitive church. These were not the same claims that the *philosophes* were making. There was enough overlap, however, for the two groups to work together in the enthusiastic days of 1789.

The government's ruling on the elections to the Estates-General made it possible for men like Grégoire to represent the church on the national stage, something that his superiors in the church would never have permitted.

But beyond the specifics of the ruling, the very act of a government decision on the elections was itself significant. The Gallican Church had long valued its independence from the government. When kings made requests, in years gone by, the episcopacy considered them; some wishes they granted, some they withheld. But the upper clergy had lost its grip on the lower clergy by 1789 and, as Aston notes, "the government had finally gained the whip hand in its dealings with the Gallican church."[16] The bishops could not say "no" to the government's order.

It was not only within the church that people were talking about the need to reform the church. Virtually everyone agreed that there was *some* need for reform, they just disagreed on what form that reform should take. If the lower clergy shared some of the third estate's views on the need to level the playing field, that does not mean that the mass of parish priests agreed with the rest of the third estates' projects. Many priests saw the Revolution as an opportunity to insert some real backbone into the state backing of religious regulations, and to make sure that the moral regeneration of the nation took place along traditional, Catholic lines – in other words, to impose their rules on those portions of the population which had no interest in them. On the priests' wish lists, along with better pay for themselves and less power for the bishops, were items like better police enforcement of Sunday rest and a crackdown on the philosophical books that were spreading through the kingdom – the same philosophical books that were so inspirational to the deputies from the third estate.

Many of those philosophical books did not have very good things to say about the first estate. In 1789, in 1790, the people who were reading those books were in more positions of power than they ever had been. Anticlericalism was more prominent than it ever had been during the Old Regime. And if the *bon curé* had made progress in the opinions of the century, he still coexisted with many old ideas about what went on in village religious life.

If the Catholic Church that entered the Revolution had gone through some major changes, those changes were far less than the ones that 1789 would bring. The events of that year would bring one change then another to the Catholic Church, most of them aimed at limiting the church's power, taking away its privileges, or simply taking away its wealth.

The night of August 4, the Decrees of August 11, these days that eliminated so many of the privileges that separated the nobility from the rest of the country, eliminated many of the church's privileges as well. Gone was the tithe, the principle source of revenue for many in the church, although the decree's odd proviso that "other means will be instituted to support divine worship" meant that the abolition was more a creation of a sort of limbo for many parish priests.[17] The Declaration of the Rights of Man, by proclaiming freedom of opinion in religious matters, disappointed those Catholics who had hoped to see Catholicism remain the official religion of the kingdom. Soon the Constituent Assembly would put new restrictions on monasteries, most of which would barely survive the year.

The Constituent Assembly's decision in November of 1789 to nationalize and sell church property was a blow, not only to the Gallican Church's prestige, but to its wealth and power. Much of the motivation for this move was practical: the government needed money. Needing money was what had gotten the monarchy into a mess in the first place; needing money was what had led Louis XVI to call the Estates-General. The men who came to Versailles, then to Paris, to take part in the regeneration of the kingdom, had brought with them grand ideas on the direction that a regenerated France should take. Those men tended to be short on specifics, though, and the kingdom was as much in need of cash as ever. Taking over the Catholic Church's lands would be an answer to that problem, albeit one that no French king could have taken on his own. That the move would so cripple the Catholic Church in France, that it would remove much of its power, that the church would no longer be able to support such lavish lives for its bishops – this was for many of the more anti-clerical deputies and their supporters a major bonus. By December, the Assembly decreed that church lands would be sold off to repay the nation's debts.

For all of the changes 1789 brought to the Gallican Church, it would turn out to be only a prelude to 1790's Civil Constitution of the Clergy. That one law would have more impact on the Revolution than any other law that the national government issued. And yet, when the Constituent Assembly issued the law, it did so with little understanding of its implications.

The Civil Constitution was the Constituent Assembly's attempt to reshape the church, to make it part of the Revolution – and, in the process, strengthen the government's authority over the church. For all of the clerical deputies, be they a Sieyes, a Grégoire, or, on the other side, a Bishop La Fare, clerics were still outnumbered. Most of the deputies were lawyers or other professionals. Most of the deputies – like most of the kingdom – believed that it was time to reform the Catholic Church. But the ideas on what that reform should look like, were far from uniform.

The most famous of these ideas came from the church's critics. And in 1790, there was no shortage of critics. True, the man who most closely identified himself with the attack on the church, Voltaire, had died; most of the great writers of the Enlightenment had not survived to see the events of 1789. But the next generation of *philosophes*, including the mathematician Condorcet, were alive and well, and eager to seize the opportunity to eliminate the Catholic Church's abuses. A believer in the potential of reason and the ability of men to use reason to reshape their world for the better, Condorcet typified the beliefs of many deputies that it was time to apply the abstractions of the Enlightenment to the real world of politics. Key to this process was removing the institutions that had prevented the spread of reason, and the Catholic Church was at the top of that list. For Condorcet, the Catholic Church's history was one long string of atrocities, examples of the horror that people could inflict on each other. Incidents like the execution of Calas were merely the latest examples of a string of violence that passed through the St Bartholomew's Day Massacre of 1572 to the crusades and on to the earliest days of the medieval church.

While few deputies possessed Condorcet's genius, many shared his views on the Catholic Church. These "Voltairian lawyers," as Michelet labeled them, saw the Revolution as an opportunity to curb the church's abuses – if not to punish it for earlier abuses – or, at the very least, to punish the chief offenders, the bishops, by removing their wealth and their privileges. And if they did not come into the Revolution with a strong understanding of the church, they did come into the Revolution with a confidence in their own abilities.

Very few of these Voltairian lawyers were atheists. Very few of the *philosophes* were atheists. Many liked to consider themselves anti-*clerical* – that is, opposed to the existing religious institutions – not anti-*religious*. Only a few, however, seem particularly pious in retrospect. Voltaire's view that religion exists to keep mankind in order was common. Some religion was good for the people, in this view, as a way of keeping them happy, or keeping them from excessive debauchery and idleness. Catholicism had gone too far, though – not only were the church's leaders abusing their position by filling peasants' heads with superstitions, but those leaders had become examples of debauchery, examples of idleness.

The creation of the Civil Constitution of the Clergy was a strange development – as if Voltaire had been put in charge of reforming the church, not only eliminating its abuses, but bringing it back to its original purity, to the purity of the early Christians.[18]

But here's the thing: the idea was not as crazy as it might have seemed. Because the *philosophes* had long argued that the church's actions were harming not only society as a whole but the church itself, that they were bringing down the religion that they were supposed to be representing. It is sometimes hard to tell if they believed this rhetoric, or if it was merely a tactic that they used to strengthen their arguments. Even a virulently anti-clerical tract like the 1789 *Le Clergé Dévoilé* – *The Clergy Unmasked* – could present itself as a defender of Catholicism. True, the bulk of the pamphlet was spent accusing priests of seducing their neighbors' wives, accusing bishops of only being interested in money, and otherwise finding fault with everyone actually in the church. But the author could claim that he was not attacking the religion itself – only the abuses done in its name. The men in the church, the author wrote, were only "covering themselves in the respectable coat of religion" in order to exercise their despotism and gain their undeserved riches. In the troubled times that the author described, he could say that his real goal was not to destroy the religion, but rather to defend it – to stand up for "this religion, so holy and so pure ... but betrayed and disfigured by its ministers."[19]

It was not only people outside the Catholic Church who thought that it needed to be reformed. Again, there were longstanding movements for reform within the church itself which had been calling for an end to the abuses, movements which had sought to limit the bishops' power and wealth. In July 1790, a group of clerics from Normandy had addressed the Constituent Assembly, praising it for having taken away the church's property, and therefore allowing the church to "simplify its mission, remove itself from the scandal of its excesses, and reclaim its 'ancient splendor.'"[20] Simplicity, a return to the primitive church – these were frequent themes in all of the discussions of church reform. They had been frequent themes in the Old Regime debates, they would remain so during the Revolution, at a time when the projects actually had a shot at happening.

The Assembly approved the Civil Constitution of the Clergy on July 12, 1790, after relatively little debate in the Assembly itself. Ten days later, the king gave the law his approval.

Reading the Civil Constitution of the Clergy today, it does not seem particularly radical. It does not seem particularly pious, either. Rather than dealing with issues of faith or doctrine, it reads like one more administrative document. Such a document could have been written for tax collectors as well as for bishops and priests (except, perhaps, for the section detailing the pope's limited role). On spiritual matters, it says little.

There were several elements to the Civil Constitution. The first was the reshaping of the ecclesiastical map of the kingdom. Gone were the old dioceses, those 130 or so units, that ranged in size from the tiniest to the grandest, the most populous to the most deserted. In their place – what else? – came the departments which the Assembly had approved earlier that year. One department, one diocese – one diocese, one department.

The new laws also called for all priests – Catholic or otherwise, it did not specify – to be paid by the national government. This move was not much of a surprise, given the abolition of the tithe in August of 1789. It was the least controversial aspect of the new system, the one that received the fewest objections, particularly from opponents of the new constitution.

If there was one measure in the constitution that did have a moral or spiritual implication, it was the "Law of Residence," which required bishops to remain in their dioceses, and required curés to remain in their parishes. Absentee bishops had long been a problem – bishops appointed to wealthy sees who accepted the payment but rarely, if ever, visited. Such bishops had few defenders in 1790, and the content of this new requirement received little criticism from any side, even if many clerical deputies found fault with the way it was unilaterally imposed. More on that below.

The Civil Constitution of the Clergy reflected the influence of the Jansenist movement, but not in a simple or straightforward way. And while

Grégoire and Camus both liked the final product, not all Jansenists did. Some of the Jansenist veterans of the quarrels of the eighteenth century were among the Constitution's earliest critics.

The most surprising aspect of the Civil Constitution of the Clergy concerned the method of choosing priests and bishops: election.

Again, there was not much of a tradition of democracy within the Gallican Church – or, indeed, within the Catholic Church as a whole. Electing bishops and priests was not particularly popular with those men who were, already, bishops and priests. It was not an idea that the upper clergy embraced, it was not an idea that the lower clergy embraced. It had not even been particularly popular with people outside of the church. The idea of elections within the Catholic Church was, to use a modern expression, completely out of left field.

The elections were not, however, the only aspect of the Civil Constitution of the Clergy that the leaders of the Gallican Church opposed. They were not even the aspect that received the most opposition. Rather, it was the reshaping of the ecclesiastical map, replacing traditional dioceses with the new departmental boundaries, that most shocked the leadership of the church. It was not surprising that it was a shock, considering that the number of dioceses – and therefore of bishops – was about to decline from around 130 to just over 80. Nearly 50 of the kingdom's most powerful men were about to lose the lucrative positions they had earned through the arduous process of having been born into the nobility.[21]

But the opposition to the Civil Constitution of the Clergy went beyond the contents of the new law. This is not to say that the contents did not upset some people; they did, but everyone in the church knew some changes were coming. The leaders of the Gallican Church, however, expected to be part of the decision-making process; they expected to have a say in the reshaping of the church. What most offended many in the church, what led many potential supporters to eventually become opponents, was the heavy-handed manner in which the Constituent Assembly imposed the Constitution.

Traditionally, the priests and bishops of Old Regime France were not a particularly rabble-rousing bunch. Yes, there were many members of the lower clergy who had enthusiastically joined the movements of 1789, who had closely allied themselves with the third estate. But overall, the message that the priests of the Old Regime preached to their parishioners was one of submission to authority, of respect for authority, and not a message of revolt or revolution. The men in the Gallican Church – the bishops, the priests, the canons, the monks – had been educated and trained to believe that the opening line from Romans 13, "Let every soul be subject unto the higher powers," was how men of the cloth should understand the relationship between their role and that of the secular authorities, and that "Whosoever resisteth the power, resisteth the ordinance of God."[22]

It was an odd sort of obedience, though, that the clergy gave to its leaders – that the bishops gave to Rome, that the lower clergy gave to its bishops, that parishioners gave to their priests. It had always included some play, some wiggle-room. And if the Gallican Church had rarely said "no" to the papacy, they had a long tradition of saying "yes, but ..." That "yes, but ..." often meant wait, and waiting often lasted long enough to thwart any possible changes. Scores of writers – theologians, lawyers, priests – would analyze every detail of the matter, consulting the church fathers, consulting the scriptures, coming up with their own responses – temporizing, perhaps, by dragging their feet. But not openly resisting, not calling into question the existing hierarchy, only seeking to temper it. It was this sort of resistance that had allowed Jansenism to continue to exist long after both the king and the pope had set out to destroy it – all while calling themselves loyal subjects and good Catholics.

The leaders of the Gallican Church at first responded in much the same way to the Civil Constitution of the Clergy. They were not happy with it, but they were inclined to make some sort of compromise, to work something out that would be agreeable to both sides.

On October 30, 30 of the bishops who were in the Constituent Assembly presented their *Exposition of Principles*. Led by Boisgelin, the talented, ambitious archbishop of Aix, they explained why they did not accept the Civil Constitution.

Some of these men were angry at any attack on the "majestic edifice" that was the church's – and particularly the bishops'–power and authority.[23] Others, like Boisgelin, had been willing to accept a certain amount of change, hoping to position themselves to best take advantage of any new developments. Back in 1775, during Louis XVI's coronation sermon, Boisgelin had spoken favorably of limited monarchy; and in his campaign for election to the Estates-General, Boisgelin had presented himself as a supporter of new ideas.[24] The extent of the proposed changes, though, surpassed anything these men had anticipated. Little of the Civil Constitution appealed to them: not the abolition of the cathedral chapters and other Catholic institutions that the Assembly had declared superfluous; not the election of priests and bishops; and not the restructuring of the church and the Assembly's decision to use departmental boundaries for dioceses. Above all, though, it was the way in which the Assembly was attempting to impose the reform on the church that the bishops found problematic. Again, everyone in the church knew that some changes were coming – the leaders of the church just expected to be part of the decision-making process. When they were not, they attacked not only the content of the new laws, but the government's authority to make those laws. "These decrees," the bishops noted, "are presented as absolute laws issued by a sovereign authority, without any dependence on the Church's authority." But for the bishops, the Assembly was not sovereign, at least not in this matter; "there is a jurisdiction that is proper to, and essential to, the Church," they wrote, "a jurisdiction that Jesus-Christ gave it."[25] No government had the jurisdiction, the authority, to go against *that* jurisdiction.

This is not to say that there was no way to make changes. The church could be changed, but only the church could change it – not the government. The authors of the *Exposition* called on the Constituent Assembly to suspend the execution of the decree until the pope stated his opinion, or until a National Council would meet.[26] In the meantime, they hoped to "use all the means of charity and wisdom" to avoid a schism and the troubles that would result. Were they willing to accept some sort of reform? Were they willing to relinquish more of their wealth, more of their power? The bishops' answer was, of course, "yes, but ..." Yes, but on their terms – and only after the deputies in the Constituent Assembly had thrown some flattery their way.

The bishops who signed the *Exposition* were not intent on bringing the counter-revolution to France – or at least, they were not *yet* intent on bringing the counter-revolution to France. They were, however, insistent that the Constituent Assembly had gone well beyond its bounds. This is not to say that none of the proposed reforms were possible, but the signers of the *Exposition* were quite clear that *the Catholic Church itself* had to approve any possible reforms. This could be done either through a General Council of the Gallican Church, or through the pope's approval. Both of these options had risks. The lower clergy was wary that a National Council would strengthen the bishops' authority. And calling for the pope's views was, in many ways, a step backwards for the French church; it had spent centuries defending its "Gallican liberties," so to call on Rome for help was something of a 180-degree turn. Oddly, though, it was a turn that the pope was not that excited about, at least not yet. With the Gallican Church facing its largest crisis since the Reformation, the pope was silent. Or, at least, he was officially silent. He had sent Louis XVI some instructions, but not only did he not publicize those instructions, they arrived too late to have any impact on the king's decisions.

For supporters of the Civil Constitution, the opposition – especially from the bishops – was not religious at all.[27] Mirabeau told the Assembly that the *Exposition* was nothing but a "ruse of an hypocrisy" which "puts in motion all sorts of trouble and sedition, while it pretends to plead the cause of God."[28] The most anti-clerical voices would see here what they had seen all along, what they had seen since the days of the Old Regime: powerful men using the cloak of religion to protect their interests.

There was not a lot of potential for compromise between these two sides. Both sides claimed to speak not for themselves, but for a higher power. The clerical deputies, the opponents of the Civil Constitution of the Clergy, claimed to be speaking for tradition, for the Catholic Church, for God Himself. Their opponents spoke for the people, for the good of the nation, for reason itself. But it was as much the temperament of these two sides that kept them from compromising. Neither side doubted their ability to determine the true wishes of their higher power. Neither side doubted that their opponents' true agenda was far more self-interested than their own. Neither side lacked confidence. For generations, royal authorities had listened when the leaders of the Gallican Church had said "yes, but ..." The leaders of the Constituent Assembly would only accept "yes."

Whatever their motives, the argument of the *Exposition*, one based on jurisdiction and traditional authority, was typical of the debates of the Old Regime. For the Civil Constitution's advocates in the Constituent Assembly, that kind of debate was now meaningless. The new plan was good for the nation, or it was not; and if it was good for the nation, then any resistance was a threat to the well-being of the nation. The Assembly, in the claims it made, had always recognized the existence of limits to the power of the government. But the Assembly, in the actions it took, had always shown itself willing to exceed – or even reshape – those limits. And it had never looked kindly on any sort of negotiation over the terms by which people would adhere to its laws.

It is worth looking back on the Declaration of the Rights of Man and of the Citizen. That Declaration had guaranteed a sort of freedom of religion, and that guarantee would be relevant in the aftermath of the Civil Constitution. But the Assembly giveth and the Assembly taketh away. "No one must be disturbed for his opinions, even in religious matters," the Declaration declared, *"provided that their expression does not trouble the public order established by the law."* The people would have freedom of religious opinions and the Assembly would decide just how much. This article was noticeably less liberal than the article guaranteeing the free communication of ideas (including freedom of speech and the freedom of the press) and calling it "one of the most precious to man." Such a full-throated freedom of religion could not pass the National Assembly in 1789, as some deputies still hoped to declare Catholicism the nation's official religion.[29] Notably, the Declaration had not given Jews French citizenship. The Assembly would debate Jews' legal status in December 1789, devoting three days to arguments about a population smaller than 40,000, before ending with the granting of citizenship to the Jews of Paris and Bordeaux (though not the much larger population of Alsatian Jews, who would only become citizens in September 1791).

But even the Declaration's article declaring freedom of communication contained the caveat that all "are accountable for abuse of this freedom." Perhaps even more telling is the article establishing that men may not be arrested arbitrarily. All arrests must be for infractions of the law. But, the declaration added, every citizen summoned by the authorities must obey at once, and anyone who does not makes himself guilty by resisting.

He makes himself guilty by resisting. This was the word of the Constituent Assembly, the deputies dictating their ideal world to the grateful nation. These deputies were not ready for a less-than-grateful nation. They could not see the attachment that so many people in France had to their religion, to their traditions. They did not understand the reactions among their colleagues in the Assembly. They did not understand the reactions throughout the country. And word started reaching the Assembly that in many parts of the kingdom, the people were not happy about the new law; in many parts of the kingdom, people were not happy about the government telling them how to practice their religion.

In some places, the passage of the Civil Constitution of the Clergy was met with open opposition – to the law, to the new church, to the Revolution as a whole. The ecclesiastical deputies might have been speaking the language of compromise; not all of their colleagues in the provinces were. Some bishops made it plain they would not recognize the new diocesan boundaries, that they would not recognize the legitimacy of the Constituent Assembly in religious matters – and that they would not recognize as their peers the priests and bishops who did adhere to the new rules. Bishops declared that new priests who had been elected were not legitimate. Priests told women in their parishes that any marriage performed by the new priest was not sacred, they would be concubines, their children would be bastards.[30] The new priests earned a nickname in the areas where they were not welcome: *intrus*, the intruders. In some regions, this name would stick, it would remain the term people gave to the new priests – especially when they would replace popular priests who had opposed the Civil Constitution. Life for these men was not easy, unwelcome in their new parishes.

All was not gloom and doom. Alongside all of the "no" responses, alongside all of the "yes, but …" responses, were the many priests who said "yes." Few bishops – but many priests. For all of the divisions in the society that would result from the Civil Constitution, in much of the kingdom it started out well. A curé named Laurent, a deputy at the Constituent Assembly, found in the Civil Constitution the answer to his prayers. "The sacred tree of religion," he wrote, "rather than being wounded in this violent operation, has gained, on the contrary, a new vigor. It has been freed from the parasites that suffocated it."[31] This attitude toward the Civil Constitution of the Clergy was common.

Such peaceful transitions grabbed fewer headlines, though, than the difficulties that began popping up elsewhere in the kingdom. On November 26, 1790, the National Assembly was not learning about the areas where things were going well; they were learning about the developments in the area around Nantes, where the old bishop was spreading publications questioning the Constituent Assembly's authority, and "raising the flag of rebellion."[32] They were learning about departments that elected bishops, only to find that no other bishop would confirm that election.[33] They were learning about similar events elsewhere in the country, where people were not happy about the changes that were taking place.

For many of the men in the Assembly, it was no longer time to debate the Civil Constitution. It was simply time to follow it.

The odd thing, though, is just how little the Assembly did debate the Civil Constitution. Pierre de La Gorce, an early twentieth-century historian of the Revolution, noted that "never has a debate been more inferior to the magnitude of its subject."[34] The Assembly's Ecclesiastical Committee had spent a good deal of time writing it, but once they presented it to the entire Assembly there was little substance to the debate. Some of the deputies who most opposed the law chose not to take part in the discussion at all, as they considered the matter to be beyond the Assembly's jurisdiction.[35] But the indifference with which it was signed did not stop the deputies from becoming upset at the difficulties they had in getting clerics to adhere to the new law. If the law had been entered into absent-mindedly, the obstinacy with which people resisted it made the deputies impatient. *He makes himself guilty by resisting.*

This impatience came to a head on November 27, 1790. The Assembly had had enough of the hesitations, enough of the foot dragging, enough of the "yes, but ..." responses. It had heard the day before of events in Nantes, and it had been hearing similar stories from other parts of the kingdom. It voted to require that all clerics swear an oath of fidelity to the nation, to the law, and to the king – and therefore, implicitly, to the Civil Constitution. The Assembly required all clerics to take the oath, and to do so *within one week* of the law's eventual promulgation, or be required to leave their parishes. The oath meant that there was no longer any room for a "yes, but ..." response. It was decision time. It was decision time for men like Boisgelin, and for his colleague the bishop of Clermont who, on the eve of the decree requiring the oath, was still calling for a General Council.[36] It was decision time for priests who opposed the oath, but who lived in regions or parishes that supported the Revolution. It was decision time for priests who would have liked to take the oath, but who knew that it would alienate them from their parishioners, grown increasingly alienated with the Revolution and its Parisian leaders.

It was decision time, too, for Louis XVI. Decisions were not his strong suit.

It was decision time – it had long been decision time – for Pope Pius VI, who had still not made clear his views on the Civil Constitution. The pope would not make any statement until March, until after events were even further underway. Louis XVI had sought his advice, sought to know whether he could sanction the Civil Constitution without putting his soul in jeopardy. The pope was less focused on the king's soul; he was more focused on the property that the papacy seemed to be losing in southern France.

The king had to seek advice elsewhere. He consulted with the bishop of Clermont, asking him, too, about his soul's fate should he sanction the new system.[37] Like many of his colleagues, the bishop of Clermont was as concerned with the bishop of Clermont as he was with the king's soul. There were plenty of people around to give the king sycophantic encouragement, or to seek favor; what was lacking, though, was good advice.

Louis XVI's indecision went almost all the way to the core of his being. Almost. Because he was, by all accounts, a pious man. His faith would make his decision on the oath that much more difficult. It would not, however, keep him from an inconsistent and ultimately unsuccessful course of action. On December 26, Louis XVI sanctioned the decree requiring the oath. It is not clear why he did so; he clearly had reservations about the Civil Constitution. He had reservations about practically all of the legislation that the National Assembly had passed. It had taken a crowd of thousands and the death of two of his personal guards to get the king to approve of the Declaration of the Rights of Man and of the Citizen, but the Civil Constitution of the Clergy hit him particularly hard. So why did he finally sanction it?

Back in October 1790, the king had sent an envoy to his cousin the king of Spain, to deliver an odd message: whatever the king publicly claimed to approve of he actually disapproved of.[38] The king specifically noted his hostility to the Civil Constitution of the Clergy.

The king was trying to play a double game.

The Civil Constitution had alienated Louis XVI even further from the events of the Revolution, it took a toll on him, began to push him past the breaking point. Was it because of his worries about his soul? Or was this simply the last straw, coming on top of his virtual imprisonment in Paris, the threats to his family, the decline of his authority? In either case, he began writing to foreign leaders, requesting help. The first was his I-do-not-really-mean-it message to the king of Spain; later would come communications with the king of Prussia, along with the queen's frequent correspondence with her brother, the emperor of Austria. The king maintained his support of the Revolution in public, while his private correspondence showed his increasing alienation from the Revolution, his increasing desire to do something other than just accept the changes as they had developed.

The king was trying to play a double game, but playing a double game is not easy. It requires having two distinct games, and keeping them separate. For Mirabeau, it was a different story. The Revolution fit his skills perfectly. He was a brilliant orator, but perhaps a better backroom dealer. More comfortable the more sordid things were, he worked with the National Assembly against the monarchy, and worked with the royal family against the Assembly. Mirabeau was a man who could play a double game. Louis XVI could not. Neither of the king's games was consistent, and that gave him away. The people of France – and particularly the people in Paris – were increasingly skeptical of his actions. The leaders of foreign nations were always hesitant to intervene in France's internal affairs, especially when they felt they could still let things deteriorate to the point that they would be able to take advantage of France's instability and annex portions of the kingdom. But Louis XVI's weakness was becoming apparent enough that foreign leaders knew not to trust any word he gave. The émigrés were increasingly frustrated with the king, seeing in him equivocacy where what was needed was clarity. The king was playing, at the least, a quadruple game.

So it was as part of this at-least-quadruple game that on December 26, 1790 Louis XVI sanctioned the decree requiring all priests to swear an oath to the nation, to the law, to the king – and, therefore, to the Civil Constitution of the Clergy. Was this because he was worried about further unrest, should he refuse? Or perhaps a desire for further unrest, making it easier for him to reassert authority? Probably, in his indecision, some of each.[39]

In any case, it made the position of the opponents of the Civil Constitution that much more difficult. The king had left them in the lurch; the pope was doing nothing to help them. The next day, 62 ecclesiastical deputies – including Grégoire – took their oaths, in front of the Assembly, swearing their allegiance to the king, the law, and the Civil Constitution. But their enthusiasm for the restructured church could not make up for the overall disappointment . Slightly over one-third of the ecclesiastical deputies had taken the oath.[40] That was not enough.

All that was left now was the seemingly endless series of decisions, oaths, refusals, and confrontations that would take place throughout the kingdom – starting on January 3, 1791 with decisions, oaths and confrontations right in the center of it all, in the Assembly itself.

The schism had arrived.

Those priests and bishops who swore the oath would henceforth be known as constitutional or "juring" priests and bishops. Those who did not take the oath would be known as the "non-juring" or "refractory" clergy. Although the tensions between the two groups would wax and wane, they remained two opposed groups for more than a decade.

On January 4, the Assembly called each of the ecclesiastical deputies who had yet to take the oath. One by one, those deputies – almost all of them – refused to take the oath. Of the bishops in the Assembly, only two took the oath. One was Jean-Baptiste Gobel, who held a position as co-bishop of Basle, an eastern diocese mostly situated outside of France, and outside of the Gallican Church, but which included some parishes in French territory over which Gobel had authority. The other bishop to take the oath was Talleyrand. Both men would go far in the Revolution (though only one would survive it). But the day was won by those who had refused to swear the oath. It was, as Michelet noted, "the victory of the priests over the lawyers."[41]

The debates from the National Assembly do not always make the most riveting reading. The deputies spent days on details that today seem unimportant; the men went on and on, all too often, about the details of their projects and lavishing themselves with self-praise. But the debates from January 3–4 are filled with a palpable sense of drama. At the center of it all, the most vociferous opponent of the oath and the Civil Constitution that day was not a bishop, but the Abbé Maury. A royalist and a long-time defender of the rights of the church, he was the right wing's best match for the oratory of the revolutionary leaders on the left. He hoped to plead the cause of the church as he understood it. He wound up instead arguing simply for his right to speak, as he was shouted down time and again, asked to stop speaking, and yelled out, "You do not have the right to interrupt me!" – before his colleagues on the left decided that they did not, in fact, wish to hear him, and were not obliged to do so.

The next step was to hear the oath itself, from the mouths of all of those men in the National Assembly required to take it, those men who would have to relinquish their offices should they refuse. (Ironically, despite his title, Maury held no such office.) One by one, those deputies were called to take the oath. When they asked to speak, to explain themselves, they were shouted down. When one bishop asked to speak, the cries rang out, "No speeches! Do you take the oath, yes or no?" Finally the president of the Assembly ended the roll call, and asked simply, "Is anyone else going to present themselves, in order to take the oath?"

And here, the yelling ceased. The debate ceased. The minutes of the discussion state simply, "there was a quarter-hour of silence."[42]

Soon after, Mirabeau would state what must have already seemed clear: "the fatal moment has arrived."[43] The Assembly became the bully. The deputies who had refused to take the oath began to see themselves as martyrs. The bishops gained the respect of the other clerics, now reluctant to abandon their superiors at the moment of crisis. The bishops had threatened to cut off communication with any clergy that took the oath, and that threat was having some success. The opponents of the Civil Constitution were standing up to the Assembly, and gaining support.

The Assembly, in voting for the oath, had believed that it would end the crisis. Instead, it made the crisis worse. The nation was now split.

And, going by the numbers, split fairly down the middle. Over the next weeks and months just over half of the priests in France would take the oath. But this was not the sort of situation where 51 percent means victory. The actual number – which was probably around 55 percent – was a defeat for the Assembly and a setback for the Revolution.

The Constituent Assembly, in the aftermath of January 4, would try to mellow its approach to the refractory priests, including the ecclesiastical deputies. The Ecclesiastical Committee issued a clarifying statement distinguishing between the private expression of religion and public worship; only the latter was within the reach of the law, the statement noted. The Assembly decided to give pensions to refractory priests who had been replaced; they soon would be allowed to stay in their parishes until replaced. Eventually, the one-week deadline would be removed. Refractory priests would be allowed to take the oath at any time, and those who had missed the deadline would be welcomed into the fold at any time.

These softening measures had little effect. For the overwhelming majority of priests, their first choice was final – they took the oath in early 1791, or they never took it.[44] Throughout the kingdom, people had made their allegiances clear, be they to the Revolution or to their old priests and bishops.

For all of the drama of the debates, events on the ground could be more heated still. Throughout the following weeks, in one parish after another, in the cities of France, in the towns, in the villages, priests made their decisions and took, or did not take, the oath. For all of France's clerics, decision time had come. And for many, the decision was clear enough. Thousands of priests were enthusiastic supporters of both the Revolution and the Civil Constitution. For those men, this was an easy decision, especially when they were in parishes that supported the Revolution – because the parish's preferences were as important as the individual priest's. As Tackett points out, "the lay populations were anything but malleable clay in the hands of clergy."[45] In areas that supported the Revolution, it was hard for priests to refuse to take the oath. Those oath-taking ceremonies – always on a Sunday after mass – were joyous occasions, as the people welcomed their priest into the revolutionary fold. Some regions managed to avoid the drama. De La Gorce, a Catholic historian whose sympathies lay with the refractory church, wrote that in many communes where the curé took the oath, "there was a sort of tacit agreement between the pastor – to swear very quietly – and the parishioners – to not pay attention."[46] In other places, the affairs were far more intense; local patriots would show up at the masses of refractory priests, heckling them, calling on them to take the oath; opponents of the Civil Constitution would call out the new priests, the *intrus*, threaten them with violence, or even worse. One woman in La Rochelle told a constitutional priest there that if she was holding his heart, she would eat it.[47] Soldiers would be called in to protect priests who stood on the other side of the political divide from their parishioners, although those soldiers could often do nothing against women and children who often made up the majority of the most visible protesters. One curé complained that the 40 years he had spent in his parish had meant nothing when he decided to take the oath – and his parishioners pelted him with stones.[48]

Each department had its internal divisions, its internal rivalries – and, therefore, its own complicated patchwork of regions more or less favorable to the Revolution and the Civil Constitution. But looking more broadly, there was a clear geography of the oath. In the region around Paris, and in the southeast, the oath was most successful. The more mountainous regions south of Paris, and the areas in eastern France, were far more hostile to the oath. But the most significant region was in the west, a huge swath of the kingdom – including Brittany and Normandy – where the oath was the least successful. Different scholars have explained this geography in different ways, from economic causes to the relative social status of priests. But for whatever reason, this geography would be the geography of the rest of the Revolution. The center, for the most part, retained its support for the Revolution. The peripheries would have, for the most part, a strained relationship with the Revolution – at best. At worst, they stood in open civil war.

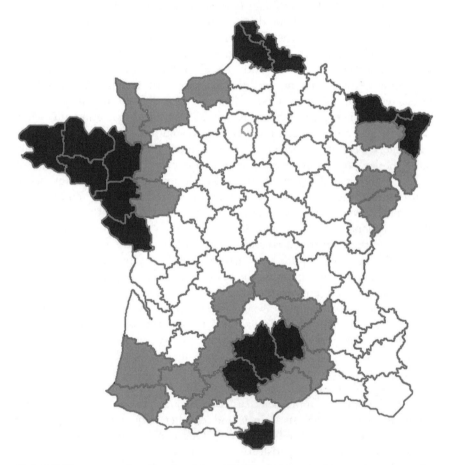

Map 3.2 The geography of oath taking. The departments where resistance to the Civil Constitution of the Clergy was the highest. In the departments shaded dark grey more than 65 percent of priests required to take the oath refused to do so; the departments in light grey ranged from 65 percent to 45 percent. Based on Michel Vovelle, *La Révolution contre l'Eglise: de la raison à l'Etre suprême* (Paris, 1988).

The case of Jacques Pierre Fleury shows some of these dynamics at work. Fleury was a priest in his early thirties at the start of the Revolution. In 1788 he was assigned to a parish in western France, on the border between Brittany and Normandy. It was not a location he had sought; in his memoirs he describes his dread in heading out to find the parish. But he was pleased on his arrival to see how the parishioners practiced their religion, and he became comfortable in his new home.

The Civil Constitution, and the subsequent oath, would cause a complete upheaval in that community. Western France was one of the regions where the fewest priests took the oath, and Fleury fit the pattern. He never did take the oath – the "criminal oath," as he called it – and, if his memoirs are accurate, never even considered taking it. Like other priests, he was facing pressure from both sides, from people who were glad that he had refused to take the oath, and from those who wished he would show his support for the Revolution. Some supporters of the oath used some rather extreme methods of persuasion. Fleury claimed that one politician offered him money, another hinted at the possibility of making him a bishop. Meanwhile, as he refused the oath, he found himself more and more strapped for cash, subject to the threat of starvation for lack of money – famine, that "most dangerous of seductions" – and was threatened at gunpoint by supporters of the oath. Some of his parishioners abandoned him. Other local priests, colleagues of Fleury's, had more trouble with their decisions; some took the oath in tears, others confided in Fleury their incertitude. Fleury does not note any doubts in his memoirs – but that is the advantage of writing one's own story.

Fleury's experiences fit the overall pattern in other ways as well. Those encouraging Fleury to take the oath were almost always men. Women were far more numerous in either encouraging Fleury to refuse to take the oath, or in supporting Fleury after he had established his position. He even wrote of a constitutional priest arriving in a neighboring parish and being chased off by women and children; at other times, women came to Fleury's defense, chasing off those who threatened him.[49]

There are no numbers, no opinion polls, there are only anecdotes. Those anecdotes, however, pile up higher and higher. The Civil Constitution, the oath, and the changes in religious practice that followed brought many, many women into the political life of the Revolution. Both sides noted the prominence of women's activism in the fights over Catholicism. For the Revolution's growing opposition, that activism was proof of the strength of the women's faith; for supporters of the Revolution, it was proof of the women's foolishness and credulity. But all agreed that women played key roles in the opposition to the Civil Constitution of the Clergy.

The men who led the Revolution had long welcomed certain political behaviors by women: donating their jewelry, playing "ornamental" roles in festivals, supporting their husbands, bearing future revolutionaries. But while it is possible to see the elements of a split between public business and private matters, between a male realm and a female one, there was no set boundary between the two, no "line," or at least not a stable one. There was rarely a perfect fit between the behavior that the men in the National Assembly expected of the women of France, and the way women actually behaved. Sometimes, there was no fit at all.

The leaders of the Revolution in the National Assembly had a tenuous relationship with all activism by the people – it had saved the Revolution, had saved the Assembly, but it was also hard to control – but they had a particularly tenuous relationship with any political activism by women. When it supported their views, they tended to praise women's generosity and their virtue, perhaps noting the way that their contributions could soften the lives of the men "leading" the Revolution. When it did not support their views, they were quick to belittle any criticism from women based, simply, on the source from which it came. Then, the women either became some sort of over-emotional group lacking in reason or else their good will had been taken advantage of, and they had been tricked, or led astray.

Even if there was no set boundary between male roles and female roles, that did not stop men from claiming that women had exceeded their roles. But it made sense that women would get involved in the reactions to the Civil Constitution – both pro and contra. The actual ceremony of oath-taking was not only something that took place in Paris, not only something that took place in the major cities; the people of France, from the biggest cities to the smallest villages, had an opportunity to see these rituals – to see the Revolution enter their lives.[50] Religion in eighteenth-century France involved far more than just people's faith and beliefs; it was a key part of community life and social interaction. Rightly or wrongly, many people viewed the Civil Constitution of the Clergy not as an attempt to reform the Gallican Church's administrative structure, but as an attempt to change their way of life. Some people were happy to see the Revolution reach into their lives, some were not. Those who were not, were, by 1791, increasingly willing to show their discontent.

That communities determined priests' adherence or non-adherence to the Civil Constitution – is known now due, largely, to the work of Tackett and other historians. It was not what the Revolution's leaders thought was happening at the time. The revolutionaries thought that priests were causing the problems, tricking people – especially women – to support them, to oppose the Civil Constitution, to oppose the Revolution. In this view, the priests were the tricksters, the women the tricked – too heavily dominated by their emotions, according to the views at the times. It was enough for the revolutionaries to disparage the women's actions; at other times they pointed to the evil machinations of the Catholic priests who had tricked them, or led them astray.

Figure 3.1 Patriotic discipline. Disputes over the Civil Constitution of the Clergy could be even more heated among the population than they were in the National Assembly. In Paris, some refractory nuns were publicly whipped by women who supported the government. From *Les Révolutions de France et de Brabant*. © Penn Special Collections.

Or, to use the term that appears far more often in the debates of the day, it was the Catholic priests who had *seduced* them – a term that both sides used, often in ways that seemed to straddle the line between literal and figurative.

Seduction was a tricky issue. No, the deputies who railed against the refractory church were not saying that all of these priests were sleeping with their female followers. But it was a word choice that led to some necessary conclusions. It required a protection that extended beyond the ability of individuals to make their own choices; it required protecting people from making choices that would not reflect their best interests. It required that people be protected from themselves, that women be protected from their own desire. The revolutionaries had, since 1789, seen their project as part of the spread of reason: reason that would make France a better place, while

France would help make the world a better place by fighting superstition and the forces of darkness. Seduction, though, was not interested in reason; it brought passions and emotions into the mix. For the revolutionaries, the people of the countryside, particularly the women, had to be protected from being led astray, just as a family had to protect its daughters, even when those daughters did not want that protection.

Eventually, the revolutionaries believed, this would not be needed. For the next generation, there would be proper education, and all citizens could be trusted to rely on their reason.

Until then, people – particularly women – needed to be protected from themselves, protected from their own desires, and protected from the priests who would lead them astray. But who would do this? Who would look after the interests of the nation?

The rise of the Jacobins

Later in the Revolution, the government itself would attempt to reach into the daily lives of its citizens, watching over their moves. In 1791, it was the most engaged citizens who took this task upon themselves – not as individuals, but as members of the clubs that had increasingly come to dominate political life, in the capital and in the provinces.

The most important of those clubs was known officially as the *Société des Amis de la Constitution*. It was unofficially known as the Jacobin club.

The name "Jacobins" was not one that the Society of the Friends of the Constitution had coined; it was the name by which people referred to France's Dominican monks. The Jacobins – the old ones, the monks – began renting space to the political club in October 1789 when, like the National Assembly, the club followed the king to Paris. Their meetings had continued, and become increasingly influential. Mirabeau, Sieyes, and Grégoire were among the more prominent men to attend the meetings. Along with them was the deputy Maximilien Robespierre, who had become a rising star of sorts in the Jacobin club. From northern France, Robespierre was a man committed to his cause and, it seemed, little else. Exceedingly serious and excessively prim, his sister would later describe him as having been the sort of child who rarely joined his friends' games – and when he did, it was to clarify the rules rather than to play himself. Robespierre was not a natural orator, lacking the sort of voice that had helped men like Barnave stand out from the crowd. Yet he had found a way to get people to listen to him.

People, yes – not only men. Already in 1790, Robespierre was far more popular than his rivals with the women who filled the galleries at the meetings of the Jacobin club. Within a few years, women would be wearing amulets with his image around their necks.

Educated largely by the church, but trained as a lawyer, there was more than a bit of the monastic to Robespierre's lifestyle in Paris. He lived modestly, he remained single (and likely celibate). There was more than a bit of the monastic to the Jacobins as a whole, too – a curious symmetry between the Jacobins of old, the communities of monks of the Old Regime, and the Jacobins of new, men who would play a major role in the Revolution. "The Jacobins," Michelet wrote, "seemed to take themselves for the direct descendents of priests. They imitated their irritating intolerance ... they ardently followed the old dogma, 'without us, no salvation.'"[51]

The Jacobins were unique among political clubs, because they were a national club. They were not the only political club in the capital, though, nor were they the only club in the provincial cities. The Revolution saw an explosion of clubs, of groups of people gathering to discuss the issues of the day. Most clubs were limited to men, although most clubs – at least, those that lasted, those that managed to have some impact – found a way to get both women and men involved.

Among the other clubs in the capital, two stand out: the Cordeliers and the *Cercle Social*.

Both, like the Jacobins, represented the political left wing. And in terms of membership, there was no clear line between those three clubs in the capital: their memberships overlapped. Leaders of both the Cordeliers and the *Cercle Social* would attend the meetings of the Jacobins, sometimes speaking there, sometimes being leaders there as well. Each club, though, managed to have its own niche, its own "vibe." The *Cercle Social* was the most intellectual, even philosophical, of the three. The Cordeliers were the least philosophical, the roughest, the closest to the politics of the street.

As with the Jacobins, the term "Cordeliers" was a nickname, taken from the religious building – a convent, this time – where the group met for the first year of its existence. The club's official name was the Society of the Friends of the Rights of Man and the Citizen. It was, according to the early twentieth-century historian Albert Mathiez, "not a political debating-society, but a fighting group," whose charter stated that their "'main object is to denounce before the tribunal of public opinion the abuses of the various authorities, and every sort of infringement of the rights of man.'"[52]

Their politics differed from the Jacobins' more in style than in substance. The Jacobins claimed to speak for the people, but were not *of* the people; the Jacobins' relatively high subscription fee meant that only men of significant means could be members. Contemporaries viewed the Jacobins as a bourgeois club, even if that word – "bourgeois" – today is out of fashion among historians of the Revolution. The Cordeliers' much lower fee meant that men of the lower middle class, and even some workers, were members. More generally, though, there was never a clear line there between member and non-member. Even the term "Cordelier" was ambiguous, meaning either the club itself or the district which had taken the convent's name. The number of prominent members of the club who lived within spitting distance of it – including Marat, when he was not in hiding – helped to maintain the links between the club and its neighborhood.

The *Cercle Social* was as far from a fighting group as any left-wing group could be. It grew out of a series of political discussions among intellectuals, discussions about Rousseau's theories, about the rights of the poor and of women. Over the course of 1790, the loose group evolved into a more formal club, eventually growing to several thousand members, and calling itself the Confederation of Friends of the Truth. The *Cercle Social* was unique among revolutionary clubs in that women could be members – not just auxiliaries of some sort. Like the Jacobins, their high membership costs meant that membership for women as for men was limited to the wealthy. The presence of so many wealthy women meant that their concerns varied from those of the women who marched to Versailles in October 1789. They advocated giving women the right to divorce their husbands and pressed for equality in inheritance rights.

Other clubs would come and go – in Paris and throughout France. They grew, loosely, out of the academies and salons that had been so important to the spread of the Enlightenment under the Old Regime. In the context of the Revolution, when a new generation of citizens was remaking its world in ways never before thought possible, though, the clubs would have a far bigger impact than any of the academies or salons had. And in this new context, none of the clubs would have a greater impact than the Jacobins.

On February 24, 1791, Talleyrand, the ambitious young bishop from Autun, returned to center stage in the unfolding Revolution. He was one of the few bishops to swear the oath, and the only one both qualified and willing to consecrate new bishops. He played his part, consecrating the first round of new bishops – including Grégoire, who was now the bishop of Blois, the capital of a department (and now diocese) not far southwest of Paris.

On March 10 the pope at last broke his silence and issued a papal bull condemning the Civil Constitution. Although the pope had signed off on similar developments elsewhere in Europe – including in Austria, where Emperor Joseph II had tangled with the Catholic Church quite a bit – he was less inclined to support decisions that seemed not to have the king's full approval. Camus, the political veteran and longtime opponent of papal interference in the French church, reminded his readers and the Assembly of how limited the pope's role was in France.[53] The journalist Brissot – not yet a major player, although he would soon become one – wrote that the pope "is an enemy who would have to be punished, if he had any strength; but since he is so weak, he deserves disdain."[54]

The pope's intervention did not change many people's minds. It did, however, harden positions on both sides. Perhaps an early intervention by the pope would have been more influential. But by the time he finally got involved publicly, there was little scope for him to change the final outcome.

Easter that year fell on April 24. In France, the tradition had long been for believing Catholics to make their annual confession. As with so much religious practice at the time, the annual confession had long combined ritual and faith, sociability and spirituality. Now, though, the confession became political. Choosing to confess meant choosing between two rival churches. Some Catholics wondered if confessing with a constitutional priest would count. Many refractory clerics warned that it would not; some even insisted, before taking confession, that the parishioners state their opposition to the new priests. Some refractory priests took confessions outside of the church, in private homes, in places where the departmental authorities would not know. This marked the early beginnings of what was becoming a clandestine church.

Such concerns about who to confess to were not limited to the people of remote villages. Louis XVI had the same decision to make. The king, however, would have to make this decision – like all of his decisions – in the gaze of the public.

And in Paris, that public was quite disappointed when, on April 17, Louis XVI confessed to the refractory bishop of Metz.

As always, the king's behavior, his intentions, were unclear. Despite confessing to a refractory bishop, the king was not setting himself up as a crusader against the Civil Constitution. Back on March 19, Louis XVI had again showed up unannounced at the Constituent Assembly. He stressed his support of the new constitution – including, he specifically noted, the Civil Constitution of the Clergy. But few believed him. The king was increasingly isolated. In February, when his aunts had tried to leave France for Italy, they had been retained by the authorities, as the Assembly debated restricting people's freedom to leave the kingdom. On April 18, the day after Louis XVI's confession to the refractory bishop, he had tried to visit his palace in Saint-Cloud, on the outskirts of Paris. The crowd, and the National Guard, had not allowed the king to leave.

The king was running out of options. Never fully comfortable with the new situation – neither with the Revolution itself, nor with the opposition to the Revolution – he was unable to embrace either side. His at-least-quadruple game had never worked well, but the Revolution was now more clearly moving in ways with which he could not coexist. The joy with which the deputies in the Assembly had greeted his appearance in February of 1790 was long gone. So, too, was the unity of the kingdom, the enthusiasm, that had spread across France in July of 1790, during the Festival of the Federation. In its place was an increasingly divided kingdom, ruled – at least in theory – by a king who was no longer allowed to leave his own palace. France was not yet at war with itself, but the battle lines were drawn.

Notes

1 Michelet, *Histoire*, I:335.
2 Louis Sébastien Mercier, *Le Nouveau Paris* (Paris, 1994), p. 77.
3 *Hommage rendu aux dames françaises sur leur patriotisme pour accélérer la fête civique du 14 juillet 1790* (Paris, 1790).
4 *Hommage rendu.*
5 Mona Ozouf, *Festivals of the French Revolution*, trans. A. Sheridan (Cambridge, MA, 1988), p. 53.
6 Michelet, *Histoire*, I:275
7 *OP* II:165.
8 Michelet, *Histoire*, I:270.
9 *Délibération des cityoyens catholiques de la ville de Nismes* (Nîmes, 1790), p. 4.
10 *Détails circonstanciés des excès qui ont eu lieu les 2,3, et 4 Mai ... 1790* (Nîmes, 1790).
11 See François Furet, *Interpreting the French Revolution*, trans. Elborg Foster (Cambridge, 1981), p. 56.
12 McManners, *Church and Society*, I:361.
13 McManners, *Church and Society*, II:727.
14 McManners, *Church and Society*, II:728.
15 Nigel Aston, *Religion and Revolution in France, 1780–1804* (Washington DC, 2000), pp. 113, 115.
16 Aston, *Religion*, p. 111.
17 Baker, ed., *The Old Regime*, p. 229.
18 Michelet, *Histoire*, I:311.
19 *Le Clergé Dévoilé* (n.p., n.d.), p. 5.
20 *Adresse de plusieurs membres du clergé de saint lo, à l'assemblé nationale* (Paris, 1790), p. 3.
21 There is no exact number of dioceses in Old Regime France. By 1789, 123 dioceses were both in French territory and part of France's 28 ecclesiastical provinces. There were other dioceses, however, which were either in French territory but not part of the Gallican Church, or else conversely were subject to archbishops of the Gallican Church but outside of French territory.
22 Romans 13:1–2.
23 D. K. Van Kley, *The Religious Origins of the French Revolution* (New Haven, 1996), p. 364.
24 Aston, *Religion*, p. 88.
25 J. Mavidal and E. Laurent, eds., *Archives parlementaires de 1787 à 1860: recueil complet des débats législatifs et politiques des chambres françaises*, first series: 1787–99 (Paris, 1879–) [henceforth *AP*], X:154.
26 See Van Kley, *Religious Origins*, p. 363.
27 Timothy Tackett, *Religion, Revolution, and Regional Culture in Eighteenth-Century France: The Ecclesiastical Oath of 1791* (Princeton, 1986), p. 24.
28 *AP* XXI:10.
29 See Michelet, *Histoire*, I: 297.
30 See *L'Abeille, ou lettre à une pieuse citoyenne chancelante* (n.p., 1791).

31 Laurent, *Déclaration d'un curé, membre de l'Assemblée Nationale, sur la Constitution Civile du Clergé* (Paris, 1790), p. 21.
32 *AP* XXI:10.
33 John McManners, *The French Revolution and the Church* (London, 1969), p. 44.
34 Pierre de La Gorce, *Histoire religieuse de la Révolution française* (New York, 1969), I:226.
35 See Van Kley, *Religious Origins*, p. 364.
36 *AP* XXI:9.
37 Michelet, *Histoire*, I:369.
38 Michelet, *Histoire*, I:369.
39 See de La Gorce, *Histoire religieuse*, I:347.
40 Aston, *Religion*, p. 158.
41 Michelet, *Histoire*, I:412.
42 *AP* XXII:16–17.
43 *AP* XXII:18.
44 Tackett, *Religion*, p. 43.
45 Tackett, *Religion*, p. 165.
46 De La Gorce, *Histoire religieuse*, I:415.
47 Jean-Clément Martin, *La Révolte brisée: femmes dans la Révolution française et l'Empire* (Paris, 2008), p. 108.
48 Tackett, *Religion*, p. 167.
49 Jacques Pierre Fleury, *Mémoires sur la Révolution, le premier Empire et les premières années de la restauration* (Paris, 1874), pp. 95, 138.
50 Tackett, *Religion*, p. 3.
51 Michelet, *Histoire*, I:429.
52 Albert Mathiez, *The French Revolution*, trans. Catherine Alison Phillips (New York, 1928), p. 122.
53 A.–G. Camus, *Observations sur deux brefs du pape* (n.p., n.d.).
54 J. P. Brissot, *Rome jugée et l'autorité législative du pape anéantie* (Paris, 1791).

4

THE KING'S FLIGHT
AND THE DECLINE OF
THE FRENCH MONARCHY
(SUMMER 1791–SUMMER 1792)

On the evening of June 21, 1791, in northwestern France, a soldier approached a large horse-drawn carriage that had recently arrived in the small town of Sainte-Menehould. "Plans have not worked out," he whispered to the passengers. "I must leave for fear of raising suspicion." He then walked away.[1] What the soldier – a German-speaking commander named Andoins, serving under the command of the French general the marquis de Bouillé – knew, and what the inhabitants of Sainte-Menehould did not, was that this was no ordinary carriage. It contained the royal family itself: the king and queen, along with their two children.

The royal family had left Paris the night before, sneaking out just before midnight. They had left an hour behind schedule, but rather than hurry to make up for the lost time, they dawdled, falling behind still further. The mastermind behind the plan, Count Axel von Fersen, did not accompany them, and the royal couple was less than fully focused on the timeline. As a result, their intricate plan, hatched months in advance, was falling apart. They had expected the duc de Choiseuil to meet them earlier in the journey. He had not; they were concerned.

So there they were. The royal family, largely on its own, traveling incognito. They had succeeded in fleeing Paris; they were now trying to reach safe haven. They were not necessarily trying to flee France – a small detail to their critics, perhaps, but an important point to the king himself and to his supporters. Their goal was to reach Montmédy, a fort near the border. There, Bouillé was waiting for them, along with his soldiers. A military leader straight out of the Old Regime, and a marquis to boot, Bouillé had been in the French army since the 1750s, and had shown no sympathy for the changes that had taken place since 1789. He was the military leader whom the royal couple trusted the most and thought could get the monarchy set up in Montmédy. From there, the king thought that they would be able to govern France free of the menaces of the Parisian mob, free from the crowds that had controlled his movements ever since October 1789. They were most of the way there. They would not, however, get much farther.

The people of Sainte-Menehould knew something was amiss. Bouillé had been preparing for the king's flight, and as a result, troop movements had increased in recent days. It was not hard to link the mysterious carriage – clearly, these were important aristocrats – to the troop movements, and conclude that the counter-revolution was on its way, with the king supported by enemy armies, perhaps sent by the queen's brother, the emperor of Austria. Their suspicions were not enough for the people of Sainte-Menehould to stop the royal family from proceeding on their journey. But there was one man in the town – a postal courier named Drouet – who had started to piece things together. He was convinced that the couple in the carriage, who claimed to be Russian nobility, were in fact the royal couple. He had once before seen the queen, and was able to recognize the king from his portrait on the paper money circulating in France.

After much hemming and hawing, the town sent Drouet off to warn other towns in the area. Drouet left Sainte-Menehould 90 minutes after the royal family. He was a strong rider, on horseback; they were traveling by carriage, with tired horses. According to the escape plan – which they had fallen even farther behind and which, by this time, everyone but them had abandoned – there would be fresh horses waiting for them just before the village of Varennes. Those horses were gone by the time the royal family arrived.

While the drivers were looking for their horses, Drouet passed the carriage. He arrived in the center of Varennes, an otherwise nondescript town near the Luxembourg border, at around 11 p.m., and informed the people there what was going on. The town sounded the alarm, ringing the church bells, the men arming themselves as best they could. When the royal family gave up trying to find the horses and headed into the center of town, they knew that they had been found out. Though they protested for some time, still insisting that they were Russian nobles (the Baroness Korff and her entourage), few were convinced. And when the local inhabitants summoned a local judge – the only local inhabitant to have seen the king before – to verify his identity, and when the judge's instinctive response to seeing Louis XVI was to bow and say, "your highness," Louis XVI could not respond otherwise: *"Je suis bien votre roi"* – yes, I am your king.

The royal family had never fully understood the Revolution. They had long been convinced that it was the plot of a few rivals, probably led by the king's cousin, the ambitious if often overestimated duc d'Orléans; they had long been convinced, too, that the Revolution was a Parisian event, that the rest of the kingdom would not approve of the demands of the citizens in the capital. Varennes would prove them wrong.[2] The citizens of that town would not let the royal family continue their journey.

Figure 4.1 The royal family leaving the Tuileries. The king and his family snuck out of their palace during the night, hoping to escape from Paris. From *Révolutions de Paris.* © Penn Special Collections.

It was not an easy decision for the town, whose inhabitants were amazed, flattered, to see their king in person. It was a small town that found itself suddenly in the spotlight; it had the power to choose whether to let the king pass or to stop him. The king asked that they be allowed to proceed, insisting that he had only the interests of his subjects, his "children," at heart. The queen asked that they be allowed to proceed, pleading with the women of Varennes, pleading to her fellow mothers. But the people of Varennes were not convinced. When messengers from the National Assembly reached Varennes on the morning of June 22 calling for the royal family's return to Paris, the citizens were faced with conflicting orders from the two main authorities in the kingdom: the king and the Assembly.

The National Assembly, like the rest of Paris, had discovered that the king was missing on the morning of June 21. Pandemonium ensued. No one knew where he was, no one knew why he had left. Had he fled of his own accord? Had he been abducted? Who else was involved? And in what direction had he gone? They were able to piece together enough information to send out two couriers – one from the Assembly, the other from the National Guard, under Lafayette's orders – to retrace the king's route. The couriers' arrival forced the people of Varennes to choose between the king and the National Assembly. The people of Varennes considered themselves "good patriots." They chose the Assembly.[3]

For the royal family, all that was left now was to turn their carriage around and start the long trip back to Paris: back to the Tuileries Palace, where their unofficial imprisonment was now that much more clear; back to the crowds who had long reviled the queen and were beginning to turn on the king; back to all that they had just risked so much to flee. And if they had fallen behind schedule on the trip *to* Varennes, that had been an all-out sprint compared to the grueling four days it took for their return journey. That trip, Michelet wrote, was "the true trial of Louis XVI." Four straight days of accusations, of condemnation, as the filial affection of his people turned into anger.[4] The crowds surrounding the carriage, joining the trip back to Paris (if only part way) numbered in the tens of thousands, following the carriages like a swarm of insects.

At the end of the second day, three men sent by the Assembly reached the royal family and its odd procession. Included among the men was the deputy Antoine Barnave, one of the most prominent members of the Jacobin club, one of the men leading the race to take over Mirabeau's place as the unofficial head of the Revolution. Still only 30 years old, Barnave's improvised speeches often outshone those of his colleagues in the Assembly who would read from their notes. He had figured out how to get himself noticed; too often, he would find that he had been played, by one faction or another. Prominent enough to set his plans in motion, he was never politically adept enough to be able to see them through. He had established

Map 4.1 The king's flight to Varennes. The royal family attempted to flee Paris for the fortress at Montmédy, and possibly leave France altogether. They only reached the town of Varennes.

himself early on as a member of the Assembly's left wing, but as the politics of the Revolution moved left he would find himself displaced toward the center and eventually the right. His encounter with the royal family, with the queen especially, would seal that transition.

The other deputy to note here was Jérôme Pétion. Like Barnave, he was a member of the Jacobin club, but his politics were further to the left, closer to Robespierre's. He considered himself a representative of the people, their "inflexible" defender. It was a political stance that kept him on the extremes in 1789, but was starting to win the love of the people of Paris in 1791.

For both men, accompanying the royal family back to Paris was not only a duty to the Revolution, it was a chance to make themselves more visible to the people of France. The race to lead the Revolution was still on, and it was as wide open as ever. Since 1789, various men had tried, and failed, to establish themselves as its leader. Louis XVI had never been that leader – a shortcoming that had only become clearer now that he had tried to flee. Sieyes and Necker had had their day, then faded into the background. To the extent that any one man had led the Revolution during its first two years, that man was Mirabeau; but Mirabeau had died the previous April, and no one had taken his place. Lafayette was still a force to be reckoned with – he was still leading the National Guard, still had armed men under his command – but he associated himself too much with the royal family to be taken as seriously as before. The other names that would rise to prominence in the coming months and years were around – including Robespierre, Marat, and Danton – and were succeeding in making themselves known, but were still far to the left. So it is hard to imagine that Barnave and Pétion did not see in this prominent role an opportunity to move up in the ranks. Barnave's actions were surprising, however. He entered the royal carriage devoted to the Revolution, and arrived back in Paris devoted to the royal family. He seems to have been touched, emotionally, by the queen and her predicament. Accompanying the royal family back to Paris would end his links to the people of Paris and the Jacobin club. Barnave would start to say what others before him had said, what others later would say: for all of the glory of the Revolution, it was time for it to end. It was time for stability to return, time for the Revolution to consolidate the gains it had made, rather than to try to make new ones.

Pétion, however, would emerge from the ordeal with his opinions little changed. He was a man of the left, a champion of the people – as "indulgent" toward the people "as others are inclined to criticize them"[5] – and would remain so for some time. Where Barnave spent the time basking in the presence of the queen, Pétion would complain that he had "never experienced a longer, and more exhausting day."[6]

When the odd procession arrived in Paris, the people stood out on the streets, watching the family, looking at and into the carriage. Unlike the rest of the trip, there were no cries of *"vive la nation."* There were no cries against the king or queen, no cries in their support. The people stood in silence, watching the king and his family arrive. In a message all too clear to the king, they kept their hats on.

The aftermath and the abduction fiction

The flight to Varennes, as it is generally called, the royal family's failed attempt to flee Paris, was a major turning point in the history of the French Revolution. The goal of the Revolution, since its beginning, since the first wave of wide-eyed delegates arrived at Versailles for the meeting of the Estates-General, had been to turn France into a constitutional monarchy. And while there are many ways to create a constitutional monarchy, they all need two things: a constitution and a monarch. France was still writing its constitution, and its monarch had just fled. But few were ready, in the summer of 1791, for a republic.

Within days, the official announcement went up. In one of the more brazen lies of the Revolution, the National Assembly's leaders made up a story to tell to the people of France – and, perhaps, a story to tell themselves. They announced that the royal family had not fled: they had been abducted, taken from Paris against their will. It was never really clear by whom, or why. Nor was it ever clear if people were actually supposed to believe the story. But now that the king had returned, everything was back to normal. And this was the charade that would go on for the next 14 months. France remained a constitutional monarchy until August 10, 1792. The game of make-believe became real enough for France to function, to pass laws and govern, even to wage war. The game of reality, though, was make-believe enough for France to embark on projects that were far more than it could pull off successfully.

As for the royal family's daily life, it quickly returned to its old patterns. Being prisoners inside the Tuileries was nothing new. Newspapers wrote of how, the night of their return to the palace, the king took the time to play with his children, as he always had before leaving. But the royal family was more isolated than they had been before, with fewer allies in the capital – and, indeed, fewer allies in the kingdom. Fersen left the kingdom. Bouillé crossed into Luxembourg once he realized that the escape plan had failed. The older of Louis XVI's two younger brothers, the comte de Provence, had also fled the same night as the king, but reached the border without difficulty. (The youngest brother had fled after the fall of the Bastille.) The king would never see either brother again. And then, there were the other émigrés, many of whom had been part of the social life in the court at Versailles – now gone, not to return until well after the royal family had perished.

The royal family's remaining friends and allies started to look like something of a junior varsity squad. Barnave was trying to recreate Mirabeau's double role, combining parliamentary leadership with backdoor dealings with the queen. An ambitious double role, indeed, but he was having little success at either part. Lafayette, whom the king had left in the most awkward of positions, was still committed to protecting the royal family. He still had armed men under his command, but he was increasingly distant from the men who were leading the Assembly – and even his control over his men was showing signs of wear. As for the royal family's friends, there were some who had stayed, friends like the princesse de Lamballe, a woman whose friendship with the queen dated back to "happier times" at Versailles. Married at 17 to the prince de Lamballe, then a widow at 18, Lamballe was a creature of the royal court, with little idea of how to get by in the outside world – but with quite a bit of wealth to her name. Pious and prudish, as a favorite of the queen she had been a frequent character in the scandalous, pornographic pamphlets that people published about life at Versailles. Unlike other friends of the queen who joined the ranks of the émigrés in 1789, Lamballe stayed in France, even following the royal family from Versailles to Paris in October 1789. She fled the Tuileries at the same time as the royal family, heading to the north of France, then toward England, but had returned upon learning of the family's troubles.

These were the people surrounding the royal family after Varennes. They were not the sort of people who could keep the royal family in power. Mirabeau and Lafayette had each tried, in his own way, to help the royal family, had but the royal family had refused. The next wave of potential assistants would be a major step down.

Perhaps the most surprising aspect of the next phase of the Revolution, which spanned June 1791 to August 1792, from the flight to Varennes until the uprising of August 10, is that the king did not immediately fall into complete irrelevancy. But again, few people in France, in June 1791, were ready for a republic. France, for the next 14 months, would remain a constitutional monarchy – with Louis XVI still the monarch.

Part of the reason for the National Assembly choosing to keep the king lay in the fear of the unknown. Another part lay in the disagreements over what exactly would replace the monarchy, or who exactly would replace the king. But from this point on, it was that much harder to believe the words of a king who had been hard to believe before he fled. Those who supported the king were now that much more opposed to the Revolution; those who supported the Revolution were now that much more opposed to the king. The Revolution and the nation were both coming apart.

And though it probably does not need to be said, the king and the National Assembly were growing apart. Over the following 14 months, the Revolution continued: the politicians continued to debate, to write new laws; the king continued to play the part of the executive, approving some laws and vetoing others. By this point, though, there were too many divisions in society, too many battle lines drawn. The minor divisions had started back in 1789, with the émigrés; the major divisions had started the following year, with the Civil Constitution of the Clergy. The divisions that the Civil Constitution had created were not going away; in many places, they were getting worse – divisions between constitutional and refractory churches, divisions between believers and unbelievers, divisions between the men who supported the Revolution and the women who supported the refractory church. France was starting to come apart at the seams. And if the Catholic Church had been the first seam, others soon followed. In the months following the king's flight to Varennes, the divisions within the National Assembly would shift left, but remain strong. The division between the Assembly and the people of Paris would also grow. This division was, above all, a social division. When the Revolution began in 1789, the third estate had been able to present a unified front against the aristocracy; now, however, its internal divisions were showing, as a new social unrest became past of France's long list of divisions. All this would go on with Louis XVI still in Paris – still king, even, until August 1792. But while he remained king of France, he had long since ceased to be a leader.

The National Assembly was now holding the cards, they just did not know how to play them. Or rather, the men in the National Assembly were not ready to play those cards, not ready to step out into adulthood and leave their paternal figure, the king, behind. Instead, they stood at the brink of adolescence – seeing all too clearly the path they knew they would eventually take, but still afraid to take it.

In the days following the flight to Varennes, the leaders of the Assembly had sent out their story of the abduction, and were trying to act as if nothing had happened. Not all of the people were buying it. People started asking two different questions. Some, the most radical, started asking: what if France were to become a republic? But most were asking: what if France were to have a different king?

A different king. But who? There were two main options, although one of them was still a child. That child was Louis XVI's son, only six years old in 1791.

The king's daughter Marie-Thérèse was older, but still only 12, in 1791. By ancient French law, not only could no queens rule, but the royal line could not even pass through a woman. No one in the Assembly seemed at all interested in changing – or even questioning – this law, even as they overhauled every other law and tradition in the kingdom. So no one was considering Marie-Thérèse for the throne. In the royal lineage, then, that left only six-year-old Louis-Charles.

France had been in this situation before – the heir to the throne too young to reign – but only when the acting king had died. There was no tradition of kings abdicating or being replaced. But then, there was no tradition of kings fleeing in the middle of the night, either.

What there was, however, was a tradition of regencies. Both Louis XIV and Louis XV had been too young to rule when they officially became king. In those situations, there were regents – an official position, given to someone who would temporarily rule until the king himself was of age. For Louis XV, who had been five years old when he became king, it was his great-uncle, the duc d'Orléans, who ruled for the eight years following Louis XIV's death. What luck! That duc d'Orléans's great-grandson was available, and presumably ready to play just such a role.

But things were a bit more complicated than that. Following in the family tradition, "Orléans," as Louis-Philippe-Joseph, duc d'Orléans was known, had been a thorn in the monarchy's side since before the Revolution began, since before Louis XVI had even taken the throne. He was the head of the Orléans family, the most powerful family in France after the Bourbons themselves. Owners of the Palais Royal, a palace across from the Tuileries in Paris (where it remains to this day), they had opened its gardens to people as a place to gather, to talk, a sort of eighteenth-century version of the ancient Agora where Socrates had roamed. Given the Orléans family's power, the royal authorities had only limited authority – at best – over what went on in the Palais Royal, making it a haven for Enlightenment writers.

Orléans was also Louis XVI's cousin, although how close exactly is complicated. Both men were descended from sons of Louis XIII, France's king in the early seventeenth century. Louis XVI was descended from the older brother and, therefore, the king; Orléans was the direct male descendent of Louis XIV's younger brother. This alone made them fourth cousins once removed; but they were actually a bit closer, on Orléans' mother's side. Royal families were like that.

If the French viewed Louis XVI – and other kings before him – as their father, Orléans seemed to spend his life jockeying for the position of coolest uncle. He was not a very serious man. He spent much of his time gambling and riding horses, and more time still chasing women. He tried to embrace the new ideas of the times, the ideas of the Enlightenment, but never in much depth. He was more comfortable as absentee patron, via his Palais Royal gardens – gardens he would later rename the "equality gardens," before eventually changing his own name to Philippe-Egalité in September 1792.

He had picked up enough of the Enlightenment, of the new ideas, to stand up to Louis XVI in the years leading up to the Revolution, and in the Revolution's early days. He had joined the third estate ahead of most of the nobility. Unlike most members of the aristocracy who, under the Old Regime, had espoused Enlightenment ideas only to abandon them after the fall of the Bastille, Orléans threw himself into the Revolution. When other nobles went conservative, he turned radical. In the aftermath of his cousin's flight to Varennes, he started attending the sessions of the Jacobin club, presenting himself there as a "simple citizen." He had not, however, done nearly as much as some people thought. As Brissot would say, Orléans was a man who liked conspiracies, as long as they lasted 24 hours or less. After that, he got scared.

Among those who overestimated Orléans's influence, two people stand out: the royal couple. They blamed him for much of what had gone on thus far, including the taking of the Bastille. Their fear that he would take over the throne in their absence prevented them from fleeing any earlier than they did. Orléans was not as powerful as the royal family believed, or as ambitious as people expected. He was not, however, likely to be content to stay as regent. No one expected Orléans to relinquish the throne, once he had it. He was not, however, one to do what it took to get the throne.

But what if there was no king at all? Rather than a regency, rather than a change in who sat on the throne, what if France were to have no king at all? This was the Big Leap, the question that people could no longer avoid. What if France was to become a republic?

The Champ de Mars Massacre

If the Festival of the Federation, held on July 14, 1790 on the Champ de Mars, had symbolized the unity of the population, there is no better symbol of the changes since then than the events that took place on that same field on July 17, 1791.

It was still in the aftermath of Varennes, and in the shadow of the Assembly's story about the abduction. Many people in the kingdom, many people in Paris, were not convinced – not convinced that Louis XVI had been abducted but, even more, not convinced that he could be trusted. And so tens of thousands of Parisians gathered once again on the Champ de Mars, where just over one year earlier the king had been part of the festivities. This time, however, they gathered to tell him to leave. Or rather, to tell the Assembly to say goodbye to the king, and find a different one.

Not all those criticizing the king were in agreement. The Jacobins had written their own petition, calling for Louis XVI's replacement. Even that had been too much for some members of the Jacobin club, who had decided that the Revolution had already gone far enough. The Cordeliers, however, had gone further, declaring that "France is no longer a monarchy, it is a *republic*."[7] "Louis," they wrote, "is nothing to us." The Cordeliers, though, were on the cutting edge here. Few in the Assembly were willing to go so far. And relatively few among the people were willing to go so far.

The people who gathered at the Champ de Mars drew up their own petition, opting – with the Jacobins – for Louis XVI's replacement. They were willing to say that which the deputies at the National Assembly, their elected representatives, were not: it was time for Louis XVI to stop reigning. Since the king had abdicated the throne, they wrote, since he was a "perjurer, a traitor and a fugitive," it was time to remove him from the throne, and to find a different king.

In retrospect, the message was not particularly radical. It was hard to argue, post-Varennes, that Louis could be trusted. But by this point, the deputies were not particularly trusting the people, either. The events of that day would only strengthen that mistrust.

As for the crowd itself, it was not a particularly angry crowd. The people had gathered as petitioners, with no intention of storming the Assembly or of gathering up arms. It was – like the Festival of the Federation the year before – a crowd of both sexes, and of all ages. People brought their families. It was a Sunday, and many of the people there had integrated their protest with their weekly Sunday stroll.

It was not, perhaps, the most innocent of crowds. In the hours before the full crowd gathered, some of the people discovered two men who had hidden below the scaffolding that supported the *autel de la patrie*, the altar of the fatherland, a large structure that the people were using for the occasion. Marat thought the men were there to blow up the structure, killing all of the good patriots on it.[8] Others thought that the men were only there to look up women's skirts.[9] The men refused to say why they were there – and when they refused, the crowd set upon them and hanged them. So it was not the most innocent of crowds, even if not all in the crowd approved of the hanging. But the hanging did not end the gathering, far from it. People continued to join throughout the day.

The details of the massacre are hazy. No one knows who started firing or how many people died. When Quinet was writing in the middle of the nineteenth century, he put it at between 12 and 400.[10] Newspapers at the time were writing of death counts as high as 1500. The most likely number is somewhere around 50.

The soldiers, Lafayette's soldiers, had arrived expecting a "furious" populace; instead they found a "peaceful people on their Sunday promenades."[11] The people did not seem too alarmed at the soldiers' arrival – and they certainly did not leave.

It was quite a surprise when, later that day, with the unarmed crowd still gathered, the soldiers began firing on the petitioners. No one knows to this day, who – if anyone – had given the order to fire. The crowd had included men and women, young and old; it had included few people who could be considered wealthy, but otherwise included a fairly wide representation of Paris's different social classes. Thus the dead as well: male and female, young and old. "The first volley," wrote Madame Roland, a woman who was becoming a force in national politics, "which should only have fired powder, was loaded with shot; five or six others followed; the cavalry charged the people fleeing, and the saber struck down those spared by the cannon."[12]

Again, the details, from this point on, are hazy. No one denied that there were casualties. The question was where to place the blame.

For most deputies in the National Assembly, the blame lay with the people. It was Bailly who presented the facts – his version, anyway – to the Assembly. Bailly had been the mayor of Paris since 1789; he still had that office, but he was no longer the people's hero he had been back then, the would-be Franklin, trusted by king and people alike. The violence of the crowd scared him, as did the violent rhetoric of writers like Marat. It was through that lens that Bailly saw the massacre at the Champ de Mars, interpreting those events as a violent crowd that needed to be controlled, not only at the Champ de Mars, but throughout the nation. So he explained to the Assembly that the "seditious" crowd had "provoked" the use of force, and that the "paternal severity" that the authorities had used was warranted. Acknowledging that persons of "the two sexes" had been at the Champ de Mars, he painted a picture of armed men hoping to avoid violence, yet forced to, due to the crowd – who had yelled insults, who had thrown rocks at the soldiers, who had even fired a pistol. Most of the deputies in the National Assembly accepted this version of events and approved the soldiers' actions, along with those of their commanders.

Barnave, too, approved the soldiers' actions, approved their "courage and faithfulness." And, he added, "it is time ... that the authority of the law exercises its absolute power." There would be no more fear of the people – the *peuple trompé*, he called them, the "tricked people." It was time for the government to rule, for order to replace chaos. Barnave was continuing to say what others before him had said: it was time for the Revolution to end, for stability to return.

In this message, in this idea of "ending the Revolution," lay a social message. The government's actions, at the Champ de Mars and in the days that followed, reinforced the message that it was no longer a time when the Revolution could be seen as a united front against the aristocracy and against the émigrés. The National Assembly was moving away from the people of Paris. Or, most of the National Assembly was, anyway. While Barnave, Bailly, and others in the Assembly were praising the soldiers, those farther to the left saw things differently.

Barnave and Bailly were not the only prominent politicians who felt that it was time to end the Revolution; other men in the Assembly, and in the Jacobin club, also saw the Champ de Mars Massacre as a signal to do just that. It was time to consolidate the gains that the French people had made, but it was also time to put an end to the leadership of the people.

The Assembly had always had a tenuous relationship with the people of Paris, a contradictory relationship even. This relationship would be one of the constants of the Revolution. The taking of the Bastille had saved the National Assembly, but it had scared the Assembly as well. The men in the Assembly claimed to *represent* the people; they did not claim to *be* the people. They were lawyers, merchants and other professionals, not workers. They spoke of the people, praised the people, but the people still scared them. The people did not scare everyone in the Jacobin club, though, or at least not to the extent that they scared Barnave and his allies. Not all of the Jacobins thought that it was time to end the Revolution.

Barnave and his cohort had learned to play the game in the Jacobin club. They could not, however, carry the day there. So they did what any mature adult would do: they took their ball and left. They left the Jacobin club and started their own club, at another former monastery: the Feuillants. Thus was born the newest political club of the Revolution, the Feuillants. Its leaders were prominent men, including Lafayette. The new club started out as the favorite to take the lead, but they would not last long. As Michelet pointed out, the Jacobins' building had a mysterious yet definitely sacred quality. One left a building like that at one's own risk.

Returning, however, to more plausible explanations for the Feuillants' future problems turned out to be the same problems that other groups would encounter: the Revolution did not want to be stopped. In 1791, as in 1789, as in 1793, the people of Paris held huge sway over the political world. It was very hard to rule without appealing to the people – and appealing to the people meant appealing to women as well as men. Political clubs had found different ways to try to appeal to women; the most frequent method, as at Paris's Jacobin club, was to restrict membership to men, but to allow women to attend and sit in the galleries. At times some of the men in the club proposed banning women from attending, but those motions never passed. The Feuillants took a different approach: they closed the club's sessions to all spectators. This eliminated the distractions, but it seems to have also eliminated the energy, the ability to influence events. That December they finally opened their sessions to spectators, but where the Jacobins had enthusiastic (if partisan) supporters, the Feuillants had only hecklers.[13]

Varennes made it hard to pretend to govern as a constitutional monarchy, with Louis XVI at the head. The aftermath of the Champ de Mars Massacre made it that much harder still. And yet, everyday business resumed. The debates in the National Assembly continued. They turned to the order of the day – new military classifications one day, on the debt another, even uniforms for soldiers.

Marat was angry. "The blood of old men, of women, of children killed on the altar of the fatherland is still steaming," he wrote, in the aftermath of the Champ de Mars Massacre. "It is crying for vengeance, and the loathsome legislators just gave their praise and voted their thanks to their cruel torturers, to their cowardly assassins."[14] Marat was often angry. His readers expected him to rail against the National Assembly, against all but the most left-wing of the deputies. But on this issue, he was not alone. "Tyranny," wrote Madame Roland, "sits on a bloodstained throne ... It is possible that we will be in the midst of a civil war here within a week."[15]

The looming war she spoke of was one between the rich and the poor, between those who would shoot at the petitioners on the Champ de Mars and those who would stand with those petitioners. And Madame Roland was right that civil war was coming. She was not right about the timeframe, though, and she was not right about its source. It was not in the main cities of the kingdom that civil war was coming. It was outside of Paris, outside of the major cities – and particularly in western France – that the kingdom was becoming harder and harder to govern. Most often, it was the continuing battles between the two churches that was making France so hard to govern.

For supporters of the refractory church, the period following January 1791 was the start of a wave of persecution. For supporters of the constitutional church, for supporters of the government, it was a time when the refractory church was bringing France closer to civil war. Legally speaking, things were not bad for the refractory priests. The government was still paying them a salary and letting them use their old churches, though in practice, local officials and local Jacobin clubs sometimes exceeded the laws.

Fleury's refusal to take the oath caused him no shortage of problems, and his case provides a good example of the discrepancies between the coexistence that the laws called for, and the way things could play out on ground level. At one point armed men – "brigands," he called them – surrounded him, held a pistol to his throat and pulled the trigger, leaving Fleury to wonder if the pistol had failed, or if the men had always known it was unloaded. Government agents continued trying to convince him to take the oath. Along with offering him money or the chance to be a bishop they threatened to incarcerate him.

For Fleury, this was persecution pure and simple. But Fleury was not trying to live in peaceful coexistence with the new priests (whom he was not slow to refer to as *intrus*). He hosted other refractory priests in his home. He refused absolution to anyone who would not denounce the constitutional church. Opponents of the refractory church would have been quick to point out that he did all of this on a government salary. He claimed to be getting poorer and poorer as the Revolution advanced. And there were hardships, of that there could be no doubt – and the events he would experience after August 1792 were much harsher – but there were also moments like Christmas 1791, when the attendance at his mass was huge.

Fleury was able to stay where he was largely because he was not without supporters, even if he did call himself "the voice yelling in the desert." People (especially women) in his village would help him when he was in need. One time, when four men showed up in his house and started singing a song in support of the Revolution, the women of the village ran out of their houses and chased down the men. He had nothing but praise for the women in a neighboring village who attacked a constitutional priest with rocks and brooms.

Such treatment for constitutional priests was not rare, particularly for the new ones. Not the established priests, the men in pro-Revolution areas who had taken the oath, remained at their jobs, and remained in their communities. But as for the men who were replacing the old refractory priests, who were facing crowds of women that insulted them, they faced serious opposition, and at times, serious risks.

This hostility was not limited to the parish priests. Claude Fauchet had been one of the most prominent pro-Revolution clerics for some time. In 1789, he had given sermons to large crowds in Paris, preaching Christianity, preaching revolution, believing that the two were part of the same master plan. By 1791 Fauchet was a bishop in the constitutional church. He also had something of a following, something of a power base as a politician, having been a key member of the *Cercle Social*. In 1791, with the anger of most revolutionaries aimed squarely at the refractory priests, he still believed that hope for peace and liberty for all nations was "a universal religion, which sees all men as brothers ... Catholicism."[16] But if his efforts were tireless, they were not always successful. At his cathedral in the Normandy city of Caen he consistently found himself facing down crowds of angry women.

This was not the treatment that Fauchet was used to. He had been a successful ecclesiastic under the Old Regime. At one point, he had even been one of the king's confessors at Versailles, although that did not last long – it was not a good role for him. Fauchet was a man who "hid the heart of a *philosophe* under the cloak of a priest."[17] This heart of a *philosophe* had gotten him kicked out of the royal court, but it made him quite popular in the days leading up to the Revolution. He gave sermons in 1789, weekly sermons that drew huge crowds, popular especially with women. His presence at the storming of the Bastille strengthened his popularity.

If Fauchet had been glad to see the women in his audience in 1789 in Paris, his experiences in Normandy left a different impression on him. In November 1791 he complained that "only the constitutional priests are hassled, are stoned, have their throats cut, while the refractory priests are never bothered." And at the heart of these conflicts were the "gatherings of devoted female dissidents," and the "heap of drunken women" that police had to disperse. "Two or three hundred of these pious women," Fauchet claimed, attacked one of the constitutional priests in his diocese, "the kindest man anyone could know, chased him, pelted him with stones in his own church, and were going to hang him by the altar when the National Guard arrived."[18]

What Fauchet saw was not unusual. These tensions were building in villages across the kingdom. But the National Assembly had stopped dealing with them as actively as they had in the past. The confrontation of January 1791 had come and gone. It had done its damage. The Assembly, in early 1791, had begun to back away from the all or nothing decrees. They continued to pay the refractory priests and allowed them to lead masses. In the months leading up to Varennes, the Assembly had decreed that constitutional churches had to be shared, that both juring and refractory priests could hold mass there. In the days before the king's flight, the National Assembly was still smarting from the days of early January 1791, when the Assembly became the bully, and the clerics became the martyrs. Some members were convinced that things would improve over time, as a new generation developed, as the old superstitions faded before the force of reason.

Meanwhile, for Lafayette, things had gone from bad to worse. The Revolution was not turning out as he had hoped; the people were not rallying to him, the king had betrayed him, and now, in many people's minds (and not without reason), he had the blood of the Champ de Mars victims on his hands. His wife would not forgive him for not doing more to help the king. Royalist, aristocratic, and devoted to the refractory church, she had never been comfortable with her husband's role in the Revolution. The openness with which women proclaimed their love for Lafayette in the early years of the Revolution had not helped matters. The Champ de Mars Massacre made things that much harder for Lafayette, whose divorce from the crowd was now complete. The Revolution was escaping Lafayette, and there was nothing he could do about it.

For the people of Paris, there were other men who could still present themselves as heroes and spokesmen. Politicians and writers from the far left were proving far more successful at gaining popular support than moderates were. Journalists like Marat, who claimed to speak on the people's behalf, took up positions more extreme than anyone in the Assembly. Then there were the various clubs. The Jacobins, since Barnave and his cohort had left for the Feuillants, had moved further to the left, as had the Cordeliers. All told, there were many factions, too many to count, all vying for the leadership of the Revolution. Some men tried to rise through the ranks of politicians, others through the streets. Left-wing politicians had to appeal too. Those who rose up through the streets had to appeal to men of the bourgeoisie and men of the streets alike, and to women as well. And this was at times a tough tightrope to walk.

Robespierre was showing that he could walk that tightrope as well as anyone.

In 1791, Robespierre was starting to emerge. He had the self-confidence that the other leaders had, despite lacking what seemed to be certain required traits. Though he was not a natural orator, and brought no renown into the Revolution, his speeches – to some extent at the National Assembly, more so at the Jacobin club – became major events.

Robespierre did not come into the Revolution with the dashing-revolutionary-hero aura of a Lafayette, nor did he have the bad-boy-aristocrat mystique of a Mirabeau. Even in 1789, he had been a bit excessively dapper; as tastes changed during the Revolution, as men began to forgo the more aristocratic stylings of earlier years, Robespierre stuck with them, giving him an oddly out-of-time look. Yet women paid attention to him – and he to them. He had argued, back in the 1780s, that female "charm," at meetings traditionally dominated by men, would get men to take the meetings more seriously – and that "encouraging talents is one of women's foremost duties."[19] During the Revolution, in the Jacobin club, and later in his speeches at the Convention, he never stopped aiming his speeches at the women in the crowd, and he never stopped cultivating female support. This is most definitely *not* to say that he was any sort of playboy. He cultivated an aura of purity, of virtue. As his sister would later write,

> his private life was so ordinary, so simple, his habits were so regular, that, from the moment when he threw himself into the world of politics, everything that was not part of the domain of history, was of mediocre importance ... His private life was but a reflection of his public life.[20]

Whatever the cause of his popularity among women, it made it that much harder for other politicians to ignore what he was saying, even if they did tend to "murmur" during his speeches. In 1791 his legislative influence was still limited. He was unable to prevent his fellow deputies from retaining the distinction between passive and active citizens. "The people," Robespierre told his fellow deputies, "this multitude of men whose cause I defend, their rights have the same origin as yours. Who gave you the right to take them away?"[21] Robespierre's single most influential move in the National Assembly, though, was a somewhat odd one. It came as the National Assembly was winding down. The Assembly's goal from the start had been to create a constitutional monarchy, and darned if they weren't going to do it, even if Louis XVI was not the ideal monarch. And they were finished writing the constitution.

That constitution called for a different sort of assembly than the National Assembly. Specifically, it called for a *Legislative* Assembly, and that Legislative Assembly was set to take over from the National Assembly in October 1791. In the waning days of the National Assembly, Robespierre made his proposal: no members of the National Assembly should be eligible for the Legislative Assembly. Politically, it was a bit of career suicide for the men in the National Assembly – the very ones affected by Robespierre's proposal – to vote for it. But these men were not lacking in idealism, and voted for it.

The Legislative Assembly and the rise of the Girondins

The Constituent Assembly's last day was September 30, 1791. The Legislative Assembly began meeting the next day. If the Revolution had an excess of leaders and wannabe-leaders before this time, now there was a whole new crop of men arriving in Paris, ready to shape the future, ready to reach for glory, ready to reap the rewards of respect from patriotic men and the devotion of patriotic women.

The new men who came to the Legislative Assembly were, for the most part, younger men. They were, on the whole, farther left than the National Assembly had been. The representatives from the clergy and the aristocracy, increasingly quiet toward the end of the National Assembly, were missing in the new group. Men whose politics would have put them in the left seats of the old assembly now found themselves on the right.

The most distinctive development, within the new assembly, was the rise of a group known as the Girondins.

The group took its name from the department in southwest France that included Bordeaux, though "group" may be too strong a term, and they certainly were not an organized political party. It was Robespierre who indelibly linked these politicians with the department when he began calling them the "faction from the Gironde," a phrase he used disdainfully but that the Girondins never escaped. A number of their leaders were deputies from the Gironde, including the lawyer Pierre Vergniaud, one of the Legislative Assembly's most powerful orators. But they might just as well have been called by any number of other names – the Brissotins was one that people used, as Brissot was one of the movement's leaders (though not from the Gironde). Fauchet was also part of this movement, and brought his own share of followers into the mix, helping cement the link between the *Cercle Social* and the Girondins. Maximin Isnard, a deputy from southeast France, also began allying himself with this faction, and would prove to be one of its most confrontational members. And then there were the Rolands, husband and wife, both of whom would play important roles in the Girondin movement. He would hold several prominent offices, including minister of the interior; she would, of course, be denied any sort of office, but that did not keep her from becoming influential among the Girondins and, from there, in the Revolution.

Politically, the Girondins could best be described as moderate left. In the context of Assembly politics, though, things were always a bit more random. Like Robespierre, they were Jacobins, men who stayed with the club after the Feuillants had left it. They were not, however, Robespierre's allies – their rivalry with Robespierre and his followers, an intra-Jacobin split during the Legislative Assembly, would grow stronger in the following years.

The Girondins were committed to the Revolution and its gains, committed to the liberty and the constitution, but also committed to the provincial elites and free trade. Unlike the Feuillants, they thought that the Revolution still had progress to make; they were less willing than Robespierre – let alone Marat – to have the crowd lead that progress.

Again, winning the support of the crowd meant winning over not only the men of Paris, but also the women. And this was where the Girondins fell short. None of their leaders had the crowds of devoted female followers that Robespierre or Marat had. Women did not carry medallions of Brissot or Roland around their necks, the way that they did Marat or Robespierre. There was a certain irony in the Girondins' inability to get women's support. At first glance, they were well positioned to get that support. The *Cercle Social* was unique in allowing women as members. The Girondins were unique in revolutionary French political life in having a prominent woman, Madame Roland, as a mover and shaker in the party, even if she was not an advocate of women's rights *per se*. The most convincing statements in favor of increased rights for women came from revolutionaries who supported the Girondins. Olympe de Gouges, author of *The Declaration of the Rights of Women*, was close to the Girondins. In her writings, she called for increased rights for women, an increased role in the political process. If women can be brought up to the scaffold, she wrote, they should be allowed to speak from the podium. The philosopher Condorcet, now a deputy in the Assembly, was a member of the Girondins, and in 1790 had argued in favor of giving women full rights of citizenship.

These appeals to the rights of women did not earn the Girondins the support of the women of Paris. Instead, the Girondins would find themselves surrounded by groups who, despite advocating more traditional relations between the sexes, gathered more support from women than did the Girondins. Fauchet's case was particularly rough – shouted down by the women in his own diocese, women who supported the refractory church, and hated by the women in Paris, who had once attended his speeches, but now preferred his political opponents on the left.

Fauchet was not the only one getting more and more frustrated by the schism between the two churches that was tearing apart much of France, particularly in the west. The biggest change, in the fall of 1791, was not the size or nature of the schism, however; it was who got to decide what to do about it. In the creation of the schism between the Revolution and half of France's Catholic Church, it was the Constituent Assembly, not the Legislative Assembly, that started the process. The Constituent had passed the Civil Constitution of the Clergy and the requirement for clerics to take the oath. But from the early days of January 1791 until it disbanded, it had tried to walk back from the precipice. This official leniency had not convinced men like Fleury, who continued to preach against the new church; nor had it always filtered down to local governments, whose actions sometimes exceeded the laws. But the Constituent Assembly had attempted *some* level of prudence in dealing with the church. That approach was not passed on to the new men of the Legislative Assembly, eager to put an end once and for all to the disturbances that the refractory priests were causing. Their efforts at cracking down on those disturbances would be as successful as their predecessors' efforts had been – which is to say, unsuccessful at best, and often counter-productive. That said, there is no sign that prudence and leniency were making things go any more smoothly. Rather, a bad situation was getting worse, and both sides were quick to place the blame.

On October 9, 1791, the Legislative Assembly heard a report from two deputies they had sent to the department of the Vendée to check on accounts of troubles there, troubles revolving around the refractory church. As the deputy Gensonné told them, there were, indeed, problems. There was a "powerful coalition" between the former bishop and the refractory clergy, who together had acted to rile up the citizens, all based on "superstitious impressions that, in the current state of things, no sort of enlightenment can destroy."[22] A Girondin, deputy (and an actual representative of the Gironde department), Gensonné had spent two months touring the Vendée, along with his colleague Guadet.

In the months and years to follow the Vendée – on the Atlantic coast, south of Brittany but north of Bordeaux – would become synonymous with refractory priests, with the women who supported those priests, with civil war. It was not yet that, though, in the fall of 1791. Many of the details of what was going on there were much like the details heard in a significant portion of the kingdom: people were still supporting the old priests; the new priests were having a hard time of it, while the old priests drew huge crowds. There were new wrinkles, though, which came from a letter that Gensonné claimed had been intercepted between the old bishop and one of the refractory priests.

According to that letter, the priests were to refuse the olive branch that the Constituent Assembly had offered them early in 1791. Rather than share the churches with the constitutional priests – a "trap," said the bishop – they were to find other places, simple places, to hold mass. The very simplicity of these locations would remind people of the simplicity of the primitive church. Priests were to stay in their parishes, if possible, and prevent any of their parishioners from any dealings with the constitutional clergy. The refractory priests were also warning women that any marriage conducted by an *intru* was illegitimate, that their children would be bastards.

These actions, Gensonné reported, were all too effective; most of the people in the department were supporters of the refractory clergy, and therefore opponents of both the constitutional clergy and, more importantly, the government.[23]

But what was the Legislative Assembly to do? Gensonné knew that some sort of show of force was needed, presumably from the army; but he was also aware of the risks of acting too harshly. His two months touring the area had allowed him to see the extent of the people's discontent, and he seemed to waver on whether he viewed their actions as rebelliousness or piety. In a letter to another deputy of the Legislative Assembly, he wrote that he "did not know how we can reestablish order in the department if we do not expel the non-juring priests."[24] And yet, when it was time for him to give his report to the Assembly, he warned that "rigorous measures, while necessary in these circumstances, against those who disturb the peace, will seem more like a persecution than a punishment inflicted by the law."[25]

Not all of the men in the Legislative Assembly were so hesitant. For some, the risks of appearing as persecutors were worth it; better, in any case, than the risks of doing nothing.

Isnard took the lead here. "Our indulgence," he said, "has augmented the audacity of our enemies."[26] It was not toleration that would solve the problem, but severity: any time a priest disturbed the public order, he claimed, "the laws, in order to be just and wise, must punish him that much more severely, as his ministry gives him many powerful means to seduce and mislead the people."[27] And the Assembly applauded.

There were reasons that cracking down made sense, within the logic of the Revolution, the logic that had been there since the start, since the first passage of the Civil Constitution of the Clergy. For the men in the Legislative Assembly, it was a matter of cracking down on behavior that was at best disturbing the public order, and at worst treasonous, counter-revolutionary. For the priests and their followers, it was a matter of the freedom of religion, a matter of saving souls. But it is hard to see how the men in the Legislative Assembly would have seen things that way, when they began hearing of events in the provinces, in the western provinces in particular, and the problems they posed for the Revolution.

The week after Gensonné's report, it was the south of France that exploded – Avignon, specifically. In a kingdom that, until 1789, had been a kingdom of exceptions, Avignon had been the most exceptional, the most particular of all. Technically speaking, it had not been part of France – its inhabitants not subject to French kings, its bishops not members of the Gallican Church – despite being surrounded by France on all sides. It had been papal territory for centuries, but in 1790 its inhabitants voted to become part of France. The pope objected, but could do little against a Revolution that was giving up on securing papal approval for anything.

The annexation did not end tensions there, though, with local supporters of Rome fighting the supporters of the Revolution. As elsewhere, the dynamic became gendered, a struggle between a disproportionately female support for the old Avignon and the pope, on one side, and, on the other side, a disproportionately male support for the government in Paris. And as often happened as well, support for the Revolution was concentrated in the city, in Avignon itself, while the surrounding countryside favored Rome. In mid-October 1791, those tensions boiled over. Word spread that the government was going to start seizing church property; word spread, too, that a statue of the Virgin Mary had been crying.

Tensions rose until a crowd set upon a local administrator named Lescuyer, beating him savagely. The men in the crowd kicked him and beat him with rocks; the women, once he was down, attacked him further, cutting off his lips, and leaving him there begging to die.[28] The doctor who reached him described his wounds as fatal "both together, and separately." Stabbed, kicked, beaten, scalped.[29] In revenge, the revolutionaries of Avignon attacked and killed 60 people, 13 of them women, then threw their bodies into a mass grave. Michelet wrote that "the inexperience of the men, so poorly armed, and with so little knowledge of how to kill, was infinitely crueler than if it had been done by executioners."[30]

The Legislative Assembly would eventually amnesty those killers. Brissot would argue that the Revolution could not happen without some damage – an argument he would move away from when he saw how savage some Parisians could become, and how hostile Paris could be to his own faction.

In a kingdom that, until 1789, had been a kingdom of exceptions, Avignon had been the most exceptional. Not everything that happened in Avignon could be generalized to the rest of France. But then, each region, each city, retained something of its own dynamic. Still, the pattern is clear enough: where there were troubles, in 1791, they were between those faithful to their own religion and those who supported the Revolution. And it was increasingly clear how key a role women were playing.

Early November 1791 – another month, another report of counter-revolutionary activity in western France. This time it was in the department of Mayenne. One by one, the reports were coming in: from the Vendée, from Mayenne, from Avignon, from Angers. There was little doubt in the deputies' minds that the Revolution was in peril. Refractory priests were leading the troubles; women were following them. And it was easier to blame the priests than the women. "A seditious, fanatical priest can do more harm to the public good than all of the most stubborn enemies of the constitution put together,"[31] claimed one deputy. Another added that "the return of peace in the interior of the kingdom depends almost entirely on these religious questions."[32]

In dealing with the refractory priests, the men in the Legislative Assembly had to respect the freedom of religion guaranteed by the Declaration of the Rights of Man. That declaration, however – that freedom – had always come with strings attached, the condition that freedom of opinion in religious matters must "not trouble the public order." And it was clear to the men in the Legislative Assembly that there were many priests who were, indeed, troubling the public order. Fauchet proposed eliminating pay for all of the refractory priests. "Let us tolerate them," Fauchet said, "but at the least, let us stop paying them to tear apart the fatherland."[33] The measure, surprisingly, was not without its critics in the Legislative Assembly – it hit those refractory priests who were not troubling the public order as hard as those who were.

The denial of payment, however, was secondary to the main feature of the latest proposal: deportation. "There is only one truly appropriate" punishment, Isnard claimed: "exile the disruptive priest from the kingdom."[34] And again, the Assembly applauded.

The final version of the law that the men in the Legislative Assembly passed included both of those elements, although the exile was toned down some. Refractory priests would no longer receive a salary from the government; they would also be declared "suspected of revolting against the law, and of bad intentions against the fatherland." Any refractory priest in a place where "religious opinions are the cause of the pretext" of any problems would be exiled from his "commune" – that is, from his village, his parish, his city – but not from France altogether.[35]

The Assembly passed the law on November 29, 1791. Three weeks later, Louis XVI vetoed it.

The people who supported the law were not pleased, but it is hard to imagine what else they could have expected. Louis XVI remained a pious man, and that was surely part of his reasoning. But it was hard to believe that he had the Revolution's interests at heart. It had been hard to believe that for some time, even before Varennes. Some even felt that he had vetoed the law because he knew that it would lead to further unrest, and that further unrest would increase the chances that the Revolution would fail, leading Louis XVI back to the sort of kingship he had known, back to Versailles, out of Paris. The month before, the king had also vetoed a decree that aimed to crack down on the émigrés' activities. While those activities did not pose the threat that the revolutionaries believed, perception was as important as reality here, and two vetoes made it twice as clear to his opponents that Louis XVI was trying to use his constitutional role in the government to bring down that government. It was cynical reasoning, but not unwarranted. If that was his goal, though, there was a far better way of bringing the Revolution to its knees: war.

The march toward war

The word – *guerre*, in French – had been on everyone's lips for some time. In 1792, that war would begin.

The people of France had expected war – or, at least, an invasion of Paris – in July of 1789, which is what had led them to seize the arms and the ammunition in the Invalides and the Bastille. They had expected war when the Great Fear raced across the countryside. But it was the flight to

Varennes that made war seem that much more likely. Everyone in France believed, once the revolutionaries had brought the king back to the Tuileries, that there would be war. Peasants started asking for arms. Villages started making preparations. War, to most of the population, was inevitable, and they could only hope for the best.

In August of 1791, a declaration from the king of Prussia and the emperor of Austria confirmed some of the people's worst fears. Here, it was beyond suspicions, as they put their intentions in writing. They declared their intention to "place the King of France in a position to be totally free to consolidate the bases of a monarchical government," and that "they shall issue their troops the necessary orders to prepare them for action." It was a strange declaration and, in retrospect, it bears the marks of the tensions between the three men – on the one hand, the king of Prussia and the emperor of Austria, on the other hand the king's brother, the comte d'Artois. Artois was urging war as soon as possible; the king of Prussia and the emperor of Austria wanted to appease the émigrés, but they were also stalling for time. Neither the king nor the emperor was ready – let alone eager – to invade France. Both were waiting for France to self-destruct further. The declaration was just enough to scare the French, just enough to satisfy the émigrés, not enough to commit to war – and certainly not enough to declare war. But the people of France were not reading the declaration with the benefit of hindsight. The Declaration of Pillnitz (its official title) scared the supporters of the Revolution. It confirmed the fears people had had since Varennes, that foreign armies would come for the king, to end the Revolution. It did not, however, scare them into submission. If anything, it spurred them into action.

For the politicians in Paris, things were less clear-cut. In retrospect, knowing how far the Revolution would go, knowing that the revolutionaries would eventually kill not only the king but the queen as well, war does seem inevitable. But in the summer of 1791 and into 1792 there was still a choice to be made. It was only civil war that, by this time, was probably inevitable, given the cleavages in France over the Civil Constitution of the Clergy. But foreign war? There was still some choice here.

Yes, foreign leaders were looking at France and, in one way or another, preparing to intervene – although not to protect the royal family. Varennes bothered them, but not as much as people in France thought. No one was on the verge of invading just to save Louis XVI. No one was on the verge of invading just to save Marie-Antoinette, including her brother. Even in February 1792, when the Austrians and the Prussians met to discuss military strategy, they were more focused on plundering Poland than they were on "saving" France.

No, it was the French government itself that started the external war. *Why* it started that war is another matter; it was not like they had nothing else to worry about. The best way to explain the decision to start the war is that everyone had their reasons; everyone did not, however, have the same reasons. Nearly everyone in power in France supported war. Not everyone wanted it to succeed.

The leaders of the Legislative Assembly saw, in war, a way to rally support to the government, a way to rekindle the patriotic spark in the hearts of the French people. Lafayette hoped to be in charge of the army, to recapture the military glory of his youth. The Girondins, by getting out in front of the war, saw a chance to get into the forefront of the political world, to be the leaders of the Legislative Assembly. But if the Girondins were cynical in exploiting the move toward war in the hopes that French success would strengthen their position in the world of domestic politics, the royal couple were even more cynical. Their hope was that the French would lose. But the king would win.

That was the plan, anyway. It was "a secret calculation, since it could not be admitted," wrote the historian François Furet, "yet it was public because it was so obvious."[36] The king and queen had no respect for the soldiers who had gone into the army to support the Revolution. They had, as always, a very limited understanding of the state of the nation, or the state of the army. But while the Girondins overestimated the army's strength, the royal couple underestimated it. By calling for war, they thought it would lead to a quick defeat; foreign armies would rush in, crush the Revolution, and put Louis XVI back on the *real* throne, the one in Versailles, the one where he did not have to reign according to the constitution and share his power with the people.

No one could say this out loud, of course. The king was trying, once again, to play a double game. With most of the émigrés stationed in German-speaking principalities just across the border from France, Louis XVI started calling for the leaders of those principalities to expel those émigrés. The people of Paris, the people of France, the men of the Legislative Assembly – saw through Louis XVI's attempted double game, but did not care. Unlike the king, they thought that they would win.

Brissot led the calls for war in the Assembly and in the Jacobin club. It was a strange, new idea of war: a war aimed at the kings of Europe, a war aimed at despotism, with France playing the part not of an invading army to rule and conquer, but of the friend of the oppressed everywhere. "The French must be the brothers of all men, of all people."[37] And the Assembly once again applauded.

As with Isnard's calls against the refractory priests, so with Brissot's calls to war against Austria: in the dynamic of the Legislative Assembly, it was boldness, not circumspection, that would carry the day, whether or not it was the wisest course of action. But were there other concerns as well?

In explaining why it was that civil war broke out in western France, Michelet had a rather unique interpretation. "Along the northern border," he wrote, "and in all the regions where troops come and go, and which breathe the air of war, the woman's ideal is the soldier, the officer; the epaulet is almost invincible. In the south, and especially in the west, the woman's ideal – the peasant woman's, at least – is the priest."[38]

An historian could say that sort of thing in the mid-nineteenth century. At the start of the twenty-first century, not so much. The claim is flawed, of course; bordering on the misogynistic, it simplifies that which is complex, it belittles the motivations of the women of both northern and western France. And yet, it points toward a phenomenon that would be one of the driving dynamics of the French Revolution: in areas hostile to the Revolution, areas where Catholic opposition was strongest, that opposition was particularly strong among women. Priests who opposed the Revolution relied heavily on women's support. This was how Michelet understood the opposition to the Revolution. More importantly, it was how the revolutionaries in Paris understood the opposition. Michelet's analysis of the women's motivation might not have been accurate, or even appropriate, but it did capture the views of the times and the concerns of many of the revolutionaries.

The strongest voice against the war? Robespierre, who could only attack the war from outside of the Legislative Assembly, from the halls of the Jacobin club. But attack the war he did.

For Robespierre, the plan to go to war was flawed on many levels. He saw war as a threat to the Revolution, one that grew out of internal issues more than external ones. He saw it as "the result of a project, long planned out, by the domestic enemies of freedom."[39] He saw the issues at stake, saw that the court was not in favor of the war because the war would help the Revolution; he saw that the court was hoping for the Revolutions's defeat. Brissot and his followers were willing to take that risk; they thought that a war of liberation would be a success, that the oppressed peoples of Europe would rise up and welcome the French armies.

Robespierre was less optimistic, because he saw the soldiers as the "missionaries of the constitution." But, said Robespierre, "no one likes armed missionaries." People would instinctively fight them, try to expel them, and the war would fail. Even if the war was successful, though, it would make domestic politics worse. War, Robespierre claimed, was good for

> military officers, ambitious men, for speculators who bet on this sort of event; it is good for ministers, whose operations it covers with a thicker, almost sacred veil; it is good for the court, it is good for the coalition of nobles, intriguers, and moderates who are governing France.[40]

In short, the leaders who were calling for war were only doing so for their own personal reasons, not for the greater good.

In a follow-up speech, Robespierre searched for a further response. He saw the dangers in war, in internal plots. As a solution, he sought Rousseau's guidance, seeing in maternal love the way to keep children from hearing the poisoned songs of temptation. The hope for the Revolution was not in external war; it was in the coming generation, and, Robespierre said, "we will have the courage to patiently wait."[41] It was a speech that lacked Brissot's dramatic threats and ultimatums. But it was also a speech that had a different audience. The men of the Legislative Assembly had interrupted Brissot's speech repeatedly with applause. After Robespierre gave his speech in the Jacobin club, all anyone could hear was the sound of women crying and blowing their noses.

In this debate on the war lay the beginnings of what would become the great political rivalry of the next phase of the Revolution. Events were not on Robespierre's side in this round. Too many other people wanted war – even if they wanted it for different reasons.

On April 20, 1792, France declared war on Austria. Fighting would begin in Belgium – part of the Austrian empire – eight days later. Many French people who supported the Revolution had greeted the coming of war with a wave of patriotic enthusiasm. Wives cried as their husbands left for war; women promised to arm themselves to protect the interior as the men left to fight abroad.

The events that followed, however, would turn more in Robespierre's favor than the Girondins'. Among the Jacobins, Robespierre was more prominent than he had ever been. He would never lose the support of the people of Paris, and the Girondins would never gain that support. Robespierre would always have more support from the women of Paris than his political opponents enjoyed. Robespierre lost the battle, when France went to war. For the Girondins, though, it was a pyrrhic victory, particularly when the fighting began badly.

From late April until late September, the war did not go well for France. Defeated at one battle, humiliated at another, the military situation was coming back to haunt those who had advocated it – Brissot and his colleagues, Louis XVI and his few remaining supporters. The enthusiasm of the kingdom would be put to the test, after the early defeats, and it would be found wanting. People panicked and began looking for enemies to attack – even people who were not themselves at the front.

As things stood, in the spring and summer of 1792, the Revolution had no shortage of enemies. The list was growing.

When the people gathered for the Festival of the Federation in July 1790, they were able to present a picture of a unified kingdom. The only real enemies were the émigrés, the aristocrats who had fled France and who tried to organize an armed response to the Revolution. However, after the passage of the Civil Constitution of the Clergy, and the decision to require all clerics to swear the oath, the list of the Revolution's enemies grew: refractory priests joined the list of the Revolution's enemies. Devout Catholics who supported the refractory church became suspect.

In 1792, foreign armies joined the list. Austrian and Prussian armies – not without reason – were now as feared as émigré armies, as feared as anybody. French people once again were worried that armies were going to march in, kill the patriotic men, rape their wives, destroy their fields, destroy the Revolution. Newspapers were filled with warnings of a St Bartholomew's Day of patriots,[42] a reminder of 1592 when Catholics had run through the streets of Paris killing Protestants. Marat had been warning of a St Bartholomew's Day for some time, but still felt the need to up the ante, warning that the king had already called on "hordes of brigands" to enter France's cities and "cut our throats."[43]

In the growing fears of the day, in the increasing inability to know accurately what was going on, subject to the latest rumors, it was easy to see enemies everywhere, but hard to know what to do. Foreign armies, émigrés, refractory priests – these groups were united in their opposition to the Revolution. Their unity, however, should not be exaggerated. Prussia and Austria tolerated the émigrés, at best, and had little interest in doing the émigrés' bidding. The refractory priests and the people who supported them were not always eager to move back to the taxes and privileges of Old Regime France. Nor was it easy for those priests to communicate with any foreign agents.

Still, the Revolution was facing enemies from without and within. More and more supporters of the Revolution viewed its enemies as one unified group. Specifically, they viewed the refractory priests as allies, as agents, of the foreign armies. This misconception was shared by people across the social spectrum, all the way up to the deputies in the Legislative Assembly. Isnard, in particular, saw all of these forces united together against the Revolution. "We are surrounded by traps and trickery," he told the Assembly. "Already the aristocrat smiles, already the fanatical priest shows his cruel joy ... all of those not content with the Revolution are united against equality; all of the kings on earth are in league against us."[44]

The Legislative Assembly had tried before to make life harder for refractory priests, only to have Louis XVI veto that law. Now it was wartime. So in May of 1792, the Legislative Assembly returned to the issue. Once more, they came up with a decree designed to crack down on refractory priests who disturbed the public, who sowed dissension and sedition in the countryside. Once more, the men in the Legislative Assembly crafted a law that called for refractory priests to be removed from their parishes, even deported. And once more, Louis XVI vetoed it.

The king made his veto official on June 11, 1792. He would remain in power for two more months. He also vetoed another measure calling for *fédérés* to protect the capital.

Louis XVI's days had probably been numbered since Varennes, if not since the taking of the Bastille. Vetoing the decrees sped up the clock. Roland, still the minister of the interior, warned the king as much, in a public letter he addressed to the king – although it was most likely penned by his wife: "there will be a terrible explosion, unless a rationally warranted confidence in Your Majesty's intentions can finally calm it."[45] The people felt that they were fighting one unified enemy – and here they were, not allowed to fight the only enemy that they could see, the only enemy within reach. The king had been given a choice between siding with the Revolution and siding with its enemies. He had chosen to side with the enemies.

On June 20, a crowd of protesters invaded the Tuileries Palace. It was, to be sure, a terrifying event for the royal family. It was not, however, a decisive event. The king stood firm. Or, mostly firm, anyway. He did play to the crowd somewhat: he drank a toast to the nation and donned a red bonnet, a sign of his allegiance to the Revolution.

It was not the first time that Louis XVI had used his choice of hat to calm the crowd, to please the crowd. Three days after the storming of the Bastille, back in July 1789, Louis XVI had traveled to Paris, to check on the capital and its people. There, before a crowd of people who still believed that the king could lead the nation, Bailly had handed the king a revolutionary cockade to wear; Louis XVI had showed the citizens of Paris that he was on their side. June of 1792 was a different time. Bailly was out as mayor of Paris, Pétion was in. The man of ideas had been replaced by the man of the people, a people of whom Bailly and many of his colleagues were increasingly afraid. But they were also a people who, since July 1789, were an established player in the politics of the Revolution.

The king's gestures in June 1792 – hat and all – may have pleased the crowd, may have even appeased the crowd, but they were not the substantive changes that the crowd had in mind. On those issues the king would not budge. He maintained his veto, his constitutional right to veto, despite being surrounded by an angry crowd. It was a far more decisive action than anything he had done in the earlier, pre-Varennes phase of the Revolution, when crowds could convince him to leave his home, to accept the Declaration of the Rights of Man.

On June 20, Louis XVI showed himself to be, for once, stronger than the crowd.[46] And the king would take that stubbornness with him in his final days as king. "The obstinacy that Louis XVI showed in his remaining months," wrote Quinet, "could not be more noticeable; for it so contrasted with the incertitudes that preceded it."[47] Louis XVI – the king who had consistently given in, only to change his mind; who had stood strong, only then to give in; who had attempted double game after double game – had finally found some sort of backbone, taken some sort of stand, even if it was only an embrace of his own inertia. It was enough to save his reign on June 20, 1792. It was far too little, and, more importantly, far too late, to save his reign much past then.

Having the king put on a red bonnet and drink a toast to the nation would not make the war go any better, it would not take away the threats that people saw all around them: refractory priests sowing counter-revolution in the countryside; émigrés, who in reality were doing little, but in people's imagination were ready to pounce; the foreign armies who – in reality, unlike the émigrés – were a real military threat. At various times during the Revolution, as during the years preceding the Revolution, people had acted on mere rumors. Such had been the case in 1789's Great Fear. But this time, the threats were real. The French armies were losing.

The Legislative Assembly did what it could to get around the impasse. In July, they declared that when "the fatherland is in danger," the Assembly could ignore the king's veto.

This was followed, nine days later, with a declaration: the fatherland is in danger.

The fatherland – *patrie* in French – was indeed in danger. But the king's defenders were fewer and fewer in the capital. The king's critics were becoming more and more vocal. Soldiers and citizens started to petition the Legislative Assembly, calling for them to suspend the king, declaring that "Louis XVI has lost the nation's confidence," that he was but a "despicable tyrant."[48]

It was not the people's words, though, but their actions that would lead the Legislative Assembly to suspend the king. The Legislative Assembly was in the same situation the Constituent Assembly had been in when the king fled, back when the people gathered at the Champ de Mars. They were caught between the king and the people, caught between a king who worked against them and a people who scared them. They could not keep the people from acting, however. Nor did they fully wish to. What was clear to them in July and August of 1792 was what had been clear to the people one year earlier at the Champ de Mars: the constitutional monarchy, led by Louis XVI, was not working.

Notes

1 Quoted in Timothy Tackett, *When the King Took Flight* (Cambridge, MA, 2003), p. 72. Tackett's account of the king's flight is excellent.
2 Michelet, *Histoire*, I:501.
3 Tackett, *When the King*, p. 23.
4 Michelet, *Histoire*, I:501.
5 Pétion, *Régles général*, pp. 10–11.
6 Tackett, *When the King*, p. 83.
7 Baker, ed., *The Old Regime*, p. 274.
8 *OP* V:3211.
9 Michelet, *Histoire*, I:552
10 Edgar Quinet, *La Révolution* (Paris, 1987), pp. 336–7.
11 Michelet, *Histoire*, I:558.
12 Baker, ed., *The Old Regime*, p. 277.
13 Doyle, *Oxford History*, pp. 175–6.

14 *OP* V:3213.
15 Baker, ed., *The Old Regime*, pp. 276–7.
16 *AP* XXXIV:512.
17 A. de Lamartine, *Histoire des Girondins* (Paris, 1984), p. 238.
18 *AP* XXXIV:512.
19 Florence Gauthier, ed., *Oeuvres de Maximilien Robespierre*, vol. XI: *Compléments (1784–94)* (Paris, 2007), pp. 193–4.
20 Charlotte Robespierre, *Mémoires* (Paris, 2006), p. 68.
21 *OMR* VII:163.
22 *AP* XXXIV:142.
23 *AP* XXXIV:143.
24 Quoted in de La Gorce, *Histoire Religieuse*, II:373.
25 *AP* XXXIV:147.
26 *AP* XXXV:67.
27 *AP* XXXV:66.
28 Michelet, *Histoire*, I:637.
29 *Procès-verbal de l'insurrection arrivée à Avignon, le 16 octobre 1791* (n.p., n.d.), p. 4.
30 Michelet, *Histoire*, I:642.
31 *AP* XXXIV:329.
32 *AP* XXXIV:614.
33 *AP* XXXIV:420.
34 *AP* XXXV:66.
35 *AP* XXXV:436–7.
36 François Furet, *Revolutionary France, 1770–1880*, trans. Antonia Neville (Oxford, 1988), p. 106.
37 *AP* XXXVII:469.
38 Michelet, *Histoire*, II:20.
39 Marc Bouloiseau and Albert Soboul, eds., *Oeuvres de Maximilien Robespierre* (Paris, 1967) [henceforth *OMR*], VIII:76.
40 *OMR* VIII:87.
41 Michelet, *Histoire*, I:669.
42 Michelet, *Histoire*, I:704.
43 *OP* V:3066.
44 *AP* XXXIX:416.
45 Baker, ed., *The Old Regime*, p. 289.
46 Quinet, *Révolution*, I:375.
47 Quinet, *Révolution*, I:384.
48 Baker, ed., *The Old Regime*, p. 293–94.

5

THE END OF THE MONARCHY
AND THE SEPTEMBER MASSACRES
(SUMMER 1792–FALL 1792)

Leading women of the Revolution

The leaders of the Revolution were men. This fact should surprise no one, given the expectations that everyone, male and female, had at the time. Not all women were unknown or anonymous, however. Aside from the women who played leadership roles in their own neighborhoods and villages, there were women who fought to rise to center stage in Paris, who tried to make themselves as famous and as influential as the men. None quite succeeded. Some came close, though – closer than most of the men who came to Versailles or Paris, hoping to become famous, only to fall back into the mass of anonymous revolutionaries.

Today, the most well known of the female revolutionaries is Olympe de Gouges, due primarily (if not exclusively) to her *Declaration of the Rights of Women*. Any fame she won during her lifetime was hard-earned. She had been an unsuccessful playwright in the years leading up to the Revolution. A widow from a young age (and a mother of one son), she had enough money to continue to write plays, but had only a few of them produced. When the Revolution came along, she threw herself into it, advocating a variety of causes, from ending slavery to cleaner streets, but primarily she advocated the cause of women. She advocated for women to get the right to divorce, and for unwed mothers to be able to name the father of their children. Above all, she advocated for women to play an equal part in the political process.[1]

As the historian Joan Scott points out, for all of her creativity, de Gouges never escaped the paradoxes of her position and her project. She believed in the power of reason at a time when women were believed to be more emotional. De Gouges remained attached to the idea that women had something valuable to say as women, due to their experiences, yet she was dissatisfied with the women that she saw around her, whom she found excessively frivolous. "Oh, women, women!" she wrote, "when will you cease to be blind?"[2]

Théroigne de Méricourt faced some of those same frustrations – desiring to start her own movement of revolutionary women, yet finding that women who supported the Revolution were more interested in supporting revolutionary men.

Théroigne de Méricourt's revolutionary activity had started back in 1789, but then took some rather strange turns. She took part in the Women's March to Versailles in October 1789, but rumors that she had threatened the royal family during that event forced her into exile in her native Belgium. That exile was not a calm retreat to her childhood home; émigrés and other supporters of the royal family in the region were convinced that she posed a threat, and several men even kidnapped her. While she was in custody, local authorities became caught up in legal wrangling over her, involving different nations and accusations that she was a French spy. She was able to make it back to Paris by 1792, where the Jacobins declared her return a "triumph for patriotism," carried her from the gallery to the center of the room, and asked her to give an account of her adventures.[3]

This victorious return would not lead to the prominence she sought. In March 1792, she called on her fellow citizenesses to rise to action. "We owe ourselves entirely to the fatherland," she wrote. "Let us arm ourselves ... let us show men that we are not their inferiors in virtue, nor in courage ... the example of our devotion will reawaken men's souls."[4] She tried to enlist the support of prominent men, but did not receive the help she had hoped for. One of the men she tried to enlist was Santerre – a wealthy brewer from the Faubourg Saint-Antoine, one of the radical suburbs (or "*faubourgs*") just east of Paris. Ambitious and handsome, Santerre was gaining a reputation and a following as a leader of the workers from his neighborhood. He would, indeed, have been a good choice as a co-sponsor of her project, but he was neither interested nor supportive. For Santerre, "when the men from these faubourgs come home from work, they prefer to find their households in good order, rather than to await the return of their women from these meetings."[5]

One incident involving Théroigne de Méricourt was particularly telling. It took place at the Jacobin club, in April 1792, when de Méricourt was sitting in the gallery. Having overheard a joke told at her expense, she threw herself over the barrier separating the gallery and the center of the room. "Overcoming the efforts made to hold her back, she approached the bureau and, with animated gestures, demanded to be able to speak."[6]

Eventually, the men there succeeded in escorting her out of the room. It was not that there was no place for women at the Jacobin club. There was: the galleries. And for the women that attended the club's meetings, this was a way for them to take part in the political process. For some of the men who attended the club, who gave speeches there, the women's presence was a key factor. Théroigne de Méricourt was one of very few women who challenged this division of labor. She did not start a movement, either among men or among women.

If her support from the left was at best tepid, the attacks on her from the right were relentless. The pamphlets portrayed her as a slut willing and eager to sleep with any deputy in the National Assembly. One pamphlet portrayed her giving birth to a child in the halls of the National Assembly itself, with all of the deputies wondering if they were the father.[7] One pornographic novel even portrayed her as Marie-Antoinette's partner, and co-hostess of a "patriotic brothel,"[8] where both women would serve the pleasures of prominent deputies. Some of these pamphlets – although never respectful – still portrayed her as having a major impact on the men in the National Assembly, and the "dangerous power that her charms had on our sensitive deputies." Even Sieyes, "that severe puritan," could not deny that "Théroigne's presence gave new energy to his constitution," according to one pamphlet.[9]

As the Revolution advanced, both Olympe de Gouges and Théroigne de Méricourt would ally themselves more with the Girondins than with Robespierre and his allies. In Théroigne's case, this seems to have been more out of personal animosity for Robespierre himself than for any sort of ideological affiliation. Wanting to lead a women's movement, but unpopular among women and facing the ridicule of men, she could only lash out against her enemies, until they, in turn, would lash out at her. It was one of the paradoxes of female participation in the Revolution: the most prominent women tended to side with the Girondins, but the Girondins had trouble garnering support from the crowds of less prominent women who took part in political life.

Madame Roland was another prominent woman who allied herself with the Girondins. Her experiences during the Revolution provide an interesting counterpoint to those of Théroigne de Méricourt and Olympe de Gouges. De Gouges had been a widow, and Théroigne had never married. Madame Roland was married, however – and married to a prominent politician. To the extent that she was able to influence political events, it was through her husband. Though she wrote that she "never deviated from the role appropriate to my sex," she was frequently a behind-the-scenes player in the politics of 1790–93.[10] She was from the start dedicated to the ideas of the Revolution, and impatient at its slow progress.[11] She sought out other revolutionary men as allies; this included Robespierre, to whom she wrote in September 1791 that she considered him one of the "small number of courageous men" who remained faithful to their principles.[12] That friend-ship would not last; by 1792 she would be firmly ensconced as a force within the Girondins. Eventually, her role within that movement would be powerful enough for Danton to tease them – particularly Monsieur Roland – for having a girl on their team. "Everyone knows that Roland was not alone in his ministry. As for myself, I was alone in mine."[13]

Thus, one more dilemma facing women who wished to be prominent individuals in the Revolution. Via her husband's influence, Madame Roland was influential. And yet, even then, more limitations: her influence would have to remain behind the scenes, and it would always threaten her husband's role. To the extent that her role was known, it left both Madame Roland and her husband open to the same criticisms that the king and queen faced, that Louis XV had faced – that women were controlling their men, that wives (or, in Louis XV's case, mistresses) were having too much influence.

These three women were probably the most prominent revolutionaries. Probably, not definitely – arguments could be made for a handful of other women as well. Etta de Palm attempted, in 1790, to create a women's equivalent to the *Cercle Social*; in 1793, Claire Lacombe and Anne Léon would found and lead the Society of Revolutionary Republican Citizenesses. Those women would have their own impacts on the Revolution; those women would come up against the same limited options.

What was the real influence of all of these women, as individuals? It is not something that can be quantified, but in most cases: not much. No woman who supported the Revolution would have anything approaching the influence that Marie-Antoinette wielded; and it was likely Madame Roland that ranked a distant second. And both Madame Roland and Marie-Antoinette were women whose influence was tied to the roles that their husbands played – influences that always posed a threat to the men on whom they depended. The other women, though, were in different situations: widows, estranged from their husbands, married to men who did not seek the spotlight. They had to fight hard to get the attention that they received. And what they found – to no one's surprise – was just how low the glass ceiling was, and just how harsh and sexualized were the criticisms they faced.

These, then, were issues facing women during the Revolution. These issues faced men, too, but far less – and quite differently. The citizens of France were quite interested in the private lives of their politicians; they had been under the Old Regime, and they continued to be through the Revolution. There is no question that many wives influenced their husbands' politics – in the French Revolution as in any society. Lafayette, in particular, was likely moved by his wife's sympathy for the king.[14] It was rare, however, that a male politician's marital status had the impact on his politics that it could on a woman's, the way it did with Madame Roland. Mirabeau had risen to a level of leadership, despite his deserved reputation as a playboy, while the monastic Sieyes had faded into the background soon after the Revolution began. Yet Robespierre, in his own way as monastic as Sieyes, would rise in prominence as the Revolution moved along. It is easy to see here an eighteenth-century version of a more long-lasting "double standard" that either ignores or rewards sexual promiscuity among men, while penalizing women for the same behavior. Things were not that simple – or, rather, things were not *always* that simple. In the eighteenth century, people were obsessed with sexual promiscuity. They often associated it with the nobility, though; and as the Revolution became more and more hostile to the nobility, leading revolutionaries became more and more critical of promiscuity.

These transitions were starting to take shape in 1792. It was becoming harder for any sort of playboy member of the nobility to play a leading role, while men like Santerre were gaining in influence. This was the time when the *sans-culottes* – about whom more is to come in the following chapters – were starting to rise to prominence, especially in Paris. With their rise came an even more thorough embrace of a traditional division of labor between the sexes, the sort that Santerre had advocated.

It was less a case of a "double standard," and more a case of shifting and unstable standards. A politician's sexual behavior was always fair game for their opponents to criticize, as it had been before the Revolution. The extent to which any of those criticisms coincided with reality was rarely a factor in the impact that those criticisms had. No case of this is clearer than that of the most influential woman in the Revolution, Marie-Antoinette.

The queen had been vilified since well before the Revolution, when anonymous pamphlets accused her of every sexual misdeed possible: orgies, lesbianism, incest. The early pamphlets – those published before 1789 – had been written by or for the queen's rivals at court. They were, in other words, still royalist, and not part of an attempt to start any sort of revolution. When the Revolution did occur, though, all of that pornographic literature suddenly took on increased importance, and the limits on the press that had kept some of the raciest works under lock and key were gone. New pamphlets claimed that the queen was sleeping with the king's brother (now in exile), or invented affairs between her and discredited revolutionaries – Lafayette, perhaps, or Barnave (or both). In other cases, though, it was simply a matter of reissuing old works. Even the nicknames barely changed. From "Madame Deficit" she became "Madame Veto," all the while remaining "*l'autrichienne.*"

For all of the roles that women could play, there would always remain the roles that women could not play. Some were obvious: representative at the National Assembly, or any other major position in the government. There was a certain division of labor within other aspects of politics as well, however. Some crowd actions were decidedly co-ed. The festivals, for instance, made a point of including women; and many protests did as well. Other crowd actions were viewed as proper to women – the March to Versailles in October 1789 being the most famous and the most important. Then there were the crowd actions that the crowd viewed as proper to men. Generally speaking, the more violent, the more war-like, the more likely that participation would be limited to men. When the crowd stormed the Bastille in July 1789, it was an overwhelmingly male crowd.

The crowd on June 20, 1792 had been fairly well mixed between women and men. Though the men armed themselves with swords and even brought cannons, it was not a hostile crowd, as far as revolutionary crowds go.[15] The next crowd, though, would be far more hostile – and far more male. If women and men could not join together to overthrow the king, then the men would have to do it themselves.

The coming of August 10

Louis XVI may have shown more courage, more decisiveness, on June 20 than on any other day of his reign. That did not make him any more capable of handling the situation he was still in. Paris was still against him, Paris was still scared. Paris was scared of the enemies that confronted it, real or imaginary: from the rumors of brigands to the overestimated aristocrats, from the armies of Austria and Prussia to the refractory priests. For many partisans of the Revolution, it was not clear where one group stopped and another group started, just as it could never be clear where true accounts stopped and rumors began.

In believing that things were amiss, however, people were right. And they were right in believing that the king did not have their best interests at heart. In the nearly three years that separated the summer of 1792 from the October Days of 1789, the king had gone from being the kingdom's first baker, and the father of the people, to being the Revolution's first enemy. (The queen's status had remained steady.)

So it was that in Paris, in this summer of 1792, the city was against the king. It was clear to all that there was a second insurrection, a second June 20, coming. The only one who tried to prevent the upcoming insurrection? Lafayette.

Lafayette had been at the front lines, leading soldiers in battle (although not particularly well).[16] He returned a week after June 20. He had two goals: to bring calm and stability to Paris; and, failing that, to convince the king to flee Paris. He succeeded in neither.

By 1792, Lafayette's reputation was fading. He was no longer a hero of the Revolution; he now stood for stability and order, not revolution. And he could not always count on the men under him. When he showed up in Paris in June 1792, he tried to get the Jacobin club shut down. He did enough to scare the Jacobins, but not enough to close their club. Nor was he any more successful in convincing the king to flee. Even with the certainty of another insurrection, the king chose to stay put, and Lafayette returned to the war.

While Lafayette was trying – ineffectively – to stamp down on the rising wave of insurrection, other leaders were trying – quite effectively – to move the Revolution forward. Marat called on the people to rise up, warning them not to fall into any of the king's "traps," as the king and the foreign powers were busy forming an "elite group of villainous soldiers without souls, ready to cut their fathers' throats."[17] (The specificity might seem surprising, but to cut someone's throat – *égorger* – was becoming the verb of choice to describe any enemy's murderous intentions.)

Robespierre, meanwhile, was not too pleased with the Legislative Assembly either. "The principle causes of our woes," he told the Jacobin club in late July, "are at once in the executive and the legislative – in the executive which wants to ruin the state, and the legislative, which does not want to save it." In his speeches he began calling for a new body to take over from the Legislative Assembly, to take over from that body from which he had voluntarily eliminated himself and his fellow deputies of the Constituent Assembly. His solution was to bring in what he called a National Convention in order to "regenerate both the executive and the legislature."[18] Robespierre was becoming more and more dominant at the Jacobin club – the leading Girondins were attending less frequently, if at all. But Robespierre knew that his influence was suffering for not being able to be in the legislature. His criticisms had merit, but were not without self-interest, as Robespierre was trying to find a way to get back onto the central stage.

The Legislative Assembly was stuck in the middle, caught between the king and the crowd, trusting neither, trusted by neither. The city was losing faith in the Assembly. Several deputies reported being attacked or threatened in the street.[19]

Late in July, a tense situation became tenser. The duke of Brunswick, leader of the Prussian army, issued a manifesto that made clear that the Prussian and Austrian armies' aims went beyond defeating the French invasion, that they intended to

> put an end to the anarchy in the interior of France, to check the attacks on the throne and the altar, to restore to the king the security and liberty of which he is now deprived and to place him in a position to exercise once more the legitimate authority which belongs to him.

Those towns and villages that submitted to their armies would be protected, the duke wrote (and he was convinced that "the sane portion of the French" opposed the Revolution, just as the royal couple had been convinced before Varennes, just as Brissot and his allies were convinced that French armies would be welcomed as liberators) – but those who "dared to defend themselves" would be punished, their houses burned or destroyed. As for Paris itself, should it try to harm the royal family, or attack the Tuileries, it would face "military execution and complete destruction."[20]

This was not another measured response, designed only to appease, written to menace without committing. The duke of Brunswick had put his cards on the table. But if he hoped to scare the people of France – and particularly Paris – it does not seem to have worked. His words seemed to instill more anger than anything else.

As for those "people," the crowds that made up the city – they were not as disorganized as they might have seemed. There was an organization to the city, to the city government, one that allowed some means of communication from the national government and to the city's government to the neighborhoods.

In May of 1790, the Constituent Assembly had divided Paris into 48 official districts known as *sections* (and *sections* is the French word here). These sections had meetings, where they made decisions and issued official statements. From their start until the summer of 1792, sections tended to have assemblies once every week or two; after June 20, however, that pace started to increase. Section assemblies gave people a way to take part in the political process, one not limited to "active" citizens. They were also open to citizens to attend. Voting, in these sections, was limited to men; attendance was open to all, though, and most sections provided space for women to follow the proceedings.[21]

As the summer wore on, from late June through July and into August, these sections became louder and louder, the people of Paris angry at both the king and the Assembly. On August 4, one of the sections issued an official decree calling for the king, the "despicable tyrant,"[22] to be deposed. The Assembly was not pleased. It declared the section's decree unconstitutional, and "invite[d] all citizens to contain their zeal within the limits of the law."[23] But the Assembly was not in control, at least not in the way that they hoped to be.

There was one more element in this already volatile mix: the soldiers who were marching to Paris. Not the foreign soldiers, this time, but French soldiers, partisans of the Revolution: the *fédérés*. Their arrival in July had become something of a summer tradition, since the first anniversary of the fall of the Bastille. This year was different, though – the Festival of the Federation became something more like an excuse for these men to march on Paris, with the goal not to attend a festival, but to overthrow the king. They were, as Jaurès pointed out, men of action, who knew that only some sort of insurrection would end the crisis. Their arrival "signaled the opening of hostilities," or at least their reopening.[24] Their presence meant that the next insurrection would be markedly different from June 20. The next time, not only would it be men alone who did the fighting, but the men had already been trained how to fight. And they even brought a song with them.

It was at this point in the Revolution that the "War Song of the Army of the Rhine" came to Paris, the song that came to represent the views not just of the arriving soldiers, but of the entire Revolution. *Allons enfants de la patrie, le jour de gloire est arrivé*. Children of the fatherland, the day of glory has come. It is France's national anthem to this day, bearing the name *The Marseillaise*. Today, of course, it is old; its lyrics are dated, its last line – "may impure blood water our furrows" – has developed a new meaning in a non-militaristic and uncomfortably multicultural society. But in the summer of 1792 the song was brand new, and bristling with energy. Like any song or poem, it loses something in the translation, but its intention was clear enough: a call to arms. The enemy was coming, to "cut the throats of your sons, of your companions," and there was no time to waste. *Aux armes, citoyens!* Arm yourselves, citizens! *Formez vos bataillons!* Form your battalions!

Marchons, marchons! The first-person plural imperative is not always effective in English, but *marchons* means "let's walk" – "march on" manages to capture the spirit. This was not the song of men who intended to "contain their zeal within the limits of the law." What's more, everyone – *everyone* – knew this. "Never had an insurrection been more plainly, more clearly announced," wrote Michelet.[25] The only question was when.

August 10 and its aftermath

On the night of August 9 actions began in the sections. They had been hoping all summer for the National Assembly to depose the king, and all summer the Assembly had hesitated. So on August 9, all 48 sections – 47 of which had officially called for the king to be deposed – named their delegates to a new municipal assembly. The problem here: there was already a municipal government, with Pétion at its head. No matter. Desperate times called for desperate measures. There were, then – for a short time – two parallel municipal governments, one of which Pétion led, and the other which was just coming into being.

That night, Pétion sent a message to his second-in-command, a man named Roederer, that although he had stationed municipal officers at the Assembly and at the Tuileries, "there are no measures guaranteed to be effective."[26] After Roederer read Pétion's report to the Assembly, the deputies declared their session "permanent." They would not break for the night, but would stay in session until the crisis had passed.

At 11 p.m., the sections' delegates – the new municipal assembly – met at the Hôtel de Ville. It was an illegal body, with the clear intention of taking over the city government, yet had it no trouble entering the building and getting a space for deliberations.

Some time before midnight the tocsin started ringing out at the Cordeliers. By morning, it would be ringing throughout the capital. Around midnight Pétion went to the Tuileries to check on the king. Pétion was in a unique position. He was a supporter of the people, and the people loved him; but he was also a man of the government, and his colleagues respected him. No one else had this much support from this many factions. And, therefore, it would be a long night for Pétion. As soon as he arrived at the Tuileries he was summoned to the Assembly. He told them that he was doing what he could to maintain order, then returned to the Tuileries.

As the night went on, the deputies would not stop worrying about him, asking periodically after him. The deputies realized that things were dangerous. They knew the threat that they faced personally. As one deputy – Basire, a deputy of the far left, more sympathetic to the demands of the crowd than many of his colleagues – put it, "something very extra-ordinary is happening." But did they realize the stakes of the evening?

After Pétion left the Assembly, what did they do? What measures did they take? Or, as Basire put it, "Do you not know that today is the big day?"[27]

After Pétion left to return to the Tuileries, with none – zero – of the major issues resolved, the Assembly's next move was to listen to Condorcet's report on the legitimate role of the people in government, and his sugges-tion that the Assembly explore the possibility of perhaps one day thinking about the issue – in the abstract – of deposing a king. And, from Condorcet, that most philosophical of deputies, a promise to speak to the people in "the language of reason."[28] In other words, Condorcet and the rest of the Girondins did not yet realize that today was, indeed, the big day.

After hearing Condorcet's report, the deputies inquired, once again, after Pétion; they heard updates on the state of affairs at the Tuileries and around Paris. Then – and this may be the most amazing aspect of the night, and is certainly the strangest – they moved on to their ordinary business. They held second readings of decrees on old debts, on tax policy, on all that is dry and boring in running a government. This went on for hours. Periodically, someone would come in, give an update on movements around the capital, on the state of Pétion, or some new news ... and then the Assembly would go back to old business.

This was the Girondins' moment to take control of the Revolution, to lead the government to a new day. They had been the first to speak of a republic; they held the leadership positions in the Legislative Assembly. On this night, they could have taken control, declared the suspension of the king, declared a republic. They had all night to do so. They did not act.

It was only on the morning of August 10, after 7 a.m., that the Assembly began to focus on that day's events again. The new Commune had not waited that long to act, however. At 4 a.m., they had called for the leader of the National Guard to appear before them. Until recently, that leader had been Lafayette; in his absence, the role had fallen to a man named Mandat. The new Commune relieved Mandat of his duties, and replaced him with Santerre. No longer just the charismatic leader of the workers from eastern Paris, Santerre now had an official (or at least quasi-official) role with the National Guard.

When Mandat was leaving the Hôtel de Ville, he was shot and killed, his body thrown into the river. It was some time before the deputies in the Assembly would learn of Mandat's fate. It was that kind of day.

By morning, people were marching on the Tuileries. At 7 a.m. the deputies received definitive notice of the existence of the new Commune.

An officer of the old municipality told the Assembly that "anarchy has come," that there is a "double municipality."

The deputies spent some time deploring this dangerous "illegal act" but seemed, at least, to realize that it was time for action. They realized, too, that the king would most certainly be in danger. They pondered inviting the king to seek refuge in the Assembly, before deciding that they would "leave [it] up to his wisdom to determine if it is appropriate for him to come here, unless he felt safer" at the Tuileries.[29] In other words, they decided to tell the king that they were in session and, if he felt like it, he could stop by.

It would not be an easy decision for the king to make. On June 20, he had stared down the crowd. On August 10, the crowd was bigger and angrier. The crowd that had consisted of the men and women of Paris was replaced by a crowd of Parisian men, and men – soldiers even – from Marseilles, from Brittany. This was not a crowd that the king could stare down. Roederer was with the king, urging him to take his family and leave. The crowds were gathered outside, and there were cannons pointing at the Tuileries.

Louis XVI blinked. Some time around 8 a.m., he decided to leave, to take his family to the Assembly. Thus the king to Roederer: *marchons*. Let's walk. So Louis XVI, along with his family, along with some of their companions, walked the short distance separating the Tuileries from safe haven in the National Assembly. They were protected by soldiers from any physical abuse the crowd might have meted out, but not from the insults that people yelled toward the king and, even more, toward the queen.

What an awkward turn of events! Awkward for the king, who was forced to seek his and his family's safety in the hands of those who had most attacked royal authority; awkward for the Assembly, which was seeing its own authority undermined by the crowd. The best it could do, in these circumstances, was to put the king in his place, by sending him and his family to the most remote room of the building available.

Awkward, though, was a fair bit better than what was going on back at the Tuileries. The king was gone, yes; but the Tuileries was still a well-defended building, and the Swiss guards were still defending it, and the crowd was still planning to take it. The crowd's first move was to try to persuade the guards that all men were brothers, and that all should rise up against the tyrant. "Fishing" for guards – it was not an unfathomable idea. In the taking of the Bastille, it was their presence on the crowd's side that had turned the day; it was soldiers' hesitancy to follow Lafayette that had stopped the king from leaving for Saint-Cloud. It looked for a while like that would save the day here, too – some Swiss guards threw down their cartridges as a sign of peace to the protesters.

Then came the order to shoot. "There we see," wrote Michelet, "the power of discipline. They shot without hesitation."[30]

The Swiss were outnumbered, but they had the guns and the strategic positions. They had the authority to use force to repel force, to use force, as Roederer had told them, "when violent acts are exerted upon you."[31] The bodies started piling up. Men in the crowd had to climb over dead bodies to get in and fight.

Some time during the fighting, the Assembly started letting go of its legalistic rationales. They knew that they had to do what they could to calm Paris, even if that meant working with the new Commune. They sent agents to talk with whatever there was of a municipal government, be it legally or illegally constituted.[32] The people at the Tuileries, meanwhile, were still fighting, still trying to reach the palace, still under fire. The Assembly would soon learn that the doors of the palace had been forced.

From a tactical standpoint, both the storming of the Bastille and August 10 involved the same sort of scenario: many people versus a well-defended building. The Tuileries was a palace, not a fortress, but being inside still gave the Swiss guards defending it a huge tactical advantage over the crowds coming in. Most of the bloodshed of that day happened, again, as it had happened at the Bastille, after the people had made it through the first gate.

At around 9:30 a.m., the Assembly heard cannons firing.

Then, from his position in the safety of the Assembly, Louis XVI issued the order for the Swiss defenders to stand down, and had the message sent to the soldiers at the Tuileries. In the confusion of leaving the Tuileries, had the order simply escaped his mind? Or had he hoped to see how it would turn out, hoped that the Swiss would emerge victorious over the crowd? Had he simply hoped to inflict some punishment on the way out?

The Swiss soon stopped shooting, but there were already hundreds of people dead. By 11 a.m. the cannons had stopped. Some of the protesters sought out the Swiss, in the same spirit of universal brotherhood that they had tried to activate before the fighting started; others sought vengeance, and the crowd killed more than a few Swiss soldiers that afternoon. The people had begun the day angry; they ended the day victorious, but no less angry.

The Assembly, meanwhile, finally started making some decisions. Whether it was the king's defeat, the Commune's swagger, or a belated recognition that it was, indeed, the big day, over the coming hours the Assembly made several decisions that changed the course of the Revolution.

The Assembly "provisionally suspended" the king. It seemed a half measure at the time, but it was clear to all but the most mistrustful that he would never again reign. They recalled several Girondin ministers whom Louis XVI had dismissed in the weeks leading up to June 20. The Assembly called for a National Convention to determine the future direction of France and the Revolution. Ending finally the distinction between active and passive citizens, the delegates to that Convention would be elected – for the first time – by universal male suffrage.

Once the Legislative Assembly decided to act, it acted; these were far-ranging decrees. Suspending the king was a major step, as were calling for a Convention and universal male suffrage. But the timing was off. The Assembly was too late to regain control of the Revolution. The Commune was not scared to stand up to the Assembly, to represent the people, to tell the Assembly that "we come here, in its name."[33] Despite the steps that the Legislative Assembly took on the afternoon of August 10, it would never regain full control of the government, and certainly not of Paris.

The Convention was coming. That much was clear; the Assembly had decreed it, and the Commune supported it. Until then, there would be a strange – and not particularly stable or effective – shared governance between the two bodies. The Commune could claim to speak for the people, but it was only Paris that had elected it; the Assembly could claim to speak for the people, but it was only the wealthier classes that had elected it. As for the people, they were free to choose to listen to both, or neither.

To clarify: in one form or another, the Commune had existed since the eve of the taking of the Bastille, when the electors had organized in Paris, hoping to protect the city from the surrounding armies. Since 1789 it had been, quite simply, the city government. By 1792 it represented 48 sections, each of which sent representatives. That Commune had helped run Paris, led by Paris's mayor – Bailly first, then Pétion, who had taken over after the Champ de Mars Massacre.

The Commune that rose up on the eve of August 10 was something different. It tied its goals more firmly to saving France, and the Revolution, as opposed to just governing Paris. For the historian Thomas Carlyle, "one may say that there never was on Earth a stranger Town-Council."[34] Michelet was more critical of the men who made up the Commune. Some, he wrote, were simple men – vulgar and angry, perhaps, but "not incapable of generous sentiments." As for the rest? He found them closed-minded, bitter, irredeemable – especially Hébert and Chaumette, the "miserable scribes" who led the Commune, and who would soon play major roles in the Revolution.[35] The Commune was not without its defenders, however. Mathiez, more sympathetic to the radical Revolution, agreed that the men in the Commune were "simple" but felt they better represented the people's will than the Assembly's deputies.[36] Jaurès went further in his praise of these men, whose "obscure boldness saved the nation."[37]

It was time for the Legislative Assembly to figure out what sharing power with this Commune would entail. Freed finally of its opponent at the Tuileries, it now found itself faced with a rival institution. It did not, for all that, simply pack up and leave. (It did consider it, though. Madame Roland

131

was among the prominent politicians calling for the government to move to southern France, out of fear of both the Parisian crowd and the advancing armies.) The king and queen were still the enemy, but they had at least been neutralized. They had traded their *de facto* imprisonment in the Tuileries for an actual imprisonment in the Temple monastery – an old building, isolated and medieval, "like an owl in the sun,"[38] as sinister in its own way as the Bastille had been. It was there that Louis XVI and his family would remain, locked in their makeshift apartment in the Temple's towers. They still played a part in political life: hostage. And with that part firmly established, it was time for the Assembly, and the Commune, to move on to the other enemies on the list.

Next up? Refractory priests. It took longer than might have been expected, but on August 26, the Legislative Assembly issued the decree that everyone knew had been coming: the decree to deport refractory priests. Stating that the troubles they caused were "one of the main causes of danger to the fatherland," the decree gave refractory priests one week to leave their district and two weeks to leave the kingdom. Those who complied could choose their destination, but those who disobeyed and were caught would be sent to French Guyana.[39]

This edict was not the watershed moment that it might have been, as many local governments had already enacted their own decrees calling for refractory priests to leave, or to gather in the department's capital city. In some departments those decrees preceded August 10, or even June 20. Other departments, as soon as they heard news of the revolt of August 10, took measures against the refractory priests, either arresting them or deporting them.[40]

Again, the freedom of religious opinions guaranteed in the Declaration of the Rights of Man had always protected "the public order established by the law," which religious opinions had no right to trouble. Who, then, was to decide when religious expression did, or did not, trouble the public order? Following the passage of the Civil Constitution of the Clergy, local governments had struggled with this question. Different locations had different dynamics. Much of France would move from relative toleration in early 1791 to more repressive measures that began in the summer of 1792. As some departments ordered all refractory priests to gather in the departmental capital, and other departments chose to issue "amicable convocations" that amounted to the same thing, for many refractory priests their next step had begun: internment, imprisonment.[41]

These amicable convocations did not always lead to amicable results. Having refractory priests gather in the departmental capital had unforeseen consequences. Refractory priests who had been living isolated lives in their villages now found themselves gathered with other like-minded men. Local patriots and Jacobins now found themselves in close quarters with those priests – sometimes even outnumbered. Peasants would come in from the countryside to check on their priests. Gathering the priests had not worked. The next step was deportation.

Fleury's journey here was typical. He had thus far managed to stay in his village, acting every bit the part of the refractory priest: living among his followers, supported by the local women, preaching against the Revolution, and refusing sacraments to those who supported the *intrus*. In his region the deportation order had preceded August 10. He received the order to leave his parish in late July. He traveled to the nearest city, Laval, where he stayed for several weeks in a monastery with 400 other refractory clerics, including one bishop. (The bishop, Fleury noted, had been given the room next to the toilets.)

There is little evidence that any of these men were actively conspiring with the enemy, as the revolutionaries claimed. On the other hand, when the priests imprisoned with Fleury heard that the Prussians were approaching Paris, they thought the Revolution would soon be over and that they could go back to their homes.[42] They may have not been collaborating with the enemy, as very few of them could, but they were rooting for the enemy. As it was, by the middle of September, Fleury would be on a boat for England. All of those who had been healthy enough to travel had left Laval, and headed north to Normandy, where they caught the boat. Those not healthy enough to leave stayed in Laval.

Fleury was not too far from the coast, and therefore able to leave France without too much delay. For other refractory priests, deportation was not as simple. All over France, these men began to find their way to the nearest border – and if not, to find their way to the nearest capital, even to Paris. The roads of France, according to de La Gorce, were filling with priests. Many areas were inhospitable to refractory priests. In July, two refractory priests in Bordeaux had been killed, their heads paraded on pikes.[43] Other stories from elsewhere in France held similar messages: refractory priests were the enemies of the Revolution, and legitimate targets for the Revolution's supporters.

Few of the priests who headed to Paris considered it the ideal destination. It was the center of the Revolution, home to many of the most anticlerical citizens in all of France. But the capital offered the possibility of anonymity, of being lost in the big city. At least, it seemed to. As it turned out, they could not have chosen a worse place. But at the time, their options were few, and traveling to Paris was not without a certain logic. Paris had tended to defend the right to freedom of religion, and they knew the dangers they faced in their own parishes. Once there, they gathered where supporters would house them. Most left their new "homes" rarely. The large numbers of new priests added to the city's anxiety. On August 29 the Commune ruled that any refractory priests in Paris who did not leave within the two weeks allowed by the decree of August 26 would be incarcerated.[44]

By this time, the number of prisoners was starting to exceed the space available in Paris's prisons. (Tearing down the Bastille had not helped.) Other buildings started serving as prisons. Temple, for the royal family – but churches, too, including former monasteries and convents like Carmes and the Abbaye at St. Germain des Prés, were turned into makeshift prisons. Both Carmes and the Abbaye Prison held large numbers of refractory priests who had run afoul of their local administrations, whether because they had been leading anti-revolutionary protests, or simply because the local administrations had wanted to crack down on any potential problems.

The events of August 10 had toppled the king; the war, though, was still going on. French armies were doing poorly. On August 20, the Prussian armies began their siege of Longwy, a fortified town on France's northeast border; three days later, Longwy fell. Allied forces from Prussia and Austria were less than 200 miles from Paris and already through France's first line of defense.

There was bad news from the west as well. In the Vendée – which had been on the Assembly's worry list since October 1791, when they heard the report on counter-revolutionary activities there – people's dissatisfaction with the Revolution had taken one more step in the move toward civil war. Peasants had taken over the town of Châtillon-sur-Sèvre. Forces from the National Guard would soon take it back, but by then the fighting had left some 200 dead. The enemies of the Revolution seemed to be acting in concert. Why else would this be happening at once? The priests in the west, the armies in the east ... the king neutralized, yes, but that was not enough.

Then more bad news arrived from the east: enemy troops had reached Verdun. Like Longwy, Verdun was a fortified town northeast of Paris – but less northeast of Paris than Longwy. Again, they held siege there, and again the town fell. Rumors spread that the women of Verdun had welcomed the foreign troops with open arms.[45] The troops were even closer to Paris, closer to the heart of the Revolution, closer to being able to deliver the Brunswick Manifesto's promise of "military execution and complete destruction."

In reality, there was little coordination between the Revolution's different enemies. The émigrés, for all of the fear that they inspired, were out of touch and ineffective, and probably hindered the Austrians and Prussians more than they helped them. The refractory priests were isolated. Fleury was typical – he hoped for the foreign armies' success, but had no way of actually aiding them. Even Lafayette, when he no longer believed in the Revolution, had no way of aiding its enemies. In the aftermath of August 10 he commanded his troops to march on Paris, in the hopes of saving the Revolution from the forces now leading it, in the hopes of saving the royal family. His troops refused to follow his command. Seeing the writing on the wall, he left, crossing the border into Austrian territory, where the Austrians promptly arrested him.

That arrest would eventually save Lafayette's reputation in France, save the legacy of a man who, despite his experience as the "hero of two worlds," was still only in his mid-thirties, and who would still have a role to play in

France's history in the years to come.[46] News of his arrest was slow in arriving, however; belief in that news slower still. For Marat and Robespierre, Lafayette was still a threat; Marat was convinced that Lafayette was "marching, at the head of his army, toward Paris,"[47] and Robespierre was equally convinced that, when that happened, most of the Legislative Assembly would join him.[48] Neither happened. Perception, though, has a funny way of becoming reality. Or, at least, of being just as convincing.

With the armies closing in from the east and the religious revolts to the west, the revolutionaries in Paris were threatened by two enemies that they imagined as one; but the armies were not yet in Paris. There were refractory priests in Paris, unarmed.

The September Massacres

It is not surprising which one they went after. The ferocity of that attack, though, was another story.

The immediate spark came on the morning of September 2 when news of Verdun's fall reached Paris. News that the people of Verdun had not put up much resistance did not help matters. Tensions were high, and authority was weak; between the Assembly and the Commune, no one quite knew who was in charge. Rumors were circulating, meanwhile, about the growing number of prisoners in the capital – that these prisoners were, from the depths of their prisons, conspiring with the enemy armies.[49]

Upon news of Verdun's fall, the tocsin started ringing out across the capital. The early afternoon sight of a convoy moving 24 prisoners across Paris was too much for some Parisians to resist, especially when many of them were dressed in their ecclesiastical garb, "the uniform that most violently energized the people's hatred."[50] When that convoy reached the destination prison – the Abbaye – these prisoners became the first victims of what would soon be known as the September Massacres. As Quinet pointed out, "once the first blood was shed, the thirst for it was awakened."[51] Soon, crowds would be killing prisoners across Paris. Later that afternoon, another group of assassins reached the convent of Carmes and its hundreds of refractory priests (and three refractory bishops), men who had arrived in Paris in the preceding weeks and months. Thus, the rest of September 2, 1792: the executions of prisoners at Carmes and the Abbaye. It started in the afternoon and would continue into the evening. At the Abbaye, Maillard – the man who had tried to bring order to the October Days – tried to bring order to the killings. It was a strange sort of order, as the assassins created a makeshift tribunal, where they could assess the guilt or innocence of each prisoner, saving some, condemning and then killing most.

The following day the massacres spread to other Paris prisons. Some of these were prisons holding other refractory priests, the targets of choice. But the assassins became less picky; common criminals, debtors, prostitutes

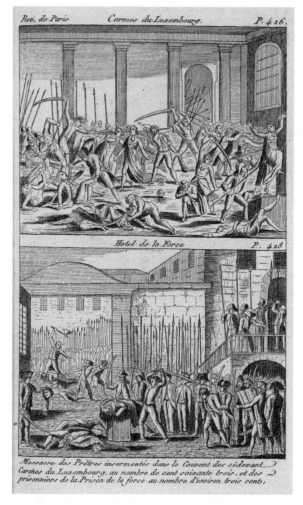

Figure 5.1 The September Massacres. The assassins of September 1792, sometimes known as *septembriseurs*, killing refractory priests in the Carmes Prison (upper) and ordinary prisoners in La Force Prison (lower). From *Révolutions de Paris*. © Penn Special Collections.

began to fall victim of the crowd's wrath. One prison – La Force – the Commune had partially cleared on the night of September 2–3, releasing the women only in prison for debts. It was a telling move, an acknowledgment that the other prisoners would be left to face the violence.

The most famous victim of the massacres was the princesse de Lamballe, killed on September 3. She had been at La Force, sent there when the Commune had sent the royal family to the Temple. It was during the massacre of La Force's prisoners and their mock trial that the mob had decided her fate. The "judges" tried, somewhat, to save her. They dared her to cry "long live the nation!" When she did not, her fate was set.[52] The assassins set upon her and killed her – most likely starting with a blow to the back of her head, before she succumbed to other weapons – perhaps knives, perhaps just fists and feet. Nor did the crowd stop at killing her, although not all of the details are clear. Her head? That much is known. Someone cut it off and (what else?) put it on a pike. Hardly the first head to be paraded on a pike during the Revolution, but in this case, the pike became particularly handy. The crowd marched from La Force to the Temple, where the pike allowed them to hold de Lamballe's head up outside of the room where the royal family was staying in the towers, in the hopes that the queen might have one last look at her old friend.

The fate of the rest of her body is less clear. Michelet wrote of the four hours that her body, nude, lay bleeding on the street, as passers-by remarked how white her skin was – a sure sign of an aristocratic, spoiled life. He also referred opaquely to a man who had "the indignity to mutilate her at the very place that all must respect (because it is from there that we all emerge)."[53] Mercier was more explicit. After de Lamballe "had been mutilated in a hundred different ways," he wrote, one of the assassins sliced up her genitals "and made them into moustaches, in the presence of horrified spectators."

"I no longer," he wrote, "have the strength to write."[54]

Most historians give some version of this story, with varying degrees of detail, though in a more recent study Antoine de Baecque has dismissed the traditional accounts of her violations and mutilations. His "defense" is relative: there is no doubting that the participants in the massacre murdered and decapitated her, then paraded her head through the streets on a pike. From what documents exist, though (and these come from the section), no one stripped or mutilated her body. Rather, people in the crowd transported her body to the section and then to a gravesite where – once its head had returned from the trip to the Temple – it was buried. This is not to say that the body was not mistreated. It was, after all, beheaded. But for de Baecque, the murder fit with the murders that had been happening throughout the Revolution.[55]

The more horrific version of this story is the more common one, hard as it may be – even in this context – to believe. There is no surprise, though, that as horrible as the events were, the stories about those events could exceed the horror. The September Massacres were borne of a convergence of circumstances: the power vacuum, the relative anarchy in Paris, the deteriorating war situation. A big part of that mix, though, was the difficulty for anyone to separate truth from fiction, news from rumor – a situation true at any time of the Revolution, but more crucial, more tragic, at key turning points. Was the war going badly? Yes. Were the armies marching toward Paris? Yes. Was there a plot among the prisoners to bring ruin to the Revolution? No. The assassins were acting on news, some of which was accurate, some of which was not; if news of their own events mixed the accurate and the inaccurate, it is hard to be surprised.

The rest of September 3, the massacres continued. That night Marat wrote an open letter to the rest of France, calling on the provinces to follow Paris's lead. He wrote that some of the "ferocious conspirators" in prison in Paris had been "put to death by the people, acts of justice that seemed necessary." It was now time that

> the entire nation ... adopt this means so necessary to public salvation, and all of the French should cry out, like the Parisians: we are marching on the enemy, but we will not leave behind us these brigands, to cut the throats of our children and our wives.[56]

By the next day things would become even worse. With few priests and few aristocrats left to kill, the crowd moved to other prisons. The number of assassins was not high; it was probably several hundred, not the sort of number of Parisians that had stormed the Bastille or the Tuileries. The mass indifference, or even the passive approval, had let this occur.

The Legislative Assembly made several attempts to talk to the people participating in the massacres, sending out deputies to address them, but to no avail. Rather than sending soldiers, the Assembly was reduced to sending an old man – Dusaulx – who stood on a chair trying, in vain, to get people to listen to him. The Commune had voted salaries for the assassins, although they had also made sure not to know too much of what was going on. The local sections had provided wine. Santerre, in charge of the National Guard, did not stop the massacres – because he chose not to, because he was waiting for orders, or because he did not have the control over his troops that he claimed. Danton, the minister of justice (and, therefore, in charge of the prisons), lay low during the whole affair. Robespierre also lay low – with no official title requiring him to act, but with enough respect from the crowd to have made it worth acting.

By the end of the three days, the people participating in the September Massacres had killed over 1000 prisoners, and possibly close to 1500. Priests made up less than half of the victims. Some in Paris were shocked, from the start, by the horror. Others viewed it as merely unfortunate and messy – but, if not necessary, not completely unjustified.

Were the refractory priests vanquished as a threat to the Revolution? No. Most of the refractory priests were not in Paris. Nor was it clear that murdering or deporting all of them would silence the counter-revolution, particularly in western France. As for the remaining enemy, nothing that the September Massacres accomplished had done anything to prevent the armies from advancing on Paris.

To portray all of Paris as bloodthirsty assassins would not be accurate – at most a few hundred took part. To portray most of Paris as not caring about those being massacred would be more accurate. The following summer, Madame Roland would write: "My blood boils when I hear the Parisians praised for not wanting another September Massacre. Good God! Nobody needs you, citizens of Paris, for another massacre. All you have to do is to sit tight, as you did last time."[57] But the Parisians' inaction was more complicated than just apathy; during the summer and fall of 1792, thousands of young men did do what they could to confront the foreign armies – they signed up to fight for the Revolution.

They may well have expected to receive some sort of martyrdom soon, given how poorly the war was going. Thus far, it was Robespierre's predictions, and not Brissot's, that had proved accurate. Not only were the peoples of the Austrian empire not greeting the French armies as liberators, but the French were not even fighting on Austrian soil. Instead, it was Austrian and Prussian troops who were fighting on French soil and marching toward Paris – until September 20, when something unexpected happened. French armies under the command of General Dumouriez engaged the Prussian forces under Brunswick. This time, however, France won. At the Battle of Valmy, French troops were able to outmaneuver and defeat Brunswick's army, forcing it to surrender and retreat.

Valmy, Verdun, Longwy – these were places that, in and of themselves, were not particularly important, at least for non-military reasons. But just as the news of Verdun's fall had sent fear into the hearts of supporters of the Revolution and had sparked the September Massacres, so news of Valmy led to a wave of enthusiasm among those supporters. Now, it turned out, France did have an army that could fight, that could win.

When Dumouriez returned to Paris in October, he was treated as a hero. By the time he returned, however, it was to a Paris that had gone through more than a few changes, and a government that had gone through quite the upheaval since it had placed him in charge of the armies of the northeast.

In the closing hours of the events of August 10 the Legislative Assembly had called for a National Convention. In the following weeks, elections had begun. Many familiar faces, from the Constituent Assembly, from the Legislative Assembly, would find their way onto the list of deputies for this, France's third legislature in four years. Sieyes, Grégoire, Pétion, Robespierre, veterans of the Constituent Assembly, were once again deputies. The duc d'Orléans was there, too, though he now went by "Philippe-Egalité" ("Philip Equality"). Brissot, Roland, Isnard, Vergniaud, veterans of the Legislative Assembly, remained deputies in the new legislature.

For all of that continuity, it was, overall, a shift to the left; the old right, once again, was gone, as it had gone during the transition from the

Constituent to the Legislative Assembly, and the Girondins now found themselves on the right.

As for the new faces, some were, genuinely, new: thus Louis Antoine de Saint-Just, young and unknown during the first years of the Revolution, but soon to make a name for himself. Some were less new, in the political scene, but were a sign of how far to the left politics had shifted. Thus Jean-Paul Marat, active, influential since the start of the Revolution, but always out of the government – always too angry, too fringe. Until now. Thus too Danton, whom the Legislative Assembly had made a minister in August, and who now became a deputy for the first time.

The Convention first met on September 20 – privately. On September 21, the Convention held its first public meeting. As its first order of business, it declared the abolition of the monarchy in France. France was now a republic.

It was quite a path that France had taken, in the years from 1789 until 1792.

It was quite a path, too, that France had taken in just two months, August and September 1792. From a monarchy, it had become a republic based on universal male suffrage.

The government that emerged from these two months, though – the France that emerged from these two months – still had no shortage of problems to deal with. These would be difficult issues for any government, but the government that emerged in late September 1792 was deeply divided, and the France that it ruled over divided more deeply still.

The Legislative Assembly had not remained idle in its closing weeks. On September 20 – the day of its last session – it passed a law legalizing divorce. Calls for the legalization of divorce were often tied to larger issues: if the French were going to end the despotism of the king over the nation, they should also end the despotism of a husband over his wife, and a father over his children. Couples could now divorce by mutual consent, or either spouse could initiate the proceedings. This did not lead to an embrace of libertinism or celibacy; many revolutionaries remained wary of bachelorhood, and continued to see the family as one of the bedrocks of society. They hoped, though, for a society that had agreed to come together and chose to stay together, rather than one that suffered under the yoke of unjust laws. Legalizing divorce was also a statement to the Catholic Church: marriage is a matter for individuals to decide as they see fit, and whether or not they choose to seek a priest's advice on the matter is up to the couple.[58]

August and September both left their mark on the new Convention. The breakdown of the government on August 10, the emergence of a new force, that of the Commune that stood up to the Legislative Assembly, the unstable and inefficient shared governance that followed – this whole rigmarole was displaced into the very politics of the Convention. On one side – the right – sat the Girondins, Brissot, Roland, Isnard, the voices that had dominated the

Legislative Assembly. On the left, Marat, Robespierre, Danton, representing the politics (if not the personnel) of the Commune. In between them, bitterness, acrimony – disputes that had been strong enough before, at the start of 1792, in the debates leading up to the declaration of war.

More than anything, though, it was the legacy of September that stood between them as the Convention began. As Quinet put it, "the massacres placed a river of blood" between the two factions.[59] The Girondins could never see past the violence and horror of those events. The left would never risk alienating the people of Paris by cracking down on the perpetrators; and for some, like Marat, there was always the risk that that crackdown would reach them.

The king in prison, the foreign armies defeated – this meant victories against two of the enemies that the Revolution had faced that summer. But as fall arrived the Convention had to govern over a France that had been divided since 1790. Killing a few hundred priests would not change that.

Notes

1 Joan Scott, *Only Paradoxes to Offer: French Feminists and the Rights of Man* (Cambridge, MA, 1997), p. 108.
2 Baker, ed., *The Old Regime*, p. 265.
3 F.-A. Aulard, ed., *La Société des Jacobins: recueil de documents* (Paris, 1891–7), III:347.
4 *Discours prononcé à la Société Fraternelle des Minimes, le 25 mars 1792, par Mlle. Théroigne.*
5 Elisabeth Roudinesco, *Théroigne de Méricourt: A Melancholic Woman during the French Revolution*, trans. Martin Thom (New York 1991), p. 99.
6 Aulard, ed., *Jacobins*, III:521.
7 Roudinesco, p. 31.
8 Anon., *Bordel Patriotique institué par la Reine des François pour les plaisirs des Députés à la nouvelle Législature* (Paris, 1791).
9 *Précis historique sur la vie de Mademoiselle Téroigne de Méricour*, p. 8.
10 Quoted in Laura Mason and Tracey Rizzo, *The French Revolution: A Document Collection* (Boston, 1999), p. 158.
11 See Michelet, *Histoire*, I:523–31.
12 Charlotte Robespierre, *Memoires*, p. 72.
13 Michelet, *Histoire*, II:57.
14 Michelet, *Histoire*, I:457.
15 Michelet, *Histoire*, I:723.
16 See Michelet, *Histoire*, I:699.
17 *OP* VII:4157.
18 B. J. B. Buchez and P. C. Roux, *Histoire parlementaire de la Révolution française* (Paris, 1834–8), XVI:222, 226.
19 *AP* 47:609.
20 Quoted in J. H. Robinson, ed., *Readings in European History*, II: 443–5 (Boston, 1906).

21 See the discussion in Dominique Godineau, *The Women of Paris and Their French Revolution*, trans. Katherine Streip (Berkeley, 1998), p. 198.
22 Baker, ed., *The Old Regime*, p. 294.
23 Baker, ed., *The Old Regime*, p. 295.
24 Jaurès, *Histoire*, II:669–72.
25 Michelet, *Histoire*, I:749.
26 *AP* XLVII:610.
27 *AP* XLVII:616, 624.
28 *AP* XLVII:615.
29 *AP* XLVII:635.
30 Michelet, *Histoire*, I:777.
31 *AP* XLVII:637.
32 *AP* XLVII:639.
33 *AP* XLVII:641.
34 Thomas Carlyle, *The French Revolution: A History* (New York, 2002), p. 511.
35 Michelet, *Histoire*, I:794, 814.
36 Mathiez, *The French Revolution*, p. 165.
37 Jaurès, *Histoire*, II:685, 688.
38 Michelet, *Histoire*, I:796.
39 Jean Robinet, *Le Mouvement religieux à Paris pendant la Révolution (1789–1801)* (Paris, 1898), II:278.
40 See Donald Sutherland, *The French Revolution and Empire: The Quest for Order* (Oxford, 2003).
41 De La Gorce, *Histoire Religieuse*, II:204.
42 Fleury, *Mémoires*, pp. 179–201.
43 De La Gorce, *Histoire Religieuse*, II:223.
44 Robinet, *Mouvement*, II:280.
45 Martin, *Révolte Brisée*, p. 114.
46 Michelet, *Histoire*, I:800.
47 *OP* VIII:4691.
48 Aulard, ed., *Jacobins*, IV:214.
49 Adolphe Thiers, *Histoire de la Révolution française* (Paris, 1844), II:311.
50 Michelet, *Histoire*, I:833.
51 Quinet, *Révolution*, I:410.
52 Michelet, *Histoire*, I:853.
53 Michelet, *Histoire*, I:855.
54 Mercier, *Nouveau Paris*, p. 99.
55 Antoine de Baecque, *Glory and Terror*, trans. Charlotte Mandell (New York, 2001), pp. 64–5.
56 *OP* VII:4313.
57 *The Memoirs of Madame Roland: A Heroine of the French Revolution*, trans., ed., Evelyn Shuckburgh (Mount Kisco, 1986), p. 31.
58 Suzanne Desan, *The Family on Trial in Revolutionary France* (Berkeley, 2004), pp. 92–8.
59 Quinet, *Révolution*, I:417.

6

THE NEW FRENCH
REPUBLIC AND ITS RIVALRIES
(FALL 1792–SUMMER 1793)

The French army's victory at Valmy gave the new government some breathing space. It did not make up for the bitter division that plagued the Convention from its first days.

There is no perfect label to give to either side in this battle, but the standard – Girondins versus Montagnards – has passed the test of time. *Montagnard* means inhabitant of the Mountain; "Mountain" referred to the upper seats where the left-wing deputies now sat, including Robespierre, Danton, and Marat. Some historians prefer the label Jacobins, and there was no small overlap between the Montagnard deputies and the members of the Jacobin club. Robespierre was becoming the most influential man in both groups. Marat sat with the Montagnards in the Convention, and the Jacobins, in late 1792, were beginning to accept him, even if most members were embarrassed by his excesses.[1] There were leaders of the Montagnards, though, who preferred to avoid the meetings of the Jacobin club, avoid its particular dynamic, what Michelet called its "inquisitorial spirit."[2] And then, the membership of the Jacobin club had changed over the years. Lafayette and Barnave were only distant memories there, but it was not that long since Brissot and Robespierre had debated at the Jacobin club.

Those days were gone, though. If the term "Jacobin" does not capture all of the Girondins' opponents, the Jacobins certainly made up a solid core. And the people who continued to meet at the Jacobin club were not lacking in animosity toward the Girondins. During the first months of the Convention, every discussion at the Jacobin club had found a way of deteriorating into a criticism of their opponents – the men on the right, the men who not too long ago had been part of the left: Brissot, Roland, Vergniaud, Condorcet, Isnard. The Girondins.

These were not "parties," in modern political terms. There was no sort of official apparatus, no official title. Nor is it possible to give exact numbers of how many deputies were on either side, although, out of the nearly 750 men in the Convention, estimates of 150 deputies on the Girondin side, at the opening of the Convention, and around 120 on the Montagnard side seem close to the mark. Make no mistake, though: these were two opposing factions. Their rivalry was such that it wound up shaping and reshaping each group, as each attempted to define itself as what the other was not. Their rivalry dominated the period from August 1792 until June 1793 in a way which in retrospect hardly seems appropriate. Major, world-historical decisions became transformed by a rivalry that was at best a rather minor distinction between two groups of committed republicans, and at worst a collection of petty personal rivalries. The fate of the Revolution was at stake on the battlefield, but politicians remained focused on this rivalry.

Nowhere was the phenomenon of letting petty rivalries control major questions more evident than in the first major question that the Convention had to deal with: the king. What should they do with Louis XVI?

On August 10, the Legislative Assembly had provisionally suspended the king. There was no talk, in the Legislative Assembly's final days, of ending that suspension. The Convention's first act had been to declare itself a republic. The king was no longer needed. But what to do with him? It would be too simple to just let him and his family walk away. Some deputies spoke of keeping the king hostage. But the general movement was toward something far more dramatic. A trial. Execution. Trial then execution. Execution without trial.

Execution without trial seems a bit extreme, but it had its defenders. Robespierre, for one. A monarchist up until August 10, he emerged in its aftermath the most strident of republicans. An opponent of the death penalty in the Revolution's early years, here he was leading the cry for at least one death penalty. "There is no trial to be conducted here. You are not judges," he told the Convention in early December. "The trial of a tyrant is the insurrection; his sentence is the end of his power; his punishment, whatever the liberty of the people demands."[3]

And then there was Louis Antoine de Saint-Just, the new arrival on the scene. If Saint-Just had not taken part in the earlier waves of political activity of the Revolution, it was because even at the start of the Convention he was barely 25 years old. From a small town in the Burgundy region, and the author of a pornographic poem he had written while in prison for stealing his mother's silver, he had begun corresponding with Robespierre during the Legislative Assembly. Saint-Just arrived in Paris as a deputy to the Convention, very much Robespierre's young protégé. He made his presence known on November 3, when he gave a speech in favor of the king's execution. "This man," Saint-Just said of Louis XVI, "must reign or die ... He must die to assure the tranquility of the people, since to assure his own, he intended that the people be crushed." And, he added, "no man can reign innocently."[4]

Thus Robespierre and Saint-Just, on the need for the Convention to execute Louis XVI. One a monarchist until recently, the other an unknown until even more recently, now together leading the charge for the king's death.

Those two were latecomers to the republican cause. Back in the summer of 1791, in the aftermath of the king's flight, some of the leading Girondins had first started calling for a republic. But in the first months of the Convention the Girondins, for little reason other than opposition to the Mountain and fear of the Parisian crowd, wound up playing the role of the king's protectors. Not that they were arguing for his return to the crown. But they were arguing for his right to a trial. The question was not as easy as it appeared. Robespierre was right on at least one point – the deputies were not judges. Second, trying the king meant ignoring many of the laws that the Revolution had enacted in earlier years. Condorcet seemed more concerned about appearances, arguing that "it is the opinion of mankind, the opinion of posterity, to which the nation is accountable."[5]

One frequent bone of contention between the two sides: the role that Paris should play in the Revolution.

In the elections to the Convention, the Girondins had dominated in most of France, but they had done dismally in Paris. Even Pétion, so recently the unofficial king of Paris and the hero of the crowd, was now siding with the Girondins, and was thus defeated on Paris's ballot. (He would be elected from his home department, nearby Eure-et-Loire.) Paris had sent the Mountain's leaders to the Convention. And of course it was Parisians who were filling the galleries at the Convention, and from the start of the Convention those galleries were decidedly pro-Mountain. Already pro-Robespierre, the audiences now had another hero to root for in Marat.

In their complaints about Paris, in their complaints about the politics of the Montagnards, the Girondins had legitimate accusations to make against their opponents – starting with the claim that the perpetrators of the September Massacres deserved to be punished. The Girondins had a position that could have been dominant as well – for all of Paris's pressure, the Girondins had more supporters among the deputies than did the Montagnards. Most of the key ministries were in the hands of the Girondins' friends and allies. But over the Convention's first eight months, the Girondins would show a knack for losing winnable battles. Whenever they attacked the Montagnards, whenever they attacked the Montagnard leaders, they went too far. The pattern began in late October, with a full-scale attack on Robespierre in the Convention from the Girondin deputy Jean-Baptiste Louvet.

Not Brissot, who had proven during the lead-up to the war that he could rally support to his side; not Vergniaud, their best public speaker; not Isnard, the most ferocious bulldog among the Girondins. Not even Condorcet, the deepest thinker, although admittedly his abstractions risked losing the deputies' attention. Not, in other words, anyone people already feared, or even respected. The lead attacker was someone whom the faction's leaders could sacrifice if need be, probably set up for the task by Madame Roland. A one-time novelist who still seemed to have trouble telling fact from fiction, Louvet had attended the meetings of the Jacobin club for months before daring to speak.

The Girondins had good reasons for attacking Robespierre. He had not been the leader of August 10 that one might have expected; he had done nothing to stop the September Massacres, and barely more to reprimand the perpetrators, let alone try to prosecute them. But Louvet's attack went beyond this. Louvet claimed, among other things, that Robespierre wanted to become a dictator; that he was working closely with Marat and Danton to form a triumvirate. He claimed, too, that Robespierre had provided the Commune with a list of people to be killed during the September Massacres.

Robespierre rarely let even minor criticisms go unanswered (he was quite thin-skinned), and he was not going to ignore an all-out attack. He took the unusual step, however, of requesting a one-week delay for his response. (Louvet, for his part, had written the speech out and carried it with him for some time before getting to read it at the Convention.)

Robespierre would give his response went November 5. On substance alone Robespierre's speech was more convincing. He had had little contact with Marat, so he was able to dispense with what he called "this bizarre project ... to identify me, at any cost, with a man who is not me."[6] Nor were the other accusations more convincing – Robespierre could deny being at the Commune during the massacres, and Louvet could not provide any proof to the contrary. It had been a vague accusation, which taught the Convention nothing new, and which required but a vague reply.[7]

Some aspects of Robespierre's response went beyond his speech's content. On the day of his response to Louvet, Robespierre had even more fans than normal in the galleries. Women had lined up early to get seats, and packed the galleries even more than usual. In his memoirs, Louvet would complain that Robespierre had brought as many "Jacobins and Jacobines"[8] as he could find to support him, but while Robespierre certainly encouraged that support, the people – women and men alike, but mostly women – came of their own accord.

Robespierre's response was enough to convince not only the galleries (who needed little convincing), but the "Plain" as well, the men who made up the bulk of the Convention, loyal to neither the Mountain nor the Girondins. Louvet had tried to respond, but was rebuffed by Bertrand Barère, a deputy from the Pyrenees. Neither Girondin nor yet Montagnard, Barère had a knack for keeping things moving. Robespierre and Louvet left the podium, the Convention moved on to other business. That evening, Robespierre celebrated his victory at the Jacobin club, while the Girondins went off to lick their wounds.

Madame Roland and the Girondins may have set up Louvet, ready to sacrifice him, but they still smarted from the defeat. Having failed to topple Robespierre via oratory or parliamentary politics, the Girondins took once more to the printed word. Condorcet, writing in the Girondin newspaper *Chroniques de Paris*, wrote:

> One wonders sometimes, why are there so many women following Robespierre around, at his home, at the podium of the Jacobins, at the Cordeliers, at the Convention? It is that the French Revolution is a religion and Robespierre is making it into a cult; he is a priest who has his devotees ... he speaks of God and of providence ... Robespierre is nothing but a priest and will never be anything but a priest.[9]

Harsh words from Condorcet – and, one suspects, not a small bit of jealousy. Condorcet was the Revolution's greatest philosopher, but also a spokesman (in 1790 at least) for the rights of women. But that support for women's rights had not brought Condorcet and the Girondins the support of women, who were siding with the Montagnards. Suddenly, the movement for women's rights was less important to Condorcet. But such was the dynamic of the Girondins–Montagnards rivalry. It transformed every issue, as each group sought to be what the other was not.

Condorcet's shift points, too, to one of the paradoxes of women's involvement in the French Revolution. Everyone who participated in the Revolution saw how much women were taking part in it – not as deputies in the Assemblies, but in the galleries (hence Carlyle's dismissive description of them as the "shrill galleries" where women would "bring their seam with them, or their knitting-needles; and shriek or knit as the case needs"[10]), in meetings, in public demonstrations, in festivals. Female activism was a major force in the Revolution, but it was not female activism in favor of women's rights, as we would define them today. There was no major movement aimed at women's suffrage, let alone female eligibility to political office. To some extent, there was more female activism aimed at what was then defined as "women's issues" – issues revolving around the home, around food or religion or children. But only to some extent. Women took sides in the major politics of the day, and in 1792 and 1793, they usually took the side of Robespierre and the Montagnards.

When the Convention replaced the Legislative Assembly, the importance of the Parisian crowd – and especially the women in the crowd – became even stronger than it had been. The spring and summer of 1793 were the high point of women's involvement and influence in the politics of the Revolution. Women's frequent interventions on behalf of the Montagnards would be a decisive factor in the course of the Revolution.

The trial of Louis Capet

On November 20, Roland told the Convention of a secret safe the king had kept hidden in the walls of the Tuileries. The Convention had been going through the royal family's papers and belongings in preparation for the trial. The discovery of the hidden safe – referred to then and since as the *armoire de fer*, the iron armoire – seemed like something out of a novel. But here, too, the parliamentary rivalry colored the whole episode. Rather than boasting about finding information against the king, Roland boasted of finding information that compromised some of the Montagnards. The Montagnards were skeptical, and assumed that he had taken away any information incriminating himself or his allies. Some thought that he had consulted his wife.[11] Marat took this a step further, accusing Roland of stealing jewelry from the safe.[12]

Marat was as caught up in the Mountain–Girondin rivalry as anyone. From his paper, the "friend of the people" hurled his invectives at Brissot, at Roland, at all of their allies, sometimes attacking them all at once, sometimes picking out individuals for special attention. He railed against "the hypocrite Isnard," or even "Isnard the trickster," or the "*Brissotin* rogues," the "vile intriguers"; he railed, too, against "Roland, who lulls people to sleep," and his wife, "the minister of the interior."[13] At this point, for Marat, there was no longer much difference in his eyes between the king himself and his "defenders" – the Girondins.

In the end, execution without trial was found wanting. The king would be tried. The Convention would try him.

It would begin with the accusations against the king, followed by the king's defense. The final part – after no shortage of speeches from deputies – would be a vote. On Marat's proposal, that vote would be individual and public. Unlike other votes, each deputy would have to appear before the Convention and state his vote. Marat "wanted to know for sure who the traitors are, for there are some in this Assembly," and thought that an individual roll call was an "infallible means" to find out. But Marat also knew that the crowds in the galleries were on his side, even if many of the deputies were not.[14]

Robert Lindet stated the case for the prosecution. A well-off former lawyer, nearing 50 as the trial began, Lindet's case was more a history of the entire Revolution thus far, portraying Louis XVI's role in as damaging a light as possible. All of the king's shortcomings were there, from his unwillingness to support the third estate in the early days of the Revolution to the troops he gathered on the eve of the storming of the Bastille, from his attempt to flee France to the deaths of August 10. Even his construction of the *armoire de fer* was there.

Louis XVI was present to hear these accusations. Or rather, Louis *Capet*, as the arrest warrant called the dethroned king, was there. "Capet is the name of one of my ancestors," he told the Convention. "It is not mine."[15] Still, though, he took part in the trial. He could not have avoided being tried, but he could have refused to take an active role. Many royalists wished he had – wished that instead of playing the revolutionaries' game, he had informed them that they had no jurisdiction over him, that it was God, not men, who had put him on the throne of France. But Louis XVI did no such thing. Instead he replied to accusations, responded – without admitting his guilt. "It was never my intention to make blood flow," he told the gathered deputies, and "the thought of counter-revolution never entered my mind." Some acts he denied doing, or denied knowing about; some, like his failure to quell early counter-revolutionary uprisings, he blamed on his ministers.[16] Others he said were constitutional, legal, and therefore not criminal.

Not all of the king's responses were credible. He denied having had the *armoire de fer* built, a claim which would have stretched the beliefs of even his strongest defenders. He took no blame for the deaths on August 10. But if the specifics of his answers did not help his cause, his presence at the trial did. The man being interrogated did not look like the callous tyrant that the revolutionaries had been denouncing. Though not many would get to see it, the king had done well in captivity. At trial, he would stay calm and collected. There was little he could do, at this point, to change his fate. There was still much he could do to change his image.

The king's lawyers pleaded his case over the following days. It was a surprising group. One, de Sèze, a well-spoken lawyer from Bordeaux; the other, Malesherbes, who was in his own way as representative of the Old Regime as Louis himself. But where the king represented all that the deputies hated in the Old Regime, Malesherbes represented much that the deputies held dear. As a minister under Louis XV, Malesherbes supported the Enlightenment and allowed the publication of books that would normally have been censored. He represented not the arbitrary and the unjust of the Old Regime, but enlightenment, progress, and much that the Revolution looked back on as its source of inspiration. Malesherbes agreed to defend the king, knowing the risks he ran, explaining them by citing his "disdain for life."[17]

A risky task, defending the king, but from a strictly legal perspective, not a hopeless one. There were some points that would have been worth making, had this been a real court case. Some were technicalities, others more valid, but points nevertheless. The king could argue convincingly enough that he had not been fleeing France, only fleeing to a fortress by the border. Such were the odd benefits of having been stopped en route. This logic could help him defend his actions during any of the half-hearted crackdowns he had begun during the earlier days of the Revolution, crackdowns he had not seen through. Such were the odd benefits of his indecisiveness. As the *London Times* wrote, "he would have reigned with glory, had he but possessed those faults which his assassins laid to his charge."[18] He could even argue that he was not responsible for the bloodshed on August 10. Though all he had needed to do was to tell his guards to stand down when he and his family walked from the Tuileries to the National Assembly, though he had left them to defend an empty palace, when Lindet told him that he "made the blood of the people flow on August 10" the king could reply, "No, Monsieur, it was not me," and his lawyers could follow up that it was the people who had attacked the palace, not the palace that had attacked the people. How could he have been guilty of something that happened, they asked, when he had left the Tuileries, when he "saw nothing, said nothing, did nothing, gave no orders, and did not leave the asylum he had voluntarily chosen" until he entered a prison?[19]

Even the documents from the *armoire de fer* were not particularly damning. The safe itself was, of course – the documents less so. Roland's meddling had not helped matters much. Marat was convinced that the most damning documents had been removed – "the evidence of all of the monarch's treasonous activities, and those of his agents, were written in his hand and contained in a safe hidden in his palace," he noted, until Roland had gotten his hands on them. And, he added, "no equitable tribunal" would accept most of the items found via such a search, where no official inventory had been taken.[20]

Not that the National Convention fit everyone's definition of an equitable tribunal. Not that the trial would be done according to the strictest notions of legality. Robespierre had already pointed it out – they were deputies, not judges.[21]

Many of the deputies, most of the leaders, were already on record about what they thought the appropriate fate. Robespierre, Saint-Just, having advocated death without trial, were not going to vote him innocent. The leaders of the Girondins were caught up in their own proclamations, their own attempts to outplay the Mountain. It was a political trial – and, as the sociologist Michael Walzer points out, it had to be a political trial.[22] Such trials are both legal and political; the biggest ones add no small amount of drama.

The first two acts of that drama came with Lindet's prosecution and with the king's lawyers' defense. The high drama came later, though. First with the voting, then with the king's execution. This drama, though – again – was only half about the king. The stakes seemed far more focused on the rivalry between the Girondins and the Montagnards, each jockeying for position. One of the most important decisions of the entire Revolution – along with the 1790 Civil Constitution of the Clergy and the 1792 decision to declare war – would be fought over not in its own right, but as if it was a smaller piece in a larger game. Neither faction, on its own, had enough men to carry the day without support. It would be up to the Plain, the mass of men who sat somewhere between the two groups, to provide a majority on one side or the other.

There were to be three questions posed to each deputy.

First: Is Louis guilty? (yes or no)

Second: Whatever your decision, shall it be submitted to the ratification of the people? (yes or no)

Third: What penalty shall Louis suffer?[23]

The second question – Should the judgment be submitted to the people? – was a Girondin proposal. Vergniaud gave the case its most powerful support, telling his fellow deputies that

> the people alone, who promised inviolability to Louis, can declare that they wish to make use of the right to punish ... if the people desire the death of Louis, they will command it; if, on the contrary, you take their power from them, you will incur at least the reproach of having strayed from your duty.[24]

Any political trial is a balance of politics and legality, no political trial is a perfect balance. But sometimes, issues are too blatantly political. Robespierre and Saint-Just's plan to skip the trial and go directly to the execution: too blatantly political. But the "appeal to the people," while less bloody, was just as political. It made the decision to kill the king more national, less Parisian. This could be one more step toward making the Revolution as a whole more national, and less Parisian. Second, it provided one more chance to try to defeat the Mountain. The king's corpse was looking more and more like a potential Mountain trophy. The Girondins were set to keep the Mountain from earning any trophies, even if it meant defending a king that they had never liked.

With Vergniaud leading the calls for the appeal to the people and Robespierre leading the opposition, it was Barère, once again, who helped move things along, arguing that in this "last battle between despotism and liberty," the appeal to the people was "contrary to principles, useless ..." and it "ties the hands of the Convention, which could no longer take the necessary measures for the public's safety."[25]

The voting for the first question was clear enough. Few if any in the Convention thought Louis XVI innocent. None of the deputies – zero – voted for his innocence. Some attached various conditions and caveats, others were missing, but out of 745 deputies, 693 voted "yes" to the question of the former king's guilt.[26] Voting on the appeal to the people was less one-sided. Of the 707 votes, 424 were against the appeal, 283 for. *Closer*, but not close. A defeat, then, for the Girondins, although not always for principled reasons. Some deputies found the idea impractical. Some viewed it as a cop-out. Even a few of the Girondins opted out, including Condorcet and Isnard.[27]

All of which led to question three, the penalty. And again, more drama – long, drawn-out drama. These were not men simply to walk up to the podium and declare "yes" or "no." They were men given to long explanations and justifications. The roll call began on the evening of January 16. It continued, overnight, into the next day, finishing some 25 hours after it had begun, long enough that people had trouble keeping count. As the final votes arrived people were still not sure of the outcome. So it was that Vergniaud, then acting as president of the Convention, announced that "in the name of the Convention, the punishment it pronounces against Louis Capet is that of death."[28]

The numbers this time were less clear. Not all of the speeches amounted to a "death" or "not death" vote. Questions one and two had called for a "yes" or "no"; question three – What penalty shall Louis suffer? – had no such requirement, and a fair number of votes could be counted as "death, but ..." Some had voted for a "delayed" death, others for a death only after certain conditions had been met (peace, for instance, or the expulsion of all Bourbons from France). Vergniaud, for instance: he acknowledged that he had hoped for the appeal to the people in the second vote, but lost. But he saw the potential contradictions between the first vote and the third. "I declared yesterday that I recognize his guilt of conspiring against liberty and the national safety. There is no hesitating today on the penalty. The law is clear: it is death."[29] But his was a "death, but ..." sentence, as he hoped that the Convention would consider examining whether or not it would be useful to delay the execution – a particular variation of the "death, but ..." verdict that 25 other deputies had also chosen.

In the end, though, death – not "death, but ..." but "death" – was the verdict. By how much depends on how some of the "death, but ..." votes are counted. Of 721 deputies voting, two voted for shackles. More deputies, though still a minority, voted for imprisonment or exile. Death – be it simple "death," or "death, but ..." garnered 387 votes, at least. Count the most far-fetched "death, but ..." votes and that figure can reach up to 455.

Those who voted for death, plain and simple – for death without conditions, without delay – numbered 361. Still a majority, yes, but a majority by the slimmest of margins, a majority of just one.

And there were votes that might have gone the other way. There was Orléans – now Philippe-Egalité – the one deputy who might have gotten a pass had he chosen not to vote, who voted for the death of his cousin. "Uniquely occupied by my duties," he told the Convention, "convinced that all who harmed or who will harm the sovereignty of the people merit death, I vote for death." Isnard also voted for "the death of the tyrant," adding that he wanted the king's two brothers killed in effigy alongside him.[30]

Then there were all of the anonymous members of the Plain, whose votes for the king's death outnumbered those of committed Montagnards. The Plain, it should be noted, was not a "middle party" – it had no real leaders, no identifiable politics. Its other nickname – le marais, the swamp – reflected its lack of initiative. It consisted of men repelled by both parties, or intimidated by the whole situation. It was not without famous names – Sieyes, for one, was there. But there was never anything resembling a "politics of the Plain." It is fair to ask what their motivations were in voting, and it is fair to ask how free their votes were. The Girondins thought that the voting was less than free – thanks to Marat's insistence on voting from the podium, thanks to the galleries who booed every vote other than death. Jaurès, who did not hide his partisanship for the Montagnards, was quick to point out that no right-wing deputy was ever injured by the crowds in the galleries.[31] But if none was injured, many were intimidated, and this Marat knew quite well.

The execution took place on January 21, 1793.

Louis XVI had requested three days to spend with his family and to "prepare myself to appear in the presence of God."[32] He also asked for a priest. The Convention did not grant Louis XVI the three days; they did grant him the priest, in the person of Henry Essex Edgeworth, an Irish priest living in Paris. A *de facto* refractory, as he had never taken the oath to the Civil Constitution of the Clergy, but a foreigner, so free of any legal obligation to do so. In other words, a wise choice.

It was with Edgeworth, along with a few remaining servants and his immediate family, that the deposed king spent his last night. Then it was Santerre, the morning of January 21, who arrived at the Temple to transport the king to the guillotine. Louis XVI stalled him, hoping to pray one last time with Edgeworth, until he realized that his time was up. Thus the king to Santerre: *marchons*. Let's walk.

The king who arrived at the scaffold was composed. From the scaffold he began to address the crowd. Edgeworth heard him say, "I die innocent of all the crimes laid to my charge; I pardon those who have occasioned my death; and I pray to God that the blood you are going to shed may never be visited on France."[33] He would have continued to speak, but one of the military leaders – perhaps Santerre – ordered that the drummers start drumming, drowning out his voice.

They put the king's head in place. The executioner pulled the cord, the blade dropped. The executioner held up the king's severed head to the gathered crowd. The Revolution had entered a new phase.

Few events cry out for Oedipal interpretations quite like the killing of a king; Louis XVI's execution was the key moment in what Hunt sees as a shift from paternal to fraternal government.[34] Kings were fathers of the people, put there both to protect and to punish, to care for and to rule over. Even Marat, back in 1789, had told his readers that the deputies of the Estates-General were "one big family, of which the monarch will show himself to be the father."[35] The revolutionaries had long since stopped talking in terms of filial devotion, though. It was fraternity that ruled the day, and it was looking like this model of fraternity had no room for a father, only for brothers.

The king's death, though, meant different things to different people. Ironically, it was probably least patricidal for those who led him to his death. Outside of Paris, outside of the ranks of the committed revolutionaries, there were many French people for whom the king was still their

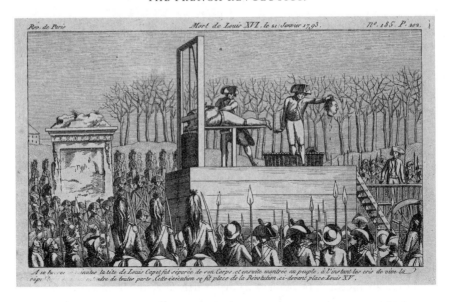

Figure 6.1 The execution of Louis XVI. The executioner shows the head of Louis Capet, formerly King Louis XVI, to the crowd. From *Révolutions de Paris*. © Penn Special Collections.

father. Those people, though, least wanted the king killed. Among those who decided to kill the king – the deputies to the Convention, the men arguing over Louis XVI's fate – it was not their Oedipal desires that led to the king's death so much as their political version of a sibling rivalry. Liberty, equality, fraternity – this new trinity of the Revolution – was still a work in progress. Their goal of fraternity, in particular, seemed to be sorely lacking. The rivalry between the Girondins and the Mountain was coloring all decisions, pushing men into positions that they had trouble embracing, pushing men to value winning the sibling rivalry over all other goals.

If there is a Freudian message in all of this, then, it lies less in Freud's analysis of the Oedipus complex than in Freud's analysis of fraternity. Brothers' love for each other, Freud notes, covers over hidden tensions, rivalries, hatreds. Cain's action may have been the exception; the desire to do so, though, was the rule. The revolutionary injunction for men to treat all men as brothers is superfluous, because when you look at how brothers behave, when you look at how close Cain and Abel are to all fraternal relationships, you realize that all men *already* treat each other as brothers.

But, again, if the king's death was not the result of an overriding Oedipal impulsion, but the collateral damage of a sibling rivalry, the people still saw it as a major occasion. The first evidence of this? Right after the king died, with the executioner still holding his head up to the crowd, with his blood flowing from both halves of his severed neck, the people closest to the scaffold grabbed whatever they had on them – paper, pikes, clothing, and especially their handkerchiefs – and dipped it in the king's blood.[36]

Politics and the people in 1793

In the weeks leading up to the king's execution, Robespierre and other Jacobins had portrayed the king's death as the answer to all of their problems. But the France that had killed the king would prove no easier to govern. There was, to be fair, a brief truce, a brief period of cooperation, following the king's execution. Enough time of cooperation to declare war on England and Holland. But the unanimity would not last long. The division between the Girondins and the Montagnards would continue to dominate French politics. In the aftermath of the king's execution, the Jacobin club, pleased with the execution, nevertheless turned immediately to their complaints about Roland.[37] It was a Montagnard victory, but not one that would satisfy the Montagnards for long.

The Montagnards, meanwhile, were facing plenty of pressure from outside as well, from the people.

"The people." This phrase hovered over every political discussion, every theory, every practical measure of the French Revolution. The government claimed its mandate from the people, the leaders claimed to act on behalf of the people. Few things were easier than justifying whatever plan a politician had than by saying that it benefited the people. But who *were* the people? The question's simplicity does not mean that its answer was also simple.

Most politicians could not claim to *be* the people. Whatever "the people" meant, it meant something other than the wealthy elites that were filling the ranks of the deputies at the Convention or the membership of the Jacobin club. Robespierre could claim to act on behalf of the people, but he was not to be found among them. He was a well-off, well-educated, primly dressed lawyer. Even Marat, whom nobody ever considered prim, called himself the "*friend* of the people." Not "the people." The *friend* of the people.

If the claim to speak on behalf of the people was a powerful rhetorical device, so too was the claim to *be* the people. But not everyone could pull that off. Most of the politicians did not even try.

The workers of Paris were different. They, indeed, could claim to be the people. And increasingly, they did. And increasingly, they began referring to themselves as "*sans-culottes*." The term lends itself to a variety of translations, although the *sans* part is simple enough: it means "without." Any exact definition of *culottes* brings with it a detailed discussion of eighteenth-century clothing styles; today the French word has a different meaning. The culotte was, in any case, the dress of an aristocrat, the dress of a wealthy man. "Stockings," perhaps, is an adequate translation. The kind of stockings that would get ripped up by the sort of manual labor sans-culottes were expected to do.

If none of the deputies actually were sans-culottes, those on the left were never sparing in their praise. In July 1793, the Jacobin club would even be graced by the performance of a song in honor of the sans-culottes:

> If we no longer see, in Paris
> Insolent dukes, petty marquises,
> nor tyrants in skull-caps [i.e. the clergy]
> In throwing off this infernal yoke
> If the poor man is now the rich man's equal,
> It is thanks to the sans-culottes!

And so on, for another ten verses (nine of which rhymed "sans-culottes" with either "despot" or "patriot").[38]

The journalist Hébert, too, threw praise toward "the honest sans-culotte, who lives from day to day by the sweat of his brow," and who "holds his head high everywhere he goes." The sans-culotte's day was simple, for Hébert – work during the day, the section meeting at night, then home to his family. *His* family, for here, too, the idea of a sans-culotte was distinctly masculine. For Hébert, the sans-culotte was not just a man, but a family man. "In the evening, when he enters his hovel, his wife rushes to greet him, his small children hug him, his dog bounds up and licks him." And though the primary childrearing responsibilities fall to his wife, the sans-culotte plays his part, making his children "promise always to be good citizens and to love the Republic above all else."[39] A pamphlet from April 1793 painted a similar portrait of the sans-culotte. A bit aggressive, even in its title – "Reply to the Impertinent Question: What is a sans-culotte?" – the pamphlet described the sans-culotte as a man who "lives simply with his wife and children, if he has any," who "is useful, because he knows how to work in the field, to forge iron, to use a saw, to use a file, to roof a house, to make shoes, and to shed his last drop of blood for the safety of the Republic." Other things that distracted from that would not be part of his life. Cafes, the theater, and gambling halls were all places where the sans-culotte would not be found. And at the section meetings, his focus was pure: "in the evening he goes to his section, not powdered or perfumed, or smartly booted in the hope of catching the eye of the citizenesses in the galleries."[40]

Generations of social historians have tried to figure out what they can about who the sans-culottes actually were: where they lived, how much they earned, what occupations they held, etc. Such research is always fraught with complications, and here is no different. Before deciding what the sans-culottes did, researchers had to decide who was, and who was not, a sans-culotte. As the historian Alfred Cobban pointed out, "what the sans-culottes wanted is almost as difficult to say as what they were. Their name indicates that they did not wear knee-breeches, which is about as useless a class distinction as could be found."[41] George Rudé, far more sympathetic, pointed out that the men who took part in sans-culotte life were not the riffraff that critics took them to be. They tended to be young men from the neighborhoods in eastern Paris or the suburbs just east of there, particularly the Faubourg Saint-Antoine.[42] Their jobs varied, but most could call themselves "artisans"– shoemakers, carpenters, blacksmiths, etc.[43] But if most sans-culottes were artisans, not all artisans were sans-culottes. Even Albert Soboul, who did more research than anyone else into who the sans-culottes were, recognized the impossibility of getting clear answers.[44] His final verdict was that it was not any objective social status, or even garment choice, but rather "a passionate desire for equality" that served as the movement's "distinctive trait."[45]

Missing from the ranks of the sans-culottes, not surprisingly, were the most well-off. There were no lawyers, no large-scale merchants, none of the kinds of men who made up the Jacobin club. Missing, too, were the poorest residents of Paris. This was not a crowd of beggars, or even of unskilled day laborers. Nor were certain other groups welcome there, including domestic servants, as sans-culottes felt that servants would be looking after their masters' interests.

The image of the sans-culotte embraced some social changes but not others. Equality, for the sans-culotte, meant equality among men, an end to the extreme divisions between rich and poor. It did not mean rethinking the relationships between women and men. In the image of the sans-culotte, work and political activity were the lot of men; housekeeping and raising the next generation of citizens the lot of women. Santerre had said as much, back in 1792, when he dismissed Théroigne de Méricourt's proposals. Chasing after women, sleeping around – these were the activities of the old nobility, of the queen, in their minds. They were not appropriate for the new leaders of the Revolution.

The reality was quite different from the image, and historians have been too quick to accept the movement's self-descriptions. Women were key players in the politics of the Revolution. Not as leaders, not in the way that Théroigne de Méricourt or Olympe de Gouges would have hoped, and not in any movement that would fit today's definitions of feminist objectives. But wherever there was popular activism, women were taking part. In the counter-revolutionary movements of western France and the fiercely revolutionary crowds of the capital and other French cities, women were taking part. As always, women attended meetings at every level of the political ladder: at the Convention, the Jacobin club, the Cordeliers club, and at just about every section meeting. And if the good sans-culotte was not showing up at those meetings "powdered or perfumed, or smartly booted in the hope of catching the eye of the citizenesses in the galleries," it is a safe guess that many less upstanding sans-culottes were doing just that. After all, if not, why mention it?

The politicians, in turn, were often hoping to catch the eye of the sans-culottes. It was a strange dynamic of politics, throughout the Revolution, but especially in 1792–3: men like Robespierre, Danton, Marat, Hébert – their politics were based on finding ways to bridge the distance between the sans-culottes and the Convention, between "the people" and the government. That distance was not always easy to bridge.

Here, Robespierre shined. No one was better at bridging those two worlds.

It was in many ways a strange partnership. If "without breeches" is ambiguous as a social marker, it is still worth pointing out that Robespierre *did* wear breeches; he did not dress the part of the sans-culotte. He did not act like Marat or Hébert, who felt that to appeal to the sans-culottes they had to make at least some attempt to speak in their language. His support, though, was enormous, his influence growing.

Robespierre's popularity bothered his opponents, who would try to belittle not only Robespierre but his followers as well. This had been Condorcet's approach, when he complained of the "many women following Robespierre around." But another part of Condorcet's claim is also worth noting: that Robespierre was "nothing but a priest and will never be anything but a priest." This was a common theme in descriptions of Robespierre. Nearly all commentators, supporters and detractors alike, have seen him as priestly. Robespierre was not alone in this; the Montagnards had many former clerics in their ranks. Robespierre may have acted like a priest; others actually had been priests. Several bishops in the constitutional church, including Grégoire and Gobel, were deputies in the Convention. Aside from Fauchet, they all sat with the Montagnards. In the person of François Chabot the Montagnards even had a former capuchin monk, albeit one who had fathered a child with his housekeeper.[46] The Girondins, though, were party of anti-clericals. True, Fauchet was a leading Girondin and a former priest at Versailles, but his status as a priest and a believing Catholic was a source of tension between him and his allies. Condorcet, especially, had been a critic of religion and especially of Catholicism since well before the start of the Revolution, and looked forward to a world with less "superstition." The Girondins had led the crackdown on refractory priests at the start of the Legislative Assembly; they had only little tolerance for the constitutional church. The Montagnards' relationship with religion would be much more complicated. Later in the Revolution it would include some of the harshest attacks on the Catholic Church (covered in Chapter 8), led primarily by Hébert and his followers. But Robespierre's relationship with Catholicism was much more subtle. When Robespierre had referred to "providence" in a March 1792 speech, the Girondin Guadet had mocked him for it. "I would never have believed that a man who has worked so hard for three years to pull the people from the slavery of despotism" would then put the people back into the "despotism of superstition."[47] But Robespierre would never endorse the more radical anti-clerical aspects of the Revolution, be they Girondist or Hébertist; nor would he ever tolerate any form of atheism.

Whatever the reason that women were on the side of the Montagnards, it was impossible to deny their visibility or the impact that they were having on politics. If the Girondins were troubled by it, it was because women were vocal in their opposition to them; and if the leaders of the Montagnards supported women's activism, it was for similarly self-interested reasons. There were times, though, when the men leading the Montagnards became concerned. Not all of the Jacobins were pleased about the events of late February and early March 1793, for instance, when there was a series of "subsistence" riots in the capital.

The rioters wanted price controls on certain things – particularly on bread and soap. Most deputies supported free-market policies, but the sans-culottes were calling for controls: for maximum prices, for assurances, for the traditional "just prices" on the necessities of life. Longstanding aims, and if the riots themselves were brief they reflected lasting goals. Here, too, in the riots, it was women leading the way – attacking merchants, distributing goods that they believed the merchants were charging too much money for.[48] Robespierre thought that these riots were unworthy of the people – "The people must rise up, not to gather sugar, but to bring down the brigands," he told the Jacobin club.[49] And the club, in its official statement, suggested that the women in the riots had been misled by enemies of the people.[50] Not all the people in the galleries thought that a fair assessment of the situation.

In spite of any such difficulties, Robespierre was still doing well in the new politics of the Convention. Louvet's attack had only strengthened his position; the king's death had been a victory as well. Not that any of this seemed to make Robespierre happy. In his speeches at the Convention, he continued to focus on the threats to the Revolution and to the republic. He continued to see these threats everywhere, to warn people about "the grave circumstances which surround us."[51]

His role in the Jacobin club was evolving. Over the course of the Revolution, he would never again stand isolated, alone, as he had when facing down the rush to declare war on Austria. He was now a dominant voice in the club. His influence would never again be limited to the galleries. Whatever position he chose, other Jacobins would line up to be on his side.

And then there was Marat. He had been a presence in the Revolution since 1789, but he had always been the outsider. Robespierre, for all his populist rhetoric, had been a deputy at the Estates-General, and had always been a member of the Jacobin club. His whereabouts had been well known. Marat had been forced into hiding at several points during the Revolution, spending months underground, unable to write his paper. People assumed that he had spent time in caves or sewers or some such unsanitary locale – hence his skin problems – but his "subterranean retreats," his "dungeons and cellars" were probably just the basement of the Cordeliers club.[52] Not that he had ever been known for his impeccable hygiene; back in 1791, *The Patriotic Brothel* called Marat "hairy," a "runt," even a "monkey," and hence the only prominent politician unwelcome in the establishment.[53] And while Robespierre had always spoken about the people's just vengeance, it was Marat who called for violence, who called for the execution of enemies of the Revolution. He had a habit of talking about the "guilty heads" of his opponents, playing on the French word for guilty, *coupable*.[54] The French verb *couper* means "to cut" so if there was a French word for "cuttable," *coupable* would be it. Marat also tended to present some twisted pay-now or pay-later offers to his readers. Early in the Revolution, he had told them that "Six months ago five or six hundred heads would have sufficed to pull you away from the abyss. Today ... perhaps you will need to fell five thousand."[55] Soon, that number would be 10,000.[56] It was Marat, too, who had sung the praises of the September Massacres, before realizing it was impolitic to do so.

Now here he was, Jean-Paul Marat, friend of the people, deputy to the Convention, and member of the Jacobin club. Marat was moving toward the mainstream – or perhaps the mainstream was moving toward Marat.

Neither the Convention nor the Jacobin club gave him a complete welcome. The Girondins viewed him as a demagogue with blood on his hands. In Marat's first speech to the Convention on September 25, he faced down the yells and murmurs of his fellow deputies. He acknowledged that he had "in this Assembly a great number of enemies" – "All! All!" his fellow deputies yelled back.[57] The Jacobins – the official members, anyway – had a more measured response to Marat's presence among them, defending his goals, if not his methods, and noting that he could get "carried away by his enthusiasm."[58]

Danton, meanwhile, had been off in Belgium. Like Marat, Danton had taken part in the Revolution from the beginning, but the Convention was his first time in the legislature. In the first years of the Revolution he had been primarily known as the leader of the Cordeliers, although he had taken part in the national government since the aftermath of August 10. He could seem like the yang to Robespierre's yin – ugly but courageous, a powerful, instinctive orator, a large man with a powerful voice and expensive tastes. While even Robespierre's critics called him "the incorruptible," Danton seemed to come pre-corrupted, and probably took more than a few bribes during his career. The first months of the Convention, though, he was more off stage than usual – first because of his government business in Belgium, then because of his wife's death in February.

Neither Robespierre nor Danton collaborated much with Marat. *No one* collaborated much with Marat, who was a loner by political inclination and, it would seem, personal inclination. He did, though, have a "wife" during the later years of the Revolution. (They were married, according to Marat, "before the Supreme Being".[59]) She would look after him, especially as his skin condition worsened, and he was largely confined to his bathtub with a makeshift writing table.

Even the "friend of the people" had rivals from his left, though.[60]

The most notable was Hébert. Though he had been a member of the Commune since August 10, his influence came primarily from his journalism. Hébert aimed for a similar readership as Marat, though his writing style was different, a "vulgar" language that he thought would appeal more to the people. "You have to swear, with those who swear," he wrote. His newspaper was *Le Père Duchesne* (*father Duchesne*), based on a fictional foul-mouthed man of the people who, over the course of the Revolution, would come to eclipse the flesh-and-blood man who had created him – an unremarkable, well-educated man who could read Latin.

Then there were the more marginal leaders. A group known as the "*enragés*" was starting to gain momentum, led by Jacques Roux, a radical priest who was developing a following, particularly among the most radical women of Paris – enough to worry not only Robespierre, but Hébert and Marat as well. Roux worked closer to ground level, at section meetings, among the people. He had been a key player in the subsistence riots that Robespierre had denounced; he would continue to be a thorn in the side of the more "establishment" Montagnards for some months to come.

The Mountain, then, was hardly one unified group. Little united them except for their hostility to the Girondins. For now, though, that was usually enough.

The Convention at war

Even before the king's death, back in November 1792, France had changed its approach to foreign policy. Having renounced wars of aggression in the earliest days of the Revolution, it now declared that it had the right to intervene anywhere where people "wanted to reclaim their liberty." Having since declared war on England and Holland, in early March 1793 France declared war on Spain.

From the Battle of Valmy through the fall of 1972, the fighting had gone well more than it had gone poorly. Verdun, Longwy, whose fall had so scared France, were French again. France was expanding in the southeast, with Nice now part of the republic. Dumouriez's invasion of Belgium, also in 1792, had been a success militarily, even if it was politically problematic: Dumouriez's views of what a French Belgium should become were not shared by the Convention. But militarily, from Valmy until the end of 1792, the French could not have asked for much more from their armies.

As the season for military campaigns began in 1793, as the winter thawed, things would not go as well for France. Dumouriez's invasion of

Holland ended poorly with a defeat at Neerwinden in mid-March. Soon after that, Dumouriez would follow Lafayette's script, rally his troops to march on the capital, fail, and flee to the Austrians. Dumouriez's betrayal hit hard, bringing fear of invasion, greater fear of all military leaders, and the touch of suspicion to all those who had cooperated with Dumouriez, including France's coolest uncle, Philippe-Egalité (*né* Orléans), long under a cloud of suspicion, now under a darker cloud.

Other fronts were faring better, but there were too many. France's armies – and France's attention – were spread too thin. On February 24, the Convention issued its first *levée*, its first decree of forced conscription. Not a small one: 300,000 men would be sent to fight on the front lines. It was a move that would eventually bring success on the battlefield, but it had its risks. Conscription was a return to the Old Regime, to the requisitions of young men from every village and every neighborhood in France. Regions that had already been unhappy about the Revolution were that much more unhappy. Regions of western France – Brittany, the Vendée – that had been upset about the Civil Constitution of the Clergy, had lived in opposition to the Revolution since then, with their priests either exiled or in hiding, performing masses in huts hidden in the countryside; these were not communities that had wanted to send their young men to the front in 1792. Conscription would bring the next phase of the Revolution to the Vendée, when the region broke out in open warfare. In March 1793 the civil war began, a full-out civil war, with guns and generals and troop movements on both sides. Atrocities, too. Here, too, the Revolution entered a new phase.

The Convention started to hear news of the events in the Vendée in March. News would come in from the west (when the insurgents had not blocked the postal routes)[61] of the uprisings there. News would soon follow of Dumouriez's failure and subsequent betrayal, followed by more news of the uprising in the Vendée. Marat told his readers that "the fatherland has never found itself menaced by such great danger ... may the skies have pity on us, if the nation does not rise up!"[62]

Even before news reached Paris of the Vendée and of Dumouriez's betrayal, Paris itself was already starting to erupt. On the night of March 8, protesters (likely followers of Hébert) smashed the presses that printed the Girondin newspapers. The first attempt at a full-scale insurrection against the Girondins came two days later, with the tocsin ringing out once again, before Santerre and his troops quelled what turned out to be a minor uprising.[63]

During these first months of 1793 the men of the Convention put some key government changes in place.

On March 9 the Convention created the "representatives-on-mission," pairs of deputies who would head off to all of France's departments to oversee conscription. In the months to follow, the representatives-on-mission would become the main links between the national government and the departments; as departments became less enamored of the Revolution, the representatives' task, power, and importance grew.

The following day, at the suggestion of Danton, the Convention created an "extraordinary criminal tribunal" meant to judge "any counter-revolutionary enterprise, any attack on liberty."[64] Later in the year it would be renamed the Revolutionary Tribunal – the name that Danton and others had proposed in the first place. It, too, would grow to exceed the role intended for it, although the Girondins saw this one coming. Vergniaud compared it to a "Venetian inquisition." Another Girondin, Buzot, facing the murmurs from the galleries, replied that "these murmurs teach me what I already know, that there is courage in opposing the coming despotism."[65] "It is time to act," someone yelled down, "not to chatter." Thus, over the Girondins' objections, the Revolutionary Tribunal.

It was, indeed, time to act. Starting on March 11, the rebels in the Vendée had taken over several towns and showed no sign of stopping. These battles – discussed at more length in the next chapter – showed the republic just how much danger it was in, attacked from within while it was at war with most of Europe.

On April 6 the Convention created the *comité du salut public*. The standard translation of this term – "Committee of Public Safety" – has passed the test of time, and there is no reason to abandon it now. It does not capture all the nuances of the French *salut*, though – the word means "safety," but also "salvation." The Committee was an attempt to streamline government decisions and take some authority away from ministers. It would have nine members, renewable each month. The Convention formed the Committee because the deputies realized that things were getting dangerous. With the nation now at war with itself in the Vendée, the Convention needed to be able to reply with something other than abstract discussions or partisan bickering.

By the height of the Terror, the Committee of Public Safety would be the most powerful group in all of France, more powerful than the Convention itself. In the first half of 1793, it was not yet that. Danton was the most prominent man on the Committee, but one of only two representatives from the Montagnards. Barère and Lindet were also there. The Girondins had no members, but unlike the Revolutionary Tribunal, the Committee of Public Safety was not a Montagnard institution at the start; its membership was dominated by relatively uncontroversial men from the Plain. Girondins had not opposed the Committee, and Isnard, in particular, had even helped shape it. It would take some time, though, for the Committee to hit its stride. It was given significant powers from the start, but its formation was not, in and of itself, a turning point in the Revolution. All of which is to say that the government was developing the tools appropriate for the straits in which the young republic found itself, but was only just beginning to figure out how to use those new tools.

The Girondins, though, remained focused on their rivalry. This was the sad paradox of the Girondins, their combination of overly abstract thought and surprisingly petty political objectives. With Dumouriez gone over to the Austrians, with the Vendée exploding, the Girondins kept their sights focused not on either war front, but on the Montagnards.

Marat was their target this time.

Guadet brought the accusation against Marat, in April 1793, accusing him of having "preached pillage and murder ... attempted to destroy the sovereignty of the people, and urged the dissolution of the Convention."[66] But in the Convention, the content of the accusation mattered little. The deputies knew Marat; the deputies each knew whether they thought that he should be brought up for trial or not. "If Marat can be denounced," Danton told the Convention, "it is not for one action, it is not after one reading."[67] Some of Marat's opponents even acknowledged that the charges were questionable; one Girondin told the Convention that "Marat must be brought before the court of public censure, which we should have established a long time ago ... but for the matters here, there is no standing. I vote against. I say, no." Isnard, too, said, "in my soul and my conscience I declare that he deserves it," but he did not understand the accusation itself, and abstained – as did Pétion.[68]

Their hesitancy was not shared by the majority of their colleagues, though. Or at least not by those who were in attendance – many deputies were missing (no small number as representatives-on-mission); 360 deputies voted, with 220 voting against Marat. It was, for once, a parliamentary victory for the Girondins over the Montagnards. Unlike the king's trial, unlike Louvet's attack on Robespierre, here, the Girondins had won. But what had they achieved? They had sent Marat to the Revolutionary Tribunal, or what would soon be called such. The problem was that, given their disapproval of it, they had never made any effort to put it under Girondin control. So they had sent him to a court that was not under their control, on flimsy charges of which he would soon be acquitted.

That was the word, on April 24, when his supporters arrived at the Convention to "bring the brave Marat."[69] Marat, who would tell his leaders that he had only appeared before the Tribunal "to make truth triumph," would devote the next three issues of his newspaper to the story of his trial and acquittal.[70] For someone who thrived on complaining of being persecuted as much as he did on defeating his rivals, his accusation and acquittal were a perfect story.

A victory, again, for the Montagnards – even if some of them were still ambivalent about Marat himself. But the people who cheered Marat's acquittal shared no such ambivalence. People – mostly, but not only, women – carried Marat through the streets to the Jacobin club for what amounted to his victory lap. Other women made it to the club before Marat, leaving him crowns of laurels. The hesitancy with which many Jacobins had greeted Marat at the start of the Convention was not gone, but it was waning. The Montagnards as a whole were stronger in the aftermath of Marat's victory.

And the patience that some had had with the Girondins was waning too.

People began speaking of "purging" the Convention. The idea spread among the people of Paris that the time for negotiating with the Girondins was done, that there was no way to govern with them.

The purge of the Girondins

Back in April, before Marat's trial, a man named Pache, the minister of war, had told the Convention that they needed to expel 22 of the deputies, the 22 leaders of the Girondins. In the weeks to follow, other groups would propose similar petitions. Tensions were higher after Marat's acquittal – particularly as more bad news came in from the Vendée.

The minutes of the Convention during May 1793 are hard to believe at times. Constant bickering, even physical confrontations, fill the pages of the discussions of a government of a nation at war, a nation whose existence was at risk. Rather than treat this as a call to action and unity, it was a call for each side to defeat the other, all this under the yells of the mostly pro-Montagnard galleries.

There would be times when the Girondins would try to deal with the galleries, would try to do something to avoid having the galleries yelling down at them. At one point, there were certain galleries reserved for supporters of the Girondins. A group of women, including members of a new club called the Society of Revolutionary Republican Citizenesses, put a stop to that, making sure that all the galleries were pro-Montagnard. The presidents of the Convention would frequently ask for quiet; when they finally got it, it would never last long.

On May 18, a disturbance in the galleries even interrupted the Convention's meeting, when disputes over a seat led to yelling that filled the hall. Isnard gave a warning to his fellow deputies. "Legislators! People!" he yelled,

> listen in silence. There's a plot going on to destroy the Convention by insurrection. A disorder will start in the Convention, serving as pretext to a riot. Women will start the movement; once their misled arms have wounded the fatherland, people will say that they are heroines who must be saved. Men will come to help them.

And he gave one final warning: "we have managed to fanaticize that portion of the people who, more virtuous than enlightened, is so easy to seduce."[71] What would follow, then, would surely be anarchy and civil war.

The Girondins took their one try at moving toward tyranny. At Barère's suggestion, the Convention formed the "Commission of Twelve" – twelve deputies who would be responsible for investigating the Commune and the capital's insurrectionary activities. Barère's ability to propose compromises, or, at the least, to get the Convention to move on, was rare in the spring of 1793, and it would eventually take him far. The Commission of Twelve, though, would not be his most lasting idea. With the twelve deputies all coming from the Plain or the Gironde, it would be the one new institution that the Girondins did control. They went to work on May 20.

On May 24, Hébert joined the cry for an insurrection, calling for the sans-culottes to rise up against the "frigging remains of accomplices of Capet and Dumouriez ... who piss ice during a heatwave, and who, instead of defending the republic, fan the flames of civil war between Paris and the departments."[72] The Girondin-led Commission of Twelve had him arrested the next day. Not without consequences: the sans-culottes may not have loved Hébert as they did Marat, but he had more than his share of followers, many of them angered at the arrest, angered at the Girondins, angered at this mysterious new Commission of Twelve.

The next day, 25 May, the first of several delegations made it to the Convention in opposition to Hébert's arrest – a deputation from the Commune. They denounced the Twelve's arrest of "a citizen who has made himself commendable, by his enlightenment and his civic virtue."[73]

If that description of Hébert drew "ironic laughter" from the Convention's right wing, Isnard's reaction was less indulgent. Isnard was, at this moment, the president of the Convention – a prestigious position, but not a particularly important or powerful one. It was the sort of position where success means being noticed less, not more – but that was not the approach that Isnard was taking on May 25.

He snapped.

In his response to the deputation from the Commune, he told them to

> listen to the truths that I am going to tell you. France has made Paris the depository of the nation's representation; Paris must respect that; Paris's constituted authorities must use all of their power to assure that respect. If ever the Convention is sullied, if ever, by one of these insurrections that have not ceased since March 10 ...

The murmurs began, from the Montagnards and the galleries. The right and the center began applauding. Fabre d'Eglantine, a Dantonist, demanded to speak – "against you, president ..."

But Isnard continued. "If by these constant insurrections, something happens which harms the nation's representatives, I declare to you, in the name of all of France ..."

Montagnards began yelling that he had no right to speak in the name of France; the center and the right yelled, "Yes, say it in the name of France!"

Isnard continued. "I declare to you, in the name of all of France, that Paris will be annihilated."

Murmurs from the Montagnards and the galleries grew loud enough to drown out Isnard's voice. Marat yelled at Isnard to descend from the podium, claiming that he "dishonored" the Assembly.

But still Isnard continued. "Soon, they will search the banks of the Seine to see if Paris had ever existed."[74]

The center and the right cheered. The Montagnards and the galleries were aghast. Danton, others, demanded to speak. News of Isnard's words spread quickly through the capital, through the faubourgs. After months of yelling down from the galleries at the Girondins, demanding their arrest, their expulsion, after months of veiled threats and unveiled threats, the Montagnards and their supporters could portray themselves as the victims, as the threatened ones. In the eyes of the sans-culottes, no longer were the Girondins just holding up progress; they were threatening Paris itself.

Deputations continued to arrive at the Convention, demanding Hébert's freedom, demanding an end to the Commission of Twelve. The following day at the Jacobin club, Robespierre announced that the "moment had arrived" for the people to rise up, for an "insurrection against the corrupted deputies" of the Convention.[75]

On May 27 Hébert was freed, although that did not calm things. The Convention voted to maintain the Commission of Twelve, by a count of 279 to 238. In other words, the Girondins' position, on May 27, was still a majority one. But if it was a majority position among the deputies, the galleries swung the *room's* majority well toward the Montagnards, and the dynamic of the room reflected that.

The deliberations of the Convention that day were as heated as ever, and as dysfunctional as ever. Isnard fought to keep Robespierre from speaking to the Convention; predictably, the right wing supported him, the Montagnards and the galleries did not. The debate continued: should Robespierre be allowed to speak? The Montagnard Thuriot claimed that Isnard was not only a counter-revolutionary, but "the head of the Christian army in the Vendée."[76] Each side accused the other of promoting civil war. A Montagnard threatened to assassinate Isnard, bringing all deputies on both sides to their feet. Elected representatives began grabbing paper out of each other's hands, getting in each other's faces, pushing and shoving. Still no definitive answer: could Robespierre speak? At one point people were in the hallways, preventing any movement in or out of the room. One deputy tried to leave, had a sword pointed at his chest, and returned to the Assembly.

Isnard got word to the National Guard to clear the corridors. Free circulation returned. The end of that session of the Convention was curious, though. Or rather, it was not clear *when* exactly the session ended. Because in the final hours, it was not the full Convention, or anything like it, but rather 100 or so Montagnards, along with the various deputations, who began sitting in the seats left vacant by the remaining deputies.

The lines between who was, and who was not, in the Convention were becoming blurred; the questions of what was and what was not proper for the Convention to do, for the Commune to do, for the sans-culottes or the sections to do – these, too, were getting blurred.

And the anger at the Girondins kept growing. Different groups made different demands: the abolition of the Twelve; the expulsion of the 22 Girondins (the names sometimes varied, but it was always 22). Along with this, the same sans-culottes demands for maximum prices for bread, for workshops, kept being repeated throughout the capital.

The revolt, when it came, took two tries.

The Parisians who led the revolt claimed to be acting in the spirit of July 14, 1789, and of August 10, 1792. But if these insurrections were no longer new, this was no well-oiled insurrection machine. The events of the next few days were sloppy.

On May 31 Paris woke to the sound of the tocsin and the alarm cannons. The insurrection was on. In a touch of irony, the people were once again marching on the Tuileries. From the National Assembly's arrival in Paris in October 1789 until earlier in May 1793, the Assembly and Convention had met in the salle du Manège, across from the Tuileries. In early May the Convention moved to a room in the Tuileries itself. It was a darker room than the Manège, built as a theater, to be lit by candles and not the sun. The dynamics overall were similar – a large room, with galleries; largely female audiences watching the debates between the men in the Convention, as they had at the two preceding legislatures.

The Convention, though, did not have the sort of armed guards that the king had had. The Convention – like the Assemblies before it – had relied on the protection of the people. But the relationship between the people in the insurrection and the Convention had changed. In 1789, the insurrection had been on behalf of the whole National Assembly; in 1792, the revolt of August 10 had reflected poorly on the Legislative Assembly, clearly unable to keep the peace. In 1793, though, it was a revolt in the name of one of the Convention's parties, against the other.

The insurrection of May 31, even if it considered itself the heir to the earlier insurrections, did not share their successes. The tocsin, it seemed, was growing old.

The day was not without its tensions. The minister of the interior began the session by admitting that he "could not hide from the Convention that there is much agitation in Paris."[77] People did march on the Tuileries, and there were a large number of armed men surrounding it. Within the Convention were the usual back-and-forth of accusations. The Girondin

Rabaut de Saint-Etienne had hoped to defend the Commission of Twelve, but was never able to speak. Vergniaud began calling for the galleries to be cleared. The president of the Convention – no longer Isnard – threatened to have them cleared, but never did.

And Vergniaud later tried to appease the crowd – saying, that day, that Paris had done well, and noting that the streets of the capital were calm. A reference, perhaps, to what he and his allies were trying in vain to prove – that the Parisians filling the galleries, petitioning the Convention, no longer represented the majority of the city, but only its most radical fringe. It was not enough for Vergniaud to win over the crowd's approval, though. A later deputation from the 48 sections still called for his arrest. Nor was it enough to win over Robespierre's approval. As Robespierre began listing the changes needed, in his long-winded style, and Vergniaud called on him to "conclude," Robespierre replied:

> Yes, I am going to conclude, and against you. Against you, who, after the Revolution of August 10, wanted to bring those who made that revolution to the scaffold ... against you who have not ceased calling for the destruction of Paris.[78]

That said, for a day that had started with the tocsin and had hoped to be the next great "*journée*" of the Revolution, the next August 10, May 31, was surprisingly ineffective. By the end of the day, the Commission of Twelve was, indeed, gone. There was, however, no purge. Earlier in the day Vergniaud had led an oath that all of the deputies had taken – to die at their post if need be. By the end of the day, no one had died, and no one had left their post.

The events of May 31 had put the Convention in a difficult position. The Plain, even the Montagnards, were not happy about being dictated to by the crowd. On May 31, the Convention stared down the crowd, a statement that the Convention believed in the rule of law, not force. It was not only the Girondins yelling "No!" to the people who marched on the Convention – those cries rang out from the center, and from the left as well. The Convention was not eager to be saved by brute force. Even Robespierre felt threatened, claiming that he felt physically weak during those days.

The tocsin would ring again, the whole night of June 1. The morning of June 2 many of the same people would again come down to the Tuileries – the deputies, the spectators, the deputations from the Commune and the sections. There were also armed troops surrounding the Convention – as many as 80,000 men in arms, some of them hoping for a change, others not quite sure why they were there.

It was an odd day, June 2, from the start, with many of the soldiers there under false pretences (they had been told of a royalist gathering on the nearby Champs-Elysées). Santerre was off in western France to lead troops against the Vendéen rebels. In charge of the troops instead was a sans-culotte named Hanriot who, on June 2, was still quite new at his job. It was one more strange aspect to June 2 – the crowd of armed men giving the appearance of a Convention under siege, an appearance that would have its own sort of impact. And a situation not unlike that of Paris as a whole – where most people were not necessarily opponents of the Girondins, but neither were they their supporters, and where an angry, vocal contingent was allowed to speak for the entire capital, making it seem that all of Paris – like all of the crowd around the Tuileries on the morning of June 2 – was, indeed, unified against the Girondins. Or, as the deputy Lanjuinais put it, "Paris is pure, Paris is good; Paris is oppressed by tyrants who want blood and power."[79]

A curious pair of days, May 31 and June 2. The first, full of drama and conflict, but lacking any real resolution. The second had a smaller share of conflict, and, over the course of it, less drama, but it did have a resolution. The most prominent Girondins – Brissot, Vergniaud, Isnard, Roland – talked little or not at all. Many were not in attendance; having sworn two days earlier to die at their posts, they were now gathered at the home of a supporter, waiting out the day.[80]

The Breton deputy Lanjuinais, less a Girondin than simply an opponent of the Montagnards, was nevertheless the most vocal defender of the Girondins that day – and perhaps the only one not intimidated by the situation. He called on the Convention to shut down the Commune, the "rival, usurping authority that is surrounding you with guns and cannons", and, he claimed, a petition which had been "dragged through the mud of the streets of Paris."[81] Several Montagnard deputies, including Robespierre's younger brother, tried to pry Lanjuinais – physically – from the podium. Pandemonium. Lanjuinais was able to resist, to keep speaking, but not to achieve the measures he called for, measures which would have meant limiting the power of the Paris Commune, the sections, all those who had been calling for the purge.

Nor were the usual leaders of the Montagnards particularly vocal. Robespierre said little, Danton was "hesitating miserably,"[82] and if he said anything, it did not make it into the official record; Marat waited until the waning moments to intervene.

Otherwise, the days were similar: bickering back and forth; circulation blocked at times, open at times; women sometimes blocking the doors to the Convention, at other times men, armed men, even. Petitions, deputations, arriving, denouncing the Girondins, denouncing the "22." The Convention deliberated under the yells of the women and men in the galleries, yells that were always in support of the Montagnards; that, after all, had been the case for some time. The Convention, again, deliberated while surrounded by soldiers – many of them brand new, but armed anyway.

The difference between the two days lay mostly in the arrival, finally, of some sort of decision from the Committee of Public Safety. It arrived in the person – who else? – of Barère, speaking for the Committee. He presented his offer as a compromise, but it hardly was. "There has been talk of arrest, we have not complied with any such measure, which would be unworthy of republicans." But that was the extent of the compromise, and the Committee's plan was hardly a way of getting the two sides to work together. "The only measure that can end these divisions which are harming the republic," was for the leading Girondins "voluntarily [to] suspend their functions."[83]

Not much of a compromise, but in its own way, successful.

Isnard led the way. Between one man and the nation, he said, "I will always lean toward the nation that I adore, that I will always adore."[84] A few others, including Fauchet, followed suit. Lanjuinais less so – "do not wait for me to demission," he told his fellow deputies, "the Convention is under siege, there are cannons aimed at this palace ... I declare that I cannot give any opinion at the moment, and I will shut up."[85] It was late that night that Lanjuinais finally agreed to walk away. By then, there was no saving the Girondins. But there was, oddly enough, a chance to save several of the men in the "22." It was here that Marat took center stage, declaring that a few of the men included were innocent. Dusaulx, for one – the old man, who during the September Massacres had stood on a chair trying, in vain, to get people to listen to him. According to Marat, he was just an "old dotard." Another of the men on the list "did not deserve to be thought of." Others Marat added, including Louvet.[86] Thus Marat, in the waning moments of an odd insurrection, held the power to convict or pardon by his very word. He proposed changes to the list, and the Convention approved them.

It was the Plain that had the power to make these decisions. Perhaps they were deciding out of fear of the crowd; perhaps they were simply deciding that they had to choose one side or another. The Convention, as Michelet noted, had a choice to make – they could let the Girondins perish, or they could let France perish, and "even the Gironde chose the Gironde."[87]

The Girondins had begun the Convention in a decent situation. True, they had emerged fairly weak in the aftermath of August 10, but the September Massacres had shown that the Montagnards were a party of violence and anarchy. Though outvoted in Paris, the Girondins were a dominant party in much of the nation, and, when the Convention opened in late September 1792, they had more deputies than the Montagnards. Just over eight months later, they were walking out of the Convention.

As on August 10, the Girondins proved to be not up to the moment. In 1793 France was in a civil war, and the desperation in the capital – some well founded, some not – led their opponents to advocate more radical positions than they might have otherwise. Meanwhile, the Girondins seemed more focused on defeating their parliamentary rivals than they were on facing the foreign armies to the east or the rebel armies to the west. As the historian R.R. Palmer wrote, "they were reluctant to adopt emergency measures in an emergency which they had themselves in large part brought about."[88] Their desire to punish the men who carried out the September Massacres was more than valid, but in the end, it prevented them from working with the Montagnards, even though they never succeeded in punishing the murderers either. They also tended to pick the wrong battles: sending Louvet after Robespierre, then hanging him out to dry; sending Marat to the Montagnard-dominated Revolutionary Tribunal; Isnard threatening all of Paris with destruction. Couple that with the inability of the Girondins' leaders to win the support of the people in Paris, and the Montagnards' victory seems all but inevitable.

The Montagnard victory meant a move toward consolidating Montagnard control over the Revolution, and a move toward consolidating Paris's control over the nation. It would mean a move toward appeasing the crowd's demands – maximums on prices, controls on the press, more taxes on the wealthy. It was a move toward consolidating more and more power in fewer and fewer hands. For Quinet, this was a step backwards. As he put it, on June 2 "it was decided that the regeneration of France would not be done by the new method, liberty, but by the Old Regime's method, tyranny."[89] It would not help that a lot of the institutional changes were already in place for a more top-down approach to government: the Revolutionary Tribunal, the representatives-on-mission, the Committee of Public Safety.

In the aftermath of June 2, in the session's final moments, some of the deputies rushed to the podium, protesting against what had happened. It was not what they had been elected for; the events of that day had not been what was expected in a republic. But the Convention was already planning ahead, discussing the business to be dealt with in the coming days, days which, for the first time in months, would not be dominated by fratricidal rivalry. The Montagnards' victory had been possible in large part because they were more popular in Paris; now, though, they were faced with the daunting task of ruling all of France.

Notes

1 Aulard, ed., *Jacobins*, IV:418.
2 Michelet, *Histoire*, I:303, II:404.
3 Baker, ed., *The Old Regime*, pp. 307, 309.
4 Baker, ed., *The Old Regime*, pp. 305–6.
5 Baker, ed., *The Old Regime*, p. 311.
6 *OMR* IX:80.
7 Michelet, *Histoire*, II:112.

8 Jean-Baptiste Louvet de Couvray, *Mémoires de Louvet de Couvrai sur la Révolution française*, ed. Alphonse Aulard, (Paris, 1889), I:60.
9 Quoted in Jaurès, *Histoire*, III:372.
10 Carlyle, *History*, p. 580.
11 Michelet, *Histoire*, II:199.
12 Paul Lombard, *Le Procès du roi* (Paris, 1993), p. 80.
13 *OP* VIIII:4668, 4739, 5324, IX:5859, 5883, 6417.
14 *AP* LIV:397.
15 Thiers, *Histoire*, III:201.
16 *AP* LV:9.
17 Michelet, *Histoire*, II:211.
18 *London Times*, January 25, 1793.
19 *AP* LV:632.
20 *OP* VIII:5130, 5452.
21 The legal issues were, in fact, surprisingly complicated. The Constitution of 1791 gave the king immunity from most forms of prosecution. The legislature could dethrone him, but once it did that, it could only try him for things he had done since being dethroned – and all he had done in that time was to be a prisoner at the Temple. In the end, the Convention decided that it was not bound by the Constitution of 1791.
22 Michael Walzer, "The King's Trial and the Political Culture of the Revolution," in *The Political Culture of the French Revolution*, ed. Lucas, pp. 188–9.
23 Quoted in David Jordan, *The King's Trial: Louis XVI vs. the French Revolution* (Berkeley, 1979), p. 166.
24 Quoted in Baker, ed., *The Old Regime*, pp. 323–4.
25 *AP* LVI:199, 205
26 Jordan, *The King's Trial*, p. 172
27 *AP* LVII:88, 90.
28 Jordan, *The King's Trial*, p. 191.
29 *AP* LVII:343.
30 *AP* LVII:366, 378.
31 Jaurès, *Histoire*, V:137–41. There would be one deputy killed by a crowd that marched into the Convention in May 1795.
32 Jordan, *The King's Trial*, p. 208.
33 http://www.eyewitnesstohistory.com/louis.htm.
34 Hunt, *Family Romance*, See the discussion in Chapter 2.
35 *OP* I:47.
36 Michelet, *Histoire*, II:262.
37 Aulard, ed., *Jacobins*, IV:689.
38 Aulard, ed., *Jacobins*, V:288–90.
39 John Hardman, *French Revolution Documents 1792–95* (New York, 1973), II:218–19; quoted in http://chnm.gmu.edu/revolution/d/373/.
40 Baker, ed., *The Old Regime*, p. 331.
41 Alfred Cobban, *A History of Modern France* (London, 1968), I:227.
42 George Rudé, *The French Revolution* (New York, 1988), pp. 94–5.
43 Albert Soboul, *The Sans Culottes: The Popular Movement and the Revolutionary Government*, trans. Remy Inglis Hall (New York, 1972), p. 40.
44 Soboul, *Sans Culottes*, p. 25.

45 Soboul, *Sans Culottes*, p. 250.
46 Michelet, *Histoire*, II:425; Martin, *Révolte Brisée*, p. 161.
47 Aulard, ed., *Jacobins*, IV:699.
48 Doyle, *Oxford History*, p. 223.
49 Aulard, ed., *Jacobins*, V:45.
50 Aulard, ed., *Jacobins*, V:53–4.
51 *OMR* IX:207.
52 Louis Gottschalk, *Jean-Paul Marat: A Study in Radicalism* (Chicago, 1967), p. 94; Carlyle, *The French Revolution*, p. 633.
53 *Bordel Patriotique*, pp. 26, 59.
54 See, for example, *OP* I:246, 537, II:791.
55 *OP* III:1927.
56 *OP* VI:3264.
57 Quoted in Gottschalk, *Jean-Paul Marat*, p. 143.
58 Aulard, ed., *Jacobins*, IV:418.
59 Gottschalk, *Jean-Paul Marat*, p. 93.
60 Michelet, *Histoire*, II:542.
61 *AP* 60:259.
62 *OP* IX:5882.
63 Doyle, *Oxford History*, p. 227.
64 Gérard Walter, ed., *Actes du Tribunal révolutionnaire* (Paris, 1968), p. 14.
65 Quoted in Thiers, *Histoire*, III:336.
66 Gottschalk, *Jean-Paul Marat*, p. 158.
67 *AP* LXI:639.
68 *AP* LXII:41, 44, 56.
69 *AP* LXIII:217–18.
70 *OP* IX:6183–98.
71 *AP* LXV:43.
72 M. Charles Brunet, ed., *Le Père Duchesne d'Hébert* (Paris, 1859), p. 161.
73 *AP* LXV:320.
74 *AP* LXV:320.
75 *OMR* IX:526–7.
76 *AP* LXV:381.
77 *AP* LXV:638.
78 *AP* LXV:653.
79 *AP* LXV:700.
80 Thiers, *Histoire*, IV:174.
81 *AP* LXV:699.
82 Michelet, *Histoire*, II:440.
83 *AP* LXV:704.
84 *AP* LXV:704.
85 *AP* LXV:705.
86 *AP* LXV:706.
87 Michelet, *Histoire*, II:407.
88 R. R. Palmer, *Twelve who Ruled: The Year of the Terror in the French Revolution* (Princeton, 1969), p. 25.
89 Quinet, *Révolution*, I:502.

7

THE FEDERALIST REVOLT, THE VENDÉE, AND THE START OF THE TERROR (SUMMER 1793–FALL 1793)

All of France, it would turn out, was not particularly interested in being ruled by Paris. Not by *this* Paris, in any case. Citizens outside Paris, reading the news, were being told of a Paris where a disorderly crowd worshipped at the altars of Robespierre, Marat, and Danton. In June and July of 1793, the chances of Paris ruling the rest of France appeared quite slim.

Since March, the long-disgruntled Vendée had been fighting back against the government in Paris. The external war was still going on, with no reason to think that smooth sailing awaited. For the Montagnards and their supporters, it was the Girondins' unwillingness to face up to the challenges bearing down on the young republic that had made it necessary to expel them from the Convention. A pyrrhic victory, then – expelling the Girondins did not make the problems go away, as the Girondins' supporters (or perhaps more accurately, the Montagnards' opponents) in much of France began to turn against Paris and the Revolution. Thus Madame Roland, whom the Paris Commune had seen fit to imprison even before June 2: "Do you think that proud Marseilles and wise Gironde will forgive the affronts committed against their representatives? Do you think they will ever again cooperate with your criminal city?"[1]

Madame Roland would not be the only Girondin leader sent to prison – though it was not clear, as the Girondins walked out of the Convention, what exactly was to happen to them. The decree expelling them from the Convention had called for them to be put under house arrest. It was a decree that some respected, but others did not. The Convention had all but announced their willingness to let the deputies flee when they decreed that only one officer would be guarding each deputy.[2] Madame Roland chose to stay, obeying – with what Thiers called a "noble indifference" – her local section.[3] Her husband, already out of Paris, chose not to return. Vergniaud was among those who chose to stay. "Let them prove that we are guilty," he wrote; "otherwise, let them bring their own heads to the scaffold."[4]

Brissot, Pétion, Louvet, Buzot, Guadet, others – they chose to flee. Traveling through France was not easy for them; they could not travel openly, nor bring much with them. Most had to leave behind their families. What some fleeing deputies found, though, was that they arrived in friendly territories. Those who made it to Caen, the capital of the Calvados department in Normandy, were even housed by the local government. The fleeing Girondins thought that they were saving the republic from the handful of deputies, and handful of Parisians, who had taken it over. As Louvet put it, "nothing but the insurrection of the departments could save France."[5]

An insurrection of the departments. For the Montagnards in Paris, this was a call to civil war, plain and simple. Marat called the Girondin leaders in Caen and Bordeaux "true counter-revolutionaries, in league with the enemies of freedom both within and without, to put the fatherland back in chains."[6] Their goal, according to Marat, was "to destroy the Republic and reestablish royalty"[7] – probably with England's help. Marat had a point; they were calling for a civil war, though the leaders of the federalist revolt were not advocating a return to monarchy. They had been republicans before most of their Montagnard opponents. Nor were the leaders of the Girondins hoping to put Philippe-Egalité (né Orléans) on the throne, as Marat claimed.[8] But the Girondins too had a point; they had been elected by their departments but were now expelled, primarily because of the actions of the people of Paris. Both sides, though, realized that this was now a civil war. And this civil war, in the summer of 1793, was not looking particularly promising for the government in Paris.

Most of France was now in open opposition to the central government.

Caen was becoming the center of a province arming itself to march on Paris. In Brittany, to Normandy's west, the countryside had long been hostile to the Revolution. Like the Vendée to the south, the people there had never accepted the Civil Constitution of the Clergy, and had taken to their own form of opposition, a guerrilla warfare known as *Chouannerie*. The cities of Brittany were supporters of the Revolution, though – or at least they had been. Now, though, the people there who supported the Revolution were siding with the Girondins.

In the southwest, Bordeaux was siding with its own Girondin deputies. By the time word of the events of June 2 had reached Bordeaux, after more than a few rounds of whisper-down-the-lane, the citizens heard not that their deputies had been expelled, but that they had been massacred, and that Marat – or perhaps Philippe-Egalité – was to be the new ruler.[9] (There is perhaps no clearer message of the fall of France's once coolest uncle than that both sides were now using his name in inaccurate attempts to smear their opponents.) The stories were not true, but it is hard to say if the truth would have been less effective. Bordeaux and the surrounding region began raising their own army to march on Paris.

Lyon, in the southeast, had not waited for the expulsion of the Girondins. On May 29 there was an uprising in Lyon, overthrowing a group of Montagnards, always a minority there, who had been ruling the city since the winter. Other cities – Marseilles and Toulon most notably, though there were others – saw similar developments.

Back in 1790, the government had divided mainland France into 83 departments, along with another 11 for its colonies. In the summer of 1793, of those 83 departments, at least 60 – if not more like 70 – were in one way or another opposed to the central government. In Bordeaux, Marseilles, and Caen, they gathered armies. Men from surrounding areas were heading to those cities, eager to march on Paris and overthrow the government there. The government in Paris would soon accuse all of these places of "federalism," and would accuse the Girondins in exile of leading this "federalist revolt."

This term, "federalist revolt," has passed the test of time, but it is not particularly accurate. It implies that the movement favored the doctrine of federalism, which is to say, relative autonomy for the different regions of France. Regional autonomy had never been a goal of the Girondins – if anything, they wanted the same central government, just with a different group of men in charge. More generally, though, there was no consistently articulated goal for the revolt. It was an opposition to Paris; it was an opposition to the Montagnards, to Robespierre, to Marat.

The expelled Girondins who had fled Paris were important leaders in this movement, but many of the men who joined the armies were royalists, supporters of the Old Regime – men not willing, perhaps, to join the ranks of the Vendéans, but still willing to fight against Paris. Such a description fit Félix Wimpffen, the army general in command of the forces in Caen. Indeed, one of the biggest problems facing the federalist revolt was that, beyond an opposition to the Montagnards ruling in Paris, little united them. Royalists assumed that the revolt was in the name of monarchy; their eagerness to support the expelled deputies vanished upon learning that their exile had not brought these men back into the royalist fold. Thus Pétion, of the leading citizens of Caen: "they detested the Mountain most cordially, but they liked republicans no better."[10]

Of the challenges that the Revolution was facing in the summer of 1793 – the federalist revolt, the external war, the revolt in the Vendée – the federalist revolt proved to have the most smoke, but the least fire. From Paris, they must have seemed a formidable foe. Marat, looking at the different threats the republic was facing, wrote that "the most imminent danger is to see new departments dragged along by the example of the Eure, Calvados, and Jura" – all departments which had declared their opposition to the Convention and their plans to raise armies – "which is to say to see the enemies of freedom raise the flag of revolt against the

Convention." The Convention's only answer, for Marat, was to send troops to stop the enemies of freedom, and to "crush them without mercy."[11]

Such fears made sense at the time, but do not fit with the picture of the revolt that the exiled Girondins gave – particularly Louvet. His descriptions of the federalist army show only a rag-tag group of men with much spirit but few resources and little leadership. Wimpffen, in particular, seemed more interested in stalling than in marching on Paris. The moment, at least in the west, was quickly passing. The only real positive memory that Louvet had from the time was when he met "a stout, handsome young woman."[12] That woman – Charlotte Corday – would soon make quite an impression on all of France. At this point, she was just one more woman from Normandy, unlikely to have made much of an impression on Louvet or anyone else.

At one point, it looked like troops would be converging on Paris from Normandy, from Marseilles and Lyon, from Bordeaux – not to mention from the Vendée. But these troops, it would turn out, did not make it far from home. Lyon's revolt – about which more below – would remain a local fight. The troops from Marseilles never made it past Avignon, which is to say, they traveled little more than ten percent of the distance to Paris. The troops from Bordeaux made it approximately 20 miles from Bordeaux before stopping and setting up their camp. Even those 20 miles were south, away from Paris, which is roughly 350 miles to the northeast.

Caen is 145 miles from Paris, Evreux less than half that, and for the Girondins' supporters, the journey from Caen to Evreux was on friendly terrain. This posed the gravest danger to Paris. Wimpffen's plan, though, was to establish a stronghold in Normandy and seek help from England. The exiled deputies were too patriotic for this. To Louvet, inviting English troops onto French soil would have been the end of the French republic – "and of our honor, in the same instant."[13] But perhaps Wimpffen understood better than the deputies the nature of the troops at his disposal. When the troops finally started marching toward Paris the trip past Evreux was not a shining moment for anyone involved. As the federalist troops approached the small town of Pacy-sur-Eure on July 13, local gendarmes were able to halt their advance.

Accounts of the battle vary. According to some, when the local troops fired their cannons at the troops marching from Normandy, those troops panicked and fled, never regrouping until they were back in Caen. According to other accounts, the local troops had not even fired their cannons at the arriving troops. They had merely made a show of those cannons, and fired them in the air.

All accounts agree on the panicked retreat back to Caen, though.

For all intents and purposes, that was that, for the northern phase of the federalist revolt. Carlyle wrote that "few wars ... were ever levied of a more insufficient character than this of Calvados,"[14] and it is hard to disagree. The troops from Brittany returned to Brittany; Caen stated its support for the Convention. Louvet wrote of seeing a poster on the government building where they were staying, declaring that they were now outlaws. He, along with other exiled deputies, left for Brittany, disguised as the Breton soldiers with whom they marched; they would soon sail down to Bordeaux. The resistance there would last longer – the Convention would not retake control of Bordeaux until September – but it would be no more effective at threatening the government in Paris. The only real damage that Normandy would do to the Montagnards in Paris came not from the men in arms, but from the young woman whom Louvet would later claim made such an impression on him.

Charlotte Corday arrived in Paris that July with a simple plan: she was going to kill either Robespierre or Marat. She chose Marat.

Marat, by that point, was not doing well. Despite the expulsion of the Girondins – and the key role he had played that day – Marat still saw threats surrounding him, threatening the Revolution. He was getting sick. He spent little time in the Convention, and most of his time in the home of his common-law wife, Simone Evrard. His years of underground living had taken their toll. He may never have lived in the sewers, but his skin was starting to look as if he had. The reason why he spent most of his time in a bathtub was to ease his discomfort. It was by this bathtub that one of the most famous conversations, and one of the most famous events, of the Revolution took place.

Corday had sent several letters to Marat. "I come from Caen," she wrote, adding that she had information about the "unhappy developments in this part of the Republic."[15] When that failed, she wrote in a manner sure to flatter a man who prided himself on defending the less fortunate, that "it is sufficient that I be quite unhappy, to have earned the right to your protection."[16] Over Evrard's opposition, Marat let Corday enter, perhaps seeing in this young woman from Caen a source of information on the events there, perhaps someone to impress, perhaps someone to save from danger. She came and talked to him, and when he asked her who was hiding out in Caen and causing the trouble there, she gave him a few names. "I will have them all guillotined," Marat replied.

Then the young woman from Caen grabbed the knife that she had bought that morning, and plunged it into Marat's chest. He died soon afterward.

Corday and Marat have become a pair, historically speaking – "hapless beautiful Charlotte" and "hapless squalid Marat,"[17] to use Carlyle's terms. Corday did little else out of the ordinary in her life. This she knew; she described herself as a "useless woman," for whom a long life "will not do any good."[18] Marat was already a prominent politician and journalist. Yet, as historical pairs go, they are not as bad a fit as it might first seem. Corday, interrogated after her arrest, gave explanations that could have come from one of Marat's papers. "I killed one man," she told her interrogators, "to save

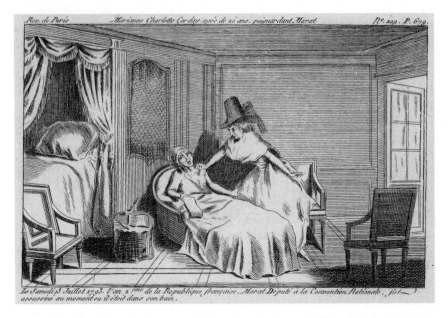

Figure 7.1 The assassination of Marat. Charlotte Corday stabs Marat as he sits in his bathtub. From *Révolutions de Paris*. © Penn Special Collections.

100,000." Here was logic that was dear to Marat's heart; he had always been creating such ratios, or saying that the number of deaths needed to save the Revolution was rising, from the hundreds to the thousands.[19]

Their deaths, meanwhile, would be within days of each other. Corday had anticipated being torn apart by an angry crowd – or, if not, fleeing to England. The crowd did form, but several men in it protected her, so that she could be brought to face the Revolutionary Tribunal. In earlier years of the Revolution, she would have more likely been torn apart by the crowd, her head paraded on a pike – like the governor of the Bastille or the king's bodyguards in 1789, like the princesse de Lamballe in 1792. Instead, she was led to the prison, able, even to write to her father, and to the exiled Girondin Barbaroux. To her father, she asked forgiveness, "for disposing of my existence without your permission." To Barbaroux, she asked that what remained of her money be given to the "wives and children of the brave inhabitants of Caen" who were marching on Paris, and to "tell General Wimpffen that I believe I have helped him."[20] It was on the same day that Corday stabbed Marat, though, that Wimpffen's troops had turned and fled at the first sound of cannon fire. She had not only gotten farther than they had; she had done more damage to the Montagnards, by herself, than all of Caen's troops.

If Corday's head was never paraded on a pike through the streets of Paris, it did not get to spend much more time attached to her body, either.

After several days of prison (including an interrogation seeking to find links between Corday and the deputies in Caen), the Revolutionary Tribunal sentenced her to death. On July 17 she was executed – guillotined, as Louis XVI had been.

It was a relatively recent invention, the guillotine. Dr. Joseph Guillotin, in calling for a device that would cut off heads "in the blink of an eye," had a surprisingly humanitarian goal: to make death equal for all, to eliminate unnecessary suffering. The Old Regime had a wide variety of punishments, depending not only on the crime but on the social status of the criminal. Decapitation was reserved for the nobility; commoners would suffer more. The guillotine brought that noble punishment to even the most humble. Dr. Guillotin did not anticipate just how many of those humble souls would perish at the hands of his instrument (which he had inspired, though technically did not invent). In the summer of 1793, though, the rate of executions was still slow, not what it would become in 1794. Its victims were relatively low profile up to that point, with the exception of the king, that highest of high-profile victims. But few people, up to this point, had died at the guillotine. Thousands had already died during the Revolution: in the siege of the Bastille; on August 10, 1792; in the massacre at the Champ de Mars; in the September Massacres; and in the war. Yet for Marat, while he was living, not enough *coupable* heads were being cut off; hence his vow to Corday to have the exiled deputies guillotined. It would be another few months before politicians would suffer that fate.

La Vendée militaire

It was in the Vendée, though, that revolutionary violence first began to reach unprecedented levels.

The Vendée was one of the departments which the Constituent Assembly had created in 1790, taking its name from the river that formed its southern border. The word itself had come to mean much more, though – and rightly so, given how often the fighting flowed over the 1790 boundaries. "While all provinces became departments," wrote the historian Jean Yole, "the Vendée is the only department that became a province. With a vigorous gesture, it upset the official geography, breaking the narrow limits that had been imposed on it."[21]

The region itself was quite varied, and never as unified as the revolutionaries would come to believe. The western part of the Vendée was known as the *marais*, or the swamp (the same name given to a now fashionable neighborhood in Paris and, at times, to the deputies of the Plain in the Convention). East of the *marais* was the *bocage*, or woodlands; and to the north was the Mauges (a regional name which does not mean anything). These regions varied culturally as well as geographically. What can be said is that the countryside, both swamps and forests, was hostile to the Revolution and vociferous in its support

181

of the refractory church. The towns and cities, though, were republican, and saw the local peasants as backward and superstitious. As one local government agent wrote, "fanatical priests have found, in the ignorance and stupidity" of the local inhabitants, "the disposition that they desire."[22]

The Vendéan countryside had not always been anti-revolutionary. It was open to many of the revolutionary changes, particularly the move toward equality.[23] The king's execution came and went there with little impact. The Revolution's religious policies turned the Vendée against the Revolution; 75 percent of the priests there had refused to take the oath. When constitutional priests were assigned to parishes in the Vendée, they had to face the insults and threats of the parishioners. The constitutional priests would face the prospect of empty churches, or even of violence. Many chose to leave.

The policy that brought the Vendée from general disgruntlement to civil war, though, was one the Convention borrowed from the Old Regime. With the wars against Austria and Prussia requiring more men than volunteers could provide, the Convention voted a conscription of 300,000 men, with quotas for each department. In communities across the republic young men would draw lots to see who would be sent off to war. This was how the monarchy had done it. Unpopular then, it was even less popular now.

The Convention announced the decision in February. In March, fighting began in two different places in the region.

One was Machecoul in the marais, where thousands of peasants descended on the town, yelling *"point de tirement"* – no drawing of lots, no military conscription – and for their "good priests" as well.[24] When a local official tried to talk to the crowd, one of the peasants stabbed him in the heart with a pike. Soon, it was a full-scale riot; local officials were targeted, beaten, killed, their homes ransacked, their papers burned. One witness described the fate of the town's constitutional priest, "hit in the head by pitchforks and bayonets" before one woman "removed his manly qualities."[25] Over the next few days, the peasants who had taken over Machecoul killed at least 40 citizens there; they would kill hundreds more in the following months, in makeshift tribunals reminiscent of those set up in the September Massacres.

Fighting also started in the Mauges, in the town of Saint-Florent. The fighting was less violent there, but the causes – and result – were similar. As at Machecoul, the peasants won; the republican forces fled, albeit with fewer losses this time.

There was no advanced planning, no conspiracy, between the people of Machecoul and the people of Saint-Florent. As the insurrection developed, and the people of the Mauges and the bocage tried to cooperate with the people of the marais, the results were mixed. But the fighting had begun. Peasants had risen up in two regions, and had done so successfully. News was reaching Paris about the events in the Vendée, and especially about Machecoul. They were hearing stories about the number of dead and their grisly fates.

Map 7.1 The fighting in the Vendée. The key battles of the *Vendée militaire*.

The story of the early fighting in the Vendée was as much about the failures of the armies of the republic as it was about the successes of the peasants. The Convention's armies, known as the "Blues" for the color of their uniforms, were outnumbered, underprepared, and undisciplined. A dynamic that was present elsewhere as well – the Vendée was not the only place upset about conscription – snowballed. The republican troops not only fled, they left their weapons, their gunpowder, even cannons. The peasants who had descended on Machecoul and on Saint-Florent, then on other villages and towns in the following weeks, found themselves in a position that they had not expected: they controlled the towns, and they had weapons. Now they needed leaders.

The Vendéan rebels chose their leaders in a way that the republican troops could not. The most famous of the bunch was a man named Cathelineau, a common citizen from the Mauges. As the story goes, Cathelineau was kneading his bread when peasants came to him, telling him of what had happened at Saint-Florent, and calling on him to lead them. His opposition to the Civil Constitution of the Clergy had earned him respect from his fellow peasants. His local refractory priest described him as a pious, dedicated Christian. His critics described him as being completely under the influence of his priest, misled, like the rest of the rebels.

Most leaders were not peasants, though. The Old Regime army, with its all-aristocrat officer corps, was becoming republican, but not without growing pains. Bouillé had fled France after the failure of the king's flight in 1791; Lafayette and Dumouriez had fled France when their troops refused to march on Paris. Below them, hundreds of other officers, thousands of soldiers, had left the royal army as it became republican.

Henri La Rochejaquelein, like Lafayette, had stayed at it through August 10. His father had emigrated years earlier, but La Rochejaquelein chose to stay, joining the king's constitutional guard. On August 10 he was in Paris, a 19-year-old royalist in the inadequate force protecting the Tuileries. He left Paris after that, returning to his family's estate. "I am leaving for my province," he announced, "and soon you will hear people talking about me." In April 1793 a crowd of peasants gathered in his courtyard and told him that, if he wished, he would have 10,000 men under his orders.[26]

In the marais, the peasants who took over Machecoul found their own leader. Charette, too, had been in the military, specifically the navy, during the Old Regime. There is no story here of bread kneading, but Charette, too, had been pushed to lead the newly formed troops despite himself. His troops, though, never fully mixed with the troops from the bocage and the Mauges, and Charette never got along with the other generals.

The Revolution provided these men with opportunities for glory that they never would have had in the Old Regime. Charette and La Rochejaquelein would have been average officers in the army, Cathelineau an average villager in a remote part of France. Instead, they would become heroes to those who supported them; villains, brigands, to those who supported the Revolution. As military leaders, their skills varied. Some had enough experience to make a difference. Others had an ability to inspire. Madame Lescure, the wife of one of the Vendée's leaders, wrote that peasants called Cathelineau the "Saint of Anjou," and believed that "one could not be wounded next to such a holy man."[27] At a time when the Revolution had to enact old-style rules of conscription, the Vendéans had a volunteer army. The goal of having all male citizens be soldiers and all soldiers be citizens – the revolutionaries tried to impose that by decree. In the Vendée, it arose spontaneously, done in the name not of progress and equality, but of tradition and hierarchy.

Thus began the first phase of fighting, the first phase of what came to be called the *Vendée militaire*, the war in the Vendée and the neighboring departments. This first phase would last until June. The rebels won far more battles than they lost; they gathered strength and took over town after town, village after village. The more the "Blues" lost, the more momentum the "Whites" gained – and the more weapons and gunpowder as well.

Not all of the victories would last. The rebels were better at taking over cities and towns than they were at keeping control. And the nature of these victories varied. In towns like Machecoul, the arrival of the Vendéan rebels meant massacres of the local inhabitants; in other cities, where the local inhabitants put up little fight, even no fight at all, the rebels simply occupied the city, looked for food to eat and places to sleep, and a church to pray in. Often, their "control" of a city would only last a few days; as the rebels would march off to fight the next battle, the town would be left with few or no guards. The republican "forces" would then reassert their authority over the town. At Easter, most of the Vendéan army returned to their villages to confess and work their fields.

Religious life continued among the rebels, even during the campaigns, to the point of ostentation. In towns and cities that the rebels took over, they would flock to the churches to pray. They gave religious nicknames to the cannons seized from the republican forces. Priests were frequently among the rebel troops, blessing the rebels' weapons, taking their confessions, leading prayers. When the leaders of the movement set up a leadership council, it included several clerics.

There was even one bishop who came to lead the rebels in prayers and processions. Or at least, he said he was a bishop. The local refractory bishops had all emigrated, and none would return during the Revolution. But some time in late May a man showed up claiming to be the bishop of Agra – claiming, too, that the pope had sent him to lead the rebels in their fight against the Revolution.

The diocese of Agra, though, did not yet exist; there was no bishop of Agra and it is not clear why anyone thought that Agra, in India, would have had a French-speaking bishop. In reality, the man was a priest named Guyot de Folleville. He had been a priest in nearby Brittany, a constitutional priest, even, though he had retracted his oath not long after taking it. The charade worked. Madame Lescure wrote that when he entered a town the bells rang out, and the peasants were "drunk with joy" at the sight of him.[28]

On June 9 the rebels reached the Loire River and took over the town of Saumur. Over the course of the eighteenth century, the royal government had improved France's road system. Rivers, though, remained crucial to trade and communications. By gaining control over the cities and towns along the Loire, the rebels were taking a step past simply massacring the local townspeople; they were threatening France's communication system, its links with the outside world.

Sensing the need for more organization, the military leaders met, declaring that Cathelineau would be the head general of what was now called the "Royal and Catholic Army," though it was still an army where generals did largely as they pleased. On June 12, the rebels took over the city of Angers, 30 miles west of Saumur, on the Loire. The largest question facing the rebels, given their unanticipated success, was what to do next. They decided to attack Nantes, the region's most important city. Charette would attack from the left bank, the other troops from different angles on the right bank. Charette's troops arrived too early, though, due to his impatience; Cathelineau's troops arrived too late, a small troop of republican soldiers having held them off for some time several miles north of the city. Both sides had taken losses by the time Cathelineau led his men into the city, as the fighting moved from the area around Nantes to the streets of the city itself.

A bullet, probably shot from a window above the street, hit Cathelineau. A fatal wound for Cathelineau, it was also a blow to the rebels' morale. Whether because it brought the realization that the "Saint of Anjou" was not invincible, or simply because they now lacked leadership, the fighting quickly turned toward the republicans' advantage, as word spread through the rebel ranks that their leader was gone. By the end of the day, Nantes remained unconquered; the Vendéans retreated to plan their next move.

"If the Vendéans had taken Nantes," Michelet wrote, "they would have become, in reality, masters of the situation. Such a major development would have given them the sea, the Loire River, several departments, and a true western kingdom, all at once." The Convention would have lost Brittany, then perhaps Normandy as well. The door would have been open for the arrival of English troops on French soil.[29]

The Battle of Nantes was the end of the first phase of the civil war. "Such a grand occasion for the Vendéans would not be found again," according to Quinet. "They would have more numerous armies, their spirits fiercer, the blood would flow with more fury; but the terrain would be lacking for a conquest, and the victory would not know where to put itself."[30] The next phase of the civil war would be more even. The leadership of the rebel army passed to Maurice d'Elbée, another former royal officer and a member of the nobility. D'Elbée's attempts to introduce military discipline took away some of what had been the rebels' strength.[31] Still, the fighting over the summer of 1793 was hardly a walk in the park for the republican forces. Even with the arrival of more republican troops – some of them experienced soldiers who had fought against the Austrian and Prussian forces – the rebels would only go down fighting.

The contrast between the civil war in the Vendée and the federalist revolt could hardly be clearer. In one case, cannonballs shot in the air sent the soldiers running; the other would endure for months, battle after battle, and would claim thousands of lives on both sides. In explaining this difference, it is hard to look past the role that religion played in motivating the Vendéan soldiers – a motivation lacking in the federalist revolt. Quinet described the fighting in the Vendée as a religious war, adding that "a religion can only be eradicated by another religion ... Vague ideas could not stand up to the force of faith."[32] One might ask today to what extent the Vendéans' religious motivations were based on faith, and to what extent they were based on more social concerns. Many Vendéans likely saw the reform of the church as an attack on their community and their way of life, rather than as a threat to their salvation. Either way, both sides agreed on the importance of religion in the Vendée – though defenders of the Vendéans saw the rebels' tenacity as proof of their piety, while defenders of the republic saw it as proof that the Vendée was a bastion of superstition and ignorance, where credulous peasants had been led astray by the forces of religion, and by "scoundrels" using the cloak of religion to defend their own interests.

Revolutionary religion

The Revolution, however, was becoming a religion in its own right. Or *rite* – the Revolution had a tradition of borrowing religious practices and putting them to revolutionary uses. The Festival of the Federation[33] was one of many festivals that the government had initiated to rally support to the Revolution, much as religious festivals during the Old Regime had helped anchor Catholicism into people's daily lives. For Quinet, this was a "constant imitation of Catholicism ... this people, who are considered skeptical, cannot last one hour without a national religion."[34] Almanacs began to appear, helping to guide people through the year as almanacs had done for the past several centuries – but replacing the traditional saints with a new set of saints, replacing the commemoration of the events of the New Testament with the events of the Revolution. Hébert had tried his hand at this genre, as had Collot d'Herbois, a future member of the Committee of Public Safety. Other authors wrote republican catechisms to teach children about revolutionary virtues just as children had previously learned about Christian ones.

In Paris, Marat's death had brought these religious elements out in a new way. At the Cordeliers club, Marat's body was presented for his followers and supporters to pay their respects. He was posed with his chest bare, his wound visible; a white sheet covered his lower body and two stones from the Bastille had been placed next to him. Due to the summer heat (and perhaps Marat's skin condition), decomposition came faster than expected. His skin turned green, his face unrecognizable. The hygiene and sanitary conditions of Paris were nothing that one might call modern, yet the smell of Marat's corpse made an impression on people in the area.[35] Observers noted the large number of women who came, who cried, who threw flowers at the corpse. One group of women paraded his bathtub around the streets of Paris, with a bloody shirt held high on a pike. Other women gathered his blood, calling for that blood to become the "seed [*sémence*] for intrepid republicans" to come, turning a funeral rite into a rite of fecundity. Over the objections of a jealous Robespierre, a movement began to have Marat's body interred at the Pantheon, a recently constructed church on Paris's left bank that the revolutionary government had transformed into a mausoleum for the great men of the nation.[36] Marat's heart – literally – would stay in the Cordeliers club. Grisly as it sounds, this was an old tradition. Catholic churches all over Europe boasted of having body parts from different saints, be it a nose, a foot (or, less gruesomely, a piece of wood from the cross).

Marat was not the only revolutionary whose death would inspire a cult of martyrs. In January, in the immediate aftermath of the vote to execute Louis XVI – before the sentence had even been carried out – a former bodyguard of the king, angry at the verdict, had assassinated the deputy

Louis Michel Le Peletier. Formerly known as Le Peletier de Saint-Fargeau, he had been an aristocrat during the Old Regime and had represented the nobility at the Estates-General. His politics had shifted to the left during the Revolution; Le Peletier had denounced his former title and supported the cause of people. He had voted for the king's execution, and royalists saw this vote as a betrayal. A solid if unremarkable deputy, the assassination made Le Peletier into a martyr. His corpse was even transferred to the Pantheon, to lie alongside Voltaire's remains, and Rousseau's, and even Mirabeau's. This was illustrious company for Le Peletier.

Another martyr's cult would spring up around Joseph Bara, a young revolutionary killed in December 1793 in the fighting against the Vendéans. Though hardly the only revolutionary killed in the civil war, Bara was only 14 years old when he died. He had been killed by thieves during a robbery, but the general in charge of his troops told the Convention that Bara was a young patriot who could have saved his own life by saying, "long live the king," but who chose instead to yell out "long live the republic." Robespierre called Bara a "virtuous child" and a hero, and asked that "the honors of the Pantheon" be given to him. He also called for the artist David to prepare a celebration in his honor.[37]

That artist, Jacques-Louis David, had emerged as *the* painter of the Revolution. Though all three of these martyrs would be the subject of many paintings, in each case it was David's painting that stood above the rest. His painting of Marat dying in his bathtub, Corday's letter in his left hand as his right falls limp toward the floor, has become one of the most famous of all paintings from the French Revolution. In his painting of Bara, David portrayed him nude and lying on his side on the ground, his genitals tucked between his legs, his long hair falling over his shoulder: neither fully child nor fully adult, neither fully male nor fully female.

Bara had been an obscure 14-year-old, Le Peletier a solid if unremarkable deputy. Their deaths turned them into martyrs; their martyrdom – and the way the Revolution celebrated their martyrdom – made them famous. Marat's case was different. He had been famous while he was alive. His death raised his profile still higher among those who had already supported him, while the Montagnards who had thought less highly of him now kept their criticisms to themselves. Before his death, some of his followers had viewed him as a prophet. Now Marat's supporters, including the women who had followed him, were treating him like a saint as well as a martyr.

The reactions to Marat's death show just how complicated understanding women's role in the Revolution can be. There is no reason that it should not be complicated – no one would try to discuss "men's role in the Revolution" without acknowledging that there were men on every side. Corday had showed a real danger. One newspaper warned of such "viragos," of the dangers presented by a woman "who was not as pretty as people said" and who, at 25 years old, was "practically an old maid."[38] (Some Jacobins may even have attended Corday's autopsy in the hopes of determining if she was still a virgin.) At a speech at a section meeting, one man spoke of the danger of a woman like Corday, guided by fanatics. Then he had to realize to whom exactly he was speaking. "Pardon, citizenesses," he told the crowd, "it is not of you that I am speaking ... you are not to blame, if nature has created a monster bearing the image of your sex."[39]

Marat's influence would live on, but day-to-day governing remained the purview of the living. But who would take Marat's place as the people's friend? Hébert seemed the best positioned; he was already a radical journalist, as Marat had been. Roux – though Marat had despised and criticized him – also seemed well positioned, given his support from the people of Paris, particularly its most radical sections. Both, in their own way, would see their profiles rise, as part of the growing influence of what Michelet called the "terra incognita beyond Marat."[40]

Robespierre, too, would see his power expand in the aftermath of Marat's death. On July 27, he became a member of the Committee of Public Safety. This would turn out to be a major shift in the Revolution; it was, from the start, a major change in Robespierre's role in the government. For years, he had been influential. He had criticized those who were running the government, and he had offered his suggestions on how to improve the government. He had spoken at the Estates-General, the Constituent Assembly, and the Convention; he had spoken at the Jacobin club and at the Commune. He had even tried his hand at journalism. What he had not yet done was govern. Now – "against his inclination,"[41] as he told the Jacobins – he was on the Revolution's most powerful committee.

The Committee, meanwhile, was starting to hit its stride and make use of its powers. The Committee of Public Safety was, in theory, answerable to the Convention – and the Convention's deputies would elect the Committee's members monthly. As the Revolution faced the crises of the summer of 1793, the Committee began to take its definitive form, its membership becoming more stable, while growing from its original nine members to twelve.

Several of the twelve men on the Committee of Public Safety were there because of their expertise in specific areas – the army, the navy, the provisioning of Paris. The Committee already included two followers of Robespierre, including Saint-Just. The other was Georges Couthon, a former lawyer from central France whose health problems had left him unable to walk. The Robespierrists were not the far left of the Committee, however; that prize went to Billaud-Varenne and Collot d'Herbois, men from the Cordeliers club politically close to Hébert.

The Committee's legacy is one of terror, executions, and insistence on political purity – and rightly so, as Chapter 8 will show. But there was always something more mundane about the Committee's tasks as well.

Beyond Robespierre's call for a virtuous public, beyond Collot d'Herbois and Billaud-Varenne's calls for executions, lay the work of men who were committed to running the government.

The Committee's powers were extensive, but so were its tasks. The military victories of late 1792 and early 1793 were distant memories; Dumouriez's defection cast a shadow over discussions of war, of strategy, of generals. Still, the French push for war had not slowed down. Back in November 1792 the Convention had declared that it had the right to intervene anywhere people wanted to reclaim their liberty. The February conscription of 300,000 men, which had sparked the armed insurrection in the Vendée, had not gotten the army the 300,000 men it had expected. By May, less than one-third of the anticipated troops were in uniform.

During the spring campaigns, French troops were on their back heels – against the Austrians, who had teamed up with Dutch and English forces, retaken Belgium and pushed onto French territory; against the Prussians, who had retaken land lost to the French in 1792; and against Spanish troops, who had crossed the eastern Pyrenees.

In August, the tide would start to turn, in part due to the efforts of the Committee of Public Safety, in part through sheer luck. The Committee was doing what it could to help the war effort. On August 4 Lazare Carnot joined the Committee, and put all his energies toward organizing the army and rethinking its strategy. The allied forces had had the upper hand but had not been able to capitalize. One problem: the allies were not that allied. Each power still had its eyes on different parts of France to take over after the republic's defeat. If France's troops had been unable to capitalize fully until that point, it was in part because they were not much more unified than their opponents. Generals had their own strategies, their own approaches. The confusion in the capital had made such maneuvers possible. The centralization of power in the Committee of Public Safety put an end to this. As Thiers wrote, Carnot conceived of "vast plans, in which prudence was mixed with daring." With Carnot in charge, "generals could no longer ... each act on their own."[42]

Barère, meanwhile, was rallying the Convention's support for stricter measures in the Vendée. Though he had never had the following of a Danton, a Brissot, or a Robespierre, Barère remained influential. He had been a member of the Committee of Public Safety since its start, and it was in the name of the Committee that on August 1 he called for an end to any half measures the Convention might have been taking against its enemies, internal or external. "We need measures that are vast, prompt, and above all rigorous," he told the Convention. "We will have peace the day the interior is pacified, the rebels are overcome, the brigands are exterminated ... No more Vendée, no more royalty; no more Vendée, and the enemies of the Republic will have disappeared." The aim, for Barère, was not only military defeat, but something far more extreme: to exterminate this rebel race … humanity need not complain; the elderly, the women, and the children will be treated with the care required by nature and by society. Humanity need not complain; it is for its own well-being that we uproot the evil; punishing the rebels will help the fatherland.[43]

By the end of the day, the Convention had decreed a series of measures, aimed at attacking both royalism and religious opposition. Marie-Antoinette (the "woman who has been the cause of all of the evils of France," according to Barère) would be sent before the Revolutionary Tribunal. The royal tombs, just north of Paris, would be destroyed. And the Convention would adopt a scorched earth policy in fighting in the Vendée. "The forests will be chopped down, the rebel hideouts destroyed, the harvest cut down."[44]

This would not lead to an immediate turn in the fighting there. The Blues were not much more organized than they had been before; they were unable to capitalize much on the victory over the rebels at Nantes. The rebels' leaders began to fight among themselves as well. Other generals were unhappy with d'Elbée's leadership. Some of the soldiers bristled under his attempts to impose military discipline on an army whose volunteer soldiers were used to coming and going as they pleased. Still, the Vendéans would score a major victory on September 19 at the Battle of Torfou. Charette's forces again joined with the rest of the army, together defeating an army composed of the best soldiers the Blues had, troops that had been sent from the war against the allies to fight in the Vendée.

Since Barère's speech of August 1, since the announcement of the coming of the scorched earth approach to the Vendée, the rebels and their supporter had been preparing for the worst. Charette's soldiers had already avoided one confrontation; they had sought to avoid another in Torfou until their flight was barred by women who supported the rebels. "If you do not want to fight," the women said, "give us your weapons."[45] The men, chastened, returned to the fighting.

The war had reshaped the role that women played in the Vendée. As often happened during wartime, when men were off fighting, women took up more of the tasks at home. In many villages, women served on leadership councils set up as local governments. That said, one might see the period from the start of the fighting in the spring of 1793 until that October as the one period when men were most setting the agenda in the Vendée. For several years, women had been the ones hiding refractory priests, the ones most opposed to the arrival of constitutional priests, the ones who were most vocal in their opposition to the Revolution. When the fighting started, that changed. Some women did participate in the fighting on the rebels' side. (Other women participated on the republicans' side, and the Convention's decree calling for the scorched earth approach in the Vendée had also noted that "the law that expels women from the army will be rigorously executed;

191

the generals are responsible for this."[46]) Mostly, though, war was the work of men. Women would be targeted by both sides, raped and killed by both sides. Word spread of Barère's speech, of the threats to the forests and the crops. Word was probably not spreading of Barère's promise, and the Convention's decree, that women, children, and the elderly would be protected. The division of labor that had developed among rebel peasant communities in the early months of the fighting in the Vendée, with men fighting and women taking care of the farms and the homes, was breaking down. Hence the women's presence at the Battle of Torfou, pushing the men to fight harder. Women were starting to stay closer to the rebel army, worried about falling prey to republican soldiers.

The Battle of Torfou would end with the Blues retreating, the Whites happy with their victory but without the strength to chase down the retreating enemy. Small victories would follow, in the coming days. The council of the rebels would meet, and decide to go back onto the offensive. Some of the peasants would return to their fields; others who stayed would attend the mass given by the bishop of Agra – conducted with so much grace, according to de La Gorce, that "one could almost pardon him for blessing without the right."[47]

Back in Paris, not only the government but the people were concerned about the young republic's many battlefronts. It was in part to appease the radicals in Paris, and in part to deal with the threats the government faced, that the Convention went back to the issue of conscription.

It was conscription that had provided the spark in the powder keg of the Vendée, the decision to draft 300,000 men into the army. The Convention's decree of August 23 went far further:

> From this moment until the enemy is driven from the soil of the Republic, all Frenchmen are in permanent requisition for the service of the armies. The young men shall go to battle; the married men shall forge arms and transport provisions; the women shall make tents and clothing and shall serve in the hospitals; the children shall turn old linen into lint; the aged shall betake themselves to the public places in order to arouse the courage of the warriors and preach the hatred of kings and the unity of the Republic.[48]

The old republican and classical ideal of every citizen a soldier, every soldier a citizen, was now law. There was a place for all French people in the military effort, as well as the start of an attempt to clarify the proper roles in the war effort for men and for women.

The law was not only a call for the French people to take a greater role in the affairs of the republic; it was also one more step in the centralization of power in the hands of the Committee of Public Safety, which was "charged to take all necessary measures to set up without delay an extraordinary manufacture of arms of every sort," including requisitioning workers "within the entire extent of the Republic." And in the provinces, the representatives-on-mission were "invested with unlimited power."[49]

In the weeks following the Battle of Torfou, leaders of the Vendéan rebels continued to fight among themselves. The army began to change, as more non-combatants flocked to it, hoping for protection. The distinction between combatant and non-combatant had never been clear in the region – the countryside overwhelmingly supported the rebels and provided what assistance they could to those fighting. But in September and October women, children, priests, and the elderly started migrating to the army, leaving their villages, bringing their possessions and even their livestock with them.

On October 1, Barère would again address the Convention, would again call for an end to the civil war in the Vendée. "The Vendée should have been annihilated long ago," he said, but progress had been slow. The Convention's generals were not cooperating with each other; some soldiers were not behaving "as the armies of a Republic must." But the Vendée remained key, remained not only "the heart of the Republic" but the "refuge of fanaticism, where priests had raised their altars ... It is therefore in the Vendée that our enemies will attack; and therefore the Vendée deserves all of your attention." Barère repeated his claims that a victory in the Vendée would hurt not only the rebels there, but Austria and England, royalism and fanaticism. But now, there was little time: "it is there that we must strike, between now and 20 October, before the winter, before the routes become impassable, before the brigands find their impunity in the climate and the season."

Barère did not repeat his guarantees for the women, children, and elderly; "the whole population is in armed rebellion," he said, and "women are playing starring roles." And he repeated his call to "accelerate the destruction of the Vendée ... The brigands must be defeated and exterminated ... they must be chased from their own territory to bring them down."[50]

Barère would get something close to his wish on October 17, in the city of Cholet. One of the main cities in the Mauges, Cholet lies southeast of Nantes, roughly 25 miles south of the Loire River. There were around 40,000 rebel troops, led by d'Elbée and La Rochejaquelein, against 25,000 Blues, but the fighting would turn against the rebels as the day went on. When it was clear that the republican forces would win, the Vendéans – combatants, non-combatants – started yelling "à la Loire" – to the Loire. The entire procession, soldiers, women and children, the elderly, many carrying their possessions, all began the trek north to the river. All those who survived – and many, including d'Elbée, did not – headed north. A procession, tens of thousands heading to the river and somehow crossing it, as if reenacting Moses' parting of the Red Sea.

The rebels had succeeded in fleeing the armies. They had bought themselves some time. But they had left their home territory, the territory where they could fade in and out of view. They were now in Brittany, hardly hostile territory, but new. La Rochejaquelein, barely 20, became their chief.

On October 1, Barère had told the Convention that the republic needed to destroy the Vendée by the end of the month, and that the rebels had to be chased from their own territory. On October 20, back at the Convention, he would tell his fellow deputies that the war was over, that "the Vendée no longer exists."[51] The rebels had indeed been chased from their own territory. The war was not over, as Barère had thought; there would be more battles, including more rebel victories. But the rebel armies were on the run.

In Lyon, too, the revolt was coming to an end. Its revolt had lasted longer than Caen's; it had not revolted in the way that the Vendée had, but neither had it folded the way that Wimpffen's armies had. It had first revolted against the Convention in late May, when a mixed group of Girondin supporters and royalists had overthrown the Montagnard-led municipal government. In July they had guillotined the former head of the government, a Montagnard supporter named Chalier. Lyon had not been much of a threat to take over surrounding areas, and it was never able to ally with troops from Marseilles, the way that the Convention feared, the way that the local Girondin supporters hoped, but it took some time before the Convention was able to deal with the situation. Local inhabitants might not have been up for marching on Paris, but they were willing to defend their city. In August, the Convention's troops arrived outside of Lyon and started a siege. On October 8 Convention troops entered the city, led by Couthon, and reinstated the Montagnards.[52]

Back in Paris, the people and the government were happy to hear the news of Lyon – but not eager to forgive the Lyonnais. On October 12 the Convention decreed that Lyon would be destroyed, and that what remained would be renamed "Freed-Town." With shades of Isnard's threats against Paris, the Convention decreed that on the debris where Lyon had once stood, a plaque would read: "Lyon declared war on liberty; Lyon is no more."[53]

Lyon and the Vendée were facing far more retaliation from the Convention than Caen had faced. Soon after the failed march on Paris, the local government in Caen had declared its allegiance to the Convention and kicked out the exiled deputies. The Vendée and Lyon were given threats of annihilation and destruction (threats that, as Chapter 8 will show, were hardly empty). Part of the explanation lies in the nature of the conflict: in one case a fight that was brief and inconsequential; in the other case, a battle that was slow, long, bloody. But another part of the explanation lies in the attitudes of the men running the government, and in the attitudes of the women and men in Paris who were keeping such a close eye on the men running the government.

In the Girondins' absence, the Montagnard government had been able to pass laws that it would not otherwise have been able to. In June, the Convention had passed a new constitution, proclaiming "in the presence of the Supreme Being" that the republic was "one and indivisible."

The Constitution of 1793, sometimes known as the Constitution of Year I, confirmed France's status as a republic; its new Declaration of the Rights of Man established a full freedom of religion, and added that insurrection is "the most sacred of rights and the most indispensable of duties." The constitution also declared that "all Frenchmen are soldiers."

The purging of the Girondins, though, had not led to a unified government, and certainly not a unified Paris. New groups were fighting with each other; radicals who had helped the Montagnards against the Girondins were now finding that the Montagnards were not as radical as they had hoped. Jaurès, describing the mood in Paris at the time, wrote that

> this was no longer the generous spirit of 1790, nor the magnificent anger of 1792; it was sometimes a grandiose and bitter fury, sometimes also the bestial and vile need to relieve one's own suffering by making another suffer ... this was, alas, for much of the crowd, the temptation of these dark hours.[54]

For many in Paris – for the militants who attended the meetings of the sections; for the leaders of the sans-culottes; for the enragés, led by Roux; for the followers of Hébert; for the Society of Revolutionary Republican Citizenesses – the Montagnard government was not doing enough to combat the forces of counter-revolution. These groups were in many ways taking on the role that Marat had played for years. They were warning not just of real threats but of possible threats, not just of possible threats but of false, imaginary threats. But they had followings, they could not be ignored. They could be placated, they could be repressed, but they could not be ignored.

On September 5, crowds marched on the Convention, largely made up of sans-culottes. Robespierre now found himself facing the demands of the sans-culottes as a leading member of the government (at the time, he was not only a member of the Committee of Public Safety, but the Convention's president). "You have passed wise laws," Chaumette told the Convention on behalf of the Commune, "which promise happiness. But they are not yet executed." Chaumette called for the Convention to form revolutionary armies, to go after hoarders. "Let this army be followed by an incorruptible and formidable tribunal, and by the fatal instrument which at a single stroke severs both the conspiracies and the days of their authors."

Billaud-Varenne was among the first to reply to Chaumette and the demands of the crowd. He replied favorably, saying that "all your enemies must be put under arrest this very day ... if revolutions drag on, it is because only half-measures are ever taken." It was Danton, though, who once again put his stamp on the day, who once again showed his ability to mix fiery rhetoric with practical measures. He proposed – and it soon became law – that the sections would meet twice a week, rather than every day. "Industrious men who live by the sweat of their brow cannot attend the sections," he told the Convention, implying that aristocrats and other men of leisure could take them over. In reality, the threat was that militants would take over the sections, something that the Montagnards used to support, but no longer did. To keep the populist spin, Danton proposed – and it soon became law – that those who attended the sections would be paid.

There was one legacy of the day that may have had less immediate direct impact, but whose symbolic impact was huge. Barère, echoing earlier statements made by representatives of the Commune and the Jacobin club, told the Convention that they should adopt the "mighty slogan we owe to the Commune of Paris: *make Terror the order of the day* ... They want to destroy the Mountain. Well! The Mountain will annihilate them!"[55]

Many of the Terror's institutions were already in place: the Committee of Public Safety and the Revolutionary Tribunal in Paris, the representatives-on-mission in the provinces, along with the armies in the Vendée and, now, in Lyon. Soon after the Convention had declared that Terror was the order of the day, the Law of Suspects of September 17 declared that "All suspected persons within the territory of the Republic and still at liberty shall be placed in custody," including people who had "shown themselves partisans of tyranny or federalism and enemies of liberty," and "those who are unable to justify ... their means of existence and the performance of their civic duties."[56] On September 29 the Convention passed a law establishing price controls for items of "first necessity." This law, known as "the Maximum," covered a wide range of items, from meat to firewood, from writing paper to shoes. It also set limits on workers' wages.[57]

Finally, on October 10, the government officially suspended the constitution. "In the circumstances in which the Republic finds itself," Saint-Just told the Convention, "the constitution cannot be established. It would destroy itself." Instead, the government would be "revolutionary until peace," with more power vested in the Committee of Public Safety.[58]

In all of these moves, the government was giving the Parisian crowd what it wanted – or, at least, managing to make it look like that was what it was doing. Drafting laws, however, was not all that the government would do.

The start of the Terror

This was the start of the time of the guillotine.

Bloodshed was not new to the Revolution; violent riots had preceded the storming of the Bastille, and there had been many deaths since then. The war had upped the ante, and the civil war in the Vendée had meant that French citizens were now killing each other in large numbers. Deaths on the battlefield – whether at war with the rest of Europe, or in the civil war – would always outnumber deaths by guillotine, but deaths by guillotine were about to rise. The notable government executions, up to this point, had been few – Louis XVI, then Charlotte Corday.

In the fall of 1793, this would change. In late August, Custine, an army general deemed to have been too timid against Austria and Prussia, was guillotined. As Thiers wrote, Custine had on his record "many mistakes, but no treason ... he suffered the pain that they had been unable to inflict on Dumouriez."[59] After Custine came more calls for punishment of those already in prison, already out of power, but still breathing. Calls for the death of the Girondins and of other revolutionaries since passed by.

In mid-October, it was Marie-Antoinette, former queen, who sat before the Revolutionary Tribunal. Like her husband, she had to face accusations that spanned the length of the Revolution. She had to defend her actions during the flight to Varennes, even during the days preceding the Women's March to Versailles, when soldiers at the palace had trampled on the revolutionary cockade. "The cockade, if it existed," she told her interrogators, "was only the error of a few men."

During the interrogation, she presented herself as a wife who supported her husband. And she presented herself as she had in Varennes – as a mother. "My family is my children; I can only be well when with them." While she presented herself as a loyal wife, she was accused of "teaching Louis Capet the art of dissimulation with which he long tricked the good people of France," and of persuading the king to veto the laws against émigrés and refractory priests.

The former queen had to answer questions from several prosecutors, but it was Hébert whose questioning stood out. He brought back the old image of the queen, the one her Old Regime opponents had presented: the sex-crazed, incestuous woman. At Versailles, it had been accusations of orgies with the princesse de Lamballe, of incest with the king's brother. Now, it was accusations of incest with her own son. According to Hébert, "there is no doubt ... that there was an incestuous act between the mother and her son."

The queen replied with a question: "Did you see this?"

"No," Hébert replied, "but the entire municipality will guarantee it."

As the interrogation went on, one of the jurors noted that Marie-Antoinette had not replied to Hébert's accusations of incest. "If I have not replied," she said, "it is because nature refused a response to such an accusation made of a mother."[60]

It was not Hébert's accusations of incest that led to Marie-Antoinette's conviction by the Revolutionary Tribunal; they played a small role in the trial. If anything, Hébert's accusations earned Marie-Antoinette some sympathy, though not enough to save her. On October 16, she was led to the scaffold, and executed.

Hébert can be given some credit – or blame – for the Revolutionary Tribunal having brought Marie-Antoinette to trial in the first place. Hébert's newspaper, Le Père Duchesne, had been growing in influence since Marat's death. The paper had always been harsh on the queen, and had not stopped since the king's death – though other topics might have seemed to be more urgent, in the summer of 1793, than any possible conspiracy between foreign powers and the imprisoned and isolated queen. But in the summer of 1793, Hébert had been beating the drum for her trial and execution. In October, he not only got that trial, he was able to participate as part of the prosecution.

He beat the drum for other trials and executions as well, including the trial of the Girondins. "Quick, grease your pulleys," he wrote, as if addressing the executioner directly, "for this gang of scoundrels 500 million devils vomited on the earth, and who should have been suffocated in their cribs, dammit."[61] Before the month was over Hébert got his wish when 21 of the Girondins, including Brissot, Vergniaud, and Fauchet, were executed. They, too, had had their trial before the Revolutionary Tribunal, as Corday had, as Marie-Antoinette had.

From its start in March 1793, the Revolutionary Tribunal had accepted no appeals; its punishments were immediate. It was becoming clearer that political disagreement alone would be enough to be brought before the Tribunal. Corday – whatever one's view of Marat – had little to protest; she had entered a man's house and stabbed him in his bathtub. In Marie-Antoinette's case the accusations of incest were false, but she *had* corresponded with foreign powers, and the jury had reason to doubt her response that her correspondence only dealt with "ties of amity, and not politics."[62]

For the Girondins, the case was less clear. The Girondins on trial were, for the most part, those who had chosen to stay in Paris. For Louvet and the others who had fled, who had raised the flag of rebellion against the Convention, the case for treason was stronger; not for these men, though, who had been elected to the Convention, who had been purged from the Convention, and who had then remained in Paris. (Brissot had fled, but to central France, not to Caen, and had kept a low profile before being arrested and brought back to Paris.) For the Revolutionary Tribunal's prosecutor Fouquier-Tinville, though, while "one part of this faction was in Caen preparing an insurrection ... the other part stayed in Paris to support those infamous projects."[63]

Hébert, whom the Girondins had had arrested in May, now stood as an accuser. Chaumette as well, represented the Commune, arguing over old debates between the Commune and the Legislative Assembly during the events of August 10. The trial deliberations show more than a bit of personal vengeance, though the Girondins' main antagonist, Robespierre, did not take part. As the deliberations went on for several days, Hébert complained in his newspaper that the trial was becoming interminable. "And one asks, why are there witnesses? ... the proof of their crimes is evident." While the Tribunal had to follow the law, Hébert noted, "it's up to the Convention to make all these formalities disappear."[64] Fouquier-Tinville not only agreed, he read Hébert's column to the court.

Figure 7.2 The sentencing of the Girondins. The Girondin deputies, out of the Convention since May 2, 1793, learning they have been sentenced to death. From *Révolutions de Paris*. © Penn Special Collections.

That day at the Convention, Robespierre and Barère declared that during a trial, after three days, the prosecutor can ask the jurors if they have made up their minds; if so, the trial would end then. The following day the jury deliberated for three hours, before sending back a guilty verdict for all the defendants. They were executed the next day, singing *La Marseillaise* on the scaffold during the 31 minutes that it took to execute all 21 men.

On November 3, it was Olympe de Gouges' turn. If women can be brought up to the scaffold, she had written, they should be allowed to speak from the podium. Now she was brought to the scaffold, without having been allowed to speak from the podium. On November 7, the Convention executed Philippe-Egalité. His attempts to be just another Montagnard had failed, his Bourbon blood and his links with Dumouriez cause for enough suspicion to warrant his death.

On November 8, Madame Roland was executed. She could well have been executed with the Girondins as her "crimes" were inseparable from theirs. She told the Tribunal that, though her husband had been a minister, she had not really followed political matters, "because, being only a woman, she was not obligated to take part in them."[65] The jury did not believe her, sentencing her, too, to death. "I will gladly leave this poor earth, that devours good people and drinks the blood of the just." The people, she wrote, would soon become victims: "you will ask for bread, and they will give you cadavers, and you will finish as slaves."[66] Hébert had argued for her execution as he had argued for the queen's; Madame Roland was even able to hear what Hébert had to say about her from criers reading *Le Père Duchesne* outside her prison window. "Nothing was spared, not even physical distortion," she wrote. "I was described as a counter-revolutionary and a toothless hag who would do well to repent her sins before expiating them on the scaffold."[67] Her husband, who had never returned to Paris after the events of June 2, committed suicide upon hearing the news.

Bailly's turn came on November 11. It was a measure of how far the Revolution had come. In the aftermath of the taking of the Bastille, when the king visited Paris, it was Bailly who stood beside him as he put the revolutionary cockade on his head. As Vergniaud put it, "The Revolution, like Saturn, devours her children."[68]

Between October 1793 and the end of the year, 177 people were executed in Paris.[69] A small number, compared to what would come in 1794, or compared to what was going on in the Vendée. It was, however, a very large number compared to what had gone before. It was a new era of politics – Terror had indeed become the order of the day.

The months that would follow would be far bloodier – even in the Vendée, which had already seen far more blood than Paris. But some attributes of the Reign of Terror were already starting to become clear. The guillotine was becoming the penalty of choice, and the nature of crimes warranting the guillotine less exclusive. Political disagreement could bring a heavy price.

The immediate crises of the summer of 1793 were mostly gone. The federalist revolt was almost over (the city of Toulon, on the Mediterranean, would not be under the Convention's control until December, but Normandy, Bordeaux, Lyon, and all other centers of federalist activity were). The Vendéan army was on the run. The external war was the biggest problem, but there were signs of improvement in the French army, the number of soldiers was growing, and Carnot was centralizing the decisions. The Girondins were not only out of the Convention – they were dead.

These developments had not made it easy for the Montagnard government to run France. The different Montagnard factions were still fighting with each other; the people of Paris, particularly those who stayed active, who attended their sections, who protested in the street – they were still not satisfied with the way that things were going.

Some of the Revolution's most prominent women were executed at this time: Marie-Antoinette, Olympe de Gouges, Madame Roland. To a large extent, this was about these women's politics as much as their gender. Political changes had not helped their situations. Marie-Antoinette first, of course, but Olympe de Gouges, like Madame Roland, was a supporter of the Girondins and an opponent of Robespierre – and for some time, organized female political activism had been distinctly pro-Montagnard. In the spring of 1793, the Society of Revolutionary Republican Citizenesses had begun organizing women. Led by Claire Lacombe and Anne Léon, the Society had supported the Montagnards during their fight with the Girondins. In the post-Girondin politics, though, the Society faced a new set of problems. Though the Jacobin club had once given them "affiliated status" and space in which to meet, by September the Jacobins were becoming wary of the Society, particularly Lacombe, and particularly her association with Jacques Roux. The following week, the Convention decreed that all women were required to wear the revolutionary cockade. The Society's members made themselves into enforcers of this law, which did not earn them many friends among other Parisian women. When they tried to force women in the markets to wear it, a fight broke out, and many of the women in the Society were badly beaten.

The politics of the market women had always fit awkwardly with some aspects of the Revolution, and particularly with a group like the Republican Revolutionary Citizenesses. The market women opposed some aspects of the Revolution; they would at times protest on behalf of their imprisoned husbands, and many of them celebrated mass at Christmas, even in December 1793. Still, they found a way to mix their beliefs with aspects of the Revolution, such as praying for Robespierre when he was ill. Even as they beat up the women from the Society, they yelled out, "Long live the Republic!"[70]

In the aftermath of the fight, the Convention turned its attention to the Society. On October 30, the Convention issued a decree banning not only the Society, but all women's political clubs. Though one deputy had pointed out that he did not know "on what principle one could lean in taking away women's right to assemble peaceably," Basire replied that "it is only a question of knowing whether women's societies are dangerous. Experience has shown these past days how deadly they are to public peace." The Convention sided against women's right to assemble and decreed that "Clubs and popular societies of women, whatever name they are known under, are prohibited." The Convention also decreed that "all sessions of popular societies must be public."[71]

In recent years, scholars have offered a number of explanations for the Convention's decision to outlaw women's clubs. Some have seen it as evidence of the Revolution's inherent misogyny, or as a sign of the revolutionaries' embrace of a particularly male version of virtue and virility. Others have seen it as a sign of Rousseau's increasing influence, and his view of the importance of women playing domestic roles, while politics was the realm of men (though Madame Roland and Fauchet themselves were both dedicated followers of Rousseau).

The ruling itself had relatively few implications; there were probably only around 30 women's political clubs in France at the time, and few of them played a significant role in politics. The Convention's justifications for closing the clubs were justifications that had been heard often during the Revolution. A deputy named Amar had done most of the speaking, saying that "since the start of the Revolution, women, more enslaved by aristocratic and religious prejudices than men, have constantly been under the hands of the priests and the enemies of the state."[72]

The decision came, though, at a time when the Convention was cutting down on political dissent of all kinds.

Back in June, the Constitution of 1793 had called insurrection the most sacred right of a people. In October, though, the Convention had suspended that Constitution. Not only was the government now "revolutionary until peace"; there was no sign that peace was imminent.

The shutting of women's political clubs was not the end of female activism in the Revolution, only a small portion of which had ever taken place in those clubs. As fall turned to winter, though, the kinds of political activism that the government would accept became more limited and the Committee of Public Safety set more stringent standards for what was considered acceptable political behavior.

Notes

1 *The Memoirs of Madame Roland*, p. 31.
2 *AP* LXVI:7.
3 Thiers, *Histoire*, IV:191.
4 Quoted in Michelet, *Histoire*, II:470.
5 Louvet de Couvray, *Mémoires*, I:93.
6 *OP* X:6512.
7 *OP* X:6544.
8 *OP* X:6513, 6631.
9 Thiers, *Histoire*, IV:198.
10 Quoted in Doyle, *Oxford History*, p. 241.
11 *OP* X:6563.
12 Louvet de Couvray, *Mémoires*, I:114.
13 *Mémoires de Louvet*, p. 67.
14 Carlyle, *The French Revolution*, p. 652.
15 Walter, ed., *Actes*, p. 50.
16 Walter, ed., *Actes*, p. 51.
17 Carlyle, *The French Revolution*, p. 646.
18 Walter, ed., *Actes*, p. 60.
19 See Chapter 6.
20 Walter, ed., *Actes*, pp. 62–3.
21 Jean Yole, *La Vendée* (Paris, 1936), pp. 17–18; quoted in and translated from Reynald Secher, *A French Genocide: The Vendee*, trans. George Holoch (Notre Dame, 2003), p. 1.
22 De La Gorce, *Histoire Religieuse*, II:382.
23 Quinet, *Révolution*, I:522.
24 De La Gorce, *Histoire Religieuse*, II:416.
25 Quoted in François-Joseph Grille, *La Vendée en 1793* (Paris, 1852), III:5.
26 De La Gorce, *Histoire Religieuse*, II:460.

27 Quoted in Marcel Lidove, *Les Vendéens de 93* (Paris, n.d.), p. 91.
28 Quoted in Lidove, *Les Vendéens*, p. 105.
29 Michelet, *Histoire*, II:485.
30 Quinet, *Révolution*, I:523.
31 Michelet, *Histoire*, II:502.
32 Quinet, *Révolution*, I:531.
33 See Chapter 3.
34 Edgar Quinet, *Le Christianisme et la Révolution française* (Paris, 1984), pp. 237–8.
35 This account of the reactions to Marat's death draws heavily on Jacques Guilhaumou, *La Mort de Marat* (Paris, 1989), pp. 52–64.
36 Aulard, ed., *Jacobins*, V:303.
37 *OMR* X:257, 292–3.
38 Quoted in Guilhaumou, *La Mort*, p. 74.
39 Quoted in Guilhaumou, *La Mort*, p. 64.
40 Michelet, *Histoire*, II:542.
41 *OMR* X:65.
42 Thiers, *Histoire*, V:101.
43 *AP* LXX:90–104.
44 *AP* LXX:108.
45 De La Gorce, *Histoire Religieuse*, II:152.
46 *AP* LXX:108.
47 De La Gorce, *Histoire Religieuse*, II:158.
48 Baker, ed., *The Old Regime*, p. 340.
49 Ibid.
50 *AP* LXXV:420–6.
51 *AP* LXXVII:451–2.
52 See Paul Hanson, *The Jacobin Republic under Fire: The Federalist Revolt in the French Revolution* (University Park, PA, 2003), p. 218.
53 See Thiers, *Histoire*, V:94; Doyle, *Oxford History*, p. 253.
54 Jaurès, *Histoire*, VI:198.
55 Baker, ed., *The Old Regime*, pp. 346–51.
56 Baker, ed., *The Old Regime*, p. 353.
57 *AP* LXXV:321.
58 *AP* LXXVI:312–15.
59 Thiers, *Histoire*, 5:73.
60 Walter, ed., *Actes*, p. 149.
61 Walter, ed., *Actes*, p. 223.
62 Walter, ed., *Actes*, p. 129.
63 Walter, ed., *Actes*, p. 323.
64 Walter, ed., *Actes*, p. 325.
65 Walter, ed., *Actes*, p. 358.
66 Walter, ed., *Actes*, p. 375.
67 *Memoirs of Madame Roland*, p. 108.
68 Quoted in Carlyle, *The French Revolution*, p. 674.
69 Doyle, *Oxford History*, p. 253.
70 Martin, *Révolte Brisée*, p. 139; Levy *et al.*, eds., *Women*, p. 211.
71 *AP* LXXVIII:49.
72 *AP* LXXVIII:48.

8

THE REIGN OF TERROR
(FALL 1793–SUMMER 1794)

No one ever said the first four years of the French Revolution were not confusing enough. Starting in the fall of 1793 they get even more confusing.

Some brief corrections from the end of the last chapter are in order.

The Battle of Cholet did not occur on October 17, 1793, but on 26 Vendémiaire II. Bailly was not executed on November 11, but on 21 Brumaire II.

These dates come from the republican calendar, which the Convention had adopted in October. Until then, France had been using the Gregorian calendar – the familiar calendar of seven-day weeks and uneven months still in use today. The republican calendar replaced that schedule with a new system of 12 30-day months, each divided into three ten-day weeks, or *décades*. The remaining five days (six, in leap years) would come at the end of the 12th month.

The new calendar grew in part out of a larger move to standardize weights and measures. French peasants had long complained of the different measurements that existed in Old Regime France. The Revolution's reform of weights and measures resulted in the metric system, the system of grams, meters, and liters that still exists today. The metric system applied one set of weights and measures to all of France, just as the Decree of August 11, 1789 declared that one set of laws would apply to all of France, a more "rational" system based in the ideas of the Enlightenment.

The republican calendar shared some of those tendencies, especially its embrace of the number 10. Its main author was Gilbert Romme, a mathematician-turned-Montagnard politician, and never a fan of the Catholic Church. Grégoire would later write what was clear from the start: the republican calendar was "invented by Romme to destroy Sundays: that was his goal, he acknowledged it to me."[1]

The republican calendar did, indeed, get rid of Sundays. It got rid of Monday through Saturday as well, along with the saints' days and other holidays that shaped the agro-liturgical calendar. In its place came a new series of names and commemorations for every day of the year, designed by the Dantonist and poet Fabre d'Eglantine. Each day would commemorate something from the world of agriculture: fennel, rabbits, plows, etc. Rest days would no longer come one day out of seven, as with Sunday, but one day out of ten – on the tenth day, or *décadi*. Commemorations of the key events of the Revolution, including the storming of the Bastille and the execution of the king, became national holidays. Years would no longer be counted from the birth of Jesus, and January 1 would no longer be the start of the year.[2] Instead, all dates would be counted from September 22, 1792, the day the Convention proclaimed that France was a republic (and, as luck would have it, the fall equinox).

According to Fabre d'Eglantine, "a long usage of the Gregorian calendar has filled the memory of the people with a considerable number of images that it has long revered and which today remain the source of its religious errors."[3] The republican calendar was the revolutionaries' latest attempt to limit Catholicism's influence further. It was not the only one.

The religious situation in the fall of 1793 was not to anyone's liking: practicing Catholics found it harder and harder to practice their religion publicly; their opponents were upset that Catholicism still existed in France at all; and France's Jews and Protestants saw growing restrictions on their activities. Many Catholics lacked any official location where they could hold mass. Most priests had left their parishes, be they refractory priests sentenced to deportation or constitutional priests who left their positions due to the hostility of the population.

Some revolutionaries, though, believed the rag-tag remains of the refractory church still posed a mortal threat to the Revolution. Since March 1793, any priest who had been sentenced to deportation yet stayed in France could be executed, and as recently as October 21 the Convention had made it easier to sentence refractory priests to deportation. Yet some disobeyed the law and remained, preaching in private homes, hiding in forests, while tending to turn more of a blind eye to traditional unofficial practices than they might have under the Old Regime.

Nor was it smooth sailing for the priests who had obeyed the deportation orders. The laws called for priests to be sent to French Guyana or to the African coast, but the French government lacked the means to get them there. There were too few boats available, and English naval superiority made French sea travel difficult. In Bordeaux and La Rochelle, on the Atlantic coast, several boats at port became floating prisons for refractory priests – prisons that became breeding grounds not so much for conspiracy and sedition, as the revolutionaries feared, but for contagion and disease. Many priests imprisoned there did not survive.

Among constitutional priests, many were pressured to marry. Back in November 1792 Thomas Lindet, Robert's brother and a bishop in the constitutional church, had married and remained a bishop. His example was rare among bishops, less so among parish priests, of whom 4,500–6,000 married during the Revolution. The Constituent Assembly had been shocked in 1790 when Robespierre had suggested priests should marry; the Convention, however, put in place laws meant to defend married priests from disapproving bishops.[4]

By the fall of 1793, critics of Catholicism were attacking constitutional priests as well as refractory ones. Constitutional priests had to decide between the church and the Revolution, a decision many must have felt they had made in 1791 when they swore the oath to the nation. That was no longer enough, and they now faced pressure to renounce their faith. In late October the Convention forbade all priests from teaching. The following month it decreed that communes – the smallest unit of local government – had the right to renounce Catholicism altogether.

Given the overall politics of the Revolution, one might be tempted to label the entire event as one big wave of de-Christianization. The events known as de-Christianization, though, took place in October and November 1793 (Brumaire and Frimaire II). They began outside of Paris, though the capital would see some of the movement's most flamboyant examples.

In the Nièvre department southeast of Paris, the representative-on-mission, a former priest named Joseph Fouché, took advantage of the unlimited powers with which he was invested to do everything he could to attack Catholicism. Chaumette, a leader of the Paris Commune but a native of the Nièvre, was visiting at the time and also took part. Fouché held a "feast of Brutus" in the local church. In the following days Fouché criticized clerical celibacy and declared that morality was the only religion in France. At the entrances to graveyards he had signs placed reading "Death is an Eternal Sleep."[5]

Other representatives-on-mission followed suit. In some regions local activists pressured priests to renounce their faith, destroyed church buildings, and held mock ceremonies in churches and cathedrals. Grégoire would later complain that in schools, children were taught to make the sign of the cross in the name of Marat.[6] In Paris, Chaumette and the Commune led the de-Christianization movement, with the help of some of Paris's most prominent clerics. In mid-October Chaumette placed restrictions on public worship in Paris, prohibited people from selling religious objects, and removed all religious symbols from cemeteries. Soon dressing in clerical garb was illegal in Paris.[7]

Chaumette and the Commune were willing to go further than were the Convention or the Jacobins. Religiously, the Jacobins and most members of the Convention were a mixed bunch, with no shortage of former clerics, but they tended to view religion as a potential source of societal unity, and atheism as a recipe for chaos. Some form of deism – the belief that God had created the world, but did not intervene – was common among the deputies and the Jacobins. Chaumette and his allies went further, embracing atheism and mocking Catholicism.

Chaumette was becoming closer allies with a man named Anarchis Cloots, a wealthy German-born former noble who called himself an "ambassador of the human race" and the "enemy of God." Both men, meanwhile, were becoming closer to Gobel, the bishop of Paris. On November 7, Gobel addressed the Convention, where he renounced his position. "I became a bishop when the people wanted bishops," he told them. "I cease to be one, now that the people no longer wish to have them."[8] His vicars also renounced their positions that day. Many of the priests in the Convention, too, took the opportunity to renounce their vocation (going further than Gobel, who had renounced his position but not his faith). Sieyes even renounced his faith, although, as Quinet pointed out, "no one thought he had any."[9] The one exception: Grégoire, who refused to renounce his position as priest or as bishop. He was the leader of a church that the Revolution had created and since abandoned, but he was ready to go down with the ship, should it come to that.

Several days later, Chaumette and the Commune held a Festival of Reason in Paris's Notre-Dame Cathedral, with an actress representing Reason appearing on the altar. It was a strange ceremony, half attempting to replace one solemn ritual with another, and half mockery. Elsewhere, statues of Marat replaced states of the Virgin Mary. Sans-culottes paraded in clerical garb. After people across France attacked religious statues and churches, Grégoire would invent the term "vandalism" to describe the destruction.

Grégoire was not, however, the only prominent politician to resist the wave of de-Christianization. On November 21, Robespierre gave a speech at the Jacobin club attacking de-Christianization. He made no personal statement of faith. He even called himself a "bad Catholic." Robespierre portrayed the refractory church as exhausted. "Fanaticism is dying; I could even say it is dead," he told the Jacobins. But providence – a term he had used in the past – was alive and well, and helping to protect the social order. Noting that the Convention had not and never would outlaw Catholicism, Robespierre asked, "by what right can people threaten the freedom of religion, in the name of freedom, and attack fanaticism with a new fanaticism?"

Atheism, Robespierre told his fellow Jacobins, was "aristocratic."[10]

Robespierre's speech was not the end of de-Christianization in all of France, where representatives-on-mission still had the power to enact what policies they chose. Nor was it the immediate end of all de-Christianization in Paris; two days after Robespierre's speech, Chaumette ordered all religious buildings in Paris closed, declaring priests "personally and individually responsible for all troubles whose source comes from religious opinions."[11] But Robespierre had taken the wind out of the movement's sails. The new rituals and the cult of reason were gone. Robespierre had placed Catholicism under his protection, and in November 1793 that protection meant a great deal. Soon Chaumette relented, reopening the churches and announcing that he had never intended to hurt the freedom of religion, "as long as the exercise of that freedom does not harm society." Hébert, too – whom Robespierre had specifically targeted in his speech – added his endorsement of freedom of religion, though it was clear that he was backing down out of fear of Robespierre, not respect for any church. "There was a profound and intimate joy in the counter-revolution," wrote Michelet. "From then on, there was not one right-minded woman who did not add in a few words for Robespierre in her nightly prayers."[12]

Robespierre's intervention was not the only thing going against de-Christianization. There had been a fair bit of resistance, even among populations sympathetic to the Revolution, even among the sans-culottes.[13] Michelet, who wrote that the Revolution had failed to "sate the eternal hunger of the human soul," regretted that it had only tried to destroy religions, not to show that its negation of an arbitrary religion that favored the few was also the "affirmation of a religion of justice and equality for all."[14] For Aston, the de-Christianizers failed in part because they made no real attempt to appeal to women.[15] Chaumette had criticized women active in politics, asking "since when is it permitted to renounce one's sex? Since when is it decent to see women abandon the *pious* cares of their household, the cradle of their children, to come into public places, to the galleries to hear speeches?"[16] He had also criticized the women who still attended churches where they "breathed the cadaverous smell of the temples of Jesus" and who took pity on wounded soldiers from the Vendée who had fought against the Republic.[17]

For Quinet, though, the failure of the leading Jacobins – especially Robespierre – to support de-Christianization doomed the Revolution. The Committee of Public Safety, according to Quinet, "used its absolute power to make sure that the old religion did not endure any lasting damage. From there, one can say that the life force of the Revolution was employed to reduce the Revolution to nothingness."[18] It is not clear, though, that Catholicism emerged as unscathed as Michelet and Quinet believed. De-Christianization achieved its maximum impact not by smashing statues but by making sure that many parishes had no priests. By the spring of 1794, there may have been as few as 150 French parishes openly celebrating mass, compared to the tens of thousands that celebrated it before the Revolution.[19] This did not always mean a full abandonment of religious practice. In many churches, lay people led mass; women from the congregation took more prominent roles in the ceremonies than they had been able to do before the Revolution (or since, for that matter). Where there were refractory priests hiding in the woods, they would lead clandestine masses that could have the excitement of the forbidden and could make participants feel as though they were part of the primitive church (something that the Civil Constitution of the Clergy had intended, albeit in a very different way). Public displays of faith, however, were dangerous. In many places, they were even illegal.

For people who wanted to display their allegiance to the Revolution, however, there was no limit on ways to do so. Wearing the revolutionary cockade or the outfit of a sans-culotte remained fashionable, but during the Terror people went far beyond this. Towns changed their names to remove any trace of Catholicism or aristocracy, or to show their allegiance to the Revolution. Some 3,000 of France's 40,000 communes changed their names, some of them removing "Saint," or the name of a local noble family, others adding "Mountain" or "People." Children's names also began to reflect revolutionary values and heroes. There were fewer Pierres and Jeans, as couples named their children "Liberty," "Mountain," or "Marat."[20]

Political rivalries

De-Christianization was not the only issue where Robespierre would be able to influence the course of the Revolution. His authority was rising past what any politician had been able to accomplish during the earlier years of the Revolution. He was the most powerful voice in both the Jacobin club and the Committee of Public Safety. He was not, however, without his concerns. He never was.

The reasons for his attack on de-Christianization lay not only in the concerns he outlined during his speech at the Jacobin club; they also lay in the partisan politics of the Revolution in the early months of the Terror. De-Christianization was a policy Robespierre's rivals had started, and he understood that its success could mean their rise to the top of the political pile. For the first years of the Revolution, Robespierre had been on the left wing. He had represented the edge of sane politics – however radical his positions, he had the status of a former deputy to the Estates-General and the speaking habits of a former lawyer. Those farther to his left – Marat, Hébert, Roux, the sans-culottes, and local leaders – had stood outside the mainstream of political life and outside of the Assemblies.

Following August 10, 1792, the dynamic had changed. The Commune included not only Robespierre, but also Hébert and Chaumette. When the Convention began the following month, Robespierre and Danton were there, but so were men more radical than they, including Marat, Billaud-Varenne, and Collot d'Herbois.

As long as the Girondins were in the Convention, the different factions of the Montagnards could work together. Once the Girondins were gone, that became harder, then impossible. Marat's death made the extreme left more extreme but no less powerful. Jaurès, who did not hide his sympathies for Robespierre, wrote that once France had "escaped from the Girondin anarchy," Robespierre "must have asked himself if the Revolution would succumb to the anarchy of demagogues."[21]

Robespierre and his followers, once the far left, now found themselves in the center of political life. They were the most powerful faction, the ones setting the tone for the Committee of Public Safety's decisions. As Robespierre's most recent biographer writes, "Robespierre's standing on the Committee was such that he exerted a powerful overall sense of purpose and direction. There were many specific matters on which he did not have his way, but the key political statements were his."[22]

They were the center, too, in that they found themselves trying to out-maneuver rivals to both the right and the left. On the right lay Danton and his followers; on the left, the Hébertists. As with the Girondins, these were still not parties in the modern sense of the word. Danton commanded the allegiance of many politicians, though his behavior at times raised questions. His tendencies toward personal excess stood in stark contrast to Robespierre. While Robespierre never stopped stressing the importance of virtue for the republic, Danton's retort was "virtue is what I do every night in bed with my wife."[23]

Second wife, that is. Danton's first wife had died in February 1793, and he had married a younger woman in June. For a leading politician in a major nation during a time of crisis, Danton was distracted, his personal life pulling him in one direction, his politics in another. In early October he left for his hometown, around 100 miles east of Paris. When he returned on November 21 he had trouble regaining the influence he had enjoyed earlier.

To the left of the Robespierrists lay the "Hébertists," though, while that term has passed the test of time, it is not particularly accurate. Jaurès preferred the term "Cordeliers," which has its own ambiguities, given the Cordeliers' history and the prominent roles that Danton and Marat had played among them in earlier years. Still, as Jaurès notes, while "Hébert could stand in for the Cordeliers group" as the publisher of *Le Père Duchèsne*, "he was in no way the leader. A good journalist, but a mediocre politician, lacking in character."[24]

Still, Hébert's newspaper was a powerful force in politics, and Hébert himself had powerful allies. In the Committee of Public Safety, Billaud-Varenne and Collot d'Herbois were close to Hébert politically, as was the minister of war; many of the representatives-on-mission could be counted as "Hébertists" as well. They had a consistent base of power in Paris's Commune, where Hébert and Chaumette both held positions. This made the Hébertist faction powerful in Paris, and, as the Montagnards had shown in May, being powerful in Paris went a long way toward being powerful in all of France.

For the next several months, the main dynamic in politics was the struggle for supremacy between Dantonists, Robespierrists, and Hébertists.

Neither Danton nor Hébert, however, was in the Committee of Public Safety. While there were men in the Committee who were allies of those two men, Robespierre and his allies played the more prominent role in the Committee – and, through the Committee, in the country. And the Committee's role was still growing. On December 4 the Convention voted to increase the Committee's authority in France. Ministries were now only to pass on the Committee's orders, local governments were only to enforce those orders, and representatives-on-mission saw their roles significantly curtailed.[25]

Meanwhile, the Vendéan army continued to wander through Brittany, and through the regions east of Brittany, with many miles – and the Loire River – separating the rebels from their home turf. This was still the procession that had fled Cholet, part army and part exodus, with families carrying their belongings walking alongside armed soldiers. It was not the force that had threatened Nantes the previous summer, but it could not be ignored, and it had its military successes. The Vendéans, though, did not know where to go or what to do with themselves. They marched to the city of Laval, which they took over, but they could not stay long. The republican armies were chasing them, and the rebels' leaders – though they were having trouble making themselves obeyed – knew that the Blues would win a direct battle.

They decided to head north, further from their homes, toward the Atlantic Ocean and the city of Granville in Normandy, in the hopes that help would arrive there from England. They heard conflicting reports of English support being on its way. The rebels tried to communicate with England, but all official lines were cut and, by this point, most of the unofficial lines were as well. During the earlier months of the rebellion, and before they left their home region, the Vendéans had developed systems of communication that alerted local inhabitants to events, to danger. Here, though, north of home, telling truth from rumor was even more difficult – and helped lead them to the unfortuitous choice of traveling to Granville.

Choosing Granville was not inevitable. They could have stayed in Brittany, headed west, where there were few republican troops, the population was sympathetic to their plight, and coordinating with English troops would have been easier. They could have picked another town on Normandy's coast that was not so well defended. Granville was among the worst choices they could have made. They arrived there on November 14 but were unable to take the town, protected by its walls and by more republican soldiers than the rebels had anticipated. With few supplies and the weather turning colder, the Vendéans were in no position to hold siege on the town; with their eyes scanning the horizon, they saw no sign of English ships coming to their aid.

They returned toward the Loire, marching in the general direction from which they had come, weaker, hungrier, colder. A bit wiser, perhaps, about their bishop, who had come close to his previous home and been identified as merely a priest, and not a particularly stellar one.

The return trip toward the Loire went badly for the Vendéans. They reached the river at Angers, but failed to take the city or to get many people across the river. They headed back away from the river, northeast to the city

Map 8.1 The Vendéans' trek. Following the Vendéans' defeat at Cholet, they traveled north to Granville before returning toward the Loire.

of Le Mans, where they fought the republican troops on December 12. Roughly 10,000 rebels died in that battle. It was for all intents and purposes the end of the rebels as a military threat – the end that Barère had believed had occurred back on October 17. Eleven days later the Blues defeated what was left of the Vendéan army at the Battle of Savenay, further east but still north of the Loire. After that Battle, one general of the Blues bragged that he had "crushed the children under the hooves of my horses and butchered the women."[26] Some bands of soldiers remained after Savenay, but they numbered in the hundreds, at most. La Rochejaquelein would live until late January, Charette for several more years. This was the end, though, of the armies of tens of thousands of rebels taking over cities and defeating republican troops, the end of the Vendée posing a threat to the Revolution.

It was not, however, the end of the worries for the people in the region. In Nantes, the local government had begun the Revolution's bloodiest crackdown on counter-revolutionary activity. Jean-Baptiste Carrier, the representative-on-mission in Nantes, had arrived in October. His task was not an easy one. The city had been through a lot during the fighting in the Vendée. Its prisons were overflowing with former rebel soldiers, refractory priests, and other refugees; people worried that diseases would spread through the cells. It was Carrier's task to bring order to Nantes and its surrounding region, bring order to the most important city in the region, sitting along the Loire River.

The Loire – "What a revolutionary torrent," Carrier would say.[27] Though it had already played a key role in the war of the Vendée, Carrier would make a different, more gruesome use of it. On several occasions he placed prisoners on boats and set them out onto the Loire, where he had them sunk. These came to be known as "*noyades*," drownings.

De La Gorce, relaying the accounts from one priest who claimed to have survived the first *noyade*, told of priests in the boat, seeing the water start to pool at their feet, then kneeling in the water to pray and giving each other absolution. Four of the men managed to swim to the shore, though three of them were killed once they reached it.[28]

Other historians gave less positive views of the priests who died. Michelet thought that they had been the "true center, the real home of the counter-revolution," and that they had conspired with the women of the region to give orders.[29] Still, Michelet praised the men who stopped Carrier, local republicans who wrote to Robespierre of what was going on in Nantes, prompting Carrier's recall to Paris in early February.

There are no official counts of the dead from the *noyades*. Martin says the number was at least 4,000, with as many as 10,000 dying during Carrier's time in Nantes.[30] The *noyades* happened on several occasions, and while they were hardly secret for the people in Nantes, some of whom could hear the screaming, Carrier was careful to avoid leaving written traces. Stories spread not only of priests, but also of women and children being drowned in the boats. Stories spread, too, of "republican marriages" that Carrier invented, tying a man and a woman together and drowning them in the river – stories that not all historians have accepted. *What a revolutionary torrent, the Loire.*

Three weeks before Carrier's recall to Paris, the republican general Turreau began a new plan for a complete destruction of the Vendée, known as the "infernal columns." Their goal was to go through the entire region systematically and carry out the goals that Barère had announced back in August: destroy the region, its hideouts, its crops. The safeguarding of "humanity," the promises to protect the women, the children, and the enemy, were long gone. The troops destroyed villages, killed inhabitants and even farm animals. Many soldiers of the republic were angry at the rebels who had threatened the republic from within at the same time as it was under such threat from without. The anger fell hard on the women and children of the region as well. Just as politicians in Paris had long blamed women for supporting the church instead of the Revolution, republican soldiers who fought in the Vendée complained, "it's the women that are the cause of all of our problems. Without the women, the Republic would already be established, and we would be at home relaxing."[31] In one town south of Cholet, republican troops shot the men and then built a bonfire for the women and children. According to one witness, "once there were no more royalist women" to throw on the bonfire, "they turned to the wives of true patriots."[32] One general had written to another that "if you come across any peasants or any women in the areas where the columns have been ... shoot them. They are the partisans of our enemies, they are also spies."[33]

In earlier years of the Revolution, critics of the refractory church had argued that women were posing a threat to the Revolution, due to their credulity, their willingness to believe the stories priests were telling them. The last weeks and months of the fighting in the Vendée can be seen as a final revenge for that support. Women in the region fell prey to the republican soldiers. Soldiers in some of the divisions, though not all, along with powerful politicians and their minions, would take advantage of their situation to rape the local women, kill them, or both. It was, according to Martin, the "explosion of deadly rivalries between different revolutionary currents, against the backdrop of an affirmation of masculine power ... that left the path open to a regression in the relations between men and women."[34]

From the battles of the *Vendée militaire*, the wandering to Granville, the end at Le Mans and Savenay, the drownings in Nantes, and the infernal columns, the fighting in the region was not only a political event, or a religious or military event. It was a demographic event. In the early nineteenth century, one historian put the number of dead in the region at 600,000.[35] Martin puts it at perhaps half that: 250,000–300,000, not counting republican soldiers who died there.[36] In the aftermath of the fighting, towns like Machecoul lay devastated, as dogs and wolves wandered through the empty streets.

No other region matched the ferocity, or the death count, of the Vendée. No other representative-on-mission matched Carrier's collection of horrors. In looking at some of their activities, though, one might come to the conclusion that it was not for lack of trying.

In Lyon, Couthon had been in charge of punishing the city for its rebellion against the Montagnard Convention, but he proved insufficiently ruthless for the task. In November he was replaced, with both Fouché and Collot d'Herbois coming in – the latter promising that the Convention's enemies would be thrown into the Rhône River "so that along the two banks, at the mouth of the river ... they will terrify the ferocious but cowardly English with the omnipotence of the French people."[37] By April, they had condemned nearly 2,000 people to death. When the guillotine proved too slow they began having people shot – some by cannons – over open graves outside the city. (Nantes had its *noyades*, Lyon had its *cannonades*.) Many of the people killed were supporters of the Girondins. There were also 100 priests among those executed. The constitutional bishop, a former deputy to the Legislative Assembly named Lamourette, was arrested and sent to the Revolutionary Tribunal in Paris, then executed in January. Critics of the repression in Lyon tended to place the blame on Collot d'Herbois, some even suggesting that it was a measure of personal revenge for the struggles he'd had there as a playwright in the years before the Revolution. But the stakes and the politics of Lyon's uprising and subsequent repression were, as its most recent historian has noted, "extraordinarily complicated." The citizens of Lyon were not as opposed to the Convention's politics as it might appear; by the time of the repression, though, the city had not only been through a siege, but had executed the local Jacobin leader – from which point "the die was essentially cast."[38] For any politician not to reply harshly would have put him at risk upon his return to Paris.

Leniency could be dangerous. In Bordeaux, the representative-on-mission was a man named Tallien, who, by the standards of normal life, was no slouch when it came to terrorism: his government had sentenced 104 people to death, including the mayor. Still, he was recalled to Paris and accused of being a moderate. Not that his conduct was beyond reproach – he had taken as a mistress a former noble who had been in a Bordeaux prison since the passage of the Law of Suspects, creating a scandal and leading people in Bordeaux to claim that she was influencing Tallien's policies. Tallien obeyed his recall, returning to Paris. His mistress followed him, and was re-arrested.

Robespierre's political morality

As with the de-Christianization movement, none of this was to Robespierre's liking. He had a particular view of what France should look like, of how French people should act in the new republic. Politics, for Robespierre, was a question of morality – and morality a matter of politics.

Mixing morality and politics was not new. Many of the accusations against Marie-Antoinette had been about her supposed debaucheries. But one of the paradoxes of the Revolution was its embrace of a relatively prim sexual morality during a time of a declining role for any sort of official religion, particularly Catholicism. For Voltairians, who liked to poke fun at the debaucheries of wayward priests and bishops – some real, most exaggerated – this made sense. But Old Regime society had been one where state and church worked together to enforce codes of morality, and the lines between sin and crime were not always clear. Many of the priests who had come to Versailles for the Estates-General in 1789, even when they sympathized with the third estate, still hoped to be able to bring about a moral regeneration of the nation based on Catholicism.

The Revolution had removed any legal backing to the church's role in enforcing morality. For Robespierre, though, the goal of a moral regeneration of France was not gone. It was still there, but it was in peril.

Robespierre had always held these views. He had not always held so much power. From the late fall of 1793 into the summer of 1794 – a period roughly equivalent to year II in the republican calendar – when Robespierre was most influential, his views and even his personality played a large role in shaping the course of the Revolution. Just as Louis XVI's hesitations and indecisions had helped shape the course of the Revolution's early years, Robespierre's strict morality and lack of perspective would help shape the course of the Terror.

In a speech he gave on February 5, 1794 before the Convention, Robespierre set out what he called the "principles of political morality." The first rule of political conduct, he told his fellow deputies, "ought to be to relate all your efforts to maintaining equality and developing virtue ... that which is immoral is impolitic, that which is corrupting is counter-revolutionary." When Robespierre complained of a representative-on-mission who "pushed his delirium to the point of commandeering women for his own use," he was not only pointing to the sort of behavior that any normal person would criticize, but arguing that such behavior posed a threat to the Revolution. For the republic to succeed, the people – and especially the leaders – would have to "substitute morality for egoism." They would have to make virtue the guiding principle in their lives.

His idea of virtue, though, was not soft or kind:

> If the mainspring of popular government in peacetime is virtue, amid revolution it is both virtue and terror: virtue, without which terror is fatal; terror, without which virtue is impotent. Terror is nothing but prompt, severe, inflexible justice, it is therefore an emanation of virtue.

In identifying the threats to the reign of virtue, Robespierre pointed in his speech less to the foreign armies France was fighting than to his rival parties among the Montagnards, whom he now called France's "internal enemies" who "march under the banners of different routes" but who both worked toward the triumph of tyranny. "One of these two factions" – and everyone in the Convention would have understood that he was discussing the Dantonists – "pushes us toward weakness"; the other – the Hébertists – toward excess. "The one wants to change liberty into a frenzied nymph, the other into a prostitute."[39]

Whether the Dantonists were pushing the Revolution toward "weakness" is an open question. Danton, since his return to Paris, had been arguing for a slowdown in the Terror. In the first months of 1794, the Revolution was not facing the threats that it had faced in the summer of 1793. But how safe was it? There were no imminent crises along the lines of the fall of Verdun, but France was not as secure as it would be by the summer. The internal threats were not at the level of the federalist revolt or the civil war in the Vendée. Danton and his allies – including Fabre d'Eglantine, Camille Desmoulins, Basire, and Chabot – felt that the time had come to lessen the rigor of the government's policies. At one point, Chabot and Basire, along with a deputy named Thuriot, had argued that any deputy brought before the Revolutionary Tribunal should be able to defend himself.[40] A reasonable proposal, but one that could seem, during year II, like a sign of weakness.

Few, however, would dispute Robespierre's claim that the Hébertists were leading the Revolution toward excess. In early 1794, though, they were a major force in political life.

Robespierre was faced with a dilemma: he could ally himself with the Dantonists, look beyond their corruption and their "indulgence" in order to strike a blow against the Hébertists; or he could ally with the Hébertists to take out Danton and his followers. Robespierre and the Committee of Public Safety wound up going after both factions. Danton and Hebert, along with many of their allies, would soon be brought before the Revolutionary Tribunal on questionable charges. As Jaurès put it, "Robespierre had the acute premonition of his terrible role. He would be the one responsible for spreading death left and right; he would be the one to balance the scaffold. He felt himself becoming the center of gravity of the guillotine."[41]

On March 21 the trial began for Hébert and some of his closest allies.

They were not Hébert's most powerful allies, or even the ones with the most blood on their hands. Collot d'Herbois and Billaud-Varenne were not on trial, remaining key members of the Committee of Public Safety; nor were any of the representatives-on-mission who shared Hébert's approach – Carrier, Fouché. Nor was Chaumette, as the alliance between him and Hébert had dissolved in recent months. Other men who had led the cult of reason were there, though, including Momoro, whose wife had played the part of Reason in the festival at Notre-Dame. Momoro had been the one who had convinced the then-mayor of Paris, Pache, to have "Liberty, Equality, Fraternity" inscribed on the walls of Paris's buildings. The inscriptions would survive the Revolution; Momoro would not. Nor would Cloots, the "ambassador to the human race" who had arrived from his native Germany to take part in the Revolution, but whose foreign roots and foreign fortune made him suspect, and whose views seemed too close to atheism for Robespierre and his followers. Robespierre had claimed that atheism was aristocratic – and Cloots, for all of his belief in equality and the Enlightenment, seemed guilty on both counts.

On March 24, Hébert and his allies were executed. Cloots remained calm on the scaffold, confident that while he would die, "the idea cannot." Hébert was in tears. The crowd that witnessed the execution, though, was pleased. One police agent there wrote that huge numbers had gathered for the occasion. "Joy and pleasure were on people's faces ... people were saying 'we would have thought that Hébert would have showed more courage ... the Girondins stood at the guillotine with more firmness.'"[42] As Quinet noted, "the people did not feel sorry for any of its leaders, even the most beloved, when the time came for them to ascend the scaffold."[43]

Several days later Condorcet was arrested. His "illegal" status dated from mid-July when Chabot had accused him of being an enemy of the republic. Condorcet had stayed hidden since then, even writing one of his most famous works, A Sketch of the Progress of the Human Spirit. The book finished, he emerged from hiding and was soon arrested. He poisoned himself while in captivity rather than die at the guillotine. He had started the Revolution as one of France's most prominent intellectuals. Intellectual prominence, though, had not saved Bailly, and it did not save Condorcet. Nor would it save France's most prominent chemist, Lavoisier, who would die several months later, with instructions to his students that they count how many times his eyes blinked after his head was severed.

In the aftermath of the Hébertists' trial, all eyes turned toward Danton and his followers. Danton had been advocating a relaxation of the Terror. "The people want Terror to be the order of the day, and they are right," he had told the Convention in November 1793. But the Terror should be aimed at "aristocrats, egoists, conspirators and traitors," not those who are merely weak. It was time, Danton said, to be "sparing of human blood."[44] He thought that the war might finally give way to peace, even if it was not a revolutionary peace that brought freedom to oppressed peoples; he thought, as the historian Palmer put it, that they could create "a vague and broad republic, in which men of all kinds, good and bad, sound and tainted, might, after disposing of irreconcilable extremists, join together by not arguing over principles." It was, as Palmer wrote, the promise of a "broad and comfortable way," as opposed to Robespierre's "straight and narrow."[45]

Retreat, though, could be tricky; acknowledging the possibility for a relaxation of laws meant that the government – particularly the Committee of Public Safety – would have to relinquish some of its power, which it was not eager to do.

It did not help matters that Danton and his followers had some other questions to attend to. Danton's potential corruption had long been a question, though one that up to this point had not caused him too many problems. Among his allies, however, corruption was doing more harm. Fabre d'Eglantine had been implicated in several scandals, and the wealth he had accrued during the Revolution – from his pen, he had told the

Jacobins – seemed suspect at best. Chabot, the former monk, was now married to the sister of an Austrian baron who had brought quite a dowry with her into the marriage, and whose two brothers were Austrian spies.

Camille Desmoulins, too, had moved closer to Danton. He had long been associated with Robespierre, as the two had known each other since their school days. While Robespierre had since grown up to become a successful lawyer before becoming a revolutionary, Desmoulins seemed not to have grown up at all. He went by his first name, Camille, unlike other politicians. Desmoulins was a talented writer, though, and quite witty, especially when compared to Robespierre's constant seriousness. When he began a newspaper named *Le Vieux Cordelier* (*Old Cordelier*) in December 1793, Desmoulins' first targets were the de-Christianizers. Soon, though, he began satirizing the Revolution (and, by implication, Robespierre), comparing it to the worst days of the Roman Empire, even writing, "you want to remove all your enemies by means of the guilliotine! What folly!"[46]

Robespierre, who had always had a thin skin, was sensitive to this sort of attack. He was particularly sensitive to satire, and to the "conspiracy of comedy," as Michelet pointed out: "The powerful head of the Jacobins ... understood that the mystery of his power lay in seriousness, and that if France lost its seriousness for a minute, the fascination would end, his prestige would vanish, and all would be lost."[47] Desmoulins kept poking at Robespierre, though, writing about him in his newspaper and arguing against him at the Jacobin club until the Jacobins expelled him. Danton, meanwhile, remained calmer than he should have. "I know they want to arrest me," he told his allies, "but they will not dare to."[48] Yet they did dare.

The trial of Danton and his allies began on April 2. The case against Danton himself was weak. The cases against some of the other 13 defendants were stronger, and some of the men tried alongside Danton were there to make Danton guilty by association. The Committee of Public Safety had put a lot on the line in calling for Danton's arrest; not only would Danton be the most significant execution since Louis XVI, but one of its members, Hérault de Séchelles, was among the defendants. The Revolution's "other" committee, the Committee of General Security, had also called for the arrests of Danton and his allies, and had as much at stake as the Committee of Public Safety. Though the Committee of General Security was overshadowed by Public Safety, its role in overseeing the police and the prisons was making it more prominent under the Terror.

Danton, on trial, looked for a way to make himself heard.

Fouquier-Tinville, the prosecutor, found himself unable to compete with Danton, and needing help from the two committees. Danton was one of the Revolution's great orators, capable of speaking all day. This posed a threat: Danton could convince the jury in a way that other defendants had been unable to. He seemed more the accuser than the accused. When asked where he lived, he replied that soon his name would be in the

Pantheon, and he reduced to nothingness. Desmoulins, when asked his age, replied, "33. The same age as the sans-culotte Jesus-Christ, when he died."[49]

The trial was turning Danton's way. So the two committees – via the Convention, which by this point was too scared to stand up to them – ordered him to shut up. Saint-Just pushed through a measure declaring that if there was any "attempt to trouble the public tranquility, or to impede the workings of justice," those responsible would not be allowed to participate in the discussions. In other words, Danton was still on trial, but he was no longer allowed to defend himself.

Vadier, a member of the Committee of General Security, had informed Fouquier-Tinville of the new ruling, telling him that "we have the scoundrels."[50] The trial would continue, but without defense it was even less legitimate than it had been, even less legitimate than the Girondins' trial had been. But, then, the Revolutionary Tribunal was Danton's own creation.

"Do not forget to show my head to the people," Danton told the executioner as he stood on the scaffold on April 5. "It is a good thing to see."[51]

Explaining the Terror

At one time, "Danton or Robespierre" was one of the great debates among historians of the Revolution. Robespierre's supporters pointed to the desperate straits in which the Revolution had found itself in 1793 and the inadequacy of Danton's response; they also compared Robespierre's probity with Danton's corruption, as Danton had made himself rich during the Revolution through questionable means. Danton's advocates pointed to Robespierre's excessive dogmatism, the carnage that would follow Danton's fall, and the need to humanize the Terror. Chief among Danton's defenders was Alphonse Aulard, who in 1885 became the first historian to hold the chair of History of the French Revolution at the Sorbonne, one of France's most prestigious universities. Aulard considered Danton the man who could have saved the Revolution. Danton's fall and Robespierre's rise, then, became the moment when the Revolution went too far. Aulard's most important student – and eventual successor in the chair – disagreed. Mathiez, in an ongoing debate with Aulard, devoted much of his career to advocating on Robespierre's behalf, and no small amount of time and effort to casting doubt on Danton's legacy.

Before Mathiez and Aulard, Michelet had also been critical of Robespierre, whom he referred to as "the tyrant," though he did not see Danton as the savior. In one passage Michelet addressed the reader directly, writing that "we must not leave our readers uncertain about the path that we would have taken, if we had sat in the Convention ... we would have been Montagnard, but not Jacobin."[52] For Jaurès, though, such a claim was a "loophole," and missed the gravity of the situation that the revolutionaries faced. "I am with Robespierre," Jaurès wrote, "and it is next to him that I would sit."[53] If these debates have faded, it is more a result of distance from the events than from any sort of resolution. Two recent English language biographies of Robespierre are a case in point, with one historian arguing that "Robespierre was a police boss and France a police state," while the other describes him as a man "not prepared to compromise the principles of 1789 in order to achieve stability, and in that lay his greatness and his tragedy" – while calling Danton's attempt to soften the Terror "courageous and humane, but stunningly inept, since the crisis was plainly far from over."[54]

Beyond the debates over Robespierre lies a larger debate – that of the origins of the Terror as a whole. The French Revolution, after all, had begun as an attempt to turn France into a constitutional monarchy, not a republic, and certainly not the radical republic of year II. Defenders of the radical Revolution – whether supporters of Danton or Robespierre – tend to point to the circumstances that the Revolution faced. As it progressed, it became necessary to centralize the government and clamp down on opposition. Between the civil war, the external war, and the problems posed by radicals in Paris, the niceties of parliamentary politics became a luxury that the Revolution could not afford. By that logic, the developments of the Revolution, from the execution of Louis XVI to the expulsion of the Girondins to the execution of Danton, were necessary to prevent France from imploding. Again, historians supportive of the Revolution will argue over which of these acts were, and were not, justified by the circumstances, though most stop short of defending the September Massacres or the *noyades*, and some find ways to blame Robespierre and his allies for such events while others seek to absolve him.

For other historians, though, the Terror was inherent in the Revolution from the start. By embracing the philosophy of the Enlightenment and doing away with tradition, the revolutionaries – even when they were writing the Declaration of the Rights of Man – were paving the way for the tyranny of the Committee of Public Safety (and even, in some accounts, the tyranny of the Bolsheviks). This interpretation had started even before the Terror had, with the writings of Edmund Burke, whose 1790 *Reflections on the Revolution in France* had set the tone for early criticisms of the Revolution. Other conservatives would pick up on these themes throughout the nineteenth and twentieth centuries, with the most recent accounts focusing on the ideologies of the revolutionaries.[55]

The disagreements tend to be as much about politics as they are about history. To defend the Revolution of 1794 is to stake out a position on the far left of the political spectrum; to attack 1789 is to stake out a position on the far right. The "theory of circumstances" does have much to recommend it, as the Revolution was indeed at risk in the summer of 1793. Those circumstances, however, were in many ways the Revolution's own doing.

The week after Danton's execution, as if cleaning up loose ends, a hodge-podge of 19 Hébertists and Dantonists were executed together. Included were Hébert's widow, a former nun, and Desmoulins' 24-year-old widow.

Chaumette and Gobel were also executed in this group. Chaumette still represented the legacy of the failed cult of reason. Gobel carried with him the double stain of having taken part in the constitutional church and then abandoning it. His sentence was, for Michelet, "a lesson to priests not to become revolutionaries" – and a chance for refractory priests to laugh at his fate.[56]

Robespierre's own religious views were rather complicated. As a "bad Catholic" who opposed atheism, Robespierre would have had to create a religion from scratch in order to help realize the virtuous society he had envisioned. Now that his main rivals were gone, though, he could do just that.

In the aftermath of the purges of the Hébertists and the Dantonists, Robespierre and his allies were able to consolidate their power. The Revolutionary Tribunal had been under their control for some time. The deaths of Hébert and Chaumette meant that the leadership of the Commune went to a man named Payan who had long been faithful to Robespierre. In April, Robespierre gained control over a new police force, even though that violated the Committee of General Security's jurisdiction. The sans-culottes were not the force they had been, having achieved many of their aims; and, as Doyle puts it, "many former 'blood-drinkers' were now in effect government employees."[57] Soon most of the political clubs would close, except for the Jacobins.

Saint-Just put it best: "the Revolution is frozen."[58] All of the main factions had been taken out except for Robespierre's. Since 1789, it had been the people's actions that had pushed the Revolution forward: on July 14, 1789, on August 10, 1792, on June 2 and on September 5, 1793. Now, the people were without their leaders. Robespierre was a man of the government, was *the* man of the government, and would not be leading any more insurrections against it. Hébert, Marat, even Danton were gone. In February Roux had committed suicide while in custody. The Jacobin club was becoming Robespierre's echo chamber. The sections were no longer the force they had been, since Danton had changed their meetings to twice-weekly. Other deputies feared for their own lives, and were not eager to rise up in protest. As Thiers wrote, the Committee of Public safety was acting in the middle of a "universal dissolution of all authorities." As a result,

> it could not reorganize without gaining power, or do good without adding its own ambitions. Its most recent measures were profitable to it without doubt, but were also prudent and useful ... but it was approaching the moment when ambition alone would reign, and where the interests of its own power would replace that of the state.

Within the Committee, Robespierre did not make all of the decisions, and he remained unaware of many day-to-day details. But when it came to major moral and political issues, the other men in the Committee "saved those subjects for him, as those most worthy of his talent and his virtue."[59]

Robespierre's personal apotheosis came on June 8, 1794, at the Festival of the Supreme Being. It was 20 Prairial according to the republican calendar – a *décadi*, and therefore a day of rest. It was also a Sunday – and not just any Sunday, but the day of Pentecost (sometimes called Whitsunday), a key day in the Catholic liturgical year.

The festival took place throughout France, at least where the men running the departments were faithful supporters of Robespierre – even if the differences between the atheistic cult of reason and the deist cult of the supreme being were lost on some of the attendees. Not that Robespierre's religion was on the verge of taking over France: one anonymous woman in the city of Auxerre, when asked why she was not taking part, replied: "It's not your God I adore. He's too young. It's the old one."[60] By all accounts, however, the festival was a joyous event – particularly in Paris, where perhaps half a million people attended on a beautiful day. One biographer called it the happiest day of Robespierre's life, which seems likely.[61] Robespierre gave two speeches that day, the first one by the Tuileries.

The speeches indicate Robespierre's goal in the festival, and in his creation of the cult of the supreme being. He was not trying to recreate either the constitutional church or the Catholicism of the Old Regime. As Robespierre had told the Convention several weeks earlier, "How different is the God of Nature from the God of priests!"[62] Robespierre was trying to create a religion that would provide unity to the divided nation, and that would instill a love of virtue among the people. He expanded on these beliefs in his speech at the festival:

> Liberty and virtue issued together from the breast of the divinity. One cannot reside among men without the other. Generous people, do you want to triumph over all your enemies? Practice justice and render to the Divinity the only form of worship worthy of him. People, let us surrender ourselves today, under his auspices, to the just ecstasy of pure joy. Tomorrow we shall again combat vices and tyrants; we will give the world an example of republican virtues.[63]

Robespierre then lit on fire a cardboard statue symbolizing atheism.

The second part of the festival took place at the Champ de Mars, a bit less than a mile away. As the current president of the Convention – and, frankly, as the Man of the Moment – Robespierre led the Convention's procession from the Tuileries to the Champ de Mars.

One thing about Robespierre: by the standards of the eighteenth century, he was rather fit, even in April 1794, when the strain of almost five years of near-constant revolutionary activity was draining his energy. His diet was as austere as the rest of his life. He drank little. He walked frequently, both to get where he needed to go and as a way of thinking through issues that troubled him. Many of his colleagues ate far more and walked far less. As Robespierre led the procession, his pace fluctuated. Whether out of habit or impatience, he would walk up ahead, opening a gap between himself and his fellow deputies, then slow down, to close the gap; but once closed, the pattern would begin again. Some deputies viewed this as Robespierre's haughtiness, his distance from the rest of the deputies.

Robespierre had always acted a bit like a priest, but the festival, where he presented himself as a religious leader, brought out his priestly traits even more. Just as Condorcet had explained Robespierre's popularity with women as "a priest who has his devotees," Robespierre accorded women a prominent place in the festival, telling them: "women of France, you are worthy of the world's love and respect! What have you to envy the women of Sparta? Like them, you have brought heroes into the world, heroes who are devoted to the fatherland with a sublime abandon."[64]

Some deputies were less impressed by the festival than were the rest of the crowd. Robespierre could hear them snickering. One of them – the Dantonist Thuriot – was heard to say, "Look at the bugger. It is not enough for him to be master. He has to be God."[65] Deputies were not eager to oppose him openly. Why would they be? So many of their colleagues had opposed him and died as a result. But many were not pleased with the festival.

The people who attended were pleased with the festival, though part of that joy came from a misunderstanding of what it meant. *"Let us surrender ourselves today, under his auspices, to the just ecstasy of pure joy. Tomorrow we shall again combat vices and tyrants."*[66] On the day of the festival, the guillotine had been given a rest, and moved out of sight. People thought that the festival represented an end to the executions, but the guillotine would reappear the next day, simply moved further east to the Faubourg Saint-Antoine, its work about to get far busier.[67]

Two days after the Festival of the Supreme Being, the Convention – with Robespierre and the Committee's strong backing – issued the Law of 22 Prairial. That law streamlined criminal procedures for the Revolutionary Tribunal, whose procedures were already quite minimal. Since the Girondins, the ability for defendants to argue their case had been limited; since Danton, more limited still. Since the Law of Suspects, the previous September, the criteria for being brought before the Revolutionary Tribunal were vast and vague; now they were more vague and more vast. Among those now deemed "enemies of the people" were

> those who have ... sought to disparage or dissolve the National Convention and the revolutionary and republican government of which it is the center ... Those who have sought to inspire discouragement ... Those who, by whatever means or by whatever

appearances they assume, have made an attempt against the liberty, unity, and security of the Republic.

If there was sufficient proof – either "material" or "moral" – then there would be neither witnesses nor any counsel for conspirators.

The only penalty was death.

The impact of the law was immediate. During the 17 months from March 1793 through July 1794, 2,627 people were guillotined in Paris. Of those, 1,376 were executed in the 47 days following the passage of the Law of 22 Prairial. The rate of executions jumped from just under three executions per day to more than 30.[68] Fouquier-Tinville began trying people in larger and larger groups, until he had prepared an amphitheater with the intention of trying 160 people at once – with the guillotine in the room with them. The Committee of Public Safety did put a stop to this, but the limit it set – "only" 60 defendants at once – indicated how hasty the process was. Fouquier-Tinville claimed that Paris's prisons would soon all have signs at the door reading, "house for rent."[69]

Meanwhile, news from the war would once again help transform the Revolution. The campaigns of 1794 had never posed the threats to the Revolution's existence that the campaigns of 1792 and 1793 had. In theory, they should have: France faced an impressive set of opponents in Austria, Prussia, Holland, England, and Spain. As Blanning points out, however, the allied forces seemed to have learned nothing from earlier campaigns, while Carnot and the French armies had learned quite a bit.[70]

On May 18, French armies defeated allied troops in Tourcoing, a town near France's northern border. This was a key victory for the French, and a key defeat for Austria. Austria had not fought alone against the French; there were British troops as well, and the duke of York, son of King George III barely avoided capture. It was Austrian territory, though, that was most threatened by French forces, and after Tourcoing, many Austrian leaders felt that Belgium was lost. On June 25 at the Battle of Fleurus, the French defeated the Austrian forces again, opening up all of Belgium for French conquest and making the foreign invasion of France, already scarcely a possibility, even more remote.

In earlier years, military developments had radicalized the Revolution. The defeats in the summer of 1792 had led to the revolt of August 10 and then the September Massacres; conscription had sparked the fighting in the Vendée, which in turn had helped lead to the Girondins' expulsion.

Victory was different, though. Tourcoing and Fleurus were different. It was no longer a case of military defeats bringing into question an insufficiently radical government; military success brought into question an overly radical government. On October 10, 1793, Saint-Just had declared that the government would be revolutionary until peace. Fleurus did not mean peace;

no lasting peace would come for another 20 years. But Fleurus did mean that the threat of invasion was over. The Terror was not. And more people began to ask why.

On June 29 – soon after the happiest day of Robespierre's life, and just three days after the French victory at Fleurus – Robespierre quarreled with Billaud-Varenne, Collot d'Herbois, and Carnot at a meeting of the Committee of Public Safety. The three men called Robespierre a dictator. The Committee had always had its factions and its tensions, but still found a way to work together (except for Hérault de Séchelles, executed with the Dantonists). Now, its *modus operandi* was breaking down. Robespierre left the meeting, and would not return to the Committee for nearly a month.

One of the strange paradoxes of the Revolution was that at the time when Robespierre was most powerful, he was also most absent. He was frustrated with some of his fellow Committee members, and with the Convention, but his health – both physical and mental – was also suffering. Aside from six weeks that Robespierre had spent in his hometown of Arras in 1791, he had been in Paris since October 1789 (and Versailles before then), constantly involved in the political life of the Revolution. Saint-Just had said that "those who would make revolutions in the world, those who want to do good in this world must sleep only in the tomb,"[71] but Saint-Just was nine years younger, had spent less time in politics, and the time he spent on missions away from Paris allowed him to recuperate. Saint-Just had the energy he needed in the summer of 1794; Robespierre did not. Not that Robespierre sat around doing nothing. He still worked from home. The Committee had papers brought to him, he read and signed what he had to, he issued orders as he saw fit. He also continued to speak at the Jacobin club, where his views still dominated opinion; the leaders of the Commune and the Committee of Public Safety's police force were still loyal to him, as was the Revolutionary Tribunal. For Thiers, should he have wished to repeat the events of May 31 and June 2, he had the means to do so. But Robespierre led by words, not by actions. As his opponents on the Committee of Public Safety conspired against him, Robespierre preferred to influence opinion through the Jacobins.[72] He was becoming more exhausted, though, as the work – and, some said, the guilt – wore him down.

The rest of the Committee of Public Safety continued to meet, and Robespierre's rivals – particularly Billaud-Varenne and Collot d'Herbois – began to rally other members of both committees to their side. Carnot had already expressed his hostility to Robespierre; Barère was wavering, ready, as always, to help move things along. The men of the Committee of General Security were mostly hostile to Robespierre. On July 22 and 23, Barère organized joint meetings of both committees in an attempt to bring Robespierre back into the fold. The first went poorly, with Robespierre unwilling to work with some of the other men there. The second went better, and they were able to make certain decisions – enough for Barère to inform the Convention that harmony reigned among the two committees – but it was not a lasting peace. Couthon, Robespierre, and Saint-Just continued to insist that there were several more deputies who needed to be executed. Their accusations were vague, though. When other deputies asked them to say who, they refused, leaving the other deputies with the sense that they might be next.

Meanwhile, strange rumors started to circulate about Robespierre.

It was hardly unusual for rumors to circulate around a leading figure; they had circulated around the king and queen, around almost every leader to rise on the revolutionary scene. In previous years, rumors about Robespierre had been a rather tepid lot. His nickname, "the incorruptible," was accurate – even his opponents accepted it. There were no rumors of Robespierre embezzling government funds or working with the enemy. The rumors about Robespierre always involved women, but even those were rather chaste, as rumors go. There had been suggestions that the daughter of the family with whom he boarded had become his wife or his lover. Given the circumstances – a single man living with a family that had a single daughter of marrying age – such rumors were inevitable. Another rumor spread that a woman named Cecile Renault, who on 22 May had feebly attempted to assassinate Robespierre, had actually been his lover. Why else, people asked, had her family been executed along with her?

Some of the new rumors were even stranger, particularly the ones concerning Catherine Théot, an old woman who called herself the "mother of God." By 1794, she had gathered a small circle around herself, and had proclaimed that Robespierre was the messiah. Vadier wanted to attack Robespierre and his allies by bringing Théot before the Revolutionary Tribunal. Robespierre and the Committee of Public Safety were able to keep her from appearing, but at the cost of more people talking about her and her relationship with him.

Other events around Paris contributed to the general dissatisfaction with the Reign of Terror. In one incident, a man named Magenthies circulated a petition that called for the death penalty for anyone who dared to say, "holy name of God." In another incident, a revolutionary committee from a section near the Tuileries arrested several drunk workers as suspects.

People in Paris blamed these events on Robespierre. He was not to blame, at least not directly; Robespierre had Magenthies sent before the Revolutionary Tribunal, and he had the members of the section's revolutionary committee arrested. For people in Paris, though, these were troubling omens. As Thiers wrote, "people said that his Supreme Being was going to become more oppressive than Christ, and that soon the Inquisition would be reestablished on behalf of Deism."[73]

Robespierre's endorsement of Barère's crackdown on "patriotic banquets" strengthened the view of Robespierre as an enemy of any enjoyable activity. Following the victory at Fleurus, some of Paris's sections began holding "civic meals" and "fraternal banquets" meant to celebrate the victory of the armies and of the Revolution. To Barère and to others in the government, these meals seemed too much like a critique of the Terror, a message that the danger had passed. Robespierre saw the danger, too – noting that the banquets were an opportunity for the Revolution's enemies to "soften public opinion, and to lull the friends of liberty to sleep ... patriots must know that their enemies are not yet vanquished, and that only virtue, vigilance, and courage can strengthen the Republic."[74]

Robespierre had offered the citizens of France – and particularly of Paris – a new religion, but that religion was not catching on. For all of the glory of the Festival of the Supreme Being, it was looking like a religion whose heyday had only been one day long, but whose leader continued to hope that France would become some sort of revolutionary theocracy. People were not only tired of the Reign of Terror; they were tired of the Reign of Virtue.

Robespierre's final days

On July 26, 1794 – 8 Thermidor II – a new rumor about Robespierre spread across Paris.

According to this one, Robespierre planned to make himself the king of France. To strengthen his claim to the throne, he would marry Louis XVI and Marie-Antoinette's 15-year-old daughter Marie-Thérèse, still imprisoned in the Temple. It was, in some ways, a natural rumor to have started – a rumor about Robespierre which combined an impending or secret marriage with his desire for power.

The rumor was not only false; it was a conscious fabrication by Robespierre's enemies in the Convention, once again concocted by Vadier, who would in later years boast that "the danger of losing one's head made one imaginative."[75] Vadier knew that a showdown was coming between Robespierre and his latest round of opponents, and 8 Thermidor was looking like the day.

One day earlier, Robespierre had attempted to get one of the deputies arrested; the deputy had demanded that the two committees make a report on his activities before the accusation. Surprisingly, this worked: his request was successful, much to Robespierre's chagrin. A deputy had stood up to Robespierre, and – at least for the moment – appeared to have defeated him. The Convention was recovering its courage. A showdown was coming. Robespierre left that evening, and went home to prepare his response: a speech.

"The remarkable character of the era!" Michelet wrote. "With so many means [available to him], he counted on a speech."[76] Rather than call on the police force under his control, or call on the Commune to start an insurrection, he worked on his speech.

As the Convention reconvened on the morning of 8 Thermidor, it was as if Basire was calling from beyond the grave, repeating what he had said on the night of August 9, 1792: "Do you not know that today is the big day?"[77] Robespierre's speech lasted two hours. He complained that he had been blamed for everything:

> they tell the nobles, *he is the one who banished you*; at the same time, they tell the patriots, *he wants to save the nobles*; they tell priests, *he is the one who is oppressing you; without him, you would be triumphant and at peace*; they tell fanatics, *he is the one who destroyed religion*; they tell persecuted patriots, *he is the one who commanded it, or who does not want to make it stop*.

From there he lashed out at his critics. He did so vaguely, though, again hesitating to name most of his enemies, leaving his fellow deputies unclear as to whether they were, or were not, on his list.

"The time has not yet come," he said at the end of his speech, "when good men can serve their fatherland with impunity. The defenders of liberty will only be banished, while the horde of scoundrels dominates."[78]

It was not the first showdown that Robespierre had at the Convention; it was not his most successful, though. It was not greeted with the thunderous applause that his recent speeches had received. Had he not been so powerful, by this point, had there not already been so much death, it might have seemed more like the speeches he had given back at Versailles in the earliest days of the Revolution – overly long declarations in which his fellow deputies struggled to remain interested.

After the speech, there was a motion to have it printed and distributed throughout France and to the armies. This was common for important speeches, but the motion, after some wrangling, did not pass. Deputies were openly expressing their hostility to Robespierre. Vadier again brought up the Théot affair, thinking that it would be the decisive piece of evidence against Robespierre. Other deputies began airing their own gripes against him, too. Collot d'Herbois, who was president of the Convention at the time, struggled to maintain control.

Some deputies yelled out that Robespierre should name the five or six deputies he thought needed to be killed. "Name them! Name them!" But Robespierre rambled, avoiding specifics. "When one boasts that they have the courage to be virtuous, they must also have the courage to tell the truth," one deputy yelled out.

"I persist in what I have said," Robespierre replied.[79]

That evening, Robespierre gave his speech again in the more comforting confines of the Jacobin club. There, he was still among his supporters, who cheered the speech. The galleries continued to show their support. Collot d'Herbois was thrown out of the club that night. The Jacobins also voted to expel any deputies who had voted against the speech being published. But Robespierre knew that his time was ending. "That speech," he told the

Jacobins, "was my last will and testament." And should this be the end, "you will see me drink the hemlock calmly."[80]

The night of 8–9 Thermidor was a flurry of activity throughout the city. Deputies communicated with colleagues, people all over the city tried to determine what was happening, what role they should play. By the next morning, though, the deputies were back at the Convention.

The day of 9 Thermidor Robespierre would be able to say little; his allies would be able to say little. Saint-Just had just begun his speech when Tallien cut him off. Tallien warned that Robespierre was trying to attack the deputies one by one, isolating them, "until one day there will only be he and the evil, debauched men who serve him." Other deputies started speaking out against Robespierre, including Billaud-Varenne. When Robespierre tried to reply, deputies yelled out, "Down with the tyrant!"

Vadier again spoke, and again brought up Théot. He claimed that he had new evidence, in the form of a letter hidden under her mattress. This claim, though, only earned the laughter of the Convention. Robespierre again tried to reply and again was unable to speak. Tallien spoke next, trying to bring things back to the point. Finally, Barère spoke, praising the two committees, calling them the key to revolutionary government, and defending them from Robespierre's attacks. Barère was eager, as always, to do what was necessary to help things move along. His critics joked that he had arrived that morning with two speeches in his pocket, one for Robespierre and one against. He could tell which way the wind was blowing.

Robespierre again tried to speak, and was again unable to. This time it was Thuriot, sitting in as the president, who would not let Robespierre take his turn. "It was the great shadow of Danton presiding," Jaurès wrote, "and it was Danton who said to Robespierre, 'you will only get to speak when it is your turn.'"[81] When Robespierre tried one last time to get permission to speak, his voice faltered. One deputy yelled out, "It is Danton's blood that you're choking on!"[82]

Before the session was over, the Convention had issued a decree for the arrests of Robespierre and his closest allies, including Saint-Just and Couthon. All were led off to separate prisons around Paris.

That night was even busier than the last, as word spread of the arrests. Robespierre's supporters soon freed him and his allies and brought them to the Hôtel de Ville. For Thiers, "If Robespierre had dared it – if he had been a man of action, showed himself and marched on the Convention, the Convention would have been in danger. But he was only a talker, and besides, he sensed, as did all of his allies, that opinion was abandoning him."[83] Jaurès put a more positive spin on it:

the Convention, in decreeing his arrest, in placing him outside the law, had committed its entire existence against him. It was the entire Convention that he would have to defeat. In the name of what principle? By virtue of what right? And what would he do in the aftermath? He would be no more than a dictator lost in the void, soon devoured by his own armies.[84]

Could Robespierre have pulled off an insurrection if he had wanted to? Until the summer of 1793, Robespierre had fought for the rights of the people to rise up and change their rulers; that changed, though, when he became one of their rulers. The Montagnards had been more successful than any of their predecessors in stifling popular activism. This had, in part, been by granting the people's demands, especially the Maximum. But it also came from stifling sources of the people's power. Some of the sans-culottes were ready for the Terror to end; others were angry about the death of Hébert; many were eager to keep their jobs as functionaries. The Commune, now under the control of Robespierre's allies, called for an insurrection to save their leaders, but few followed. The Commune reached out to the Jacobins, asking them to send over Robespierre's supporters from the galleries – citizens and citizenesses alike – to rise up and free Robespierre. But the insurrection never gained the momentum it needed. The sections did not rise up as they had so many times over the previous years. "The tocsin of Thermidor," Quinet wrote, "was only heard by Robespierre's enemies. The people ... seemed no longer to exist."[85]

Some time during that busy night, Robespierre was wounded. Either he had attempted to drink the proverbial hemlock by shooting himself, or a police agent shot him. In either case, the bullet went through his cheek; painful, but not life-threatening. Robespierre spent the rest of the night in pain, waiting for his execution.

On July 28, 1794 – 10 Thermidor II – Robespierre, Saint-Just, and Couthon were all beheaded. So, too, were 19 others. They had been carted to the scaffold along the same path that so many earlier prisoners had taken; women followed along behind, dancing while hurling insults at the condemned men.

On the scaffold, the executioner tore away the bandage that was holding Robespierre's jaw together. Robespierre screamed out in pain. They put Robespierre's head in place. The executioner pulled the cord, the blade dropped. Robespierre's head fell into the basket. The Revolution had entered a new phase.

The deaths of Robespierre and his allies were not the end of the killing. The next day 70 more would die on the scaffold. The fall of Robespierre – known as "Thermidor," for the month in the republican calendar when it occurred – would, however, mean a return to more moderate policies from the government, and less emphasis on virtue and equality. It would mean less influence from the sans-culottes, and more influence from the wealthier classes. Soon the Convention would dismantle the Revolutionary Tribunal and free the suspects still in prison. (Fouquier-Tinville would live on for almost a year, until he was found guilty after a legitimate trial lasting over a month.) Even the galleries of the Jacobin club, where the audience had been a consistent source of support for Robespierre, were restructured in the wake of his fall. At the request of the two committees, the Jacobin club changed its policies on who would be allowed to attend the sessions, eliminating reserved seats for its regulars. The deputy who had delivered the committees' request, a Dantonist named Legendre, addressed the women in the galleries directly before leaving the club with the phrase that politicians had been using about women since the start of the Revolution: "You were misled."[86]

If moderates were the eventual winners of the events of 8–10 Thermidor, they were not its instigators. Billaud-Varenne and Collot d'Herbois helped lead the charge against Robespierre. Fouché, too, was one of the leaders of Robespierre's overthrow. Carrier, still alive, was happy to see Robespierre executed. These were men with blood on their hands, eager to escape prosecution. Their goal was not to end the Terror; it was to save themselves. "Nothing gives more honor to Robespierre," Michelet wrote, "than that the main authors of his downfall were some of the worst men in France."[87]

No, it was not the moderates, and especially not the men of the Plain, who had risen up. The men who initiated the events of 8–9 Thermidor were Robespierre's fellow Montagnards. The one quote that best sums up the attitude of the men of the Plain – the moderates, still present in the Convention in the summer of 1794 – came from the Abbé Sieyes. When asked what he had done during the Terror, he replied: "I survived."[88]

Notes

1 *Mémoires de l'Abbé Grégoire* (Paris, 1989), p. 57.
2 James Guillaume, *Procès-verbaux du Comité d'instruction publique de la Convention nationale* (Paris, 1891), I:236.
3 Baker, ed., *The Old Regime*, p. 365.
4 Aston, *Religion*, p. 213.
5 McManners, *French Revolution*, p. 88.
6 *Mémoires de l'Abbé Grégoire*, p. 57.
7 Thiers, *Histoire*, V:195.
8 Quoted in Thiers, *Histoire*, V:199.
9 Quinet, *Révolution*, II:618.
10 *OMR* X:194–201.
11 Jaurès, *Histoire*, VI:339.
12 Michelet, *Histoire*, II:644.
13 Albert Soboul, *Les Sans-culottes Parisiens en l'An II: Mouvement populaire et gouvernement révolutionnaire* (Paris, 1958), p. 310.
14 Michelet, *Histoire*, II:616.
15 Aston, *Religion*, p. 262.
16 Chaumette, "Speech at City Hall Denouncing Women's Political Activism", (November 17, 1793), available at http://chnm.gmu.edu/revolution/d/489/

17 Aulard, ed., *Jacobins*, V:522.
18 Quinet, *Révolution*, II:623.
19 Aston, *Religion*, pp. 215, 276.
20 Serge Bianchi, *La Révolution culturelle de l'an II* (Paris, 1982), pp. 228–32.
21 Jaurès, *Histoire*, VI:305.
22 Peter McPhee, *Robespierre: A Revolutionary Life* (London, 2012), p. 164.
23 Quoted in Ruth Scurr, *Fatal Purity: Robespierre and the French Revolution* (New York, 2006), p. 279.
24 Jaurès, *Histoire*, VI:305.
25 Doyle, *Oxford History*, p. 263.
26 Quoted in T. C. W. Blanning, *The French Revolutionary Wars, 1787–1802* (London, 1996), p. 98.
27 David Bell, *The First Total War: Napoleon's Europe and the Birth of Warfare as we Know It* (New York, 2007), p. 182.
28 De La Gorce, *Histoire religieuse*, III:388.
29 Michelet, *Histoire*, II:689.
30 Jean-Clément Martin, *Blancs et bleus dans la Vendée déchirée* (Paris, 1986), p. 103.
31 Quoted in Michelet, *Histoire*, II:696.
32 Quoted in Blanning, *Revolutionary Wars*, p. 98.
33 Quoted in Martin, *Blancs et bleus*, p. 106.
34 Jean-Clément Martin, "Femmes et guerre civile, l'exemple de la Vendée, 1793–96," *CLIO. Histoire, femmes et sociétés* [En ligne], 5 | 1997, mis en ligne le 01 janvier 2005, consulté le 30 juin 2013. URL: http://clio.revues.org/410; DOI: 10.4000/clio.410.
35 Martin, *Blancs et bleus*, p. 146.
36 Martin, *Blancs et bleus*, p. 151.
37 Quoted in Hanson, *Jacobin Republic*, p. 220.
38 Hanson, *Jacobin Republic*, p. 220.
39 Baker, ed., *The Old Regime*, pp. 370–7.
40 *AP* LXXVIII: 204–6.
41 Jaurès, *Histoire*, VI:395.
42 Walter, ed., *Actes*, p. 505.
43 Quinet, *Révolution*, II:703.
44 *AP* LXXX: 164–5; Norman Hampson, *Danton* (London, 1988), p. 139.
45 Palmer, *Twelve*, p. 257.
46 Quoted in McPhee, *Robespierre*, p. 179.
47 Michelet, *Histoire*, II:671.
48 Quoted in Thiers, *Histoire*, V:386.
49 Thiers, *Histoire*, V:399.
50 Thiers, *Histoire*, V:409.
51 Walter, ed., *Actes*, p. 584.
52 Michelet, *Histoire*, II:404.
53 Jaurès, *Histoire*, VI:202–4.
54 John Hardman, *Robespierre* (London, 1999), p. x; McPhee, *Robespierre*, pp. 180, 232.
55 See the useful account in Hugh Gough, *The Terror in the French Revolution* (New York, 1998), pp. 1–9.

56 Michelet, *Histoire*, II:768.
57 Doyle, *Oxford History*, p. 271.
58 Jaurès, *Histoire*, V:487.
59 Thiers, *Histoire*, VI:15, 22.
60 Suzanne Desan, *Reclaiming the Sacred: Lay Religion and Popular Politics in Revolutionary France* (Ithaca, 1990), p. 206.
61 Scurr, *Fatal Purity*, p. 326.
62 Quoted in McPhee, *Robespierre*, p. 159.
63 Baker, ed., *The Old Regime*, p. 387.
64 *OMR* X:461.
65 Quoted in McPhee, *Robespierre*, p. 198.
66 Baker, ed., *The Old Regime*, p. 387.
67 Michelet, *Histoire*, II:801.
68 Gough, *The Terror*, p. 57. See also Donald Greer, *The Incidence of the Terror during the French Revolution: A Statistical Interpretation* (Gloucester, MA, 1966), p. 119.
69 Thiers, *Histoire*, VI:134, 138.
70 Blanning, *Revolutionary Wars*, p. 112.
71 Baker, ed., *The Old Regime*, p. 359.
72 Thiers, *Histoire*, VI:157.
73 Thiers, *Histoire*, VI:182; *OMR* X:540–1.
74 *OMR* X:534–5.
75 Quoted in Bronislaw Baczko, *Ending the Terror: The French Revolution after Robespierre*, trans. Michael Petheram (Cambridge, 1994), p. 16.
76 Michelet, *Histoire*, II:854.
77 *AP* XLVII:616, 624.
78 *OMR* X:558, 576. Emphasis in original.
79 *AP* XCIII:532–5.
80 Aulard, ed., *Jacobins*, VI:289.
81 Jaurès, *Histoire*, VI:512.
82 McPhee, *Robespierre*, p. 216.
83 Thiers, *Histoire*, VI:224.
84 Jaurès, *Histoire*, VI:512.
85 Quinet, *Révolution*, II:684.
86 Aulard, ed., *Jacobins*, VI:296.
87 Michelet, *Histoire*, II:706.
88 Furet, *Revolutionary France*, p. 45.

9

AFTER THE TERROR
(FALL 1794–1799)

The five years following Robespierre's fall have long been the ignored middle child of the era, trapped between the revolutionary drama that preceded them and the Napoleonic era that followed. It is an era that the classic historians paid less attention to. Michelet and Jaurès both ended their accounts with Robespierre's execution and the ensuing celebrations that broke out across Paris. For all of Michelet's disdain for Robespierre, he had little enthusiasm for the reappearance of wealth during the following months. "Let us turn our eyes away," he wrote.[1]

More recent historians, though, have reshaped the way that people think about this era. Deprived of the guillotine as a penalty for minor offenses, the men of Thermidor, and of the Directory era that followed, had to reshape both the government itself and the way it interacted with its population. Here, too, religious questions were paramount; and here, too, women often played leading roles in popular opposition to new policies, until the policies became so far-reaching that they faced the opposition of nearly the entire nation.

In the aftermath of Robespierre's fall, the men now in charge of the government dismantled many of the most radical aspects of the Revolution. Not only did they put an end to the Terror and the Law of 22 Prairial, they also eliminated the Maximum and the Revolutionary Tribunal. Many of the mainstays of political life of year II were now gone.

Gone, too, was much of the drama that had characterized the first five years of the Revolution. The personalities who dominated political life between 1795 and 1799 were not the larger-than-life characters of 1789–94; there were no Marats or Héberts, no Madame Rolands or Vergniauds. Those who had been most likely to stand out in the first five years of the Revolution were also least likely to survive.

For the most prominent revolutionaries who had made it this far alive, another group was about to be removed from the scene as well. A coalition of moderates and extremists had led the events of 8–10 Thermidor, but it was the extremists – Collot d'Herbois, Billaud-Varenne, Tallien, Fouché – who had been the instigators. The way the population reacted to

Robespierre's fall, however, made it clear that the France that would emerge from those events would be a moderate France, not a radical one. The coalition between moderates and extremists soon broke down.

The radicals had been eager to place all blame for the Terror on Robespierre, now that he was unable to defend himself. Tallien – who had brought the Terror to Bordeaux – told the Convention that the Terror "was Robespierre's system, he was the one who put it into practice with the help of a few subordinates ... the Convention was a victim of it, never an accomplice."[2] Politicians of all stripes began speaking out against Robespierre, ignoring that many of them had been singing his praises weeks (if not days) earlier. Before summer was over, a somewhat shady character named Mehée de la Touche published a book called *La Queue de Robespierre* (*Robespierre's Tail*), playing on the ambiguities of the word *queue*, which could mean an animal's tail, a line (as in the British "queue up," referring to the people who had lined up to support Robespierre before his fall), or something a bit more phallic. The book not only provided the otherwise unnoteworthy Mehée de la Touche his 15 minutes of fame but also led to a mini-genre of satirical political texts: *Response to Robespierre's Tail*, *Let's Cut off His Tail*, *Give Me Back My Tail*, *Robespierre's Flayed Tail*, and *Robespierre's Naughty Bits* were all examples of this genre.[3] Robespierre's critics were aware of the support that he had from some women in Paris, and were eager to use it against him as a way of propping up their own claims to authority.

The Montagnards who had cooperated with Robespierre and his allies were particularly eager to pass on all of the blame for the Terror to their now-deceased colleagues. Sometimes, they succeeded. Some of the leaders of Thermidor – including some of the men whose earlier actions warranted punishment – would survive well after Robespierre's death. For instance, Fouché's political career would last into the first decades of the nineteenth century, bringing him an enormous amount of success and power. Tallien, too, would remain in politics, although with less success.

Others, though, were not able to bury all of their crimes with Robespierre. In December, Carrier was executed. The following April the Convention deported Barère, Billaud-Varenne and Collot d'Herbois to Guyana.

Meanwhile, the Convention began the process of reinstating the surviving Girondins, including those who had been expelled on June 2, 1793. Louvet, Isnard, and Lanjuinais, among others, were once again serving as deputies; Louvet would even spend some time as a member of the post-Robespierre Committee of Public Safety.

Several long-time leaders of the Revolution remained in politics. Grégoire was still in the Convention. He continued to preside over the constitutional church, rescuing it from what seemed like imminent irrelevancy. Sieyes, too, remained in politics, and even began to recover his voice. Carnot, known mostly for his success in reorganizing the army, was alone among members of the Committee of Public Safety in being able to continue his political career. Overall, though, it is hard to disagree with the sentiment held at the time – even by many royalists – that the transition from the Terror to Thermidor had been a victory of mediocrity over talent.

Socially, Thermidorian France was a time when the wealthy again began showing off their wealth. The *muscadins* – also known as the *jeunesse dorée*, or "gilded youth" – became the era's answer to the sans-culottes. These were wealthy young men who, like the sans-culottes, used their choices of clothing to express their politics. But while the sans-culottes used plain clothes to express their leftist politics and working-class status, the muscadins dressed elaborately (if not pretentiously) as a way of showing their hostility toward the radical Revolution and their indifference to the issues facing poorer citizens. They were not genteel tea-drinking denizens of the salons and theaters who limited their activism to discussions and writing; in November they physically attacked the Jacobin club, throwing stones, breaking the windows and beating up many of the people inside.

Though the Jacobin club had been attacked, most deputies were not interested in hearing the victims' story. The day after the attack, one deputy told the Convention he had seen a woman outside of the club bleeding, disheveled, and in tears. When the deputy said that he had heard the muscadins telling the women there that they should not be in the galleries of either the Jacobin club or the Convention, the Convention applauded.[4]

On November 12, 1794 (22 Brumaire III), the Convention ordered the Jacobin club closed. It was not the complete death of Jacobinism, which continued to exist as an ideology and a legacy, and would find ways to make itself heard in the coming years; it was, however, one more sign of the end of an era. The Jacobin club had been a powerful society since the early days of the Revolution, back when Mirabeau and Barnave were its leading lights. The Convention decreed, however, that henceforth the building would be used to store weapons.

As for the sans-culottes, they never regained the influence they had had earlier in the Revolution. Conditions were otherwise ripe for an uprising of the people: the winter of 1794–5 was the coldest of the century, and there was not enough wood to burn for people to keep warm. Bread was scarce, especially in Paris, with army provisioning demanding more and more of what had been an average harvest. There was rice available, but without fuel, people struggled to find ways to cook it.

People wanted bread. The Maximum had never worked smoothly, but its absence seemed to be making things worse.

There was anger, there was cause – and there was a tradition of popular action, of insurrections led by sans-culottes putting pressure on the Convention. As lines at bakeries grew longer and longer, small-scale disturbances started breaking out across the city. The deputies realized that this was a situation they had to deal with, and tried to make sure that bread was reaching people. They were not fully successful, though; nor were they able to do away with all of the people's concerns or hunger. The government began rationing bread for Paris, but distributed it in amounts too small to sustain or satisfy most recipients. In March, posters around Paris called for the wives of sans-culottes to attend the sessions of the Convention, and, from the galleries, to thwart the actions of deputies deemed counter-revolutionary.[5]

The people's leaders, though, were lacking. Marat, Hébert, Robespierre, Chaumette, even Roux, all gone – and new leaders had not emerged. As Quinet wrote, "all their idols had fallen, one after another," and in 1795 the people "felt alone and misled in the Revolution ... deprived of the scaffold, insulted by the gilded youth, dethroned from its ephemeral royalty, the people returned to their bloody, sad, deserted, miserable homes; and there, they felt their hunger."[6]

In October 1789, when bread had been lacking in Paris, the women of Paris had marched to Versailles in an attempt to get the king to provision the city, and to help the Revolution and the National Assembly move forward.

The events of April 1, 1795 can be seen as a distant echo of the October Days of 1789. A mostly female crowd marched on the Convention, invading the hall and calling for bread. And just as the women of October 1789 had linked the demands for royal approval of the Declaration of the Rights of Man to their demands for bread, there were political demands here as well – along with the cries of "bread! bread!" people started to yell, "Bread, and the Constitution of 1793."

The October Days had succeeded. The riots of April 1795 – 12 Germinal III, according to the republican calendar – did not. No one in the Convention approved the rioters' actions, not even the remaining Montagnards, who called on the women to return to their homes. The underlying problems, though – especially the scarcity of bread – remained.

On May 20–23 (1–4 Prairial), another crowd – still largely female – invaded the Convention. One officer assigned to protect the Convention wrote of having only 1,200 men under his orders, against "twenty thousand armed men and forty thousand furies – for they cannot be referred to as women." These "shrews," he added, "were a thousand times more atrocious than the men."[7] This time the crowd did something that no crowd had yet done: they killed a deputy in the halls of the Convention itself. They even put his head on a pike, paraded it through the hall, and presented it to the president of the Convention, the deputy Boissy d'Anglas, who managed to stay calm and give the head a respectful salute.

This insurrection, known as the "Prairial Days," while it went farther than earlier revolts had in its violence against the deputies, was not more successful in achieving its aims. If anything, it marked a final gasp by the sans-culottes and the women of Paris to impose their will on the Revolution, and to make the Revolution pay attention to the lower classes. It did not move the Revolution to the left. If anything, it sped up a move toward the right that was already well underway. The Convention henceforth banned women from its galleries; several days later, it would attempt to ban women from attending any political assemblies. The Convention even decreed that "all women will retire to their respective domiciles until otherwise ordered ... those found in the streets, gathered together in groups of more than five persons will be dispersed by armed force and placed under arrest until public tranquility is restored to Paris."[8]

The Prairial Days meant the end of the line for some Montagnard deputies who had supported the insurrection. In the aftermath, several deputies – including Romme, the creator of the republican calendar – were sentenced to death by a military commission; they committed suicide while in custody. There was no longer any tolerance in the Convention for the sort of allegiance between parliamentary politics and street fighting that the Jacobins and the Montagnards had fostered. The government sent troops to surround the militant neighborhoods of the Faubourg Saint-Antoine, which, "starved and unarmed, surrendered the following day without a fight." For Lefebvre, "this is the date which should be taken as the end of the Revolution. Its mainspring was now broken."[9]

Radical women had been a force to be reckoned with in Parisian political life; now, the Convention was doing everything it could to keep them down. Many of the women who took part in the Prairial Days were arrested and sentenced (though not to death; most sentences were two months in prison). The women of Paris never regained the role that they had played in the politics of the French Revolution up to that point. As Godineau wrote, "the first of Prairial saw the high point of a mass female movement and sounded its knell." In place of women's vocal activism came "the greatest tranquility" and "women's silence."[10]

There would only be one more attempt to build a mass movement of the people in Paris, the self-proclaimed "conspiracy of equals," led by Gracchus Babeuf. The goals of Babeuf's movement were indeed radical – promises of a vast redistribution of wealth to help the poor, replacing current land ownership with a community of land and an equal distribution of its products – but this was never a mass movement with widespread support. Though its leaders talked of conspiracy and attempted to set up a shadow government, the actual government had always been well aware of what was happening and had little trouble putting an end to Babeuf's plans. It is more accurate to see it as "the first 'red peril' in modern history," a movement whose main impact was to provide the government with an excuse to crack down further on political activity.[11] Babeuf was executed in May 1797; his ideas became more influential for later radicals than they had been while he – or the Revolution – was alive.

The outlook going forward

Militarily, the era was enormously successful for France. Again, it has been overshadowed by France's later victories, when Napoleon's armies conquered most of continental Europe in the first decade of the nineteenth century, but from 1794 to 1799 French troops won far more battles than they lost. The French government annexed some conquered areas, creating new departments and making the citizens of those regions subject to the same laws as the rest of France. In other areas, including much of Italy, the Netherlands, and Switzerland, France set up "sister republics." Other parts of Europe were occupied by French troops. France was able to push back the armies allied against it. None of this came without crises, times when defeats followed other defeats, when the French armies were dangerously overextended. There were even times, as in 1799, when the reappearance of foreign troops on French soil became a distinct possibility. French plans to invade England, or to weaken it by invading Ireland or Egypt, were less fruitful, and France was never able to challenge England's naval superiority. On the continent, however, republican France was turning out to be far more successful than monarchical France had been.

There were several reasons for France's military success. The first was the size of the armies it was able to put on the battlefield. More often than not, it was able to outnumber its opponents. The mass conscription and the work that the Committee of Public Safety had done in reshaping the army gave the later governments better-trained and larger armies to work with. France also, by this time, had a new cohort of talented military leaders. The old guard – the Bouillés, the Lafayettes, the Dumouriezes – were now gone, and their departure had left open spots for men of talent. Under the Old Regime, being an army officer was reserved for men born into the aristocracy. Republican France left those positions open to all, and the best leaders were able to rise to the top. France had squandered some of that talent during the Terror by executing generals simply for losing battles, but as conditions stabilized, the new cohort had emerged: generals like Jourdan, Moreau, and Joubert – and, above all, Napoleon Bonaparte, a former supporter of the Jacobins who was proving to be not only a brave soldier, but a brilliant military strategist with an innate gift for self-promotion.

France's military success made things easier on the government domestically – though not, it would seem, easy enough. France did not have to deal with another crisis along the lines of the fall of Verdun in 1792 or the breakout of civil war in 1793. After the violence of Germinal and Prairial III, French politics during these five years were stable if compared to the five preceding years, although that was a low bar to clear. But the government was never able to capture the enthusiasm of even a significant portion of the nation. The men who led the governments during this time were eager to avoid extremes. They did not want a return to monarchy; nor did they want a return to the Terror. In the aftermath of Robespierre's fall, the character of Thermidorian politics began to take shape. This was a government committed to some form of republic, one that maintained many of the gains of the first years of the Revolution while hoping to avoid a repeat of the Terror. It remained far to the left of anything that had existed in the first few years of the Revolution. Even with the surviving Girondins reinstated, it was still a Convention dominated by men who were committed to the cause of republican France. It was also a Convention dominated by men who, in January 1793, had voted for the death of the king.

Of all events from the first five years of the Revolution – from the fall of the Bastille to the fall of Robespierre, passing through the revolt of August 10, the September Massacres, the expulsion of the Girondins – it was the execution of Louis XVI that became the touchstone for political participation during Thermidor, what Furet called "the demarcation line between the sure and the unsure."[12] For the men in the government, their goal was to move the Revolution forward, preventing any return of the monarchy while emphasizing the protection of property and preventing the crowd from influencing politics as it had in earlier years. There was not, however, a stable or strong enough middle whose support the government could rely upon. As a result, the primary political dynamic was known as "see-saw politics" – once things veered too far to the right, the men leading the government would re-correct left; once things veered too far left, they would re-correct right.

Historians have associated this see-saw politics with the personnel of the government, which was purged periodically (although bloodlessly), but it was true of the religious policies as well. The government tried various ways to find the balance between freedom of religion for its citizens and the legacy of anti-clericalism that it had inherited from the first phases of the Revolution. Every time the government tried to allow people more leeway in practicing their religion, though, it became concerned by the results; then, when it cracked down on religious practices, it ran into a different set of problems, as people expressed their resentment at the new rules and local government officials tired of trying to impose unpopular policies on their communities.

Once the Terror was over people again started attending church on Sundays and on traditional holidays. There were movements toward a reconciliation of sorts between the government and the refractory priests. Carnot sought to make peace with what remained of the insurgency in the Vendée; soon, there was an amnesty for Vendéan rebels and for *Chouans*, and the official establishment of freedom of religion in Brittany and the Vendée. The republican calendar, whose legal status had always been somewhat unclear, fell into disuse among all but members of the government and the most committed revolutionaries. In March 1795, a newspaper noted that "a foreigner arriving in Paris right now would have no trouble realizing that today is Sunday. Most of the stores are closed, and ... you can see that most of the people have chosen this day as their day of rest."[13]

The men who had led the overthrow of Robespierre had not been doing so in order for there to be a religious revival, and the Convention's religious policies after 9 Thermidor were somewhat ambivalent. In September 1794, the government decreed that it would no longer pay the salaries of any priests or other ministers. In reality, the priests of the constitutional church had not been paid for several months; nor had the government done much else in that time to support the church that it had created. Still, this was an official declaration that church and state were now separate entities.

On February 21, 1795, the Convention reemphasized its commitment to the freedom of religion, although not in a way that would have satisfied many of the practicing Catholics of the day, refractory or constitutional. People were now officially free to practice the religion of their choosing in approved locales. This was, in some ways, official government neutrality: the government still did not pay any ministers of any religion, nor did it provide locations for worship. It also prohibited anyone from interfering with anyone else's religious practice. But the limitations were more severe than might have been expected. It was a grudging acceptance of the need for some sort of end to the persecution of religions, if only for practical reasons. "Listen to the voice of reason," said Boissy d'Anglas, who presented the law, "it will tell you that only time, the spread of Enlightenment, and the progress of the human spirit will destroy all of these errors."[14]

According to the law, "every gathering of citizens for the practice of any religion is subject to the surveillance of the authorities." Permissible religious practice could be in the church or in the home, but not elsewhere, and certainly not outside. External signs of religion were prohibited: there were to be no crosses or clerical garb outside of the church, nor were religious processions permitted. Private piety was allowed, but the gregarious religion of Old Regime France with its processions and bell ringing was not. "What?" Grégoire responded. "The declaration of rights, the constitution ... have as their goal that I can do what I want in my own room?"[15] The law was, according to de La Gorce, "freedom hidden under a layer of servitude so thick that one could barely recognize it."[16] And yet, for Quinet, this was still too much. "Through these liberal laws, the ancient spirit returned ... all of France came back to the spirit of the Middle Ages, and the formula of tolerance brought back the religion of intolerance ... on one side, a magnanimous law, on the other, the victory of the reaction, as the Revolution surrenders."[17] Harsh words, but they do point to one accurate assessment: as limited as the freedoms that the law provided were, people leapt to them across France.

Enough people began expressing their preference for Catholicism that the deputies decided that the limited freedom of religion provided in February 1795 was too much. The government began requiring all priests to swear oaths to submit to the law. Finally, in October 1795, during the Thermidorian Convention's final days, it reestablished the laws against refractory priests that the Legislative Assembly and Convention had passed in 1792–3, making any refractory priest subject to deportation or execution.

The Directory

In October 1795, the Convention gave way to the newest political establishment of the Revolution, the Directory. France was still a republic, though it was no longer one based on universal male suffrage. The Directory was the first French government to have a bi-cameral legislature; that is, one with two distinct chambers (like Britain's House of Lords and House of Commons, or the USA's Senate and House of Representatives). The first chamber was the Council of 500, which initiated the laws; the second was the Council of Elders, which approved (or did not approve) the laws that the Council of 500 had passed. Terms in each chamber lasted three years, with one-third of the chamber renewable each year; the constitution also called for two-thirds of the members of the original councils to be deputies from the Convention.

Executive power lay in the five directors, men chosen through a joint process of the two legislative chambers, with one of them to be replaced each year. In the first election, Sieyes was chosen as one of the five, but declined to serve; Carnot took his place instead. The other four – La Révellière-Lépeaux, Reubell, Le Tourneur, and Barras – were a far cry from the men who had served with Carnot in the Committee of Public Safety. It was, as one recent historian wrote, a group of men "impressive only by its banality."[18] La Révellière-Lépeaux had served in the Convention, was a strong critic of the Catholic Church, and a supporter of the Girondins who had been too low profile to be included in their expulsion. Barras would go on to be the most successful politician of the bunch, guided more by a search for power and self-preservation than by principles. Le Tourneur and Reubell were competent, but forgettable politicians.

Most notably, all of the five were regicides. They had been deputies at the Convention in January 1793; four had voted for Louis XVI's death. The fifth, away at the time, had indicated his support for the execution. The regulations requiring the continuity of personnel from the Convention to the Directory assured that moderate regicides would remain the dominant force in the latter.

During the start of the Directory era, the relative revival of religious life continued as it had during Thermidor. "Revival" might not be the appropriate term; the religious practices in France during Thermidor and the first years of the Directory were something quite different from the religious practices of the Old Regime. In many places, there were no priests to lead the mass, so parishioners took it upon themselves to do so. In places where there were priests, those priests often found that they had less ability than before to impose their version of Catholicism on their parishioners.

Episcopal oversight for the priests who were still active was often minimal, whichever side of the schism the priest belonged to. All but a handful of the refractory bishops had long since left France or died – some of natural causes, some of not so natural causes. On the other side of the schism, of the 82 constitutional bishops in place in 1792, 10 had died (6 of them executed), and another 47 had left their positions – if not the church as a whole. Grégoire had worked hard to reconstruct the constitutional church, and succeeded in keeping it relevant after it had been disowned by the government that had created it; he could not, however, fill the tens of thousands of vacancies across France, nor could his church provide the sort of supervision of priests that had previously existed.

The lack of priests – and the lack of supervision for the existing priests – was not always unwelcome in many communities. Suzanne Desan's research into the religious behavior of the era has shown that this "religious revival" was one that the laity led not just in the hopes of regaining the freedom to practice their religion privately, but in order to "make religion public and official ... motivated not solely by spirituality but also by habit, politics, sociability, or fear of change."[19] As with the first opposition to the Civil Constitution of the Clergy in 1791, and as with the early opposition in the Vendée, this was a defense of a traditional culture as much as it was a defense of religion; it was a defense of processions and masses and the agro-liturgical calendar, as much as it was a defense of sacraments and Catholic doctrine. In other words, this sort of revival was precisely what Boissy d'Anglas and the Convention had *not* had in mind in February 1795 with their decree on the freedom of religion. But most surprisingly, Desan shows that much of the activism in favor of reestablishing a public practice of Catholic rituals was not even counter-revolutionary. Many of the people protesting considered themselves republicans, not monarchists; moreover, they were able to use revolutionary ideas, like the freedom of religion and popular sovereignty, to argue for their right to practice their religion as they saw fit. "The Directory," Desan wrote, "was in some ways an extremely fertile and creative period for lay religiosity."[20] One major aspect of this creativity was the "white masses" that took place in many parts of France – masses held without priests, where a member of the laity (often a school-teacher) would lead the service. And as had been the case in so much of religious life during the Revolution, women played a key role, participating in all aspects of communities' attempts to "reclaim the sacred," taking part in the riots that occurred and dominating attendance at mass – though not, it seems, actually leading the white masses.[21]

Again, this was not what the men who had overthrown Robespierre had had in mind; nor was it what their successors in the Directory were aiming for. The men in the government began asking, again, just what freedom of religion meant, and how far it extended.

One of the persistent issues that the Directory faced was its inability to see Catholicism as anything other than counter-revolutionary and royalist. The men making the laws – the Council of 500, the Council of Elders, the directors – had an innate ability to misunderstand the nation that they were governing. Some of the local administrators seemed to have a better handle on what was going on: in northern France, one local government agent wrote to the minister of the interior, "give back the crosses, the church bells, Sundays, and above all, those who live off all those childish behaviors, and everyone will cry *vive la République!*"[22] But while local administrators had a better understanding of people's priorities than did the national legislature, they had only limited leeway in determining the priorities for their local governments.

The politicians in Paris, though, saw a population that was slipping away from them.

The elections of year V, held in the spring of 1797, only confirmed this suspicion. The makeup of the councils shifted to the right, and royalists – *royalists!* – made major gains. The system of elections to the Council of 500, with one-third replaced each year, had been meant to ensure continuity dating back to the Convention. But the majority that the Convention had bequeathed to the Directory, that of regicide deputies hoping to steer a path between counter-revolution and anarchy, was already in danger.

This was not, to be sure, the most organized group of royalists. One of the surprises of this era is that the monarchists did not have more success than they did, given the relative weakness of the Directory. Their one military attempt at taking over France was a full-fledged disaster. In the summer of 1795, 3,000 émigrés had sailed from Britain to the Quiberon peninsula in Brittany, hoping to team up with the *Chouans*. There were even plans in place for Louis XVI's brother, formerly the comte d'Artois, to come (via England) and lead the troops himself. This was to be a full restoration of the Bourbon throne, if successful. In the weeks before Quiberon, Louis XVI's son had died in prison. Upon the boy's death, Louis XVI's other brother, the comte de Provence, had declared himself to be King Louis XVIII – declaring, that is, that, despite having been in a prison the whole time, Louis XVI and Marie-Antoinette's son had reigned as Louis XVII. There was always something delusional about some aspects of royalism in the 1790s – as seen in the idea that a boy-king could reign from prison, and also in the idea that a few thousand émigrés could land in distant Brittany and march on Paris. By July, the republic's armies had soundly defeated their foes and executed several hundred of the émigrés.[23] For Louis XVI's brothers, it would be another 19 years after Quiberon until they made it back to their homeland.

The royalists' chances in the parliamentary arena seemed much better in the aftermath of the elections of 1797, but they could not agree among themselves on what path to take. Some advocated a coup d'état that would bring Louis XVIII to the throne; others preferred working within the law. They were disorganized, but that did not allay the fears of the republican leaders of the Directory, who were faced with the specter of the two councils voting to invite Provence back to France to rule as Louis XVIII.

The left-wing directors began working with the army to organize their own coup d'état to eliminate the royalists from the Directory and the Councils. See-saw politics indeed.

Fructidor and its aftermath

On September 4, 1797 – 18 Fructidor V – army forces loyal to the republican directors occupied Paris. The coup d'état was on. Two of the directors were replaced, including Carnot, the former member of the Committee of Public Safety, now deemed too pro-royalist. (The other was a royalist who had recently been added to the directors.) The leaders of the coup also reshaped the Councils, sending the most prominent royalist deputies into exile. The Revolution no longer ate its young; it now just sent them to French Guyana.

The government also took steps to "correct" the results of the elections, and to reshape both the national government and local governments, ensuring that all would be hostile to any sort of reestablishment of the monarchy. It was not a return to the social policies of year II; the Directory remained a government hostile to the claims of the poorer classes, unsympathetic to the sort of people who had invaded the Convention in Germinal and Prairial. It was, however, a return to some of the religious policies of the radical Revolution. Here, too, the tendency of the republicans of the era to assume that any support for royalty meant support for Catholicism – and vice-versa – had a major impact on the policies of what would be called the "Fructidorian Directory."

In the days before the coup d'état – that is, in the period between the elections and their "correction" – the councils had started easing the laws against refractory priests. Deputies had proposed legalizing ringing bells for mass and for processions.[24] In June, they repealed the law of October 25, 1795 against refractory priests. "Let the priests be punished if they are guilty," said one deputy, "but persecution should not be confused with justice."[25]

With the coup d'état of 18 Fructidor V, the see-saw swung back in the other direction. The government reinstated the law of October 25, 1795. Refractory priests were again subject to deportation and, in some cases, execution – though the body count for the Directory's "Fructidorian Terror" never remotely approached that of year II. "The hunt commenced," according to de La Gorce, and many refractory priests again started heading for the borders.[26]

Deporting refractory priests and closing churches could only go so far, however. For all of the Fructidorian Directory's inability to understand the nation that they were trying to govern, they did realize that there was a fundamental issue at stake: the nation was not yet republican enough. The task at hand, then, was to make France more republican, so that it might merit the government it had. The question was how.

Some in the government hoped to accomplish something along the lines of what Robespierre had attempted: to create a new religion, one which would unite the people and bring unity to the nation without the baggage that Catholicism, or any other form of Christianity, brought. The two main attempts at such a religion, though, did not go far.

One of the attempted religions was called Theophilanthrophy. Like the cult of the supreme being, this was a religion based on deism. It recognized the immortality of the soul and the existence of God. It had the backing of the director La Révellière-Lépeaux, and after Fructidor the government promoted it. Soon, there were more than a dozen churches in Paris devoted to Theophilanthrophy, with outposts in several other cities. Its expansion stopped there, though. This was always a religion of the elite – and even a religion of those among the elite who felt that the masses, not the elite, needed a religion. The other attempted religion, the *culte décadaire*, was based on the sanctification of the *décadi* instead of Sunday. The fortunes of the *culte décadaire* were tied to the republican calendar, which few were following by the first half of 1797.

The coup d'état of 18 Fructidor would try to change that, though.

The centerpiece of the Fructidorian Directory's attempt to regenerate France, to inspire its citizens to be better citizens and republicans, lay in its attempt to resurrect the republican calendar and spread its use throughout the nation.

The republican calendar had never officially left; it had been included in the Constitution of the Year III (which is why it was not known as the Constitution of 1795), and the government still officially scheduled all of its activities according to the ten-day week. But most of the population had gone back to the traditional seven-day cycle once the Terror had ended. Even during the Terror, the adherence to the republican calendar had been sporadic and uneven. Put simply, most people did not like the republican calendar.

That did not stop the government. Starting in December 1797, the Council of 500 began exploring and debating ways to bring the republican calendar into people's lives. The laws would come out in several stages. First, in April 1798, came a decree from the directors. "Considering that the republican calendar, the only one that the constitution and the laws recognize, is one of the best institutions for erasing the last memories of the royal, noble, and priestly regime," the decree reinforced the importance of the calendar within the government. It brought the ten-day schedule to commercial activities, social life, and even fish markets, which were no longer allowed to correspond to traditional Catholic fast days.[27] Three laws passed in August and September expanded on the April decree, requiring shops to close on the *décadi* and national holidays, and prohibiting people from working in public on those days as well. The new laws also required stores to remain open on Sundays and required weddings to take place on the *décadi*.

The impact of these laws was predictable, or at least unsurprising, in hindsight. An unpopular government took unprecedented steps in rearranging its citizens' schedules without the threat of the guillotine to back up its laws.

In past opposition to the government's religious policies, women had taken the lead. When it came to the republican calendar, though, women and men alike found ways to oppose – or even mock – the laws. Many local government officials often did not want to follow the laws, let alone enforce them, and those officials who did try to enforce them found that there was little they could do against communities who united in their desire to avoid overhauling their schedules.[28]

For ordinary citizens, the laws regarding the republican calendar were the most intrusive laws that the French state had enacted since the fall of Robespierre, but overall, they failed to make the French state more tyrannical. If anything, the overall impact of the laws – and of the Directory's attempt to reinvigorate the republican calendar – was to make the French state more irrelevant.

It did not help matters that the see-saw politics of the Directory had not ended with the coup d'état of Fructidor V. There were two more overhauls of the government during the Directory – one in May 1798 (22 Floréal VI), the other in June 1799 (30 Prairial VII) – although neither was as decisive as Fructidor, and both, unlike Fructidor, could at least make some claim to legality. Both, though, grew out of the same goal that Fructidor had: to continue to maintain the same sort of politics, the republican politics hostile to the masses that had emerged during Thermidor. In May 1798, the government again "corrected" election results. With royalist candidates hesitant to try to get elected after the purges of the previous election, the left – and even pro-Jacobin candidates – scored major victories across France. This was a prospect with which the men currently in the government were not comfortable; just as Fructidor had struck the royalist right, Floréal struck the Jacobin left. The electorate, and the population at large, took little notice. Apathy, it seemed, was the order of the day.

The coup of 1799 occurred during a rare time of bad military news. Several areas under French control were rising up. The previous years' victories had left French armies overconfident and overextended, and it looked at that point like things were going to unravel. It was, in a way, Fructidor or Floréal in reverse: instead of the directors reshaping the councils, it was the councils that pressured three directors to resign. The resulting Directory maintained only Barras from the original group of five. Sieyes was again offered a place on the Directory; this time, he decided to serve.

By this point, Sieyes had realized that the Directory's outlook was not favorable. Having never been satisfied with the form of the government, it had not taken much to convince him of the need to restructure it once more. Sieyes wanted a stronger executive. When the Thermidorians had written the Constitution of the Year III in the shadow of the Committee of Public

Safety's Reign of Terror, a stronger executive was impossible; after four years of see-sawing back and forth, a government with a strong executive was an easier sell. But Sieyes realized that this change could not be accomplished simply through parliamentary politics. He would need another coup d'état, and he would need military help to accomplish it. He would need a general.

As luck would have it, Napoleon Bonaparte had just returned to France from Egypt. Soon, Sieyes and Bonaparte began coordinating their plans for the end of the Directory.

The rise of Napoleon Bonaparte

Bonaparte already had an impressive list of achievements by 1799, even if, at 30 years old, he was not yet eligible to be a director. He had been an army officer since before the start of the Revolution. Unlike many of his fellow officers, he had looked positively at many of the developments of 1789, and even in 1793 had sung the praises of Robespierre and the Jacobins. That year, he had helped reconquer the Mediterranean port of Toulon from British occupation. His success there helped start his rise through the military ranks. Though his support of the Jacobins in 1793 and his hesitancy to fight in the Vendée made some in the Thermidorian government wary of him, he later earned their trust – and that of the Directory – by helping put down an attempted insurrection by royalists in Paris in the closing days of the Convention. Promoted to the head of the army of Italy, Bonaparte continued to show his ability to win battles. In May 1796, he led his troops into Milan.

His next major expedition – to Egypt – was less successful, and would end with Bonaparte having to return to France without establishing French control over the country. Bonaparte, though, had showed himself at least as capable at self-promotion as he was at military strategy. The French population back home was hearing less of how the British navy was destroying the French fleet, and more about how Bonaparte had won several battles despite being outnumbered – with one of the battles being fought in the shadow of the pyramids themselves. When Bonaparte returned to France in 1799, he was greeted as a hero.

Sieyes expected to be able to take advantage of Bonaparte's reputation by making the general a puppet and himself the puppet master. The plan was halfway successful; Bonaparte's popularity did make the coup possible. But subsequent events would make it clear that it was Bonaparte, not Sieyes, who was pulling the strings.

Sieyes was not the only figure from the earlier days of the Revolution to take part in the coup. Roederer, the man who had walked with Louis XVI from the Tuileries to the National Assembly on August 10, 1792, participated as well. When Bonaparte asked him if the coup would be difficult,

Roederer told him it would not – because it was already three-quarters complete.[29] Fouché, the former de-Christianizer who had managed to survive the purges that swept away Carrier and Collot d'Herbois, also took part. He had briefly been imprisoned during Thermidor, but after Fructidor had gone on to become the minister of police. Even Talleyrand, the former bishop, was part of the plot. He had spent much of the decade in England, somehow managing to avoid both the turmoil of the radical Revolution and the taint of émigré status.

As with the events of 9 Thermidor, there was little that united the plotters except for a desire for change. The stakes were lower this time around, though, as was the resistance. Not that the coup itself went smoothly. It took place on October 9–10 (18–19 Brumaire VIII), and at several points it was touch and go. Most of the Council of 500 were unhappy about the coup, but, as Bonaparte himself reminded the deputies, their position as defenders of legality was not that strong. When one deputy brought up the constitution, Bonaparte's retort was: "You violated it on 18 Fructidor, you violated it on 22 Floréal, you violated it on 30 Prairial. The Constitution has been invoked and then violated by every single faction."[30] In the end, though, it was military force, not reasoning, that made "Brumaire" successful. And when it was done, the Directory was no more. The Directory had never been popular, and in 1799 there was no widespread basis for any sort of opposition to the takeover. Nor was there much reason to believe, in October 1799, that this coup was that different from the last. In place of the five directors there were now three provisional "consuls": Bonaparte and Sieyes, along with a man named Roger Ducos, a former regicide deputy. "Presumably, they were equal," wrote Lefebvre, "but nobody was deceived. This day of lies, with daggers added to the conspiracy, was also a day of dupes. Bonaparte put Sieyes into eclipse."[31]

De facto leader from the start, Bonaparte's primacy soon became official. In December, Bonaparte became first consul; Sieyes, once again, was out of the picture. It was soon clear, too, that this coup was indeed something different, and that Bonaparte's government was not merely the next iteration of Thermidor and the Directory. Bonaparte was far more popular than anyone in the Directory had ever been, and this popularity gave him the ability to make decisions on behalf of France. Soon he showed that he would not hesitate to make major changes in French law or in French institutions.

Napoleon Bonaparte would go on to rule France for the next decade and a half. In 1802, he became consul for life; in 1804, in the presence of the pope, he crowned himself emperor. The Estates-General, the Constituent Assembly, the Legislative Assembly, the Convention, the Directory had all come and gone; Bonaparte would rule longer than all of them put together.

Bonaparte owed his longevity in part to his military success and the glory he brought to the French nation, but he also owed it to his ability to bring relative domestic stability to France. He did something preceding regimes had not wanted to do: he made peace with the Catholic Church. In 1801–2, Bonaparte and the Vatican agreed on a "Concordat" – a new agreement on the rules and regulations of the Gallican Church. Bonaparte had not sought peace between church and state out of his own sense of piety or faith; he sought it in order to govern France better, saying that he saw in religion, "not the mystery of the incarnation, but the mystery of social order."[32] Napoleon brought an end to state-sponsored anti-clericalism. In return, he was able to benefit from a schism-free church that preached obedience to the government. Catholicism was now recognized as "the religion of the majority of the French." It was not an official state religion, as it had been under the Old Regime. But it did become the dominant religion that Boissy d'Anglas feared it would.

This was not a return to the Gallican Church of Old Regime France. The church was now subject to state laws in ways it never had been before. The personnel of the new church was composed of both constitutional priests and refractory priests, and the two groups did not always get along. The departmental boundaries remained the diocese boundaries. These were policies few Old Regime bishops would have agreed to in 1789, or even 1792, but ten years later any offer of legal protection for Catholicism made Bonaparte look like the church's savior. Soon, there was an Imperial Catechism which taught children that taxes and military service were "obligations imposed by God."[33]

Bonaparte, as a ruler, would limit freedom of the press, and eventually do away with democratic participation in the government. This did not, however, happen all at once. In 1799, he was still only first consul, and France could still make some claim to being a republic, albeit one now led by a general. When Bonaparte became consul for life in 1802 the claims to be a republic were weaker, and they vanished two years later with the proclamation of the empire. Yet even the empire retained its ties to the legacy of the Revolution. It retained the equality before the law and the uniformity of law across France that the revolutionaries of 1789 had established. It provided the sort of protection of property and free trade that most liberal and moderate revolutionaries had supported – though not the demands for greater social equality of the sans-culottes or the radical revolutionaries. In family law, Napoleonic France retained the government's primacy over religious regulations, and it still permitted some divorces. For women's rights, it represented a significant step back from earlier revolutionary legislation: it limited acceptable causes for divorce and proclaimed the "supremacy of the husband" within the family.[34] Napoleonic France did not see the vitality of female activism that had characterized the first years of the Revolution. Scholars often attribute this lack of female activism to the paternalism of the regime, but much of the cause lies in the overall lack of any sort of popular activism during the Napoleonic era. The civic equality of 1789 lasted through the Napoleonic era, but the mass participation in political life in all its myriad forms – the demonstrations and the riots, the assemblies and the gatherings in the galleries, the section meetings that ended with marches on the Convention – was over. The women of Paris had their strongest influence on events when there were links between the world of the street and the world of high politics. With those links gone, they struggled to make their voices heard.

***

The French Revolution had begun in 1789, with the meeting of the Estates-General and with the taking of the Bastille. In asking when the Revolution ended, however, there are several dates worthy of consideration. The fall of Robespierre ended the radical phase of the Revolution; the crushing of the last popular insurrection in 1795 brought an end to the Parisian uprisings that had characterized the Revolution since its start. Bonaparte's rise brought an end to the revolutionary anti-clericalism that flourished after Fructidor, by bringing peace with the Catholic Church. From 1804 on, France was no longer a republic. Bonaparte became an emperor with a crown on his head. Even the Empire had ties to the Revolution's legacy, however: the Civil Code that Napoleon first introduced to France, and then exported to other parts of Europe, maintained the civil equality that had first come to France in 1789. When Bonaparte's drawn-out fall in 1814 and 1815 brought Louis XVIII to the throne, even the restoration of the Bourbon monarchy showed signs of the changes that 25 years of revolution, upheaval, and war had brought. All of which is to say that revolutions are not required to come to a definitive end. Books, however, are – and for this book, 1799 is it. The drama of the Revolution continued after that year, but it was displaced from the streets of Paris, the meetings of the Assembly and the sections, the battlefields of the Vendée, onto the battlefields of Italy and Prussia, the Habsburg lands in Austria and eventually all the way to Russia. Back in France, the religious debates seemed settled and political activism was a shadow of its former self.

France today, like most nations, celebrates those whom it has chosen as heroes. Streets are named after those deemed worthy enough – usually men, though not always – and monuments are erected in their honor. Anyone walking around Paris can cross the Seine on the Mirabeau Bridge, or walk along the Rue Condorcet. Other streets recall battles that the French armies won, like the Rue de Fleurus or the Quai Valmy. And every year tourists wander the Place de La Bastille searching in vain for the old prison, demolished shortly after its fall. These choices of names for streets and parks act as a sort of selective memory: Paris, like most major cities in France, has no Rue Robespierre, no Rue Marat or Rue Jacques Roux. The Rue Danton in central Paris acts as a sort of limit, separating the now politically acceptable from a past that Paris is not eager to celebrate. Streets named after Robespierre and other radical leaders do exist in France, but only in working-class towns with strong traditions of leftist politics.

252

Paris is a city of history, though not only the history of the Revolution. Here and there, remnants of the medieval past remain, from fragments of old city walls to the cathedral of Notre-Dame, still towering above all that surrounds it. The nineteenth century left quite a mark on Paris, carving wide straight boulevards through neighborhoods that had only known small, twisted streets. The Champ de Mars is still there, popular with tourists picnicking under the shadow of the Eiffel Tower. The Place de la Révolution, where Louis XVI was executed, is also still there. Rechristened the Place de la Concorde, it sits across from the Tuileries gardens. To get to the spot where the king and so many others died, however, requires traversing that most modern of deathly perils, the traffic roundabout. The trip is hardly worth it. There is little to see there, no shade, no benches on which to sit, no life-size recreation of the scaffold. From there, however, one is not far from either the Elysée Palace, home to the president of the republic, or the National Assembly, which now holds its sessions just across the Seine. Those who want to see the Assembly in action need not crowd into its galleries; highlights of its sessions will be on the evening news.

Nineteenth-century France would see three kings, two emperors, one republic and one commune. Since 1871, though, France has chosen to be a republic, and that republic traces many of its roots back to 1789. The national flag is still the tricolor. *La Marseillaise* remains the national anthem. French citizens will not hesitate to remind visitors that France is indeed the *pays des droits de l'homme* – the nation that gave the world the rights of man.

Notes

1 Michelet, *Histoire*, II:896.
2 Quoted in Mason and Rizzo, *The French Revolution*, p. 267.
3 See de Baecque, *Glory and Terror*, pp. 162–3.
4 Aulard, ed., *Jacobins*, VI:650.
5 Dominique Godineau, "Masculine and Feminine Political Pratice during the French Revolution, 1793–Year III," in *Women and Politics in the Age of Democratic Revolution*, eds. H. B. Applewhite and D. G. Levy (Ann Arbor MI, 1990), pp. 61–80.
6 Quinet, *Révolution*, II:802–3.
7 Quoted in Levy *et. al.*, eds., *Women*, p. 296.
8 Quoted in Mason and Rizo, *French Revolution*, p. 275.
9 Georges Lefebvre, *The French Revolution from 1793 to 1799*, trans. John Hall Stewart and James Friguglietti (London and New York, 1964), p. 145.
10 Godineau, *Women*, pp. 354, 363.
11 Furet, *Revolutionary France*, p. 176.
12 Furet, *Revolutionary France*, p. 154.
13 From F.-A. Aulard, ed. *Paris pendant la réaction thermidorienne et sous le Directoire: Recueil de documents*, (Paris, 1898), I:566–7.
14 Boissy d'Anglas, *Rapport sur la liberté des cultes* (Paris, III).

15 Abbé Grégoire, *Discours sur la liberté des cultes* (Paris, III), p. 20.
16 De La Gorce, *Histoire religieuse*, IV:47.
17 Quinet, *Révolution*, II:835.
18 Martyn Lyons, *France under the Directory* (Cambridge, 1975), p. 21.
19 Desan, *Reclaiming*, pp. 16, 18.
20 Desan, *Reclaiming*, p. 16.
21 Desan, *Reclaiming*, p. 104.
22 Archives Nationales F1CIII Nord 7, Compte mensuaire Brumaire VII.
23 Doyle, *Oxford History*, p. 313.
24 Lyons, *France*, p. 105.
25 Quoted in de La Gorce, *Histoire religieuse*, IV:213.
26 De La Gorce, *Histoire religieuse*, IV:235.
27 *Bulletin des lois*, No. 194, p. 11.
28 Noah Shusterman, *Religion and the Politics of Time: Holidays in France from Louis XIV through Napoleon* (Washington DC, 2010), ch. 6.
29 Martyn Lyons, *Napoleon Bonaparte and the Legacy of the French Revolution* (New York, 1994), p. 35.
30 Quoted in Lyons, *Napoleon*, p. 40.
31 Lefebvre, *The French Revolution*, p. 256.
32 Quoted in Lyons, *Napoleon*, p. 85.
33 Jean Tulard, *Napoléon* (Paris, 1977), p. 365.
34 Lyons, *Napoleon*, pp. 94–9.

GUIDE TO FURTHER READING

There is an astonishingly large amount of material available on the French Revolution. The following are some suggestions for further reading, provided as a way to help readers new to the subject know where to start. It will only cover materials available in English.

The single best way to study the French Revolution is by reading texts that were written during the Revolution itself. There are several primary text readers available, including *The Old Regime and the French Revolution* (Chicago, 1987), edited by Keith Michael Baker, and *The French Revolution: A Document Collection* (Boston, 1999), edited by Laura Mason and Tracey Rizzo. Both of these are excellent; Baker tends to focus more on political issues, Mason and Rizzo on cultural issues. There is also an older reader, *Women in Revolutionary Paris, 1789–1795* (Levy *et al.*, eds., Urbana and Chicago, 1980), which has an impressive collection of texts. Not surprisingly, there are a growing number of online resources, and the site *Liberty, Equality, Fraternity: Exploring the French Revolution* (http://chnm.gmu. edu/revolution/about.html) is especially useful. There are also longer primary texts, particularly from the years before the Revolution, that have long been available in English. The works of the major Enlightenment writers are widely available, as are many popular novels from the era, and there is no better way to enter into the world of eighteenth-century France. Among some of the classics: Voltaire's novels *Candide* and *Zadig* are both available in multiple translations, and much of his *Philosophical Dictionary* is available online. Rousseau's classic works, including *On the Social Contract*, *Emile*, and *La Nouvelle Héloïse* are also all available in translation. Among novels, *Dangerous Liaisons* (translations often retain the French title *Les Liaisons Dangereuses*) gives a glimpse into the lives of the more promiscuous members of the aristocracy.

Unfortunately, when it comes to the classic nineteenth-century histories of the Revolution, reading them in English is not always easy. Thiers' *History of the French Revolution* (New York, 1897) is available in English and, though long, is quite readable. A significant portion of Michelet's history is, too, though not all of it, and one must pull together different parts from different partial translations. Thomas Carlyle's 1837 *The French Revolution: A History* (New York, 2002) is a difficult read and more valuable for students of England than those of France. Parts of Jaurès' 1908 *Socialist History of the French Revolution* are available online in English, but not the full work; nor is Quinet's 1865 history available to English readers. The one classic history that remains easily accessible is Alexis de Tocqueville's *The Old Regime and the French Revolution* (New York 1955), a book that has aged quite well, even having something of a rebirth in the decades following the Revolution's bicentennial in 1989. It is an analysis of the Revolution, not a narrative history, but it is an analysis well worth studying.

Turning to more recent secondary works, for an understanding of Old Regime society, the single best history available is John McManners' *Church and Society in Eighteenth-Century France* (Oxford, 1998). The book's title is misleading, and while it has more than enough to say on church history and on religious history, its chapters on sexuality, the theater, and other aspects of popular culture are as well-researched and informative as anything else around. For understanding other aspects of Old Regime society, Robert Darnton's works, especially his classic *The Literary Underground of the Old Regime* (Cambridge, MA, 1985), provide a great starting point. For the causes of the fall of the Old Regime and the start of the Revolution, George Lefebvre's *The Coming of the French Revolution* (Princeton, 1947) and William Doyle's *The Origins of the French Revolution* (Oxford, 1988) remain classics, though the more recent *From Deficit to Deluge: The Origins of the French Revolution* (Palo Alto, 2010), edited by Thomas Kaiser and Dale Van Kley, provides a strong updated view of the field.

There are some excellent studies devoted to key events of the Revolution. Timothy Tackett's *When the King Took Flight* (Cambridge, MA, 2003) is a riveting account of the flight to Varennes. David Jordan's *The King's Trial: Louis XVI vs. the French Revolution* (Berkeley, 1979) focuses on exactly what one would expect, but also says quite a bit about the dynamics of the Revolution at that time. David Andress's recent *The Terror* (New York, 2006) gives an updated account of the events of 1793–4. For that same period, R. R. Palmer's much older *Twelve Who Ruled: The Year of the Terror in the French Revolution* (Princeton, 1969) stands up quite well, though it tends to de-emphasize Robespierre's role more than most other accounts. For the external war, the best account is T. C. W. Blanning's *The French Revolutionary Wars, 1787–1802* (London, 1996). For the France that emerges out of the Revolution, Isser Woloch's *The New Regime* (New York, 1995) has become the classic account, and rightly so.

Among works devoted to individual revolutionaries, the best biographies available focus on Robespierre. Two of the most recent are quite good: Ruth Scurr's *Fatal Purity: Robespierre and the French Revolution* (New York, 2006) and Peter McPhee's *Robespierre: A Revolutionary Life* (London, 2012). Other options include Alyssa Sepinwall's *The Abbé Grégoire and the French*

Revolution (Berkeley and Los Angeles, 2005), and William Sewell's *A Rhetoric of Bourgeois Revolution: The Abbé Sieyes and What is the Third Estate?* (Durham, NC, 1994). The introduction to this last work contains one of the best explanations of how interpretations of the Revolution evolved during the late twentieth century.

The best guides to the religious history of the French Revolution are Dale Van Kley's *The Religious Origins of the French Revolution* (New Haven, 1996), Nigel Aston's *Religion and Revolution in France, 1780–1804* (Washington, DC, 2000), and Tackett's *Religion, Revolution, and Regional Culture in Eighteenth-Century France: The Ecclesiastical Oath of 1791* (Princeton, 1986). Michel Vovelle's *The Revolution against the Church* (Paris, 1988) gives a good study of the de-Christianization movement. For studies in the history of women and gender during the Revolution, Lynn Hunt's *The Family Romance of the French Revolution* (Berkeley and Los Angeles, 1993) and Suzanne Desan's *Reclaiming the Sacred: Lay Religion and Popular Politics in Revolutionary France* (Ithaca, 1990) are both fascinating analyses – the latter one of the few books that manages to synthesize religion and gender in its analysis. For some time, the "exclusion" thesis dominated the history of women during the Revolution; while that dominance is fading, those studies – especially Joan Landes' *Women and the Public Sphere in the Age of the French Revolution* (Ithaca, 1988) – remain relevant and important. Dominique Godineau's *The Women of Paris and Their French Revolution* (Berkeley, 1998), though a bit difficult to read cover to cover, contains a wealth of fascinating details culled from extensive archival work.

Finally, there are a number of novels – both classic and recent – that take place during the Revolution. If used carefully, these novels can provide some sense of life during the Revolution. The classic English language novel set in the Revolution is Charles Dickens' 1859 *A Tale of Two Cities* (available in many editions). Dickens' analysis of the Revolution leaves much to be desired (and relies too much on Carlyle), but it is careful in its chronology and gives a good sense of English responses to the events in France. Other older novels worth a read include Anatole France's 1912 *The Gods Will Have Blood* (New York, 1980) (French: *Les Dieux ont soif*) and Balzac's 1829 *The Chouans* (New York, 1972). More recently, Hilary Mantel's *A Place of Greater Safety* (New York, 2006) tracks the lives of leading revolutionaries during the Terror.

Many of the secondary works listed here have their own bibliographies and guides to further reading, as do Francois Furet's *Revolutionary France, 1770–1880* (Oxford, 1988) and Doyle's *The Oxford History of the French Revolution*, 2nd ed. (Oxford and New York, 2002) – the latter being particularly strong in English language texts. In any detailed research of a particular topic, eventually a reading knowledge of French will become necessary. But for an understanding of the Revolution, its major characters, events, and interpretations, there is enough available in English to satisfy all but the most ravenous appetites.

INDEX

Abbaye at St Germain des Prés 134–35
abduction theory 93, 95, 97
academies 12, 84
Agra, bishop of see Guyot de Folleville
agro-liturgical calendar 11, 204
Aiguillon, Armand Desiré, duc d' 42
almanacs 187
Alsace 6, 9, 71
American Revolution 18, 21, 24, 25, 33
Angers 109, 185, 211
armoire de fer 148–50
Artois, Charles Philippe, comte d' 38, 59,
   93, 111, 123, 197, 245
Aston, Nigel (historian) 5, 64, 208
atheism 12, 66, 159, 206, 207, 217, 222–23
August 10 1792 124–31, 149–50, 169,
   184, 209, 222
August 11 1789, Decrees of 43–44, 50, 51,
   64, 67, 204
August 4 1789, night of 42–43, 64
Aulard, Alphonse 220
Austria 1, 18, 19–20, 59, 74, 84, 89, 111,
   112, 114–15, 124, 125, 134, 139, 162,
   164, 182, 190, 193, 197, 219, 225, 252
Auxerre 223
Avignon 108–9, 178

Babeuf, François Noel "Gracchus" 239
Bailly, Jean Sylvain: Champ de Mars
   Massacre and 99; execution of 200, 204,
   218; as intellectual 28; mayor of Paris 39,
   116, 131
Bara, Joseph 188
Barbaroux, Charles Jean-Marie 180
Barère, Bertrand: and Convention 146, 151,
   163, 166, 196; and Committee of Public
   Safety 171, 199, 226–27, 230; exile of
   236; and Vendée 190–91, 193, 212

Barnave, Antoine-Pierre 28, 34, 59, 82,
   91–92, 94, 99–100, 103, 123, 143,
   237
Barras, Paul, vicomte de 243, 248
Barry, Jeanne Bécu, comtesse de 19
Basire, Claude 128, 201, 217, 228
Bastille; storming of 1, 35–39, 42, 47, 49,
   50, 53, 55, 56, 60, 93, 96, 97, 99, 102,
   110, 115, 116, 123, 126, 129, 130, 132,
   134, 148, 168, 181, 187, 200, 205, 241,
   252
Belgium 114, 120, 160, 161, 190, 225
Billaud-Varenne, Jacques Nicolas 189, 190,
   195, 209, 210, 217, 226, 230, 232,
   235–36
Blois 84
Boissy d'Anglas, François Antoine 238, 242,
   244, 251
Bonaparte, Napoleon 1, 235, 240,
   249–51
Bordeaux 107, 215, 236; federalist revolt
   and 177, 178; Jews and 9
Bouillé, François Claude, marquis de 88–89,
   93, 183, 240
bourgeoisie 14, 32
bread 23, 49–51, 159, 168, 183, 199–200,
   237, 238
Brissot, Jacques-Pierre 84, 109; calls for war
   112, 114, 125, 139; Girondins and 105,
   140, 143, 145, 170, 176, 198; during
   Old Regime 31
Brittany 7, 57, 78, 107, 129, 162, 179,
   186; Chouans and 176; Vendéan army in
   194, 211–13
Brunswick Manifesto 125
Burgundy 57, 144
Burke, Edmund 221
Buzot, François 163, 176

Caen 176, 177–79, 181, 194
cahiers de doléances 21, 43
Calas, Jean 17, 66
Calvados 176, 177–79
Camus, Armand Gaston 28, 68, 84
cannonades 214–15
Carlye, Thomas (historian) 131, 147, 178, 179
Carmes 134–36
Carnot, Lazare 190, 200, 225–26, 236, 241, 243, 246
Carrier, Jean-Baptiste 213–14, 217, 232, 236, 250
Cathelineau, Jacques 183–86
Catholic Church: decline of 13–14, 60; during Old Regime 9–12, 24; in 1789 53–54, 60,61–65; official religion vs. custom 9–10,80, 186, 187, 244; and sexual behavior 15–16, 61, 140; role in society 9–10, 23, 158, 215–16; after the Terror 235, 241–45, 246–47, 251
centralization 44, 172, 192
Cercle Social 83, 84, 102, 105, 106, 122
Chabot, François 158, 217–19.
Chalier, Joseph 194
Champ de Mars 55–57, 60, 97–99, 223
Champ de Mars Massacre 97–101, 131
Charles X *see* Artois Charles Philippe, comte d'
Charrette, François 184–85, 191, 212
Châtillon-sur-Sèvre 134
Chaumette, Anaxagoras: and Commune 131, 195, 198, 209–10, 217, 238; and de-Christianization 206–8; execution of 222
Cholet, Battle of 1, 193, 204, 211–12, 214
Chouans 176, 241, 245
citizens and citizenship 13, 30, 44, 47–49, 56, 71, 97, 104, 106, 126, 130–31, 157, 184, 192, 240, 247
Civil Constitution of the Clergy 2–3, 54, 65–81, 132; community reactions to 4, 57, 60, 70, 72–73, 80, 103, 109–10, 162, 176, 182, 183; geographic breakdown of reactions to 77–78; oath to 73, 75–79, 80; papal response 84; and women 1, 79, 102
class: definitions of 14, 25–26, 32; relations between 42–43, 98–99, 131, 155–58, 237–29; resentment 29, 100–101
Cloots, Jean-Baptiste "Anarchis", baron 207, 217–18

clothing 155, 158, 209 *see also* cockade; *sans-culottes*; *muscadins*
clubs *see Cercle Social*; Cordeliers; Feuillants; Jacobins; Society of Revolutionary Republican Citizenesses
cockade 39, 51
Collot d'Herbois, Jean-Marie 187, 189–90, 209–10, 214–15, 217, 226, 229, 232, 235, 236, 250
colonies 7
Commission of Twelve 166–68, 169
Committee of General Security 219–20, 222, 226
Committee of Public Safety 171, 209–11, 219; created 163; composition of 189–90; tasks of 192–93, 196, 202, 222–23, 225–26; during Thermidor 236–37, 240
Commune, Paris 127–32, 133, 141, 168, 170, 209–10, 222, 228, 231
concordat 251
Condorcet, Jean Antoine Nicolas de Caritat, marquis de 65–66; death of 218; and Girondins 128, 143, 145, 151; on women 13, 106, 147, 158
conscription 162, 182, 190, 192, 195, 225
Constituent Assembly *see* National Constituent Assembly
Constitution: of 1791 93, 104, 110, 112, 116, 149, 173 n21; of 1793 194–95, 196, 202, 238; of year III 238, 247–48, 250; writing 50–51, 57–58
constitutional church 242, 244; formation of 75; reception by communities 102, 107; revolution turns against 205–6.
Convention 173, 204–32; clampdown on political dissent by 201–2, 222; divisions in 143–44, 145–47, 154, 160–61, 164–72, 216–20, 228–32; opening of 125, 130–31, 139–41; and Reign of Terror 194–202; after the Reign of Terror 236–39, 242–43; and trial of Louis XIV 144, 148–53; and war 161–63, 182, 190, 192–93
Corday, Charlotte 178–81, 188–89, 196, 198
Cordeliers 83–84, 97, 103, 127, 157, 160, 187, 189, 210
coup d'état: 18 Fructidor V (September 4 1797) 246, 247; 22 Floréal VI (May 11 1798) 248, 250; 30 Prairial VII (June 18 1799) 248, 250; 18 Brumaire VIII (November 9 1799) 250

Couthon, Georges 189, 194, 214, 227, 230–31
cult of martyrs 187–88
culte décadaire 247
curés, revolt of 61
Custine, Adam Philippe, comte de 197

Danton, Georges Jacques 92, 121, 141, 158, 164, 175, 195–96, 209, 210; advocates relaxation of the Terror 216–17, 221; Girondins and 163, 167, 170; rivalry with Robespierre 160–61, 220–21, 230; trial and execution of 218–20
Dantonists 166, 210, 216–22, 224, 232
David, Jacques Louis 188
De Baecque, Antoine (historian) 137
deaths, number of 37, 196–97, 200, 214, 223
de-Christianization 206–9, 215
Declaration of Pillnitz 111
Declaration of the Rights of Man and Citizen 1, 44–48, 50–51, 53, 64, 71–72, 109, 132, 221, 238, 242
departments 57–58, 67, 181
Desan, Suzanne (historian) 5, 244
Desmoulins, Camille 31, 47, 217, 219–21
Desnot 37–38
diamond necklace affair 20, 24, 27
dioceses 7–8, 61, 62–63, 67–69, 86 n20, 251
Directory 243–50; see-saw politics of 241, 246
divorce 84, 119, 140, 251
Doyle, William (historian) 222
Drouet, Jean-Baptiste 89–90
Ducos, Pierre Roger 250
Dumouriez, Charles François 139, 161–62, 164, 166, 183, 190, 197, 199, 240
Dusaulx, Jean Joseph 138, 171

Easter 85, 185
Edgeworth, Henry Essex 153
Egypt 240, 249
Elbée, Maurice Joseph Louis Gigost d' 186, 191, 193
émigrés 38, 56–57, 59, 63, 75, 93–95, 99, 110–12, 114–15, 117, 120, 134, 197, 245
ending the Revolution 99–100, 239, 252
England 18, 24, 133, 155, 161, 176, 178, 180, 186, 190, 193, 205, 211, 225, 240, 245, 250

Enlightenment: during Old Regime 12–13; criticisms of Catholicism 63, 65–66; influence on Revolution 30–31, 96
enragés 161, 195
Estates-General 18, 215, 250, 252; becomes National Assembly 34; calling of 21, 23, 26–29; composition of 29–30, 62–63, 69; opening of 31–33
Eure 177
Evreux 178
Exposition of Principles 69–71

Fabre d'Eglantine, Philippe François 166, 205, 217–19
Fauchet, Claude 102–3, 105, 106, 109–10, 158, 171, 198, 201
federalist revolt 176–81, 186, 194, 200, 214–15, 217
fédérés 55–57, 115, 126–27
Fersen, Alex, comte de 88, 93
Festival of Reason 207, 217
Festival of the Federation 55–58, 60, 85, 97, 98, 114, 126, 187
Festival of the Supreme Being 223–24, 228
Feuillants 100, 103, 105–6
finances 18, 21, 24, 26, 65
Fleurus, Battle of 1, 225–26, 227–28, 252
Fleury, Jacques-Pierre 79, 101–2, 106, 133, 134
Foucault, marquis de 42
Fouché, Joseph 206, 214–15, 217, 232, 235–36, 250
Fouquier-Tinville, Antoine 198, 219–20, 225, 231–32
freedom of religion 3, 44, 64, 108, 132, 208, 242
freedom of speech 44
Freud, Sigmund 153–54
Fructidorian Directory 246–48
Furet, François (historian) 112, 241

galleries 49, 53, 100, 120, 145, 146–48, 153, 156–57, 163, 165, 167–70, 208, 229, 231–32, 237–39
Gensonné, Armond 107–8
Germinal riots (April 1 1795) 238, 246
Girondins: advocate war 112–14; arrest of 175; August 10 and 128, 130–32, 169; and Convention 140; expulsion of 165–72, 241; reinstatement of 236; reasons for their fall 171–72, 175; rise of 1, 105–6; rivalry with Montagnards

143–44, 145–47, 150–53, 158–60, 162, 163–72, 194, 209, 221; support from provinces 145, 166, 170; trial and execution of 198–99, 218; women and 106, 120–21, 159, 165

Gobel, Jean-Baptiste Joseph 75, 158, 207, 222

Godineau, Dominique (historian) 239

Gouges, Olympe de 106, 119, 121–22, 157, 199, 200

Granville, Battle of 211, 212

Great Fear 40–42, 50, 60, 110, 117

Greece, ancient 47, 224

Grégoire, Henri Baptiste: background 63; and Constitutional Church 68, 75, 158; and freedom of religion 206–8, 242

Guadet, Marguerite Elie 107, 158–59, 164, 176

Guillotin, Joseph 181

guillotine 181, 196, 200, 215, 235

Guyana 132, 205, 236, 246

Guyot de Follevillle, Gabriel Pierre-François 185, 192, 211

Habsburg dynasty 18, 19

Haitian Revolution 4

Hanriot, François 170

harvests 23, 41, 50, 191, 237

Hébert, Jacques-René: and Commune 131; execution of 217–18; and Girondins 166–67; politics of 156, 158, 161, 162, 187, 189, 197–98, 200, 208, 209, 210

Hébertists 210, 217–18, 221

Herault de Séchelles, Marie Jean 219, 226

horses 14, 51, 52, 88–89, 96, 212

Hôtel de Ville 36–37, 50, 127–28, 230

Huguenots 9, 17, 59, 115, 205

Hunt, Lynn (historian) 5, 48, 153

infernal columns 213–14

Isnard, Maximin: accused of leading Vendéan army 167; criticizes refractory priests 108, 110, 115; and Girondins 105, 139–41, 143, 145, 148, 151, 152, 163, 164, 170, 171, 172; during Thermidor 236; threatens Paris 165–67

Jacobin club 96–97, 103, 124, 156; attacked by muscadins 237; composition of 143, 157; closed by the Convention 237; critical of Louis XVI 97; and Girondins 105, 167; origins 82; and

Robespierre 82, 155, 189, 206, 207, 209, 222, 226, 229–31; and women 120, 164

Jansenists 10–11, 18, 28, 62, 63, 67–68, 69

Jaurès, Jean (historian) 43, 126, 131, 153, 195, 209, 210, 217, 220, 230, 235

Jesuits 10, 16

Jesus Christ 11, 47, 70, 205, 208, 220

Jews 9, 17, 71, 205

Joubert, Barthélemy Catherine 240

Jourdan, Jean-Baptiste 240

June 2 1793 169–72

June 20 1792 116–17, 123–24, 129, 130

Jura 177

La Barre, Jean François Lefebvre, chevalier de 17

La Fare, Anne Louis Henri de 27, 63, 65

La Force 136–37

La Gorce, Pierre de (historian) 73, 77, 133, 192, 213, 242, 246

La Révellière-Lépeaux, Louis Marie de 243, 247

La Rochejaquelein, Henri, comte de 184, 193–94, 212

La Rochelle 77, 205

Lacombe, Claire 122, 201

Lafayette, Gibert du Motier, marquis de 27, 112, 122, 128, 129; and American Revolution 24; as celebrity 33, 104; and Champ de Mars Massacre 98, 103; and Jacobins 100, 124, 143; leaves France 134–35, 183–84, 240; and royal family 56, 59, 90, 92, 94, 123

Lamballe, Marie-Thérèse princesse de 20, 94, 136–37, 180, 197

Lamourette, Antoine Adrien 215

Lanjuinais, Jean Denis 170–71, 236

Launey, Bernard René Jourdan, marquis de 36–38

Lavoisier, Antoine Laurent 218

Law of 22 Prairial 224, 235

Law of Suspects 215, 224

Le Mans, Battle of 211–12, 214

Le Peletier, Louis Michel 187–88

Le Tourneur, Louis François Honoré 243

Lebrun, François (historian) 11

Lefebvre, Georges (historian) 41, 239, 250

Legislative Assembly see National Legislative Assembly

Léon, Anne 122, 201

Lescure, Marie Louise Victoire de Donnissan, marquise de 184, 185

Lescuyer, Nicolas Jean-Baptiste 109
Lindet, Robert 148–50, 163, 205
Lindet, Thomas 205
Loire River 185–86, 193, 211–13
London Times 149
Longwy, Battle of 134, 139, 161
Lorraine 6, 63
Louis XIV 9, 18, 52, 96
Louis XV 18, 19, 21, 48, 96, 122, 149
Louis XVI, execution of: 153–55, 182, 188, 196, 221; as touchstone after the Terror 241, 243
Louis XVI: and August 10 129–30; calls for demission 97–98, 126; and Catholic Church 23; double game 74–75, 85, 112, 114; as father 48–49, 153–54; indecisiveness 20, 49, 56, 73–74, 216; during Old Regime 17, 26; opposition to the Revolution 34–35, 110, 115–16, 124; sexual difficulties 20; support for the Revolution 39, 52, 57–58, 95; suspension of 130; trial of 144, 148–53; *See also* Louis XVI, execution of
Louis XVIII *see* Provence, Louis-Stanislas Xavier, comte de
Louis-Charles (son of Louis XVI) 95, 245
Louvet, Jean-Baptiste, in Convention 145–47, 159, 164, 171, 172; and federalist revolt 176, 178–79, 198; during Thermidor 236
Lutherans 9
Lyon 14, 177, 194, 214–15

Machecoul 182–84, 214
Magenthies 227
Maillard, Stanislas 50, 135
"make Terror the order of the day" (Barère) 196
Malesherbes, Guillaume Chrétien de Lamoignon de 149–50
Mandat, Antoine Jean Gailliot, marquis de 128
Manège, salle du 52–53, 168
Marat, Jean-Paul 30–31, 48, 92, 158, 161, 175, 206, 207, 209, 210, 222, 235, 238; death of 1, 178–81, 187–89, 195, 197, 198; as deputy at Convention 141, 143, 145, 146, 150, 153, 159–60, 162, 165; and Girondins 148, 167, 170, 171, 172, 176, 177–78; and Jacobins 143, 160; trial of 164, 165; as journalist 58–59, 98–99, 100, 103, 115, 124, 135, 155;

and September Massacres 138; and women 106, 164
Marie-Antoinette 122, 191; opposition to the Revolution 34, 59, 111, 198; perceptions of 20, 24, 39, 48, 51, 52–53; and pornography 4, 53, 123, 215; trial and execution of 197, 200
Marie-Thérèse (daughter of Louis XVI) 95, 228, 245
Marseillaise 126–27, 199, 253
Marseilles 14, 129, 175, 177–78, 194
Martin, Jean-Clément (historian) 213, 214
Mathiez, Albert (historian) 83, 131, 220
Maury, Jean Siffrein 76
Maximum, the 235, 237
May 31 1793 168–69, 170, 226
Mayenne 109
McManners, John (historian) 10
McPhee, Peter (historian) 210, 221
Méhée de la Touche, Jean-Claude Hippolyte 236
Mercier, Louis Sébastien 55, 137
metric system 204
Michelet, Jules (historian) 35, 42, 83, 112–13, 127, 143, 171, 186, 208, 222, 228, 232, 235
Mirabeau, Honoré Gabriel Riquetti, comte de 33, 34, 70, 76, 82, 91, 94, 104, 122, 237, 252; and royal family 59, 74; death of 92, 188
Momoro, Antoine François 217
monks 55, 62, 68, 82–83, 158, 219
Montagnards: and Jacobins 143–44; Montagnard government 172, 194–96, 209, 216; rivalry with Girondins 143–44, 145–47, 150–53, 158–60, 163–72, 194; support from Paris 145, 166–67; after the Terror 236; and women 147, 159, 165
Montauban 59
Montmédy 88, 91
Moreau, Jean Victor 240
Municipal Revolution 39
muscadins 237–38

Nancy 27
Nantes 1, 15, 72, 73, 185–86, 191, 193, 211–13, 214, 215
National Assembly 34
National Constituent Assembly 38, 42–48, 51–54, 57–58, 85, 98–99, 206; and Civil Constitution of the Clergy 65–67, 69–77; creation of 34–35; closing of

104–5; and flight to Varennes 91,
93–95, 97–98
National Legislative Assembly: and August
10 125, 127–32, 138; end of 139–40;
and Girondins 105–6; and refractory
church 106–10, 132; rivalry with
Commune 129–32, 140–41; start of
104–5; and war 112–15
Necker, Jacques 25, 27, 33, 35, 39, 92
Neerwinden, Battle of 162
Netherlands 155, 161–62, 190, 225, 240
Nièvre 206
Nîmes 9, 59
nobility 14, 25 27, 38, 40, 42–43, 57, 99
Normandy 78, 176, 177–79, 186, 211
noyades 212–13, 215, 221

October Days *see* Women's March to
Versailles
Oedipal complex 153–54
Orléans, Louis Philippe Joseph, duc d' 162,
176 changes name to Philippe-Egalité 96,
152; execution of 199; overestimation of
89, 97; relation to king 96

Pache, Jean Nicolas 165, 217
Pacy-sur-Eure, Battle of 178
Palm, Etta 122
Pantheon 187–88, 220
parlements 18–19, 21, 23, 25–26, 28,
30, 44
patriotic banquets 227–28
Payan, Claude François de 222
peasants 3, 6, 9, 14, 21, 40–43, 111,
132–33, 182–84, 185–86, 192, 204
Pétion, Jérôme 28, 92, 116, 127–28
Philippe-Egalité *see* Orléans, Louis Philippe
Joseph, duc d'
philosophes see Enlightenment
pikes, heads on 38, 51, 133, 137, 180, 238
Plain, the 146, 150, 152, 163, 166, 169,
171, 181, 232
Pompadour, Jeanne Antoinette Poisson,
marquise de 19
pope, the 10, 67, 69–70, 73, 75, 84,
108,185, 250–51
population 14–15
pornography 2, 4, 16, 53, 94, 121, 123,
144
Prairial days (May 20–23 1795) 238–39,
246
primitive church 63, 67, 107, 208

prisons: 36, 134–39 *see also* Bastille; La
Force; Carmes; Abbaye at St Germain des
Prés; Nantes; La Rochelle; Temple
privileges 6, 18, 29, 40, 42–44, 64, 66, 115
Provence, Louis-Stanislas Xavier, comte de
93, 123, 245
Provence 7
provinces 23, 57; and departments 57, 181;
discontent with Paris 101, 172; support
for Girondins 151, 166; opposition to
Convention 175–79
Prussia 74, 111, 115, 124, 125, 133–34,
139, 182, 190, 197, 225, 252

Quiberon 245
Quinet, Edgar (historian) 5, 98, 116, 135,
141, 172, 186, 187, 207, 208, 218, 231,
238, 242

Rabaut de Saint-Etienne, Jean Paul 59, 169
refractory church 75, 101–2, 107–8,
109–10, 182, 185, 205, 208, 214, 244
refractory priests 75, 85, 153, 213, 222,
251; called to department capitals
132–33; deportation of 205, 246; head to
Paris 133–34; laws about 110, 132, 133,
158, 205, 241, 246; and September
Massacres 135–39; support from
population 107–8, 109–10, 182, 183
regencies 96
Reign of Terror 204–32; end of 228–32,
235; interpretations of 220–21, 235–38;
start of 196–200
Renault, Cécile 227
representatives-on-mission 162–63, 196,
206, 207, 213, 226
Republic: advocacy of 97; birth of in France
140, 144; fear of 94, 96
republican calendar 204–5, 216, 223, 231,
238, 239, 241, 247–48
republican marriages 213
Reubell, Jean-François 243
revolutionary religion 187–88, 247, 223–24
Revolutionary Tribunal 163, 180–81, 191,
196–200, 215, 224–26, 231, 235
Richerism 76
Robespierre, Augustin 170
Robespierre, Maximilien 28, 92, 150, 161,
175, 177, 179, 187, 188, 218, 238, 241,
242, 244, 247, 248, 249; and Danton
160, 210, 216–17, 219–21, 230; and de-
Christianization 207–8; execution of 231;

fall of 226–30; and Festival of the Supreme Being 223–24; and Hébertists 210, 217; interpretations of 220–21; and Jacobin club 82, 125, 135, 143, 159, 229–30, 232; Louvet's attack on 145–47, 159, 164, 172; opposition to war 113–14, 139; rise of 1, 103–4, 122, 155, 158, 222; rivalry with Girondins 113–14, 141, 143, 167, 169, 170, 198–99; role in Committee of Public Safety 189–90, 195, 209–10, 213, 215–16, 222–23, 226–27; as scapegoat 235–36; and women 104, 106, 146–47, 200–201, 206; as priest 158–59, 224.

Roederer, Pierre Louis 127, 129–30, 249–50

Rohan, Louis René Edouard, Cardinal 20, 27

Roland de la Platière, Jean-Marie 105, 115–16, 121–22, 140, 143, 148, 150, 170, 175, 200

Roland, Manon Jeanne Pilipon, Madame 98, 100, 116, 139; execution of 199–200; and Girondins 105, 106, 121–22, 131–32, 147, 148, 175

Rome, ancient 30, 47, 219

Romme, Gilbert 204, 239

Rousseau, Jean-Jacques 12–13, 31, 44, 48, 49, 84, 113–14, 188, 201

Roux, Jacques 161, 189, 195, 201, 209, 222, 238, 252

royal tombs 191

Rudé, George (historian) 157

rumors 20, 35, 39, 41, 115, 117, 120, 124, 134–35, 137–38, 211, 227, 228

Saint Cloud 85, 129

Saint-Florent 182–83

Saint-Just, Louis 140, 144, 150, 151, 189, 222, 225–26, 230, 231

Sainte-Menehould 88–89

salons 12

sans-culottes 123, 155–57, 167, 209, 222, 231

Santerre, Antoine Joseph 120, 123, 128, 138, 153, 157, 162, 169–70

Savenay, Battle of 212, 214

Scott, Joan (historian) 119

sections 126, 168–70, 189, 195–96, 200, 222, 227, 231

seduction 79, 81–82

Seine River 8, 128, 167

September 5 1793 195, 222

September Massacres 135–39, 141, 145, 146, 160, 171, 172, 181, 182, 221, 225, 241

sexuality 15–17, 122–23; and Catholic Church 15–16, 61

Sèze, Romain de 149–50

Sieyes, Emmanuel Joseph 34, 62, 65, 82, 92, 121, 122; during Convention 139, 152, 207, 232; during Directory 236, 243, 248–50; and "What is the Third Estate" 28–29, 32–33

Soboul, Albert (historian) 157

Society of Revolutionary Republican Citizenesses 122, 195, 200–202; oppose Girondins 165; overemphasized by historians 201

soldiers: 34–35, 51, 56, 98–99, 112–13, 126, 129–30, 169–70, 178–79, 183, 184–86, 192–93, 195, 197, 200, 213–14; protecting priests 77; shifting allegiances of 36–37, 117, 129 see also conscription; fédérés; war

Spain 74, 161, 225

Stael, Germaine de 33

Sundays 10, 13, 64, 98, 204–5, 223, 241–42, 245, 247–48

Swiss guards 36–37, 129–30

Tackett, Timothy (historian) 5, 77, 80

Talleyrand, Charles Maurice de 56, 61, 75, 84, 250

Tallien, Jean Lambert 215, 230, 235–36

taxes 21, 24, 26, 43

Temple monastery 132, 134, 136–37, 153, 228

Tennis Court Oath 34

Terror, Reign of see Reign of Terror

Theophilanthrophy 247

Théot, Catherine 227, 229, 230

Thérèse Philosophe 16

Thermidor 231, 235–42

Théroigne de Méricourt, Anne Josèphe 119–21, 157

Thiers, Adolphe (historian) 5, 175, 190, 197, 222, 226, 227, 230

third estate 28–30, 32, 34, 39, 53, 62, 64, 95

Thuriot, Jacques Alexis 167, 217, 224, 230

tocsin 35, 127, 135, 162, 168–69, 231

Torfou, Battle of 191–93

Toulon 177, 200, 249

Tourcoing, Battle of 225

Tuileries 23, 51, 53, 91, 93, 116, 125, 127–32, 148, 149, 168–70, 184, 223

Turreau, Louis Marie de 213

Vadier, Marc Guillaume Alexis 220, 227, 228, 229, 230

Valmy, Battle of 1, 139, 143, 161, 252

Van Kley, Dale (historian) 5

Varennes 89–8, 100, 103, 110–11, 115, 116, 125, 197

Vendéan armies: in Brittany 211–12; religious life in 185–86; as volunteer army 184, 193

Vendée: civil war in 1, 3, 134, 162, 163, 164, 175, 177, 182–86, 188, 190–94, 196, 208, 211–14; opposition to Civil Constitution of the Clergy 107–8, 162, 176, 183; regional variations in 181–82; and women 191–92, 193, 212

Verdun, Battle of 134, 135, 139, 161, 217, 240

Vergniaud, Pierre 200; execution of 198, 200; and Girondins 105, 139, 143, 145, 163, 169–70, 175, 145, 169, 170, 175, 198; and trial of Louis XVI 151–52

veto 51, 93–94, 109, 115–17, 123, 197

Virgin Mary 109, 207

Voltaire, François Marie Arouet 12, 13, 36, 65, 66, 188

Walzer, Michael (sociologist) 150

war 1, 161–62, 182, 200; after the Terror 240, 249; causes of 110–14; impact on Revolution 134–35, 137, 139, 143, 190, 225; push for from Girondins 112–14

weapons 35–37, 39, 111, 123–24, 129–30, 167, 168, 170–71, 178, 185

Wimpffen, Georges Félix, baron de 177, 178, 180, 194

women: blamed for Vendée 213–14; and Civil Constitution of the Clergy 1, 79, 102; influence of 19–20, 48, 112, 208; leading women 119–24; legal status of 16; limits on 47–48, 121–23, 156, 200–202, 251; participation in Revolution by 49, 50–53, 79–80, 126, 146–47, 157, 159, 164, 187–89, 191–92, 208, 224, 238, 239

Women's March to Versailles 1, 50–53, 120, 124, 135, 238

Yole, Jean (historian) 181

York, duke of 225